JOURNAL FOR THE STUDY OF THE NEW TESTAMENT
SUPPLEMENT SERIES
124

Sheffield Academic Press

'I Am' in John's Gospel

Literary Function, Background and Theological Implications

David Mark Ball

Journal for the Study of the New Testament
Supplement Series 124

Copyright © 1996 Sheffield Academic Press

Published by
Sheffield Academic Press Ltd
Mansion House
19 Kingfield Road
Sheffield, S11 9AS
England

Typeset by Sheffield Academic Press
and
Printed on acid-free paper in Great Britain
by Bookcraft
Midsomer Norton, Bath

British Library Cataloguing in Publication Data

A catalogue record for this book is available
from the British Library

ISBN 1-85075-587-6

CONTENTS

Part I
SUGGESTED BACKGROUND TO 'I AM':
A SURVEY OF SCHOLARSHIP

Part II
THE WORLD OF THE TEXT: A LITERARY ANALYSIS
OF THE FUNCTION OF ἐγώ εἰμι IN JOHN'S GOSPEL

Part IV
THE WORLD BEYOND THE TEXT:
CONCLUSIONS AND IMPLICATIONS

Any attempt to give a history of such a study as this may lay the author open to several dangers. One such danger is that the following study may be interpreted in the light of its pre-history rather than in its final form. Since a basic tenet of the following study is that we should study the final form of the Fourth Gospel rather than its history, it may seem self-defeating to provide a history of the study itself. A second danger is that of authorial intention and its importance (or unimportance) in understanding any text. However, with the question of the 'intentional fallacy' ringing in my ears, I will provide a brief outline of what has led to this study. For those who believe that the meaning resides in the text of the study itself, I make a profound apology.

As an undergraduate, my interest in the 'I am' sayings of the Fourth Gospel was stirred by two events. The first was a lecture course on John's Gospel given in the Sheffield University Biblical Studies Department by Dr Andrew Lincoln. This was the first time I had been exposed to a 'literary' approach to the Gospels. However, rather than neglecting the concerns of history and theology, this course attempted to integrate the approaches of the more traditional theological schools with those of modern Narrative Criticism. The second event was an Evangelistic Mission led by Dr Billy Graham in Sheffield at about the same time. This mission raised the issue of how Jesus' words in John relate to the Jesus of history; an issue that is not restricted to the Evangelical wing of the church, but has repercussions for all those concerned with what is taught in university and what is believed by the majority of church-goers.

Both of these issues led me to want to find out more about the 'I am' sayings. After an undergraduate dissertation on the subject, Dr Lincoln graciously agreed to supervise my postgraduate studies as well. I have therefore subjected not only myself, but my teacher to living closely with these sayings for seven years. This study of the 'I am' sayings will show that the second event which led to this study has still not adequately been dealt with. However, my concern for biblical studies that is accountable to the average church-goer has only been enhanced by my studies and for this I am especially grateful to Rev Dr Bruce Winter of Tyndale House, Cambridge.

Neither my undergraduate nor postgraduate studies would have got anywhere without the constant support and encouragement of my parents. I have also met many friends along the way, including my wife Angela, who was willing to marry into this project and who has proof-read the final stages of this project. I am grateful also to the examiners of my thesis, Dr Stephen Smalley and Dr Margaret Davies for the helpful comments made on areas for improvement. I am, of course, thankful that Sheffield Academic Press, and particularly Professor Stanley Porter, have accepted this study for publication.

My postgraduate work proceeded without any help from Mrs Thatcher's government. I am especially grateful therefore to Mrs G. Brown and Miss D. Everett as well as Elite Valeting for the finances to help me through (though cleaning Mercedes, BMWs and Toyotas are not the stuff Biblical Studies PhDs are usually made of). Tyndale House, Cambridge supported my second and third year's work. Other unsung heroes include Mr John Weston who gave help with my German; Ron Elsdon, who voluntarily converted my original discs from an Amstrad to a PC and Dr G. David Samuel for allowing me time to complete this work. A final word must go to my brother and the BSA Bantam which shares its renovation with this work. To both of these as well as many others, I owe my sanity.

ABBREVIATIONS

AB	Anchor Bible
AnBib	Analecta biblica
BAGD	W. Bauer, W.F. Arndt, F.W. Gingrich and F.W. Danker, *Greek–English Lexicon of the New Testament*
BDB	F. Brown, S.R. Driver and C.A. Briggs, *Hebrew and English Lexicon of the Old Testament*
BEThL	Biblotheca ephemeridum theologicarum lovaniensium
BJRL	*Bulletin of the John Rylands University Library of Manchester*
BTB	*Biblical Theology Bulletin*
BZ	*Biblische Zeitschrift*
CBQ	*Catholic Biblical Quarterly*
ConBNT	Coniectanea biblica, New Testament
ConNT	*Coniectanea neotestamentica*
EvQ	*Evangelical Quarterly*
ExpTim	*Expository Times*
ETL	*Ephemerides theologicae lovanienses*
HTR	*Harvard Theological Review*
ICC	International Critical Commentary
JBL	*Journal of Biblical Literature*
JETS	*Journal of the Evangelical Theological Society*
JSNT	*Journal for the Study of the New Testament*
JSNTSup	*Journal for the Study of the New Testament,* Supplement Series
JSOT	*Journal for the Study of the Old Testament*
JSOTSup	*Journal for the Study of the Old Testament,* Supplement Series
JTS	*Journal of Theological Studies*
LCL	Loeb Classical Library
NCB	New Century Bible
Neot	*Neotestamentica*
NICNT	New International Commentary on the New Testament
NICOT	New International Commentary on the Old Testament
NovT	*Novum Testamentum*
NovTSup	*Novum Testamentum* Supplements
NRT	*Nouvelle Revue Théologique*

NTS	*New Testament Studies*
NZTR	*New Zealand Theological Review*
RB	*Revue Biblique*
ResQ	*Restoration Quarterly*
RSR	*Recherches de science religieuse*
SBLDS	Society of Biblical Literature Dissertation Series
SE	*Studia Evangelica I, II, III* (= TU 73 [1959], 87 [1964], 88 [1964], etc.)
SJT	*Scottish Journal of Theology*
SNTSMS	Society of New Testament Studies Monograph Series
SNTU	*Studien zum Neuen Testament und seiner Umwelt*
ST	*Studia theologica*
TDNT	G. Kittel and G. Friedrich (eds.), *Theological Dictionary of the New Testament*
TZ	*Theologische Zeitschrift*
TLZ	*Theologische Literaturzeitung*
TSK	*Theologische Studien und Kritiken*
WBC	Word Biblical Commentary
WUNT	Wissenschaftliche Untersuchungen zum Neuen Testament
ZKT	*Zeitschrift für katholische Theologie*
ZNW	*Zeitschrift für die neutestamentliche Wissenschaft*

INTRODUCTION

It is now over half a century since the thorough investigation of the Johannine 'I am' sayings by E. Schweizer.[1] Although many important articles on them have appeared since then, scholarship on the Fourth Gospel has changed in so many ways that a full study of these sayings is long overdue. This is all the more important considering the significance of these sayings in the Gospel of John. The phrase is used in various forms, settings and among diverse narrative audiences.[2]

When Schweizer wrote, the general consensus was that the Gospel of John should be understood against a background of Gnostic and Mandaean literature.[3] However, many of the concepts that were thought to derive from a Gnostic milieu have since been found within Judaism. The Jewish nature of the Fourth Gospel has especially been confirmed by the discovery of the Dead Sea scrolls and by the rise in the study of Jewish material as a possible background to Johannine thought. This has led to a re-appraisal of the origins of the Gospel as a whole.

A recent trend in Johannine scholarship has been to accept that, although the text of the Gospel may have had a complex history, it should be interpreted in its final form.[4] This trend has been prompted by

1. E. Schweizer, *Ego Eimi: Die religionsgeschichtliche Herkunft und theologische Bedeutung der johanneischen Bildreden, zugleich ein Beitrag zur Quellenfrage des vierten Evangeliums* (FRLANT, 56; Göttingen: Vandenhoeck & Ruprecht, 1939).

2. Cf. P.B. Harner, *The 'I am' of the Fourth Gospel* (Facet Books; Philadelphia: Fortress Press, 1970), p. 2.

3. This was the consensus of the 'history of religions' school as advocated by R. Bultmann, who held that Mandaean Gnosticism antedates Christianity and is determinative in the shaping of Johannine Christology ('Die Bedeutung der neuer-schlossenen mandäischen und manichäischen Quellen für das Verständnis des Johannesevangeliums', *ZNTW* 24 [1925], pp. 100-46, esp. pp. 115-17). Although Schweizer (*Ego Eimi*, p. 108) did not accept that the extant Mandaean texts influenced John, he saw many parallels in Mandaism and concluded that John and Mandaism drew from a common source.

4. The development of this trend is outlined in the works of S.D. Moore (*Literary*

the rise in various forms of literary criticism,[1] which assume that the extant text is ordered to convey a message and which attempts to discover how that message is conveyed as well as what the message is.[2]

In the light of such major changes in Johannine scholarship, a new study of the 'I am' sayings is needed. However, such a study should not ignore the importance of several of Schweizer's findings about John's use of ἐγώ εἰμι. Schweizer made a nearly exhaustive survey of different uses of 'I am' in various cultures (including examples from India, Iran and Egypt as well as modern usage),[3] and drew the highly significant conclusion that formal parallels to a phrase do not necessarily denote interdependence.[4] It is therefore not necessary to discuss all the possible occurrences of 'I am' unless some sort of dependence can be established or is at least plausible. This will be particularly important in view of the following survey of possible parallels to 'I am' (Chapter 1). Secondly, Schweizer discovered that the Fourth Gospel displayed an essential unity from which it is difficult to extract particular sources for the 'I am' sayings. In other words the sayings form an integral part of the Fourth Gospel and as such cannot readily be removed from it.[5] This will be confirmed by the literary studies in Chapter 3.

Finally, Schweizer maintained that the 'I am' sayings with an image should not be regarded as allegory or parable but as 'real speech'.[6] This

Criticism and the Gospels [New Haven: Yale University Press, 1989], pp. xv-xix) and M.W.G. Stibbe (*John as Storyteller: Narrative Criticism and the Fourth Gospel* [SNTSMS, 73; Cambridge: Cambridge University Press, 1992], pp. 5-12).

1. Moore, *Literary Criticism*, p. xvi, lists 'a bewildering variety of names', by which the new literary approach may be categorized.

2. Moore points out that much biblical literary criticism has been based on the theories of new criticism. He observes that, 'a fundamental New Critical tenet was the inseparability of form and content. Form was not to be thought of as instrumental, the vehicle for ideational or propositional content or cultural or historical reality, separable from the literary text and independent of it. Rather, the meaning of the text was indissolubly bonded with its form' (*Literary Criticism*, p. 9).

3. Schweizer, *Ego Eimi*, pp. 12-14 (also pp. 14-21).

4. Schweizer, *Ego Eimi*, p. 21.

5. Schweizer, *Ego Eimi*, pp. 82-112. He concludes (p. 108): 'The style is generally unified... a) The Gospel is very probably not a completely free creation, but is written on the basis presumably of a written tradition. b) But this tradition is very strongly imbued with the evangelist's own style and is assimilated into the whole so that it is hardly possible to separate it any more.' All translations of German and French texts are my own, except where the work is cited from a published English translation.

6. Schweizer, *Ego Eimi*, pp. 112-24.

means that the 'I am' sayings do not simply compare Jesus with various images but actually unite Jesus with the term.[1] Jesus is not just like a vine (parable—cf. Mt. 13.24, 31, 33), he is the vine. Likewise he is not simply *a* vine (allegory), he is *the* vine.

> It is not Jesus who is the shepherd in the unreal, metaphorical sense—he is the only real and right one—, it is not Jesus who is the bread in the unreal, metaphorical sense—he is the only true and right one—, but all that we humans ('in reality') call shepherd and bread is only this in respect to him in an 'unreal, metaphorical' sense.[2]

1. *The Reasons for the Present Study*

From previous critical studies of the use of ἐγώ εἰμι in John's Gospel, two main categories of form have emerged:

a. The use of ἐγώ εἰμι accompanied by an image. This is the simplest category to define. Starting with the claim to be the bread of life (6.35, 41,48,51.), Jesus takes various images upon himself by means of the words ἐγώ εἰμι ending with the claim to be the true vine (15.1, 5). In all, there are seven distinct images accompanied by the words ἐγώ εἰμι in six different passages.

b. The use of ἐγώ εἰμι without an image. Brown further divides these sayings without an image into '(1) The absolute use with no predicate.'[3] '(2) The use where a predicate may be understood even though it is not expressed.'[4] A satisfactory definition of which among this second category of 'I am' sayings should be regarded as absolute (i.e. which 'I am' sayings stand alone with no further explanation of who or what Jesus is claiming to be) is hard to obtain (see Chapter 5).

Such a distinction in the use of ἐγώ εἰμι in the Fourth Gospel has led scholarship to look for formal parallels to both types of saying. A glance at the possible parallels (outlined in Chapter 1 below) shows that, while the closest formal parallels to the use without an image are in the Old

---

1. Schweizer, *Ego Eimi*, p. 122.
2. Schweizer, *Ego Eimi*, p. 124.
3. R.E. Brown, *The Gospel according to John* (AB, 29; New York: Doubleday, 1970), I, p. 533.
4. Brown, *John*, I, p. 533.

Testament and Judaism, the closest formal parallels to the sayings with an image lie in Mandaism. This has tended to result in scholars studying the different forms separately.[1] It must, however, be asked from the outset whether the use of ἐγώ εἰμι in the text of John allows such a sharp distinction between the forms of 'I am' which even permits an entirely different background to the two types of saying.

Although Schweizer warns against the danger of thinking that a parallel form of saying necessarily implies dependence,[2] his study assumes that the background to the 'I am' sayings consists of formal parallels. He is representative of many scholars in thinking that it is primarily the form of John's ἐγώ εἰμι sayings which provides the key to the correct background by which the phrase may be understood. Such an assumption leads to the danger that otherwise close parallels are excluded because they do not concur with the Johannine form. It is the contention of this investigation that conceptual parallels may prove to be as important as, and in some cases more important than, formal parallels for determining the correct background by which the ἐγώ εἰμι sayings of John's Gospel may be understood. For this reason it is important to study the way ἐγώ εἰμι is used in the Gospel itself before looking for material which is in agreement with such a use of 'I am'.

The belief that ἐγώ εἰμι in John is a formula leads to a further danger that where ἐγώ εἰμι in John does not fit the formula that has been assumed, it may be excluded from discussion.[3] This investigation will thus study every occurrence of ἐγώ εἰμι on the lips of Jesus before determining whether 'I am' is a fixed formula.

As the survey in Chapter 1 will show, scholarship has tended to concentrate on the background to the sayings in John.[4] As a result, there

---

1. Thus Schweizer (*Ego Eimi*) Bultmann (*Mandäischen und manichäischen Quellen*) and S. Schulz (*Komposition und Herkunft der Johanneischen Reden* [Stuttgart: Kohlhammer, 1960]) concentrate on the 'I am' sayings with images. The following, however, concentrate on those 'I am' sayings without images: C.H. Dodd, *The Interpretation of the Fourth Gospel* (Cambridge: Cambridge University Press, 1953), pp. 93-96; Harner, *'I am'*; J. Richter, 'Ani Hu und Ego Eimi' (unpublished dissertation, University of Erlangen, 1956); and E. Stauffer, 'The Background to the Revelation', in *idem, Jesus and his Story* (trans. D.M.Barton; London: SCM Press, 1960).

2. Schweizer, *Ego Eimi*, pp. 37, 38. Cited below in Chapter 1, 'Possible Parallels: Gnosticism and Mandaism'.

3. See below in Chapter 5, 'Delimiting the Sources: Implications of Form'.

4. By concentrating on the role of the 'I am' sayings in the Gospel of John, the

is a danger of imposing on the text ideas which were never implied. The emergence of literary criticism has both challenged the excessive preoccupation of scholarship with the background to Johannine thought and at the same time provided new tools to look at how the Gospel functions as a whole. Owing to the above considerations, the 'I am' sayings of the Fourth Gospel are ripe for re-investigation. It is important to study the context of ἐγώ εἰμι in the Gospel itself. The text of the Gospel will then be used to judge the possible background material in accordance with how the words are used in the Gospel.[1]

2. *Intention and Plan of Action*

The following study of the 'I am' sayings in the Fourth Gospel will be divided into four parts. The first (Chapter 1), entitled 'Suggested Background to "I am"' is a brief, but not exhaustive survey of the various parallels that have been suggested as possible background to the ἐγώ εἰμι sayings of the Fourth Gospel. This part is not intended as a critical history of the study of 'I am', but instead is an overview of the diverse backgrounds that may be pertinent to such a study.[2] The second part (Chapters 2–4), entitled 'The World of the Text', will entail a literary study of each pericope in which the words ἐγώ εἰμι occur. This part will concentrate on how 'I am' works in the Gospel itself[3] and will form a major part of the investigation. The third part (Chapters 5–8), entitled 'The World behind the Text', will draw on conclusions from the second part in order to investigate the background from which the 'I am' sayings derive. In other words, it will be argued that the literary function of ἐγώ εἰμι itself points to the likely sources upon which the writer

work of B. Hinrichs has gone some way to redressing this imbalance (*'Ich Bin': Die Konsistenz des Johannes-Evangeliums in der Konzentration auf das Wort Jesus* [Stuttgarter Bibelstudien, 133; Stuttgart: Katholisches Bibelwerk, 1988]).

1. Cf. W.C. Van Unnik, 'The Purpose of St John's Gospel', *SE* 1, p. 386: 'the final word of John himself' should 'offer the pattern for the reproduction of John's theology'.

2. For a brief critical history of the study of ἐγώ εἰμι , see R. Schnackenburg, *The Gospel according to St John* (trans C. Hastings *et al.*; London: Burns and Oates 1980), II, pp. 81-83.

3. By 'how it works' I intend (following R.A. Culpepper, *Anatomy of the Fourth Gospel* [Foundations and Facets: New Testament; Philadelphia: Fortress Press, 1983], p. 5) questions regarding how the narrative components of the Gospel interact with ἐγώ εἰμι and involve and affect the reader.

drew when using the phrase. The concluding part (Chapter 9), entitled 'The World beyond the Text', will then draw together implications of the investigation for the study of 'I am' and also raise possible implications of such a study for other spheres of Johannine scholarship.

This plan of action may at first seem somewhat clumsy as it involves two (and sometimes three) separate studies of the pericopes which contain ἐγώ εἰμι. However, while a more popular presentation may wish to combine the implications from a literary study with the study of background material in one smooth presentation, the following structure has two distinct advantages. The first is that this structure clearly shows the process of the investigation. In other words, it follows the structure of the investigation as it was carried out and therefore it is possible to trace how each layer of study led to another. Secondly, and more importantly, the following structure begins with the text of the Gospel. The way that 'I am' functions in the Gospel itself is then used to delimit the possible background material. This means that the function of ἐγώ εἰμι in John can be used to sift the enormous amount of possible parallels. This will show that the text itself points to a certain background by which the 'I am' sayings should be understood and will thus suggest that it is not necessary to look to every possible formal parallel before being able to determine what is meant by the use of such a phrase.

Since the term 'literary study' may be defined in several different ways, it is important to clarify the method which was adopted in examining each pericope. In what follows the concept of a 'literary study' of the Fourth Gospel is indebted to the work of Culpepper,[1] which seeks to bring tools from the field of narrative criticism to bear upon the final text of John's Gospel.[2] According to the model which Culpepper and, consequently, the following studies adopt, 'dissection and stratification have no place...and may distort and confuse one's view of the text. Every element of the Gospel contributes to the production of its meaning, and the experience of reading the text is more important than the process of its composition.'[3] However, it is not the intention of the following studies to contend that such 'dissection and stratification have no place in the study of the gospel', nor to contend that the 'process of

1. Culpepper, *Anatomy*.

2. Following Culpepper, *Anatomy*, p. 5: '"Text" here means simply the words or signifiers of the story as recorded in the 26th edition of the Nestle-Aland, *Novum Testamentum Graece*' (Stuttgart: Deutsche Bibelstiftung, 1979).

3. Culpepper, *Anatomy*, p. 5.

its composition' is not important. In fact it may be that in certain
circumstances a 'literary study' of the text sheds new light on the
process of composition, either by confirming or calling into question
previously held views. For this reason Culpepper is correct to call for a
dialogue between 'historical-critical scholarship' and 'the approach of
literary criticism'.[1] Later he further acknowledges that

> Once the effort has been made to understand the narrative character of the
> gospels, some rapprochement with the traditional, historical issues will be
> necessary. Questions about how the story is told inevitably raise interest in
> why it is told and why it is told as it is.[2]

It is therefore the intention of this investigation that such a dialogue will
begin to take place in the study of background material.

While it is important to note that the Gospel of John takes the form of
a Gospel and not of a novel, it is believed that, if used carefully, the tools
developed from the study of modern literature may also throw new light
on the study of ancient literature which conforms only to certain aspects
of the modern genre.[3] It is hoped that the literary studies will show the
particular worth of using such modern tools not only for an
understanding of the text itself but also for their implications for an
understanding of the background from which the text was written.
These literary studies will therefore prove to be a 'way in' for the
background studies which follow them.

In defence of applying the tools of modern narrative criticism to the
text of John's Gospel, it should be stated that, while such tools have
been refined and redefined in the study of various genres (such as the
folk tale and the novel),[4] many of the definitions go back to the ancient

---

1. Culpepper, *Anatomy*, p. 5.
2. Culpepper, *Anatomy*, p. 11.
3. Stibbe points out the importance of recognizing that the Gospel genre is quite
different from that of the novel and that 'Culpepper takes it too much for granted that
a gospel can be studied as if it were a novel' (*John as Storyteller*, p. 10) so that
'Culpepper's method is fundamentally anachronistic' (p. 11). The following study
has attempted to use narrative criticism only in as much as it sheds light on the
Gospel genre. It has not been possible to integrate all the implications of Stibbe's
observations of the flaws in Culpepper's method into the present study.
4. See the seminal works of V. Propp, *The Morphology of the Folktale* (trans. L.
Scott; Austin: University of Texas, 2nd edn, 1968 [1928]) and E.M. Forster, *Aspects
of the Novel* (Harmondsworth: Penguin Books, 1962); cf. also S. Chatman, *Story and
Discourse: Narrative Structure in Fiction and Film* (London: Ithaca, 1978).

study of Greek literature and much is owed in particular to Aristotle's work on poetics.[1] Thus Aristotle deals there with the concepts of plot (6.19–8.4), characterization (15.1-8) and (elsewhere) with irony.[2] Other such tools are derived from the study of ancient as well as modern literature.[3] Thus Moore is correct to observe that:

> Over the past three decades, the theory of narrative has displaced the theory of the novel on the international scene as a central preoccupation of literary theory...Over roughly the same period, narrative theory has become an interdisciplinary project, making important inroads in fields as diverse as anthropology, historiography, psychology, and, of course, theology and biblical studies. The literary study of the Gospels and Acts, in consequence, need by no means be chained to the novel.[4]

Moreover, some of the tools of more traditional historical-critical scholarship (such as form or redaction criticism) are as alien to the ancient world as are concepts derived from poetics (such as point of view or narrative time).[5] It is a question of how these tools are applied to the text of the Gospel and whether they are adapted in the light of the Gospel genre which determines how appropriate and helpful they may be in the understanding of the text.[6]

---

1. Aristotle, *The Poetics: 'Longinus' on the Sublime: Demetrius on Style* (LCL; Aristotle 23; trans. W.H. Fyfe; London: Heinemann, 1927). Aristotle is cited by Culpepper, *Anatomy*, pp. 80 and 101 on plot and characterization respectively.

2. For 'Plot' and 'Characterization' see Aristotle, *Poetics*, pp. 26-34 and p. 55 respectively. For 'Irony' see Aristotle, *The Nicomachean Ethics* (LCL; Aristotle 19; trans H. Rackham; London: Heinemann, 1926), IV, pp. 14, 16. P.D. Duke summarizes the origin and development of irony, showing that both the concept of irony and its study is firmly rooted in the ancient world, even though it has been more precisely defined by 'New Criticism' (*Irony in the Fourth Gospel* [Atlanta: John Knox Press, 1985], pp. 8-13).

3. Thus modern scholars such as Scholes and Kellogg studied Homer as well as other Hellenic and Hebraic literature in their attempt to define different types of characterization (R. Scholes and R. Kellogg, *The Nature of Narrative* [London: Oxford University Press, 1966]. For Homeric characterization see pp. 161-64; for biblical characterization see pp. 165-67).

4. Moore, *Literary Criticism*, p. xviii.

5. Moore, *Literary Criticism*, pp. xiii, xiv, makes the same point.

6. In the wake of literary studies of the Gospels, the question of genre has taken on renewed significance. For a recent study of the Fourth Gospel's genre, see M. Davies, *Rhetoric and Reference in the Fourth Gospel* (Sheffield: JSOT Press, 1992), pp. 66-109. Having shown the importance of the question of genre for the study of the Gospel, Davies is still happy to use modern concepts such as 'the

After studying the literary function of ἐγώ εἰμι in the Gospel of John, the next question to ask is what the background to the Johannine use of 'I am' may be. Drawing on its literary function and context, the possible background can be further defined. Three points suggest that it is appropriate to pursue the thesis that all the 'I am' sayings of John's Gospel derive their meaning from the Old Testament and Judaism:

1.   Old Testament and Jewish concepts are explicitly alluded to in the context of ἐγώ εἰμι;
2.   scholarship has become more and more conscious of the Jewish nature of John;
3.   literary study shows the two types of ἐγώ εἰμι to be inter-related in such a way as to suggest a similar conceptual background.

Constant reference to the context and function of ἐγώ εἰμι in John will attempt to ensure that the findings on the background to the phrase are set in their right context, not as an imposition on the text but as parallels which may shed light on the term as used in John. The question of what is meant by 'I am' on the lips of Jesus (i.e. its theological implications) in John can then be addressed in conclusion.[1]

---

implied reader' and 'the implied author' and also to make use of what is best from reader-response theories.

1.   To look at the background of the text is not in itself a departure from the concerns of narrative criticism, for a knowledge of first-century culture and history is essential to understand the Johannine story. Where this study departs from pure narrative criticism is in the belief that 'the meaning resides in the text's theological (or ideational) content. This content is separable in principle from the narrative form; narrative is the vehicle of theology. Narrative criticism in contrast, is a formalist criticism; the meaning of the biblical text is located in the details of its structure. What the text says cannot legitimately be extrapolated from how it is said' (Moore, *Literary Criticism*, p. 10). Although the following study accepts that the meaning of the text is located in the details of its structure, it views the text as the vehicle of theology so that, at least in principle, it is possible to speak of meaning conveyed by the text but which is distinct from it. In this respect the following study thus comes somewhere on the line between what Moore regards as 'compositional' and pure 'narrative' criticism. The latter has the declared intention of bracketing the author's intention with a list of extrinsic approaches inappropriate to a literary study of the text. Instead it looks at the closed universe of the story world (cf. Moore, *Literary Criticism*, pp. 8, 12). While the following study accepts that author's intention is not the primary locus of meaning, it also acknowledges that 'the text produces specifiable effects on the reader, which implicitly originate in an author's intentions' (Moore, *Literary Criticism*, p. 12).

3. *The Limitations of this Investigation*

The following investigation is not an attempt to study all the possible parallels to 'I am'. Such a study has already been carried out by Schweizer.[1] It is the thesis of this investigation that such a study is unnecessary since John itself points to a particular background by which the 'I am' sayings should be understood. It will be seen that the background for the Johannine 'I am' sayings is primarily in the Old Testament. However, this investigation does not attempt to study all the occurrences of 'I am' in the Hebrew or Greek Old Testament, but only those passages that may be alluded to in John's use of the phrase.[2] It will be argued that the formulation of the 'I am' sayings in John alludes to particular passages and themes from the Old Testament and Judaism.

This study has deliberately been restricted to the occurrences of ἐγώ εἰμι on the lips of Jesus in John. Therefore certain possible 'I am' sayings are not included in this study either because they do not fit this precise form of words or because they occur on the lips of others. The following sayings on the lips of Jesus which may be related to ἐγώ εἰμι, have been disregarded for the purpose of this study because they do not fit the precise formulation and raise issues that would need to be addressed as part of a separate study: (1) ἐγώ ἐκ τῶν ἄνω εἰμί, 8.23; (2) ἐγώ οὐκ εἰμι ἐκ τοῦ κόσμου (τούτου), 8.23; 17.16; (3) ὅπου εἰμι ἐγώ, 7.34; 12.26; 14.3; 17.24.[3] In addition, possible uses of the phrase on the lips of others have not been studied (the man born blind, 9.5; John the Baptist, 1.20; 3.28).[4] It is not a problem for the following investigation that John

1. Of the studies since Schweizer, as we have seen, only those of MacRae and Schulz have brought forward any new material. Schulz finds parallels in further Mandaean texts (*Komposition*, pp. 96, 97) as well as in material from Qumran (*Komposition*, p. 118). The material from Qumran does not contain 'I am' sayings. MacRae, *The Ego-Proclamation* (see above), suggests Gnostic material from Nag Hammadi as further parallels to the ἐγώ εἰμι of John.
2. Cf. Schweizer, *Ego Eimi*, pp. 21-27; A. Deissmann, *Light from the Ancient East* (New York: George H. Doran, 1927), pp. 139-40; and J. Richter, 'Ani Hu', pp. 19-46, for use of 'I am' in the LXX and Hebrew Old Testament; also W. Zimmerli, *I am Yahweh* (trans. D.W. Scott, ed. W. Brueggemann; Atlanta: John Knox Press, 1982) for the use of 'I am Yahweh' in the Hebrew Old Testament.
3. Brown, *John*, I, pp. 314, 347, hints at a link between these sayings and ἐγώ εἰμι.
4. Cf. E.D. Freed, 'Ego Eimi in John 1.20 and 4.25', *CBQ* 41 (2,79), pp. 288-91; P. Borgen, *Bread from Heaven: An Exegetical Study of the Concept of Manna in the*

is able to use a 'profane' ἐγώ εἰμι on the lips of the man born blind, since neither the context of that saying nor its formulation point to the background which makes the use of the phrase on Jesus' lips so profound.

Gospel of John and the Writings of Philo (SNT, 10; Leiden: Brill, 1965), p. 72; Hinrichs, *Ich Bin*, pp. 19-22, 66-69.

Part I

SUGGESTED BACKGROUND TO 'I AM':
A SURVEY OF SCHOLARSHIP

Chapter 1

POSSIBLE PARALLELS IN THE ANCIENT WORLD

The enigmatic character of the 'I am' sayings in the Fourth Gospel has caused scholars to search in every direction to understand better the implications of ἐγώ εἰμι for the 'original' audience.[1] As a starting point, a survey of the diverse opinion may show the need to delimit such background material on the basis of how 'I am' functions within the text of John itself.

1. *The Greek World*

Hellenism in General

G.P. Wetter began by looking at the occurrences of ἐγώ εἰμι in John's Gospel.[2] He then studied the incidence of 'I am' in the Synoptics before looking at its use in Judaism and the LXX.[3] Finally he investigated texts outside the sphere of the Israelite religion in the ancient world at large. He claims to have found an occurrence of the absolute 'I am' in an Egyptian text, which he cites in translation:

> I am the God Atum, who alone was…I reach this Land of the Transfigured Ones and enter in through the magnificent gateway. You who stand outside, stretch out your hands to me; I am he, I have become one of you. I am together with my Father Atum daily.[4]

Apart from this isolated occurrence of an absolute 'I am' in Egypt,

---

1. Dodd, *Interpretation*, p. 6, points out the danger but necessity of searching for background material in John.

2. G.P. Wetter, '"Ich bin es", Eine Johanneische Formel', *TSK* 88 (1915), pp. 224-38.

3. Wetter, 'Ich bin es', p. 233.

4. The translation Wetter quotes ('Ich bin es', p. 233) is by A. Erman, *Aegypten und Aegyptisches Leben im Altertum* [zweiter Band] (Tübingen: H. Laupp'schen, 1885), pp. 459-60.

Wetter also sees examples of an absolute ἐγώ εἰμι in the Magical
Papyri:

Leiden Papyrus. W. VII 33:
καὶ μηδείς με καταβιάσαιτο, **ὅτι ἐγώ εἰμι·** λέγε τὸ ὄνομα...
Leiden Papyrus. Z. 39:
οὐ μή μου λυμάνης σάρκα· **ὅτι ἐγώ εἰμι·** λέγε τὸ ὄνομα...[1]

For Wetter, these texts present evidence for a non-Jewish background to
the ἐγώ εἰμι in John. Yet Zimmermann rightly argues that the magical
texts cannot be accepted as an absolute ἐγώ εἰμι.[2] While they certainly
contain the phrase ἐγώ εἰμι, this is followed immediately by the phrase
λέγε τὸ ὄνομα. From this it is apparent that the magician was expected
to supply the name of the power whom he was invoking. Although
Wetter acknowledges that in the LXX the formula ἐγώ εἰμι clearly
signified an attribute of Yahweh and also possessed the same solemn
tone as in the text of John, he concludes that:

> In my opinion, the author of John's Gospel did not take it from the Old
> Testament... but from his environment, from the religious life bustling all
> around him, whether it had more of a Judaeo-hellenistic or more of a
> generally Hellenistic-syncretic character.[3]

Deissmann quotes three texts containing ἐγώ εἰμι[4] and sets them
alongside Jn 10.7-14. The two Isis inscriptions, the first, an inscription
from Nysa quoted by Diodorus Siculus, and the second, an inscription at
Ios, are very similar:

Ἐγὼ ᵉἸσίς εἰμι ἡ Βασίλισσα πάσης χώρας... **Ἐγώ εἰμι** ἡ τοῦ
νεωτάτου Κρόνου Θεοῦ θυγάτηρ πρέσβυτάτη. **Ἐγώ εἰμι** γυνὴ
καὶ ἀδελφὴ Ὀσίριδος βασιλέως. **Ἐγώ εἰμι** ἡ πρώτη καρπόν

---

1. Wetter, 'Ich bin es', p. 233, quotes from the *Leiden Papyrus* W. VII.33 and
Z.39.
2. H. Zimmermann, 'Das Absolute "Ego Eimi" als die neutestamentliche
Offenbarungsformel', *BZ 4* (1960), pp. 54-69, 266-76. See especially pp. 55, 56.
3. Wetter, 'Ich bin es', p. 234.
4. Deissmann, *Light*, pp. 133-40. Deissmann usefully lays out the texts in
Greek: none of these contain an absolute ἐγώ εἰμι.

p. 138	Diodorus Siculus	[6 × ἐγώ εἰμι]
pp. 139-40	The Inscription at Ios	[5 × ἐγώ εἰμι; 22 × ἐγώ]
p. 142	London Magical Papyrus No.46	[7 × ἐγώ εἰμι]

ἀνθρώποις εὑροῦσα. Ἐγώ εἰμι μήτηρ. Ὧρον τοῦ βασιλέως Ἐγώ εἰμι ἡ ἐν τῷ ἄστρῳ ἐν τῷ κυνὶ ἐπιτέλλουσα.[1]

Εἶσις ἐγώ εἰμι ἡ τ[ύρανν]ος πάσης χόρας... Ἐγὼ νόμους ἀνθρώποις ἐθέμην... Ἐγώ εἰμι Κρόνου θυγάτηρ πρέσβυτάτη. Ἐγώ εἰμι γυνὴ καὶ ἀδελφὴ Ὀσείρεος βασιλέος. Ἐγώ εἰμι θεοῦ Κυνὸς ἄστρῳ ἐπιτέλουσα. Ἐγώ εἰμι ἡ παρὰ γυναιξὶ θεὸς καλουνένη...[2]

Deissmann remarks more on the similarity between these texts and the LXX than concerning their possible influence on John:[3]

> I was anxious to show how close the resemblance can be between the Hellenised Old Testament and Hellenised Egyptian religion. The actual relationship of ideas being so close, how easy it must have been for Hellenistic Judaism and Christianity to adopt the remarkable and simple style of expression in the first person singular.[4]

The implications of Deissmann's observations are twofold. First, he allows for the possibility that Judaism itself may have been influenced by the Hellenistic 'I'-style in much the same way that he thinks the religions of Egypt were. This would mean that it would be dangerous to draw a strict line between Jewish and Hellenistic influences on John.[5] Influences in John that appear at first to be of Hellenistic character, may in fact have been filtered through Judaism and may not have been borrowed directly from the religions of Hellenism. Secondly, by placing the Isis sayings alongside John 10, he implies a conceptual correspondence

---

1.   Deissmann, *Light*, p. 138, taken from Diodorus Siculus, *History* 1.27 (trans. H. Voegel; Leipzig, 1888). Also in *Diodorus of Sicily* (LCL; trans. C.H. Oldfather; London: William Heinemann, 1933), I, pp. 86-88.

2.   The Ios inscription is presented in full by Deissmann, *Light*, pp. 139-40. The validity of Diodorus Siculus (27 BCE) for this discussion is confirmed by the text at Ios, although the latter is not dated earlier than the second or third century CE; cf. Deissmann, *Light*, p. 135.

3.   Deissmann, *Light*, pp. 139-40, points to more than 20 LXX references in which he sees stylistic parallels with the inscription at Ios.

4.   Deissmann, *Light*, p. 141.

5.   Cf. M. Hengel, *The 'Hellenisation' of Judaea in the First Century after Christ* (London: SCM Press, 1989). Hengel suggests that the distinction between 'Palestinian Judaism' and 'Hellenistic Judaism' should not be overemphasized. See esp. chapter 6, pp. 52-56: 'The Consequences: Palestinian Judaism as Hellenistic Judaism'. Hengel thinks that even in Palestine, 'people probably read the Septuagint and other edifying "Jewish-Greek" literature, but very rarely the Greek classic writers and philosophers in the original' (p. 56).

between the religions of Hellenism and the language of John. Deissmann's final text, a magical text from the fourth century CE, simply shows the continuation of this 'I'-style beyond the time of the New Testament.

Harner, who is seeking parallels to the absolute use of ἐγώ εἰμι, points out that 'no clear, unambiguous use of the phrase "I am" in an absolute sense' is found in any of the texts examined since Deissmann and Wetter.[1] Harner does acknowledge the use of 'I am' with a predicate in *The Hermetica*.[2] Barrett too suggests the Hermetic Corpus, where Poimandres reveals himself to Hermes through an 'I am' formula:

Corpus Hermeticum:
1,2:   Ἐγώ μέν, φησίν, εἰμι ὁ Ποιμάνδρης, ὁ τῆς αὐθεντίας
         νοῦς...
1,6:   Τὸ φῶς, ἐκεῖνο, ἔφη, ἐγὼ Νοῦς σὸς θέος...[3]

Barrett also thinks that the 'I'-form may indirectly stem from magical formulae dependent on the Isis aretalogy cited by Deissmann.[4]

Gnosticism and Mandaism
Besides those who admit influence of a general Hellenistic character, are those who have seen Gnostic or Mandaean stylistic features in John's language (of which 'I am' is especially characteristic). With the support of a scholar such as Bultmann, it is not surprising that possible Mandaean influence on John became widely accepted.

In a study which looked at the possible influence of Mandaean texts on the Fourth Gospel as a whole, Bultmann remarked that the revelatory style of speech is typical in Mandaism.[5] Bultmann cites what he regards as examples of real revelatory speech in which 'I am' occurs several times:

---

1.   Harner, *'I am'*, pp. 27,28.
2.   Harner, *'I am'*, p. 28.
3.   C.K. Barrett, *The Gospel according to St John* (London: SPCK, 2nd edn, 1978), p. 292. The two Hermetic references are translated in full in C.K. Barrett, *The New Testament Background: Selected Documents* (London: SPCK, 1957), pp. 82, 83. The texts are laid out in Greek in A.D. Nock and A. Festugière, *Corpus Hermeticum. Tome I. Traités I-XII* (Collection des Universités de France; Paris: 1945), pp. 7, 8.
4.   Barrett, *John*, p. 292.
5.   Bultmann, *Mandäischen und manichäischen Quellen*, p. 115.

The Envoy of Light am I, whom the Great One has sent into this world
(*Right Ginza* II, p. 64, 17-18).[1]

The Envoy of Light am I; each one, who smells his fragrance, receives
life... (*Right Ginza* II, p.64, 23-24).[2]

The true Envoy am I, in whom there is no deceit,
The True One, in whom there is no deceit, there is no fault or lack in him
(*Right Ginza* II, p. 65, 1-3).[3]

The Envoy of Life am I... (*Right Ginza* II, p. 65, 15).[4]

Bultmann claims these sayings result in the fact that 'the johannine
images of Shepherd, Vine etc. belong in a fixed context of tradition'.[5]
The belief that the words 'I am', as well as the concepts that go with
them, are indebted to Gnosticism and Mandaism is also characteristic of
Bultmann's commentary.[6] In his comments on ch. 4, for instance, he
states that 'this mode of speech about "living water", "bread of life",
"true light", "true vine" comes from the sphere of Gnostic dualism'. [7]

Schweizer took up the Mandaean question in terms of the 'I am'
sayings and their attached predicates. For Schweizer, the 'I am' sayings
of John differ structurally from all the literature that he cites in his first
chapter.[8] The few sayings in the Old Testament, which are predicated

---

1.   Bultmann, *Mandäischen und manichäischen Quellen*, quoting from
M. Lidzbarski, *Ginza, der Schatz oder das große Buch der Mandäer* (Göttingen:
Vandenhoeck & Ruprecht, 1925), p. 58.

2.   Bultmann, *Mandäischen und manichäischen Quellen*, pp. 110-11. In
Lidzbarski, *Ginza*, p. 58.

3.   Bultmann, *Mandäischen und manichäischen Quellen*, p. 113. In Lidzbarski,
Ginza, p. 59.

4.   Bultmann, *Mandäischen und manichäischen Quellen*, p. 110. In Lidzbarski,
Ginza, p. 59.

5.   Bultmann, *Mandäischen und manichäischen Quellen*, p. 116.

6.   See the long note on ἐγώ εἰμι in R. Bultmann's commentary, pp. 225-26,
where he draws many parallels with Mandaism (*The Gospel of John* [trans.
G.R. Beasley-Murray; Oxford: Basil Blackwell, 1971]). The parallels he draws from
varied backgrounds (including the Old Testament) suggest that he does not regard the
Mandaean sayings as the exclusive influence on John's ἐγώ εἰμι.

7.   Bultmann, *John*, p. 182.

8.   Schweizer, *Ego Eimi*, p. 33. He sets out what he sees as an important formal
difference between the religious-historical and Old Testament 'I am' sayings and
those in John, which have a fourfold structure: (1) ἐγώ; (2) εἰμι; (3) the 'image-word';
and (4) an adjective with the article repeated, or a genitive expressing uniqueness.

with an image, argue against finding there the background for ἐγώ εἰμι in John:

> It is striking...that even in the OT quite a selection of images would have been available, which as ever recurring terms describe the being and activity of God: 'Shepherd', 'Rock', 'Fortress', 'Shield', 'Lion' etc., but that of these predicates only the first occurs in John, while all the other johannine concepts are either completely foreign to the OT or else [when they do occur in the OT] imply something quite different.[1]

It may be true that John does not take up these predicates of the Old Testament in his 'I am' sayings, but, whether the Old Testament can be so swiftly dismissed as background to the imagery connected with the sayings, is to be seriously doubted. That Johannine terminology is really foreign to the Old Testament or even meant in a completely different way, is a matter to be discussed below. To argue that the absence of certain Old Testament predicates necessarily rules the Old Testament out as background to the sayings in John, is unconvincing. On the same premise it could be argued that the absence of the following Mandaean predicates rules Mandaism out as a source of background material:

> A house am I, which has been abandoned by its master and whose builder has deserted it (*Book of John* 65.12).[2]

> A Fisherman am I, a fisherman, chosen from among the fishermen. A fisherman am I, chosen from among the fishermen, the chief of all the fisherfolk (*Book of John* 143.1).[3]

For Schweizer, as for Bultmann, it is in the remarkably similar nature of the Mandaean literature that the key to the Johannine 'I am' sayings is to be found. He particularly concentrates on the similarity in imagery between Mandaism and John:

> A shepherd am I, who loves his sheep and cares for his sheep and lambs. Around my neck (I carry) the sheep, and the sheep do not stray from the village (*Book of John* 44.27-30).[4]

> A vine are we, a vine of life,
> A tree, in whom there is no deceit.

1. Schweizer, *Ego Eimi*, pp. 37, 38.
2. M. Lidzbarski, *Das Johannesbuch der Mandäer* (Giessen: Töppelmann, 1915), p. 69.
3. Lidzbarski, *Das Johannesbuch*, p. 144.
4. Schweizer, *Ego Eimi*, p. 64. In Lidzbarski, *Das Johannesbuch*, p. 44.

The Tree of Praise,
from whose fragrance each receives life (*Ginza* 65.39-40).[1]

The major problem with much of the Mandaean literature is that it is
difficult to date accurately. Indeed, there is an obvious Christian
influence on much of it. For example, earlier in *Ginza* (55.149), just
after a statement about Sunday observance, come the words 'I am the
true God, whom my Father has sent hither. I am the first, I am the last
Envoy; I am the Father, I am the Son, I am the Holy Spirit...'[2] Since
Schweizer acknowledges that the extant Mandaean texts are from
Babylonia of the eighth century,[3] he has to argue for an early date and a
Western origin for the essentials of Mandaism in order to be able to
assert that it is linked to the thought of John.[4] As a result he concludes
that

> It is very probable that the Evangelist is either tied to a Christian sayings-
> source, whose author was or had been very close to the Mandaean
> religious community and their texts, or even more likely (since we could
> not extract such a sayings-source) that he himself is this author and either
> he freely models his speeches according to the usual Mandaean texts, or
> he permeates existing material very strongly with his own style.[5]

In claiming to be the light of the world, the bread of life etc. Jesus is,
according to Schweizer, standing over and above those redeemers of
Mandaism.

   Against Schweizer, Yamauchi does not believe there is sufficient
evidence to support 'the development of Mandaeanism prior to the
second century AD'.[6] He correctly recognizes that parallels between
John and Mandaism 'can be significant in providing us insight into
John's *Vorlage* only if Mandaeanism was a pre-Christian movement'.[7]
Firm evidence for the existence of Mandaism in the third century CE

   1.   Schweizer, *Ego Eimi*, p. 67. In Lidzbarski, *Ginza*, pp. 59, 60.
   2.   Lidzbarski, *Ginza*, p. 50.
   3.   Schweizer, *Ego Eimi*, p. 46.
   4.   Cf. Schweizer, *Ego Eimi*, p. 62.
   5.   Schweizer, *Ego Eimi*, p. 108.
   6.   E.W. Yamauchi, 'Jewish Gnosticism? The Prologue of John, Mandaean
Parallels, and the Trimorphic Protennoia', in R. Van Den Broeck and M.J. Vermaseren,
Studies is Gnosticism and Hellenistic Religions: Festschrift Gilles Quispel (Leiden:
Brill, 1981), p. 473. Cf. also E.W. Yamauchi, *Gnostic Ethics and Mandaean Origins*
(Cambridge, MA: Harvard University Press, 1970), pp. 68-89.
   7.   Yamauchi, *Jewish Gnosticism*, p. 473.

was found in a supposed link with Mani. The similar language of Manichaeism and Mandaism had led to the theory 'that Mani (AD 216–275) had been raised among the Mandaeans'.[1] This belief was undermined by the publication of the *Cologne Codex* in 1970, which showed Mani was raised by the Jewish-Christian Elchasaites.[2] Any interdependence between the language of John and that of Manichaeism therefore probably stems from Mani's knowledge of John rather than from a mutual dependence on Mandaism. However, McArthur still contends for the possibility of a proto-Mandaism which existed in the first century and which influenced the predicated 'I am' sayings of John's Gospel:

> Certainly the evangelist would not have supported an ultimate dualism, but the radical contrast that is expressed exceeds what might have been expected from the Jewish tradition or popular Platonism (see 3.3, 7, 13, 31ff.; 6.35, 38, 41-42, 50-51, 58, 62; 7.29; 8.23, 42).[3]

More recently MacRae took up the similarities of the 'I'-form in John and in Gnostic literature. He acknowledges that, but for one exception,[4] it is hard to find any evidence for the use of an absolute 'I am' and suggests that 'There is no positive indication in this Gnostic *mythologoumenon* that the Gnostics were aware of the absolute use of ἐγώ εἰμι as a claim to divinity...'[5] MacRae argues that the Coptic Gnostic literature from Nag Hammadi contain 'I am' sayings with a predicate similar to those in the Fourth Gospel:

---

1. Yamauchi, *Jewish Gnosticism*, p. 474.
2. Yamauchi, *Jewish Gnosticism*, p. 474.
3. H.K. McArthur, 'Christological Perspectives in the Predicates of the Johannine Ego Eimi Sayings', in R.F. Berkey and S.A. Edwards (eds.), *Christological Perspectives: Festschrift H.K. McArthur* (New York: Pilgrims Press, 1982), p. 85. McArthur gives a very good overview of the Mandaean/Gnostic question as it affects ἐγώ εἰμι in John, though he admits to going against modern trends in acknowledging a proto-Mandaean influence on John. See also more recent research in which some are again arguing for an early Palestinian provenance of Mandaism independent of John. E.g. G. Widengren (ed.), *Der Mandäismus* (Wege der Forschung, 167; Darmstadt: Wissenschaftliche Buchgesellschaft, 1982).
4. In the *Pseudo-Clementine Homilies* 2.24,6: B. Rehm (ed.), *Die Pseudoklementinen*. I. *Die griechische christlichen Schriftsteller der ersten Jahrhunderte* (Berlin: Akademie Verlag, 1969), p. 45.
5. G.W. MacRae, 'The Ego-Proclamation in Gnostic sources', in E. Bammel (ed.), *The Trial of Jesus* (London: SCM Press, 1970), p. 129.

Codex VI Tractate 2: *The Thunder: Perfect Mind.*
For I am the first and the last.
I am the honoured one and the scorned one.
I am the whore and the holy one.
I am the wife and the virgin.
I am the mother and the daughter...[1]

Codex II Tractate 5: *On the Origin of the World.*
It is I who am part of my mother;
And it is I who am the Mother;
It is I who am the wife;
It is I who am the virgin...[2]

The dubious foundation of attempts to link the Mandaean literature to the time of the Gospel prompts MacRae to suggest that discussion should move from Mandaism to the 'I am' in these Gnostic sources.[3] He concludes that

> it may be that the Fourth Gospel...uses the form of ἐγώ- proclamation not merely to assert that Jesus must be recognised as or identified with the variety of human symbolism: bread, light, shepherd, life, etc but that Jesus in his truest reality transcends all of this and is revealed only in the moment of his return to the Father.[4]

Thus, for MacRae, 'the evangelist is not merely influenced by a complex and syncretistic religious background, but...deliberately makes use of such a background for his interpretation of the meaning of Jesus.'[5] However, the paradoxical nature of the 'I am' sayings cited from *On the Origin of the World* is quite unlike John's use of 'I am'. In addition, more recently both MacRae and his editor call the Gnostic nature of the cited text into question.[6] Doubts about the Gnostic nature of the text combine with doubts about how close a parallel they are to John's style to suggest that Gnosticism may not be such a fruitful sphere for the understanding of ἐγώ εἰμι in John.

1. Translated by G.W. MacRae, in J.M. Robinson (ed.), *The Nag Hammadi Library in English* (trans. Members of the Coptic Gnostic Library Project of the Institute for Antiquity and Christianity; Leiden: Brill, 1988), p. 297.

2. Translated by H.G. Bethge *et al.*, *The Nag Hammadi Library*, p. 181.

3. MacRae, *The Ego-Proclamation*, p. 133.

4. MacRae, *The Ego-Proclamation*, p. 133.

5. MacRae, *The Ego-Proclamation*, p. 133.

6. Cf. MacRae, *The Nag Hammadi Library*, p. 296; also Parrott, *The Nag Hammadi Library*, p. 296.

2. *Judaism*

The Old Testament[1]

Lightfoot suggested that, although each 'I am' saying should be decided by the context, the occurrences of the absolute ἐγώ εἰμι in John 8 and 13.19 should be translated 'I am', since 'the two words in the Greek are the same as those of the LXX in certain O.T. passages, e.g. Deut. 32.39, Is. 46.4 where Yahweh is the speaker, and thus emphasises his Godhead'.[2] He also reasoned that this interpretation should be kept in the reader's mind in Jn 18.4-8 while accepting the RV's rendering 'I am he'.[3] A far more detailed investigation into the relationship between ἐγώ εἰμι and the *ani hu* (אני הוא) of the Old Testament was undertaken by J. Richter in his dissertation.[4] With Wetter, he regards ἐγώ εἰμι as a fixed formula. Richter sets out to investigate in detail the thesis, which had been hinted at many times, that this formula refers back to the Old Testament formula *ani hu*.[5]

Richter looks at the idea of *ani hu* as a divine revelation formula. In a comprehensive study of the use of 'I am' in the Old Testament, he argues that the 'profane' (i.e. the human), which is limited to 'identification and emphatic self-statement',[6] and the 'divine' usage of *ani hu* are parallel in form.[7] By an individual exegesis of the divine occurrences of *ani hu* in Deutero-Isaiah and Deuteronomy, he is able to distinguish the peculiarities of the divine revelation formula. His conclusion is that *ani hu* is a code-word of absolute monotheism and thus it becomes 'by its breadth and all-embracing significance the sum of all God's statements about himself.'[8] By reasoning that ἐγώ εἰμι in the New Testament does indeed point back to *ani hu* in the Old Testament, he maintains that Jesus speaks as God.[9]

---

1. The division of Judaism into two sections is merely for the ease of categorization. It does not intend to imply that there are clear borders dividing Old Testament influence on John from that of the Jewish religion in general.

2. R.H. Lightfoot, *St John's Gospel* (ed. C.F. Evans; Oxford: Clarendon Press, 1986 [1953]), p. 134.

3. Lightfoot, *St John*, p. 134.

4. J. Richter, 'Ani Hu'.

5. J. Richter, 'Ani Hu', p. 17.

6. J. Richter, 'Ani Hu', p. 21.

7. J. Richter, 'Ani Hu', p. 24.

8. J. Richter, 'Ani Hu', p. 43.

9. J. Richter, 'Ani Hu', p. 85.

Zimmermann looks at the Old Testament use of the term '*ani YHWH*' (אֲנִי־יהוה) which he regards as the Revelation Formula of the Old Testament.[1] He wishes to build a bridge between that formula and the ἐγώ εἰμι of Jesus. He finds such a link in the LXX translation of Isaiah where the absolute ἐγώ εἰμι becomes the translation of *ani hu*. This in turn is connected with the formula *ani YHWH*. The LXX of Isa. 45.18 shows an even clearer link between the formula *ani YHWH* and the ἐγώ εἰμι of the New Testament since the *ani Yhwh* there is translated with an absolute ἐγώ εἰμι.[2] To those who focus on Deutero-Isaiah for an understanding of the 'I am' sayings of John can be added the names of Feuillet,[3] Brown,[4] Coetzee[5] and many others. Harner sees Deutero-Isaiah as the main influence on the absolute 'I am' of John, but does not rule out a link with the Tetragrammaton of Exod. 3.14 nor with the interpretation given to the words by Rabbinic Judaism.[6]

Both Smalley[7] and Painter[8] concentrate on the 'I am' sayings with predicates. Smalley thinks that there is more than a superficial contact between the miracle at Cana and the image of the true vine in John 15. Using Ps. 80.8 and Isa. 5.1 as examples, he thinks that, 'the thought of Israel as the vine of God is characteristically Jewish'.[9] By drawing on such a background he suggests that, 'the manifestation of the glory of Jesus in this first sign (Jn 2.11) makes clear that in him the life of the

---

1. Zimmermann, *Das Absolute 'Ego Eimi'*, pp. 64-69.

2. Zimmermann, *Das Absolute 'Ego Eimi'*, p. 68. S. Pancaro, *The Law in the Fourth Gospel: The Torah and the Gospel, Moses and Jesus, Judaism and Christianity according to John* (SNT, 42; Leiden: Brill, 1975), p. 59, builds on Zimmermann's results.

3. A. Feuillet, 'Les ego eimi christologiques du quatrième evangile: La révélation énigmatique de l'être divine de Jésus dans Jean et les Synoptiques', *RSR* 54 (1966), esp. pp. 11, 12.

4. Brown, *John*, I, Appendix IV, pp. 535-37. Brown suggests, like Zimmermann, that 'the absolute use of "I am" in John is the basis for the other uses, in particular the use... with a nominal predicate' (p. 537).

5. J.C. Coetzee, 'Jesus' Revelation in the Ego Eimi Sayings in John 8 and 9', in J.H. Petzer and P.J. Hartin (eds.), *A South African Perspective on the New Testament* (Leiden: Brill, 1986), pp. 170-77.

6. Harner, '*I am*', pp. 17 and 26 respectively.

7. S.S. Smalley, *John: Evangelist and Interpreter* (Exeter: Paternoster Press, 1978), pp. 90-91.

8. J. Painter, *John: Witness and Theologian* (London: SPCK, 1979), pp. 37-49.

9. Smalley, *Evangelist*, p. 90.

new Israel (the true vine) has come to birth'.[1] Smalley also finds that the shepherd imagery of John 10 is best explained by reference to such passages as Ps. 80.1 and Ezek. 34.12.[2] Painter thinks that many of John's images reflect the Old Testament concept of Law. He finds the Law symbolized as bread (Sir. 15.3; 24.19-21) and as light (Ps. 119.105).[3] 'The contrast with Moses and the Law is [also] suggested by the symbol "the way" which is frequently used in the Old Testament as a symbol for the Law (Deut. 1.30ff.; 5.32f.; 31.15-19; 31.29 and in numerous Psalms).'[4] For Painter, the claim to be the true vine finds its meaning in various Old Testament passages (Hos. 10.1; Ezek. 15.1-8; 19.10-14; Ps. 80.8-16) and in later Judaism was used as a symbol for the Messiah (2 *Bar.* 39.7 and Ps. 80.14 [LXX]) and for the Law (Sir. 24.17, 23-28).[5] Even though the concept of the Law is absent from the shepherd imagery, that too derives from the Old Testament (Ps. 23; 78.70-72; 80; Isa. 40.11; Jer. 31.10; Ezek. 34; 37.24).[6] The concept of truth also finds expression in the Old Testament (Ps. 119).[7]

Davies thinks that all the 'I am' sayings in the Gospel derive from the Wisdom literature of the Old Testament.[8] She argues that

> In Scripture prophets do not use this ['I'-] form, but, on the contrary, point away from themselves by introducing their oracles, 'Thus says the Lord'. The form 'I am...' is found in Scripture, however, in the Wisdom writings, where personified Wisdom speaks of her attributes.[9]

Davies then quotes from Prov. 8.12-21 and Sir. 24.3-31, arguing that Jesus in the Fourth Gospel 'declares who he is in the manner of personified Wisdom, using the same "I am" formula, and combining it with images and concepts from other parts of Scripture'.[10] Davies is aware that many have pointed to passages from Second Isaiah to understand the 'I am' sayings without an image. She refutes such a suggestion, arguing that the sayings without an image can be understood in their

---

1. Smalley, *Evangelist*, p. 90.
2. Smalley, *Evangelist*, p. 91.
3. Painter, *Witness*, pp. 39, 40.
4. Painter, *Witness*, p. 41.
5. Painter, *Witness*, p. 48.
6. Painter, *Witness*, p. 42.
7. Painter, *Witness*, p. 46.
8. Davies, *Rhetoric*, pp. 82-87.
9. Davies, *Rhetoric*, p. 83.
10. Davies, *Rhetoric*, p. 83.

own context without reference to such passages.[1] She therefore concludes 'that the Johannine Jesus' use of the "I am" form draws on Wisdom declarations from its Scripture, and does not assert Jesus' divinity'.[2]

Judaism in General

Dodd takes the *ani hu* of the Old Testament as the starting point for understanding the ἐγώ εἰμι of John. However, he looks to Rabbinic texts to elucidate the words in John further. He refers to Pinchas ben Jair (c. 130–160 CE) who takes Isa. 52.6 in the following way: 'Therefore my people shall know my name, therefore, that *Ani-hu* is speaking: here am I'.[3] Dodd goes on to argue that the translation of certain verses in the LXX bear out an interpretation in which *ani hu* is seen as a name. He thinks that the LXX version of Isa. 45.19 (ἐγώ εἰμι ἐγώ εἰμι κύριος ὁ λαλῶν δικαιοσύνην) has rendered YHWH twice, 'once by ἐγώ εἰμι and once by κύριος'. For Dodd, the second ἐγώ εἰμι becomes a name: 'I am "I AM" the Lord, who speaks righteousness'.[4] From a contemporary of Pinchas ben Jair, R. Judah ben Ilai, Dodd argues that the term *ani wehu* also became used in much the same way even before the destruction of the Temple in 70 CE. In the light of the Rabbinic interpretation of *ani hu* and of the connected *ani wehu* (אני והוא), which both came to refer to the secret name for God, Dodd suggests that the presupposition when Jesus uses ἐγώ εἰμι is that 'the eternal glory of God is given to Christ, and in the same act the Name of God is glorified'.[5]

Stauffer combines the rabbinic interpretation of *ani hu* with that of the Dead Sea sect[6] and comes to a similar conclusion to that of Dodd. In regard to the Dead Sea sect's understanding of *ani hu*, Stauffer asserts,

> The Manual of Discipline states in 8.13 f.: 'They are to be kept apart and to go into the wilderness to prepare the way of the HUAHA there, as it is written: "Prepare in the wilderness the way of..."' Here the name Jahweh is replaced in the quotation by the four points (JHVH), and in the Dead Sea text itself by the secret name HUAHA. Presumably this is made up of the HUAH (HE) and A (signifying Elohim, God).[7]

---

1. Davies, *Rhetoric*, pp. 84-86.
2. Davies, *Rhetoric*, p. 87.
3. Dodd, *Interpretation*, p. 94.
4. Dodd, *Interpretation*, p. 94.
5. Dodd, *Interpretation*, p. 95.
6. Stauffer, *Jesus* , pp. 145-46.
7. Stauffer, *Jesus* , p. 145.

Using other references from Qumran (e.g. Damascus text 9.5) as well as rabbinical writings (e.g. Sukkah 53a[1]), Stauffer suggests that

> Isaiah 40-55 was much read and quoted. The emphatic 'HU' was a favourite designation of God. Theology was occupied with the divine self-affirmations 'ANI' and 'ANI HU'. The Hallel psalms, where 'HU' means 'God', belonged at that time to the regular features of the ritual for the two great pilgrimage feasts...[2]

The very words ἐγώ εἰμι are full of meaning for both Dodd and Stauffer, and, because of rabbinic interpretation of them the implications would be automatically clear to the readers of John.[3] This depends on whether the Rabbinic usage of such a term is pre-Johannine and whether John was aware of such traditions.[4]

Schulz suggests that the Qumran texts present a plausible background to many of the images attached to 'I am'.[5] Although he allows for more than one influence on the formation of the ἐγώ εἰμι sayings,[6] he thinks it significant that many of the images used by John can be found in the Qumran literature. For example, the light/darkness dualism of John has parallels in such passages as 1 QS 3.25–4.1:

1. Sukkah 53a in I. Epstein (ed), *The Babylonian Talmud* (London: Soncino Press, 1984):

> It was taught, of Hillel the Elder, It was said that when he used to Rejoice at the Rejoicing at the place of the Water Drawing, he used to recite thus, 'If I am here, everyone is here; but if I am not here, who is here?' He also used to recite thus, 'To the place that I love, there My feet lead me; if thou wilt come into My House, I will come into thy house; if thou wilt not come into My House, I will not come to thy house, as it is laid In every place where I cause my name to be mentioned, I will come unto thee and bless thee.'

The first part of this quotation is cited by Harner, *'I am'*, p. 18, from an earlier edition of Epstein (1939), p. 253.

2. Stauffer, *Jesus*, p. 149. Stauffer admits that 'the dating of some of the psalms, of the texts of the ritual and of the Haggadah sayings,' which he uses, 'is still vigorously debated' (p. 148). Cf. Harner, *'I am'*, p. 36 n. 67.

3. With some reservations, Harner (*'I am'*, p. 26) acknowledges the possibility that such a Jewish interpretation may have been in John's mind.

4. If the Sukkah reference (above) is correctly attributed to Hillel then it is at least plausible that such a use of *ani* influenced John's use of ἐγώ εἰμι.

5. See Schulz, *Komposition*, p. 118, for a convenient summary of his conclusions concerning the background for the imagery linked to ἐγώ εἰμι.

6. Schulz, *Komposition*, pp. 91, 92, sees a distinction between the different parts of the 'I am' sayings with predicates and thus suggests that it is possible that the 'form' of the sayings may stem from a different source than the imagery.

> Truly the Spirits of light and darkness were made by him...
> The one, God loves everlastingly,
> and delights in all his deeds for ever,
> but the counsel of the other he loathes,
> and he hates all his ways for ever.[1]

Schulz suggests that Qumran is of greater importance than Mandaism for understanding the terms used by John, although this does not mean that it is the exclusive influence on Johannine thought.[2]

Daube concentrates on the Rabbinic background to the 'I am', which has been preserved in the Passover Haggadah.[3] Verses from Deuteronomy referring to Israel's deliverance from Egypt are expounded in the Haggadah so that 'the words "I am" are used to denote the personal presence of the redeeming God on that occasion'.[4] Daube cites the following passage:

> For I will pass through Egypt—this means, I and not an angel; and I will smite all the firstborn—this means, I and not a seraph; and I will execute judgement—this means, I and not the messenger; I the Lord — this means I am and no other.[5]

Daube argues that in the 'I am' of the Passover Midrash is the model for understanding that of the New Testament.[6] 'I the Lord' implies God's own personal intervention and 'consequently when they say it means *'any hw' wl' 'hr* [אני הוא ולא אחר], we must translate "I am and no other", in the sense of "God's own person being present and no other"'.[7] It is for this reason that the soldiers coming to arrest Jesus fall down in his presence when he utters ἐγώ εἰμι (Jn 18.5, 6).[8] It should be stated that Daube argues for an early date to this part of the Passover

---

1.　Schulz, *Komposition*, p. 99. The English translation is from A. Dupont-Sommer, *The Essene Writings from Qumran* (trans. G.Vermes; Oxford: Basil Blackwell, 1961), p. 79.

2.　Schulz, *Komposition*, p. 99.

3.　D. Daube, 'The "I am" of the Messianic Presence', in *idem*, *The New Testament and Rabbinic Judaism* (London: Athlone, 1956), p. 325.

4.　Daube, *The 'I am'*, p. 325.

5.　Daube, *The 'I am'*, p. 326.

6.　Daube, *The 'I am'*, p. 327.

7.　Daube, *The 'I am'*, p. 327. Recently, Braine has taken up Daube's conclusions on the significance of 'I am' in John. See D.D.C. Braine, 'The Inner Jewishness of St. John's Gospel', *SNTU* 13 (1988), p. 145 n. 64.

8.　Daube, *The 'I am'*, p. 329.

Haggadah.[1] According to Daube the reason that this is the only extant occurrence of such a use of *ani hu* is because 'the Rabbis found it dangerous and were afraid of abuse...They eliminated the expression as far as possible. But in liturgy, in the Passover-eve service, it withstood the pressure.' [2]

Borgen suggests that Midrash can supply a Jewish background to the ἐγώ εἰμι with a predicate.[3] Since his argument is important for the present investigation it will not be dealt with here but in connection with the use of ἐγώ εἰμι in John 6 and its possible implications for the background of the other 'I am' sayings with an image.

3. *The New Testament and Early Christianity*

The Synoptics

Freed argues that the words ἐγώ εἰμι should be taken to refer to Jesus' messiahship.[4] In Jn 1.20, John the Baptist denies the fact that he is the Christ with the words ἐγὼ οὐκ εἰμι ὁ Χριστός. In Jn 4.26, Jesus acknowledges his messiahship to the Samaritan woman.[5] Freed points to a similar episode concerning John the Baptist related in Acts 13.24, 25 as evidence for his case. Primarily, however, he notes occurrences of the phrase ἐγώ εἰμι in the Synoptics, which he suggests imply a messianic interpretation of the term. Freed cites the example of Mk 14.61, 62: 'Again the high priest asked him, "Are you the Christ the Son of the Blessed?" And Jesus said, "ἐγώ εἰμι; and you will see the Son of man sitting at the right hand of Power, and coming with the clouds of heaven".' Although some take Jesus' words as absolute (i.e., with no predicate, implied or unimplied), Freed suggests that 'since Jesus' reply is to the question if he is the Christ, it is more natural...to take it as meaning "I am the Christ"'.[6] This is confirmed for Freed by the fact that both Luke and Matthew seem to take Jesus' answer in this way. Thus he

---

1. P. Alexander suggests that the text shows 'all the marks of a work which has grown up over a long period of time' (P. Alexander [ed.], *Textual Sources for the Study of Judaism* [Manchester: Manchester University Press, 1984], p. 9). It may therefore be difficult to be so confident about an early date for the words cited by Daube.

2. Daube, *The 'I am'*, pp. 327-28.

3. Borgen, *Bread*, esp. pp. 72-73.

4. Freed, *1.20 and 4.25*, pp. 288-91.

5. Freed, *1.20 and 4.25*, p. 290.

6. Freed, *1.20 and 4.25*, p. 290.

concludes that 'in at least two passages in John (1.20 and 4.26) the words *ego eimi* are a part of traditional Christian terminology with respect to Jesus as Messiah'.[1]

The Risen Jesus

Kundzins discusses the possibility that the 'I am' sayings may have come from Gnostic (particularly Mandaean) sources. He rejects this on the grounds that it would demote these classic theological statements to no more than 'a transference of several important predicates and titles to Jesus', and thus they would be neither truly Christian concepts nor truly revelatory.[2] He does not see the primary function of the 'I am' sayings as one of antithesis in which the sayings always imply a contrast.[3] Furthermore he sees a difference from the Mandaean sayings in that the *logical* subject of all the statements is the 'I' of God's ambassador and not the accompanying noun.[4] He thinks that, while Schweizer has convincingly emphasized the development of the 'I'-predication in pre-Christian times, there is something entirely new in the Johannine 'I am' sayings:

> Certainly, these also begin with 'I am'. Their first half is an absolute parallel to the formulae outside Christianity. However, this 'ontological' clause, which contains a disclosure of being, is followed almost without exception by a sub-clause, which offers eternal life and salvation to those who believe.[5]

While he does find parallels in the 'I am' sayings of Mandaism, sayings with soteriological sub-clauses, such as he sees in John, only occur in late layers of the Mandaean tradition.[6] The real key to the understanding of

---

1. Freed, *1.20 and 4.25*, p. 291. In two other articles, Freed builds on this idea of ἐγώ εἰμι as a formula for the Messiah, bringing support from Old Testament and other Jewish writings: E.D. Freed, 'Ego Eimi in John viii:24 in the Light of its context and Jewish Messianic Belief', *JTS* 33 (1,82), pp. 163-67; and E.D. Freed, 'Who or What was before Abraham in John 8.58?', *JSNT* 17 (1983), pp. 52-59. Harner (*'I am'*, pp. 30-36) discusses the possible influence of the Synoptics on the 'I am' of John. He alludes (p. 35) to a possible connection between the 'I am' of 6.20 and that of Mk 6.50 but does not explain the significance of such a parallel.

2. K. Kundzins, 'Zur Diskussion über die Ego-Eimi-Spruche des Johannes-Evangeliums', in J. Köpp (ed.), *Charisteria* (Stockholm: 1954), p. 101.

3. Kundzins, 'Die Ego-Eimi-Spruche', p. 99.

4. Kundzins, 'Die Ego-Eimi-Spruche', p. 99.

5. Kundzins, 'Die Ego-Eimi-Spruche', p. 102.

6. Kundzins, 'Die Ego-Eimi-Spruche', p. 103.

the 'I am' sayings, he claims, is to be found in the New Testament and particularly in the 'I am' sayings of Revelation.[1] In the seven letters addressed to the churches in Asia, the promises made to the one who conquers, stem from the self-predication of the Risen One: 'Fear not, I am the first and the last, and the living one; I died and behold I am alive for evermore...' (1.17).[2] From this he concludes that:

> The 'I'-sayings of the Gospel and of Revelation have flowed *from one and the same source*, and this common source or root is the revelatory sayings of the risen Christ.[3]

The Parousia

Manson started by looking at the occurrence of ἐγώ εἰμι in Mk 13.6. He questioned whether this could 'really mean, as the author of Matthew took it to mean [Mt.24.5], "Ἐγώ εἰμι ὁ Χριστός"'.[4] Instead, he suggested that the meaning is that 'the Christ is come, the Parousia has arrived'.[5] Manson argues that the Matthean interpretation of the Marcan passage does not make sense because it is unlikely that those who could be said to 'come in the name of Jesus' (i.e. Christians) would claim to be the messiah, saying: 'This is to put a very strained and unnatural sense on the phrase ἐπὶ τῷ ὀνόματί μου'.[6] Using 2 Thessalonians 2 as an analogy, Manson proceeds to argue that the church was being warned against those within its number who may believe that the Parousia had happened and Christ had returned. Thus the phrase ἐγώ εἰμι in Mk 13.6 is the phrase expected to identify the presence of Christ at his return. The warning in Mark is therefore against those who may think the Parousia has happened. The ἐγώ εἰμι in John also represents the presence of Christ. Manson interprets Jn 4.26 as 'The Messiah is here, he is present in Him who speaks to you'. The ἐγώ εἰμι thus 'indicates

1. Kundzins, 'Die Ego-Eimi-Spruche', pp. 105-106. K.N. Booth argues that the 'I am' sayings in John are the words of the Risen and Exalted Lord who speaks to a universal context ('The Self-Proclamation of Jesus in St. John's Gospel', *Colloqium* 7,2 [1975], pp. 36-47).
2. Kundzins, 'Die Ego-Eimi-Spruche', p. 106.
3. Kundzins, 'Die Ego-Eimi-Spruche', p. 106.
4. W. Manson, 'The ΕΓΩ EIMI of the Messianic Presence in the New Testament', *JTS* 48 (1947), p. 139.
5. Manson, 'ΕΓΩ EIMI', p. 139.
6. Manson, 'ΕΓΩ EIMI', p. 139.

an existential situation, not merely an historical claim'.[1] He attributes a similar interpretation to the 'I am' in John 8, where he thinks the occurrences of ἐγώ εἰμι mean, 'that "God has come" to men in Jesus, the Incarnate Word. There is an intentional contraposition of "existence" and "becoming" in the last two examples [8.28 and 58].'[2]

Manson thinks that such an interpretation of 'I am' is present in the Old Testament, and in fact it is to the Old Testament that his interpretation looks for its roots. Manson points back to the call of Moses in Exodus 3, where he sees the presence of God being expressed in the words אהיה אשר אהיה. However, in light of the fact that LXX translates the Hebrew as ἐγώ εἰμι ὁ ὤν and not as ἐγώ εἰμι ἐγώ εἰμι (Exod. 3.14), it must be questioned how closely the phrase ἐγώ εἰμι should be connected with the name of God in Exodus. Manson also looks to the *ani hu* of Second Isaiah, which he regards both as expressing 'the self-manifestation of the God of Israel in the redemption of His people from Babylon' and as being 'especially associated with the Divine Presence or self-disclosure of God in History'. [3]

4. Hellenism and Judaism

In the light of the above evidence, there are those who are unwilling to restrict the background for the 'I am' sayings to either a Jewish or a Hellenistic milieu but prefer to see a dual influence. While Barrett sees Hellenism as the predominant influence on the 'I am' sayings with a predicate, he looks to Judaism for the interpretation of the absolute ἐγώ εἰμι.[4] Kysar when discussing the 'I am' sayings agrees 'that the milieu of the evangelist was of a mixed nature'.[5]

Both Schnackenburg and Becker express this mixed influence in a more precise way. Schnackenburg suggests that both the absolute ἐγώ εἰμι and much of the imagery come through the Old Testament but the

1. Manson, 'ΕΓΩ ΕΙΜΙ', p. 141.
2. Manson, 'ΕΓΩ ΕΙΜΙ', p. 141.
3. Manson, 'ΕΓΩ ΕΙΜΙ', p. 142.
4. Barrett, *John*, pp. 292 and 342 respectively.
5. R. Kysar, *The Fourth Evangelist and his Gospel* (Minneapolis: Augsburg, 1975), p. 122. A similar view was expressed as long ago as 1928 by J.H. Bernard (*The Gospel according to St John* [ICC, 30; ed. A.H. McNeile; Edinburgh: T. & T. Clark, 1928). Bernard regards ἐγώ εἰμι with a predicate as possibly having 'been cast into this special form by the evangelist, it being a form whose significance would be instantly appreciated by his readers, whether Jewish or Greek' (p. cxxi).

form of the sayings is influenced by Hellenism: 'the formal structure of the revealer's utterance was probably influenced by the soteriological type of discourse current in Eastern Hellenism.'[1] Becker takes this one stage further, suggesting that John used Old Testament tradition but in a Gnosticizing way.[2]

Another example of this mixed background for the 'I am' sayings is seen in the work of Bühner[3], who suggests that John is using a messenger formula common in the Ancient World. Bühner thinks that the 'I am' sayings should be understood in the context of prophecy. Ashton summarizes Bühner's argument:

> The *Sitz-im-Leben* is prophecy and in particular the prophet as a messenger. The broader background is not properly religious but political and social—the convention obtaining throughout the Ancient Near East whereby one man was entrusted by another with a task to perform or a message to deliver in a different place. The messenger first received his errand, then carried it out, and finally returned to report on it.[4]

Bühner argues that the Fourth Gospel has a 'Sending Christology' and that this messenger formula is central to understanding John's whole Christology.[5] Two forms of saying that are found in John conform to the understanding of a messenger in the ancient Near East: 'the "I have come" sayings (ἦλθον-*Sprüche*) and the "I am" sayings'.[6]

The main examples of 'I am' sayings which Ashton quotes are from the sphere of Judaism, such as when the angel Raphael discloses his identity to Tobit:

1.   Schnackenburg, *John*, II, Excursus 8, p. 86. Cf. also Schulz, *Komposition*, pp. 85-131, who sees a complex relationship between the content and form of the 'I am' sayings and their respective origins.

2.   J. Becker, 'Die Ich Bin Worte' in *idem*, *Das Evangelium des Johannes I. Kapitel 1-10: Ökumenischer Taschenbuch zum Neuen Testament* (Gütersloh: Gerd Mohn, 1979), p. 209.

3.   J.A. Bühner, *Der Gesandte Und Sein Weg* (WUNT, 2; Tübingen: Mohr, 1977), pp. 166-80. Bühner's suggestion has recently been taken up by Ashton, who regards the messenger formula as the best way of understanding John's 'I am' sayings. J. Ashton, *Understanding the Fourth Gospel* (Oxford: Oxford University Press, 1991), pp. 184-89.

4.   Ashton, *Understanding*, p. 185.

5.   For an excellent summary of Bühner's 'Sending Christology', see G.R. Beasley-Murray, *The Gospel of Life: Theology in the Fourth Gospel* (Peabody, MA: Hendrickson, 1991), pp. 15-33.

6.   Ashton, *Understanding*, p. 185.

I was sent to you to test you. And at the same time God sent me to heal you and Sarah your daughter-in-law. I am Raphael, one of the seven angels who stand ready and enter before the glory of the Lord (Tob. 12.14).

While Ashton acknowledges that the form of the 'I am' sayings with an image is indebted to a messenger formula used throughout the ancient Near East, 'the actual symbols are, with one exception [that of the door], abundantly attested in the Old Testament'.[1] The similarities of the sayings with those of Gnosticism, he thinks is because 'the Gnostic texts are mostly independent variants upon the same tradition'.[2]

While Bühner and Ashton are undoubtedly correct to see an influence of the messenger concept in John's Christology as a whole, in John's Gospel the 'I am' sayings with an image seem quite different from the messenger formulae in the way they are used. The messenger normally identifies himself by name, as in the example above. The 'I am' sayings in John, however, could hardly be seen to be 'names' of Jesus but rather define who he is in relation to his role among humanity.[3] Besides, the question of whether these sayings are prophetic or self-revelatory in character has to be addressed. The sayings in John, the example of Raphael given above, as well as the examples of 'I am' sayings from within Gnosticism are not in the form of traditional prophetic speech in which the prophet speaks on behalf of the one who has sent him.[4] Rather they are in the form either of self-identification (Raphael) or self-revelation (Gnosticism). It remains to be seen into which of these categories the sayings of the Fourth Gospel fit.

The above survey does not attempt to be exhaustive nor to evaluate rigorously the suggested parallels, but attempts to show the immense diversity of possible parallels by which the Johannine 'I am' sayings may be interpreted. In the light of such diverse parallels, all of which may throw light on John's use of ἐγώ εἰμι, it becomes apparent that there is

---

1. Ashton, *Understanding*, p. 187.

2. Ashton, *Understanding*, p.187.

3. See Chapter 5 Below.

4. The Old Testament prophetic formula is spoken introduced in the third person: 'thus says the Lord' (e.g. Jer. 29.4, 10, 25, 31). 'I am' sayings are either spoken on the lips of the LORD himself (see Isa. 40–55), or by angels (see the example of Raphael), or in a purely human context as a means of identification or recognition (e.g. Abraham's servant). In such a context they are usually accompanied by a name, or possibly a person's role.

an urgent need to discover how the words are used in the Fourth Gospel itself. By means of such a study, it will be easier to delimit which parallels can be discarded as background material to the Gospel, and which parallels should be studied further. It will become clear in the course of studying the function of 'I am' in John that the Gospel itself provides many clues as to the correct background by which the term should be understood.

Part II

THE WORLD OF THE TEXT: A LITERARY ANALYSIS
OF THE FUNCTION OF ἐγώ εἰμι IN JOHN'S GOSPEL

Chapter 2

Literary Criteria

Chapter 3 of this investigation contains a 'literary study' of each pericope containing the words ἐγώ εἰμι. Each study will examine the literary structure and style of the passage concerned in order to ascertain
how the words 'I am' function in their context; it is not a literary study
of the passage for its own sake. Before such studies can take place, it is
necessary to delineate the criteria adopted when looking at the text.

Outlined below are seven categories that have been used in these literary studies. While some of these categories prove useful throughout,
others are more useful in certain contexts than in others. For this reason,
certain categories are dominant in one literary study while they may be
entirely absent from another. For instance, John's use of irony in
connection with ἐγώ εἰμι may be particularly relevant to the episode
with the Samaritan woman in ch. 4 and so is dealt with in some detail in
the study on that chapter. On the other hand, irony may be of little or
no significance in Jesus' claim to be the true vine in ch. 15 and so can
be passed over without much comment. Moreover, several of the
categories below overlap, so that the writer's point of view is seen in the
way individuals are characterised as well as in the use of irony. Likewise,
irony itself may be found in the characterization of individuals as well as
in how the text interacts with the reader. For this reason the studies
themselves will not be ordered according to the categories below.
Instead, the following are given to show the various literary criteria used
as tools in examining the way ἐγώ εἰμι functions in each episode.

1. *Setting*

Since these studies assume that no word or phrase can be truly understood by itself but only as it relates to the words and phrases in which it

stands,[1] it is of first importance to ascertain the setting in which ἐγώ εἰμι occurs. This is particularly significant for the following studies since they are restricted to pericopes in which 'I am' occurs on the lips of Jesus and so there is a constant danger of losing sight of the larger context of the Gospel. The question of setting thus attempts to discover where the pericope (and subsequently where 'I am') belongs in the narrative of the Gospel as a whole. In other words, where and how does the episode in question fit into the plot and narrative time of the Gospel?[2] For this it is important to ask: What has already been revealed in the previous text? At what point in John's story of Jesus does this episode occur? How does the particular episode or pericope set the scene for what follows? For instance, it may be of great significance that Jesus' claim to be the good shepherd in ch. 10 occurs straight after his assertion to the Pharisees that, because they claim to see, their guilt remains (9.41). Or, it may also be of significance that, long before Jesus claims to be the light of the world (8.12), the prologue speaks of the light that was coming into the world (1.9).

2. *Structure*

The second literary category used in these studies is that of structure. There may be a particularly interesting or intricate structure of a passage in which ἐγώ εἰμι has a role to play. Whether or not this is so, implications of such a structure for the significance of the use of ἐγώ εἰμι must be addressed. While questions of structure are not unique to a literary study, they are essential in helping to determine how the Gospel attempts to convey its message. For instance, the fact that the discourse of John 8 begins and ends with a statement by Jesus containing 'I am' may (and will be shown to) prove significant in determining the way ἐγώ εἰμι functions.

---

1. Cf. Culpepper, *Anatomy*, p. 5.
2. The importance Culpepper attaches to narrative time and plot is shown in the fact that he devotes consecutive chapters to each (chapters 3 and 4 respectively). Culpepper (*Anatomy*) defines 'narrative time' on pp. 53, 54. See also p. 80, where he defines the central features of 'plot'. For another discussion of 'plot' in the Fourth Gospel, see A.T. Lincoln, 'Trials, Plots and the Narrative of the Fourth Gospel', *JSNT* 56 (1994), pp. 3-30.

3. *Characters and Characterization*

It has been noted above that the study of characterization in literature is
not new and goes back at least as far as the observations of Aristotle on
the Greek theatre. It may, however, be felt that addressing the question
of characterization in the Gospel of John is inappropriate since it implies
that the characters in John are fictitious, mere inventions of the author's
mind, bearing no resemblance to and having no respect for history. It
must therefore be emphasized that the following studies do not imply
that the Gospel is fictitious, nor do they deny that the text may be
portraying historical persons in an historical context. Rather,

> We are presently interested in characterization as the art and techniques by
> which an author fashions a convincing portrait of a person within a more
> or less unified piece of writing. Even if one is disposed to see real, histor-
> ical persons behind every character in John and actual events in every
> episode, the question of how the author chose to portray the person still
> arises.[1]

According to these terms, any study of how different people are portrayed in the Gospel (whether theological, historical or literary) must
directly or indirectly address questions of characterization. Titles attributed to Jesus, such as 'the word' (1.1-14), 'the lamb of God' (1.29),
'messiah' (1.41) and 'king of Israel' (1.49), all concern John's characterization or portrayal of Jesus whether they were actually attributed to
the historical Jesus or not.

While any studies of the Johannine Jesus will touch on his character,
the focus of the following studies is on how the characterization of Jesus
is achieved and particularly whether the 'I am' sayings play a part in this
characterization. Thus it may be asked whether the characters of the
Fourth Gospel are portrayed as 'flat' or 'round'.[2] A flat character is a
type or a caricature showing only one idea or quality. For example, one
of the characters of the Fourth Gospel is popularly immortalized as

---

1.   Culpepper, *Anatomy*, p. 105.

2.   Following Forster, *Aspects* , esp. pp. 73-89. It may be thought that Forster's
categorisation of characters into 'flat' or 'round' according to the complexity of their
characterization is unsuitable for studying biblical narrative. While it is acknowledged
that the biblical writers would not have made such distinctions and that the biblical
characters do not always sit easily with Forster's distinction between 'flat' and
'round', Forster's observations continue to be the most convincing and simple way
of distinguishing between different types of characterization.

'doubting Thomas', for this is seen to be his trait.[1] On the other hand a 'round' character is 'complex in temperament and motivation' and is 'like most people...capable of surprise'.[2] It may be that someone such as Nicodemus, who is one of the Pharisees (7.50) but who shows great interest in Jesus' teaching (3.1-15) and who even shows great concern for Jesus after his death (19.39), should be seen as a 'round' character in this sense for he is both complex in temperament and motivation. He is willing to stand up for Jesus at one moment in front of the Pharisees (7.50) and yet afraid (along with Joseph of Arimathea) to be an open follower at another (19.38).

Questions of characterization in John's Gospel need to focus not only on the person of Jesus but on how Jesus is shown to be who he is. This may involve other characters, or it may involve the narrator. For instance, the prologue plays a major part in determining the reader's view of Jesus right from the start. It may in some ways be likened to the omniscient prologue of the Greek theatre, where the narrator sets out his point of view to the audience.[3] It is the purpose of the following studies to determine how the words ἐγώ εἰμι may likewise further the characterization of Jesus. At the same time it is necessary to see how Jesus' narrative audience is characterized. It may be found that the other characters in John often act as a foil to Jesus, leading him to make a claim for himself by means of ἐγώ εἰμι (cf. 14.6). In such cases the role that Jesus' audience play in the narrative actually furthers his characterization. It may also be found that the reaction to the claims that are made through Jesus' 'I am' sayings furthers the characterization of his narrative audience (cf. 8.58).

4. *Irony*[4]

Since the following studies are not concerned with an investigation of irony itself but with what role ἐγώ εἰμι may have in the Fourth Gospel's use of irony, it is necessary to have a working definition of the nature of irony. For this the following studies are highly dependent on

---

1.   Whether Thomas is in fact such a 'flat' character as the caricature portrays him may be called into question in his bold statement of loyalty in Jn 11.16.

2.   Forster, *Aspects*, pp. 73, 81 (cited in Culpepper, *Anatomy*, p. 102).

3.   Cf. Duke, *Irony*, p. 24.

4.   Davies, *Rhetoric*, pp. 363-38, includes a discussion of 'Irony' and 'Double Meanings' under her discussion of the Implied Reader.

the work of Duke, which not only defines what is meant by irony but also shows the subtlety with which irony opens the door to a deeper understanding of the Gospel as a whole.[1] Following Muecke, Duke suggests that there must be three criteria in operation in order for irony to take place: (1) irony is double-layered; (2) irony presents opposition; (3) irony contains an element of unawareness.[2] In other words irony cannot take place unless there are two possible levels of meaning in a statement or situation. It cannot therefore be ironic that Jesus claims to be the good shepherd unless at the same time there is an allusion to false shepherds. Yet just because there are two possible meanings to any given statement or situation does not make it ironic. Thus the word λόγος may be a designation for Jesus (1.1ff.) or it may simply refer to Jesus' words (e.g. 5.24) but this duplicity in meaning does not necessarily mean that John's use of λόγος is ironic.[3] For irony to take place the two levels of meaning have to be in some sort of opposition. Such a contrast takes place in the two levels of meaning simultaneously expressed in the verb 'to lift up' (ὑψόω, 3.14). By this word the writer may at one and the same time refer to Jesus' exaltation in glory and also his 'lifting up on the cross'.[4] However, irony only takes place when the two contrasting levels of meaning are played off against each other so as to cause some sort of surprise (whether the surprise occurs on the part of the narrative audience or the actual reader). Thus there is an element of unawareness in the fact that when the Jews lift up the Son of man in crucifixion they are simultaneously lifting him up in glorification. Likewise Jesus' claim to be the good shepherd only becomes ironic because such a claim exposes the fact that it is the very people with whom he speaks (i.e., the Pharisees, 9.49) who are the thieves and robbers of whom he speaks (10.1, 10). While there are many more complex issues involved in irony,[5] such a working definition enables the following studies to ask what role irony plays in any pericope and how

---

1. Duke, *Irony*.

2. Duke, *Irony*, pp. 13-18.

3. Hinrichs (e.g. *Ich Bin*, p. 37, cf. also p. 35-36), implies that there is a deliberate interaction in John between the logos who Jesus is and the logos which Jesus speaks.

4. Cf. Barrett, *John*, p. 214.

5. Cf. Duke, *Irony*, pp. 18-27, for examples of different types of irony that may be encountered in the Gospel of John, and pp. 28-42, for the function of such irony. Cf. also Culpepper, *Anatomy*, pp. 165-80.

the 'I am' sayings of Jesus function in the use of irony.

Much of the irony that takes place in the Fourth Gospel depends upon the reader being placed in a privileged position of knowledge by the writer. Because of this, the reader's knowledge can be played off against the apparent lack of knowledge on the part of Jesus' narrative audience. Thus not only is the reader aware that Jesus is to be identified with the messiah when he speaks with the Samaritan woman, but she is entirely unaware of this fact. The reader's knowledge is played off against the lack of knowledge on the part of the Samaritan woman when she declares 'I know that messiah is coming (he who is called Christ); when he comes, he will show us all things' (4.25). The reader is aware that she says far more than she knows, for the reader already knows that Jesus is the Christ. It will be seen in the following studies that the use of ἐγώ εἰμι on the lips of Jesus is linked on several occasions with John's use of such 'dramatic' irony.[1]

A second form of irony which takes place in John is that in which the 'implied meaning intended by the speaker differs from that which he ostensibly asserts'.[2] This is what Duke designates as 'verbal irony' in which he suggests 'the speaker...stands protected behind the screen of ostensible meaning, while the silent intent of the word shoots beyond to do its piercing work'.[3] Such a use of 'verbal irony' will be seen to be particularly important in the study of background material where the 'I am' sayings act as a clue to a deeper level of meaning which is played off against the surface level of the text. While Jesus is seen to hide behind the surface meaning of 'I am' when the Jews ask him who he is in 8.25, it may be that the formulation of his ἐγώ εἰμι saying actually points to 'the silent intent of the word' which 'shoots beyond to do its work'.

5. Point of View

Before discussing what is meant by 'point of view' it is important to note that any narrative

---

1. Duke, *Irony*, p. 23: 'Dramatic irony employs a speaker or actant who knows less than is apparent and whose involvement in the irony is quite unintentional'. The Samaritan woman is the victim of such dramatic irony.

2. M.H. Abrams, *A Glossary of Literary Terms* (New York: Holt, Reinhart and Winston, 3rd edn, 1971), p. 80; quoted by Duke, *Irony*, p. 21.

3. Duke, *Irony*, p. 23.

is not perceived by the reader directly, but rather mediated or filtered through the telling of the (implied) author, the narrator or another character. For the reader is shown only what the author wishes to show. Never can the reader step behind the story to know a character other than in the way the narrative presents him.[1]

This is true whether the narrative is recording historical events and characters or not. The purpose of studying point of view is therefore to understand how the narrative is mediated through the telling of the story.[2] Is the narrator looking back on the episode with insight gained afterwards or showing the readers the story without such knowledge (temporal point of view)? Does the narrator depict the episode from one vantage point, or do the readers travel with the characters (spatial point of view)? Does the narrator portray the characters from the outside or are the readers allowed a glimpse into their thoughts (psychological point of view)? Finally, and most importantly for a study of the Gospel of John, it may be asked what are the narrator's hidden presuppositions and motivations in the narrative? In other words, what is the conceptual (or, in John's case, theological) worldview of the narrator?[3]

As with a discussion of characterization, it may seem that an investigation into such a modern concept as 'point of view' is somewhat anachronistic when dealing with biblical texts. However, Berlin points out that the works of Uspensky and A. Renoir have shown that the adoption of various 'points of view' by a narrator is not limited to modern literature.[4] While such a technique may not have been studied before the critical study of the novel, authors were already consciously or unconsciously using differing points of view from which to narrate their stories.

The first three categories of point of view outlined above are simply the techniques that the narrator uses in painting the Johannine picture of Jesus. In the study of John's Gospel it soon becomes apparent that the

---

1. A. Berlin, *Poetics and Interpretation of Biblical Narrative* (Sheffield: Almond Press, 1983), p. 43.

2. Berlin, *Poetics* , p. 43.

3. For a fuller discussion of point of view in John's Gospel see Culpepper, *Anatomy*, chapter 2, 'Narrator and Point of View', pp. 15-49.

4. Berlin, *Poetics*, p. 43, cites B. Uspensky (*A Poetics of Composition* [Berkeley: University of California Press, 1973], p. 171) who has studied the varying points of view adopted in Russian epic literature; Berlin also refers to the work of A. Renoir on Beowulf (A. Renoir, 'Point of View and Design for Terror', *Neuphilologische Mitteilungen* 63 [1962], pp. 154-67).

temporal point of view of the narrator can generally be defined as 'retrospective'. That is, the narrator has been through the events which are described in the narrative (21.24) and, from a point in the future, wishes to explain their significance (20.30, 31).[1] For this reason he/she is quite content to add narrative explanations to assist the reader in understanding the story (e.g. 7.37-39).

Berlin likens the spatial point of view in biblical narrative to the 'camera eye' view in modern cinema. Sometimes the narrator can give the reader a close up view of events, while sometimes the 'camera' draws back so that the reader can get a wider view of the scene.[2] However, a study of John's Gospel soon reveals that Jesus is the main focus, often the only focus, of the narrative. The reader's spatial point of view is therefore generally that of an observer of Jesus.[3] Where the phrase ἐγώ εἰμι occurs on the lips of Jesus, the reader's point of view is always that of Jesus' own audience, even though there are important instances in the Gospel as a whole where the reader leaves Jesus and observes some other characters.[4] Since, like a fly on the wall, the reader always listens to Jesus' ἐγώ εἰμι sayings from the same point of view as a silent observer, it is not necessary to address the question of spatial point of view in the following studies. It is sufficient to note here that, with the exception of 6.41 and the narrator's comment in 18.6, the 'I am' sayings of Jesus are presented to the reader unmediated, as if the reader were present to hear them.

Although there are occasions within the Gospel where the narrator reveals the 'secret thoughts' of Jesus (e.g. 6.15), more often than not Jesus' thoughts are mediated through his words. This is the case with the 'I am' sayings. In other words, the reader gains access to Jesus' thoughts only through what Jesus says. Jesus, on the other hand, often knows the inmost thoughts and motivations of his narrative audience (e.g. 6.26) and by implication possesses knowledge of the thoughts of the reader too. Since all occurrences of ἐγώ εἰμι express such a psychological point of view mediated through Jesus' own words, the following studies do not need to address the form of psychological point of view adopted by

1. Cf. Culpepper, *Anatomy*, p. 28.
2. Cf. Berlin, *Poetics*, p. 44.
3. Cf. Berlin, *Poetics*, p. 44. Also Culpepper, *Anatomy*, pp. 20, 26.
4. Notably in following the Samaritan woman from the well to her village (4.28-30, 39-42) and in following the movements of the man born blind after his sight has been restored (9.8-34)

these sayings. Discussion needs only to show what thoughts and motivations may be revealed through Jesus' use of 'I am' and whether a different psychological point of view is adopted in its immediate context.

The narrator's conceptual point of view is 'the perspective of his attitude to the story he is telling'.[1] In John's Gospel the narrator openly declares his conceptual point of view in the narrative comment of 20.31. The narrator states openly that his story of Jesus is not impartial, it is written in order that 'you may believe that Jesus is the Christ, the Son of God, and that by believing you may have life in his name'. The narrator declares that it is his intention to persuade the readers to his own point of view. Understanding that the narrator is not impartial, however, is only the beginning of understanding his conceptual point of view. This concerns not only the narrator's purpose in writing but the way this is achieved as well as the thought world out of which the narrative is written and is to be understood.

Therefore, the narrator's conceptual point of view is not only shown in explicit narrative comments concerning the purpose of writing, but also in the use made of background sources to illustrate who Jesus is. The following studies must therefore ask how the 'I am' sayings share the narrator's conceptual/theological point of view with the reader. It may be found that Culpepper is only partially correct when he suggests that 'from the beginning, the narrator shares his omniscient vantage point with the reader, so the reader is immediately given all that is needed to understand the story'.[2] While it is certain that the prologue divulges many of the narrator's beliefs about Jesus right from the start, it will be argued in the study of background material that the narrator's conceptual point of view is only fully understood with reference to the Old Testament. Jesus' 'I am' sayings appeal to the Old Testament in order for the reader to join the theological/conceptual point of view of the narrator.

6. The Implied Reader

Culpepper defines the implied reader in the following terms: 'The implied reader is defined by the text as the one who performs all the

---

1. Berlin, *Poetics*, p. 47. Culpepper (*Anatomy*) calls this the ideological point of view of the narrator, but it is probably better to refer to it as the theological or conceptual point of view since 'ideology' has come to refer to a systematic form of (political) ideas imposed on a minority in order to suppress them.

2. Culpepper, *Anatomy*, p. 19.

mental moves required to enter into the narrative world and respond to it as the implied author intends'.[1] It also follows, conversely, that if an explanation is not offered, the intended reader would have understood that point without it. In other words the implied reader is the ideal reader, who perfectly understands the narrator's conceptual point of view and enters into the worldview of the narrator.[2] A 'narrative inevitably projects a picture of the reader for which it was intended. When an explanation is offered, for example, the intended reader would not have understood that point without it.'[3]

The implied reader, however, differs from the intended reader in the fact that the implied reader is defined by the text. That is to say that the text of John's Gospel only gives the modern reader hints to suggest who the intended readers might be. From these hints, scholars may try and reconstruct who they think the intended readers may have been and how they may have understood the text. However, the implied reader is to be equated with the picture of the reader projected by the text. Such a reader understands the mind of the (implied) author perfectly but actually describes 'qualities residing in the medium itself.' [4] Such a reader is also the one who 'at any moment of the act of reading is able to situate the given part of the text not only with regard to the left—that is, to the section of the text which has already been perused—but also with regard to its context to the right—the section which has not yet been covered'.[5]

A study of the implied reader is therefore an attempt to understand the 'hints' and 'clues' within the Gospel of John so that it is possible to make the mental moves required by the (implied) author to understand the text. The implied reader is defined by those 'clues' and unanswered questions in the text which point to a meaning beyond the surface level

1. Culpepper, *Anatomy*, pp. 7, 8.
2. Culpepper, *Anatomy*, p. 208, equates this with the ideal narrative audience: 'In John the ideal narrative audience adopts the narrator's ideological point of view, penetrates the misunderstandings, appreciates the irony and is moved to fresh appreciation of transcendent mystery through the Gospel's symbolism'.
3. Culpepper, *Anatomy*, pp. 7, 8.
4. J.L. Staley, *The Print's First Kiss: A Rhetorical Investigation of the Implied Reader in the Fourth Gospel* (SBLDS, 82; Atlanta: Scholars Press, 1988), p. 34.
5. K. Stierle, 'The Reading of Fictional Texts', in S.R. Suleiman and I. Crosman (eds.), *The Reader in the Text: Essays on Audience and Interpretation*, (Princeton: Princeton University Press, 1980), pp. 94, 95.

of the text.[1] Such clues may include the reactions of those in the narrative. For example, there are two occasions where the utterance of the words ἐγώ εἰμι provokes a strange response on the part of Jesus' narrative audience (8.59; 18.5, 6, 8). Since the narrator offers no explanation of why Jesus' narrative audience reacts in this way, the text can be seen to offer a picture of a reader who understands the reason for such a reaction. If the implied reader is seen as someone who understands the author's goals, a study of the 'hints' and 'clues' within the text must lead into questions of background of the writer's thought and into a need to investigate his worldview. In other words, the study of the implied reader within the text leads to questions concerning the conceptual worldview of the narrator and should in turn lead to a better understanding of the text.

It should be noted that this definition of an implied reader is dependent on Culpepper and not on Staley. The latter sees the implied reader neither as a 'real reader's first and second reading experiences of texts nor an ideal reader's response'.[2] For Staley, the implied reader is not only defined by the text but restricted to the text:

> An implied reader must also gain all its knowledge of the story from the narrative medium itself, even if the general outline of the story is known in a culture, as is most likely the case with the first readers of the Fourth Gospel.[3]

In addition Staley's 'implied reader', unlike that of Culpepper or Stierle, is a concept that perceives all the narrator's comments and explanations, only from what has gone on before in the text.[4] Thus for Staley the 'implied reader is the affective quality of a text. It is an entity evoked and continually nurtured by the text's strategies and moved towards the implied author's goals.'[5] To study any background material implied by

---

1.   Davies (*Rhetoric*, pp. 353-59) includes the Gospel's use of Scripture under her discussion of the implied reader as one of these 'clues', suggesting that 'knowledge of those Jewish Scriptures is required for understanding the text of the Fourth Gospel' (p. 354).

2.   Staley, *Kiss*, p. 34.

3.   Staley, *Kiss*, p. 35.

4.   Staley, *Kiss*, p. 35: 'While the implied author knows the text both forward and backward, the implied reader only has knowledge of what has been read up to the given moment'.

5.   Staley, *Kiss*, p. 33.

this affective quality of the text is therefore to go beyond Staley's definition of the implied reader.

7. *Other Themes and Titles*

The final literary consideration of the following studies concerns how ἐγώ εἰμι functions in relation to the other theological/Christological themes of the Gospel. Here the question to be considered is whether there are any particular titles or themes with which ἐγώ εἰμι is particularly associated. At the same time it may be asked whether the use of ἐγώ εἰμι constitutes a theme in itself. This second consideration will have to be addressed once the literary studies have been completed, along with other general conclusions to be drawn from the following studies.

Now that the literary criteria used in the following studies have been defined, it is possible to address the literary function of the 'I am' in the Fourth Gospel. It has already been hinted that such a study of the 'I am' sayings will naturally lead into the study of background material in order to understand the narrator's conceptual point of view. In addition, such a study of how ἐγώ εἰμι functions in the Gospel will necessarily project a picture of the reader for whom such sayings were intended. It is therefore logical that the chapters which follow will address the conceptual and theological point of view assumed by the 'I am' sayings. In turn it is logical to ask in conclusion what sort of reader may have made sense of such sayings.

Chapter 3

LITERARY STUDIES

1. John 4 : The Samaritan Woman (4.26)

The words ἐγώ εἰμι first occur on the lips of Jesus in the episode of the Samaritan woman. The controversy that leads to Jesus' decision to leave for Galilee is the Pharisees' knowledge that Jesus is making more disciples than John the Baptist (4.1, 3). John emphatically denies to his own disciples that he is the Christ (οὐκ εἰμι ἐγὼ ὁ Χριστός, 3.28).[1] This is a repetition of his words to the priests and Levites sent by the Jews from Jerusalem to enquire about his identity (1.20). There he had also testified to his disciples that Jesus was the 'Lamb of God' (1.29), the one who was to baptize with the Holy Spirit (1.33) and the 'Son of God' (1.34). Immediately preceding Jesus' meeting with the Samaritan woman, John the Baptist also declares that the one to whom he had earlier borne witness is to be seen as the bridegroom (3.29).

As well as the titles given to Jesus by John the Baptist, the reader has already encountered several other christological titles: the word (1.1, 14); the true light (1.9-11); the only Son (1.14, 18); rabbi (1.38); messiah/ Christ (1.41); and the king of Israel (1.49). By these titles the narrator has placed the reader in a privileged position by bestowing knowledge of who Jesus is. In addition the reader has witnessed Jesus' first 'sign' (2.1-11) and the Temple incident (2.13-23), as well as Jesus' debate with Nicodemus about the need for rebirth (3.1-15). This means that, unlike the woman of the story, the reader is aware of the narrator's conceptual point of view about Jesus from the beginning of the episode. Such privileged knowledge allows the reader to participate in the irony that

---

1.   Hinrichs (*Ich Bin*, p. 18ff.) regards the negative 'I am' sayings of John the Baptist as a compositional preparation for the positive 'I am' sayings of Jesus. Freed thinks that 'the words *ego eimi* are part of traditional Christian terminology with respect to Jesus as Messiah' (*1.20 and 4.25*, p. 291).

takes place as the woman's understanding of Jesus unfolds.

The episode of the Samaritan woman is presented as an aside in Jesus' ministry. It happens because he is on his way to Galilee and has 'to pass through Samaria' (4.4).[1] The episode runs from Jn 4.3, where Jesus leaves Judea for Galilee, to Jn 4.43, where the objective of the former verse is finally realized. Verses 4-6 give a reason and a setting for what takes place in the rest of the pericope and so act as an introduction. The main section of the episode concerns Jesus' conversation with the Samaritan woman (vv. 7-26). The woman then departs to her village to tell of the conversation with Jesus (vv. 27-31). Meanwhile, the provision of food by the disciples leads into a short discourse on heavenly food (vv. 31-38).[2] Finally, because of the woman's witness, the people of the town come to Jesus and request that he stay with them for two days (vv. 39-42).

Jesus' discussion with the Samaritan woman will be the focus of the following study, since the words ἐγώ εἰμι conclude that dialogue (vv. 7-26). Eslinger suggests that this section is structured chiastically and that Jesus begins and concludes both halves of the dialogue:

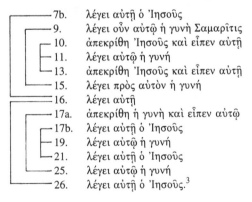

7b.	λέγει αὐτῇ ὁ Ἰησοῦς
9.	λέγει οὖν αὐτῷ ἡ γυνὴ Σαμαρῖτις
10.	ἀπεκρίθη Ἰησοῦς καὶ εἶπεν αὐτῇ
11.	λέγει αὐτῷ ἡ γυνή
13.	ἀπεκρίθη Ἰησοῦς καὶ εἶπεν αὐτῇ
15.	λέγει πρὸς αὐτὸν ἡ γυνή
16.	λέγει αὐτῇ
17a.	ἀπεκρίθη ἡ γυνὴ καὶ εἶπεν αὐτῷ
17b.	λέγει αὐτῇ ὁ Ἰησοῦς
19.	λέγει αὐτῷ ἡ γυνή
21.	λέγει αὐτῇ ὁ Ἰησοῦς
25.	λέγει αὐτῷ ἡ γυνή
26.	λέγει αὐτῇ ὁ Ἰησοῦς.[3]

---

1. For discussion of whether this is a theological or a geographical necessity cf. Brown, *John*, I, p. 169; G.R. Beasley-Murray, *John* (WBC; Waco, TX: Word Books, 1987), p. 59; E. Haenchen, *John* (2 vols.; Hermeneia; trans. R.W. Funk; Philadelphia: Fortress Press, 1984), I, p. 218.

2. G.R. O'Day rightly argues that the discussion with the disciples concerning food should not be regarded as a separate unit but as part of the whole pericope (*Revelation in the Fourth Gospel* [Philadelphia: Fortress Press, 1986], pp. 49, 50).

3. L. Eslinger, 'The Wooing of the Woman at the Well: Jesus, the Reader and Reader-response Criticism', *Literature and Theology* 1.2 (1987), pp. 171.

The structure which Eslinger suggests may be helpful in identifying v. 16 as the hinge on which the two parts of this dialogue turns. It may further be important that the sentence which contains ἐγώ εἰμι acts as an inclusio to the dialogue begun in v. 7. This would suggest that the ἐγώ εἰμι saying is in a position of particular emphasis in the discussion. The fact that Eslinger also places vv. 19 and 20 at the centre of the second section of the dialogue may also suggest a special emphasis on the issue of true worship, which the Samaritan woman introduces there.

It must be doubted, however, whether the phrases 'he said to her' and 'she said to him' can bear the structural weight that Eslinger places on them.[1] After all, such phrases are necessary for a narrative conversation to take place. Furthermore the fact that the phrases alternate says no more than that this is a dialogue and not a monologue or a discourse. As such, Jesus' words are naturally interspersed with those of the Samaritan woman. It is therefore probably wise to agree with Eslinger's general structuring of this dialogue into two complementary parts while doubting the strict pattern that his chiastic structure places on the text. In this it may be significant that the words of Jesus open and close both parts of the dialogue. In between, the Samaritan woman's understanding of Jesus progresses from 'a Jew' (v. 9), through 'Sir' (v. 11) and 'a prophet' (v. 19) and reaches its peak with Jesus' declaration by means of ἐγώ εἰμι in v. 26.[2] There the woman asserts that when the messiah comes, he will explain all things (v. 25). Jesus' 'I am' saying concludes their discussion by declaring that he is the messiah of whom she speaks.

Hinrichs points out that several features of the dialogue with the

---

1.   Eslinger's further suggestion (*Wooing*, p. 168) that this whole episode is to be interpreted in the light of an Old Testament betrothal type-scene, is unconvincing. Although parallels exist between Jn 4 and Gen. 29, these make a comparison between Jesus and 'our father Jacob' (Jn 4.12) rather than between Jesus and the patriarchal bridegroom. Jesus is indeed greater than Jacob 'who gave us this well' because he offers a greater well; a well of living water which will quench thirst for ever (vv. 10,13). If the reader were really 'intended to believe that Jesus and the Samaritan' were 'heading towards betrothal', the narrator, following such a type-scene, would surely make this clear as happens in Gen. 24 and 29. It seems better to observe obvious parallels with Jacob in Gen. 29 without allowing the structure of that episode to impose an allegorical interpretation on Jn 4. Cf. J.H. Neyrey, 'Jacob traditions and the interpretation of John 4.10-26', *CBQ* 41 (3,1979), pp. 419-37.

2.   Cf. R. Schnackenburg, *The Gospel according to St John.* I (trans K. Smith; London: Burns and Oates, 1968), p. 420.

Samaritan woman prepare for the 'I am' saying of 4.26.[1] From a formal point of view this happens in the fact that Jesus' ἐγώ εἰμι saying occurs between two questions concerning Jesus' identity (vv. 10, 29).[2] The 'I am' saying answers the first indirect question formulated by Jesus and so acts as the structural climax of the main part of the episode in Samaria. It is after this 'I am' saying that the woman departs to tell the villagers about this man who knows all about her (v. 28). Although the reason the woman gives for the fact that she thinks Jesus may be the messiah is his knowledge of her life (v. 29) and not his claim in v. 26, without Jesus' climactic words in that verse his knowledge of her life suggests no more to her than that he is a prophet (v. 19). Because of his climactic claim, made by means of ἐγώ εἰμι, she wonders whether he may indeed be the Christ (v. 29).

O'Day makes much of how the interaction between the Samaritan woman and Jesus is the way in which the character of Jesus is revealed.[3] The disciples and the Samaritan woman in John 4 are tools to help the reader understand the person of Jesus. Although they are characters in their own right, their reactions and misunderstandings enable the reader to see Jesus for whom the evangelist believes he really is. The characterization of the Samaritan woman thus acts as a foil to further the characterization of Jesus. After Jesus' initial request for a drink (v. 7), he introduces a second type of water which he claims to offer to the woman (v. 10). His cryptic statements (initially about water) force the woman to ask more questions about who he is. These are the very questions that the narrator regards as of importance for the reader to consider. Thus the woman's questions are not primarily to reveal her character or her ignorance about spiritual things but to draw out the character of Jesus.[4]

Even though the woman lacks the insight that the reader has concerning Jesus, she is not portrayed as ignorant or stupid; in fact it is possible that she knows that Jesus is talking on a different level and her

---

1.   Hinrichs, *Ich Bin*, pp. 23, 24.

2.   Hinrichs, *Ich Bin*, p. 25. Also, O'Day, *Revelation*, p. 72.

3.   O'Day, *Revelation*, p. 50.

4.   Although the Samaritan woman may on one level be 'a model of the female disciple' (Culpepper, *Anatomy*, p. 137), her primary role is as a foil to the revelation of Jesus' identity. Cf. Moore, who suggests that 'characterisation in the Gospels tends toward the "flat" and the "static" end of the spectrum. Gospel characters are plot functionaries first and foremost...' (*Literary Criticism*, p. 15).

remark of v. 12 'may be meant to sound mocking'.[1] It is as much obvious to her as to the reader that his offer is not one of normal water as he has nothing with which to draw (v. 11), and even if it was normal water, he would have to be greater than Jacob to be able to give it to her. However, even when she knows that Jesus cannot be talking of ordinary water from the well, the woman chooses to take Jesus' words literally. The irony is not in the fact that the woman is completely ignorant of a deeper level of conversation, but that she is ignorant of who it is that is conducting that conversation. Unlike the discerning reader who has knowledge of Jesus' person from the preceding chapters, she does not realize that Jesus is greater than Jacob (v. 12) and that her question actually requires a positive rather than a negative answer.[2] Until she does, she cannot know that the mysterious water he offers meets a need that even Jacob's water could not. At this point the woman does not know what the water Jesus is talking about consists of.

Although the reader knows from the preceding chapters who the narrator believes Jesus to be, it is through interaction with the narrative that the narrator's beliefs become the reader's. The narrator has set out his claims about the person of Jesus in ch. 1. Now through the narrative any doubts about the validity of those claims are addressed. The reader's lingering questions about whether Jesus is who John claims him to be are the questions which the woman too addresses, namely, 'Who is this man and what is he really offering?' O'Day rightly argues that the *who* should not be separated from the *how* of Jesus' revelation and so it is essential to understand how the person of Jesus is revealed in order to understand who he is.[3] It is therefore important to recognize that the Samaritan woman's interaction with Jesus plays a role in revealing who he is. While the discovery of Jesus' true identity is the plot of the narrative, the character of the woman is an agent of that plot.[4]

1.   Schnackenburg, *John*, I, p. 429, on 4.12.
2.   Cf. Culpepper, *Anatomy*, p. 172.
3.   O'Day, *Revelation*, p. 50.
4.   Likewise, the characterization of the disciples and the people of the village in this episode serves to further the characterization of Jesus. For this reason it is minimal. While the disciples' unstated questions are recorded, which gives the reader an inside view into their prejudicial thoughts, in this episode they are little more than a collective group (cf. vv. 8, 27, 31, 33). Even their command that Jesus should eat, which brings about a discussion of Jesus' ultimate source of nourishment, is a collective action. The narrator portrays them as acting (vv. 8, 27), thinking (v. 28) and speaking (v. 31) as a group. Likewise the villagers believe the woman and Jesus as a

In this revelation of Jesus' identity the ἐγώ εἰμι saying of 4.26 is of utmost importance, for its function is to resolve the irony created by the two indirect questions about Jesus' identity (vv. 10, 12) as well as by the woman's statement about the messiah (v. 25). The fact that the reader already knows the narrator's conceptual point of view concerning the character of Jesus, enables that knowledge to be played off against the Samaritan woman's lack of knowledge. This creates an irony as she twice says more about Jesus than she could possibly imagine. Not only is he greater than Jacob, but his ἐγώ εἰμι reveals to her that he is the very one whom she expects to show her all things (v. 25). He is the Christ.[1] If she had really known who it was who had asked her for a drink, she would have asked him to give her living water (v. 10). Through the statement containing ἐγώ εἰμι, the Samaritan woman discovers the irony of her situation and joins the conceptual point of view of Jesus, the narrator and the reader.

While the narrator has already asserted that Jesus is the messiah, this is the first (and only time) that it is explicitly acknowledged by the character of Jesus (v. 26). By means of ἐγώ εἰμι he confirms the narrator's conceptual point of view. The fact that the Samaritan woman uses the Semitic form of the title, which is immediately explained, may reveal the conceptual background of both the narrator and the implied reader. Jesus is characterized as one who accepts a Semitic title by means of the words ἐγώ εἰμι. However, the narrator feels it necessary to explain that messiah is the same as the Greek term Christ. Furthermore, Jesus is compared with the patriarch Jacob, an ancestor shared by both Jews and Samaritans alike. These references to Jewish figures suggest that the implied reader knows about traditions associating Jacob with the well at Sychar (cf. vv. 5, 6) as well as traditions about the messiah who was expected to reveal all things. It is even possible that

group. The primary role of the Samaritans is that they believe (vv. 39, 41, 42). As a result of this they also make a profession of faith that goes beyond the woman's. They too reveal something more of the person of Jesus, for they 'know that this is indeed the Saviour of the world' (v. 42).

1.   Freed is thus correct to maintain that: 'Certainly one way ... to convey the meaning of *ego eimi* in this context is to understand *messias/christos* of the sentence before it as the predicate with which *ho lalon soi* is in apposition. In contrast to the Baptist's negative statement, Jesus is reported as affirming his messiahship through the use of *ego eimi*.' (*1.20 and 4.25*, p. 290). Cf. also Barrett, *John*, p. 239; Haenchen, *John*, I, p. 224

the implied reader knows of traditions connecting the two.[1] By means of ἐγώ εἰμι Jesus acknowledges that he is to be identified with the Jewish messiah and simultaneously claims to be greater than the Jewish patriarch Jacob. It should, however, be noted that the Samaritan woman's assertion that Jesus may be the Christ and Jesus' own identification with that title do not conclude the episode. The people of the village come to believe that Jesus is not only a Jewish figure but is in fact the saviour of the world (v. 42). Thus the episode as a whole urges the reader to adopt a point of view that acknowledges that salvation comes from the Jews (v. 22). However, Jesus is not only the saviour of the Jews but the saviour of the world.

Although the words ἐγώ εἰμι in Jn 4.26 associate Jesus with the concept of the messiah, it is possible that their formulation is a hint to a further implied meaning. A case for a double meaning in Jesus' words will be argued in the discussion of background in Chapter 6 on Jesus' identity. What needs to be noted here, however, is the strange way that Jesus' affirmation of his messiahship is formulated. While John the Baptist states clearly 'I am not the Christ' (1.20), Jesus does not state 'I am the Christ'. Instead he says 'ἐγώ εἰμι who speaks to you' (v. 26).[2] Although a predicate should be supplied from the context, Jesus' words themselves are without a predicate.[3] Thus there is room for ambiguity in the understanding of ἐγώ εἰμι, even if the most obvious meaning is 'I who speak to you am the Christ'.[4]

While the focus of this study has been Jesus' claim to messiahship

---

1.   Cf. Neyrey, *Jacob Traditions*, p. 431.

2.   I am grateful to Margaret Davies for pointing out my reticence to translate ἐγώ εἰμι here and on several other occasions. It is precisely because of the ambiguity of the Greek words used in John that I have often left the words untranslated. The fact that a simple meaning 'I am he' is sometimes being played off against a far deeper meaning, will be argued for in the discussion of background material. I do not think that there is a suitable English translation to convey this ambiguity.

3.   O'Day's comment (*Revelation*, p. 72) that 'John does not intend for us to supply the predicate from the woman's statement in v. 25', is not entirely correct. While John may intend the reader to interpret the words on a deeper level, it is apparent from the following narrative that the woman took Jesus' words to imply a predicate (cf. v. 29). It is also apparent that Christ is a title which the narrator is willing to affirm in connection with Jesus (e.g. 20.31).

4.   Brown (*John*, I, p. 172) and Beasley-Murray (*John*, p. 63) allow for the possibility of a double meaning here. Harner (*'I am'*, p. 47) argues that such a double meaning is intentional.

through the words ἐγώ εἰμι, there are other important Gospel themes discussed in the pericope. What prompts the woman's mention of the messiah is the discussion of what God requires of true worshippers (v. 23). Such worshippers are described as those who worship in spirit and in truth. Thus Jesus' claim to messiahship occurs in the context of a discussion of truth. Furthermore, Jesus claims that the Samaritans worship in ignorance, while the Jews worship what they know. The knowledge of God and Jesus' identity is in fact one of the main themes of their dialogue, for it is the woman's ignorance about who Jesus is that prevents her from asking him for living water (v. 10). The Samaritan woman claims to know that messiah is coming (v. 25), but again she is ignorant of who the messiah really is. These themes tie Jesus' 'I am' saying to the themes with which the Gospel is occupied. Thus the result of Jesus' time in Samaria is belief on the part of the villagers. In fact they come to know that Jesus is the saviour of the world (v. 42).

It may be concluded that the literary function of the ἐγώ εἰμι saying in Jn 4.26 is to take a Jewish title and apply it to the person of Jesus. This takes place as the climax and conclusion of Jesus' discussion with the Samaritan woman. In this dialogue Jesus' characterization has been developed through the ironic interplay with the Samaritan woman until by means of the 'I am' saying the Samaritan woman is allowed to participate in the privileged point of view which Jesus, the narrator and the reader already share. As a result Jesus' 'I am' saying confirms the narrator's conceptual point of view. However, the question of whether this 'I am' also functions on a deeper plane must be reserved for a discussion of background material.

2. *John 6 : The Bread of Life (6.20, 35, 48; cf. vv. 41, 51)*

Immediately after the Third Discourse (5.19-47), John narrates his version of the feeding of the five thousand (vv. 1-14) and the walking on the water (vv. 17-21), in which Jesus declares himself to the disciples by the words ἐγώ εἰμι (v. 20). This is followed by a discourse (vv. 26-59), which resumes the theme of bread introduced by the feeding miracle. Here Jesus identifies himself three times with the concept of bread by means of the words ἐγώ εἰμι (vv. 35, 48, 51). This is repeated once by the Jews who murmur against such a claim (v. 41). The whole episode is set in Galilee at the season of Passover (6.4).[1]

Three themes tie ch. 6 to the previous discourse. Jesus' discussion with the Jews refers to their ancestor Moses (6.32-34) and so recalls Jesus' claim that the writings of Moses speak of him (5.45, 46). The person of Moses also ties the Bread of Life discourse with the following discourse at the feast of Tabernacles (cf. 7.19-24). The discussion of Jesus' works forms a second link with ch. 5 where Jesus asserted that his works themselves bear witness to him (5.36). In spite of this, Jesus' narrative audience still want to know what work he is doing to prove that he is working the works of God (6.30; cf. v. 28). Thirdly, Jesus' discourse on bread (esp. vv. 36-40) builds on the question of his relationship with the Father which has been developed as one of the main themes of ch. 5.[2] In addition to themes, which link his discourse to what immediately precedes, the discussion on the nature of true food in John 4 has already given the reader special insight into Jesus' perspective that the narrative audience of John 6 lacks. Not only does the reader already know that Jesus offers living water to others (4.10, 13, 14), but he/she has also overheard Jesus' statement that his food is to do the will of the one who sent him (4.34). Consequently it is not a surprise when Jesus offers the crowd bread that will endure to eternal life (6.27).

The literary unity of John 6 is evident both from its internal subject matter and because the same chronological indicator used at the beginning of ch. 6 also marks off the beginning of ch. 7 (μετὰ ταῦτα, *after this*).[3] This larger unit of John 6 can be broken down into the three main sections outlined above. These are linked together by connecting verses so that the broad structure may be seen as follows:

Introduction	vv. 1-4
The feeding miracle	*vv. 5-14*
Link: Jesus withdraws	v. 15
Disciples go to sea	v. 16
The incident on the lake	*vv. 17-21*
Link: The crowds seek Jesus	vv. 22-25
The bread of life discourse	*vv. 26-59*
Conclusion: Response	vv. 60-71

---

1.   For a discussion of the problems raised by the geographical and temporal setting of John 6 see Barrett, *John*, pp. 23, 272-73.

2.   These repeated themes warn against removing this episode from the context of the Gospel as a whole.

3.   Cf. J.D. Crossan, 'It is Written: A Structuralist Analysis of John 6', *Semeia* 26 (1983), pp. 3-21.

Since ἐγώ εἰμι does not occur until the end of the second scene where Jesus walks on the water, the feeding of the five thousand need only be discussed in relation to the literary function of ἐγώ εἰμι in the rest of the chapter.

The chapter's unity is affirmed by Crossan who suggests that mention of the disciples in vv. 1-15 and the Twelve in vv. 60-71 acts as an inclusio, framing the chapter.[1] Against the structure above he argues that John 6 should be divided into four sections. For him the chapter is ordered according to the characters involved and their reaction to Jesus' deeds and words:

	Jesus' Deeds	Jesus' words
a) Jesus and the crowds	6.1-15	6.22-59
b) Jesus and the disciples	6.16-21	6.60-71[2]

However, such a division of structure fails to give sufficient weight to the assumption in the final section (vv. 60-71) that Jesus' words to the crowds (vv. 22-59) were also uttered in the presence of those disciples who take offence at them (v. 61).[3] Besides, the disciples were not only present but actually took part in the feeding miracle (vv. 5-10). Neither is the relationship between Jesus' deeds and his words as obvious as such a structure suggests. Although there is a clear connection between the feeding miracle and Jesus' words to the crowd, such a connection is not apparent between the walking on the water and his words to the disciples. A view of structure based on a firm distinction between Jesus' narrative audience in relation to his deeds and words in each section is therefore not as helpful as Crossan supposes.[4]

1. Crossan, *It is Written*, p. 4. See also G.A. Phillips, '"This is a Hard Saying. Who Can Be a Listener to it?": Creating a Reader in John 6', *Semeia* 26 (1983), pp. 23-56, where Phillips thinks that the inclusio consists of vv. 1-13 and vv. 66-71.

2. Crossan, *It is Written*, p. 4.

3. Crossan (*It is Written*, p. 7) acknowledges that the disciples are present throughout though they are not mentioned.

4. If a division of structure is to based on characters alone, Phillips's model, in which there are seven divisions, is perhaps more helpful than Crossan's. Phillips, *A Hard Saying*, p. 38, suggests that the chapter displays a concentric structure:

The 'I am' sayings of John 6 further confirm the unity of the chapter. For, just as bread is the theme which links the feeding of the five thousand to Jesus' discourse, so ἐγώ εἰμι functions as a link between the incident on the lake and the discourse. Though different from those 'I am' sayings of Jesus' discourse on the bread of life, the ἐγώ εἰμι of 6.20 provides a verbal link between the two episodes.[1] The theme of bread in the first part of the chapter (ἄρτος, vv. 5, 7, 9, 11, 13) and the words ἐγώ εἰμι in the second part (v. 20) are combined as a single phrase in the third (ἐγώ εἰμι ὁ ἄρτος, vv. 35, 41, 48, 51). The words which identify Jesus to the disciples on the lake therefore show that this same Jesus is also the God-sent nourishment of the world. Consequently the words ἐγώ εἰμι are part of an intricate structure in which John introduces a theme and returns to it later in order to develop its meaning further. The full content of what is meant by the words ἐγώ εἰμι in John 6 cannot be determined until its last occurrence in 6.51.[2]

Borgen has shown that this intricate style of repetitive themes has similarities with passages in Philo as well as the style of Palestinian midrash.[3] The discourse is thus ordered with each new section building upon the last in such a way that it falls into the pattern of a midrash of the synagogue homily type (cf. v. 59).[4] As with the rest of the chapter,

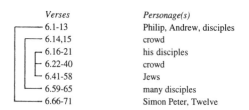

Verses	Personage(s)
6.1-13	Philip, Andrew, disciples
6.14,15	crowd
6.16-21	his disciples
6.22-40	crowd
6.41-58	Jews
6.59-65	many disciples
6.66-71	Simon Peter, Twelve

The reasons given above still hold for rejecting such a view of structure.

1.   Schnackenburg (*John*, II, p. 11) believes that the occurrence of ἐγώ εἰμι is the sole reason for the inclusion of the walking on the water in Jn 6. Cf. also J.P. Heil, *Jesus Walking on the Sea: Meaning and Gospel Functions of Matt. 14.22-33, Mark 6.45-52 and John 6.15b-21* (AnBib, 87; Rome: Biblical Institute Press, 1981), p. 154; Crossan, *It is Written*, p. 14.

2.   Cf. Phillips (*A Hard Saying*, p. 50) who suggests that the meaning of ἐγώ εἰμι is developed in the course of the chapter. On this reasoning the full meaning of ἐγώ εἰμι cannot be determined until the last ἐγώ εἰμι of the Gospel in 18.8.

3.   Borgen, *Bread*, pp. 1-97.

4.   It may be argued that a literary study should not look to other material to determine its structure. However, it is important to be aware of literary genre.

the theme that links the whole discourse is that of bread. This is mentioned first in v. 26 when it refers to the bread which the crowds have
eaten earlier and is developed through several stages until the promise
that 'whoever eats this bread will live for ever' (v. 58).

The apparently 'midrashic'[1] exposition of the text in 6.31 develops in
two important stages:

1. Borgen suggests that vv. 32-48 of Jesus' discourse paraphrase
   and discuss the first part of the crowd's quotation from Exod.
   16.4: 'He gave them bread from heaven' (v. 31).[2] The text
   from Exod. 16.4 thus becomes the text for Jesus' 'sermon'. He
   tells them that it was not Moses who gave them bread from
   heaven but his own Father. By his 'I am' saying Jesus
   identifies himself with the manna of the Old Testament. This
   saying in turn introduces the next subsection of the discourse
   (vv. 35-40). Jesus responds to the murmuring of the crowd
   (vv. 41, 42) by referring to another Old Testament text (v. 45),
   this time from Isa. 54.13. He also re-iterates his claim to offer a
   better bread than that of which Exodus 16 talks (vv. 48, 49).
2. Building on this, the final part of the discourse (vv. 49-58) can
   then be seen to paraphrase and expound the word 'eat'
   (v. 31).[3] Those who eat the true bread which comes down
   from heaven will not die (v. 50). Jesus takes his claim further
   with the assertion that the bread he offers is his flesh (v. 51). In
   conclusion he talks of his flesh and blood which offer life in
   contrast to the bread that the fathers ate which was to no avail
   (vv. 52-59).

It can therefore be seen that the text from Exod. 16.4 is reinterpreted by
Jesus and then applied to himself. The repetition of his ἐγώ εἰμι saying
plays a part in the developing exposition of Exod. 16.4 which is echoed

---

Borgen's analysis does not impose a rigid structure upon the text but suggests that
the step by step exposition of an Old Testament passage has its closest parallel in
midrashic exegesis. Cf. esp. Borgen, *Bread*, pp. 28-58.

1. 'Midrashic' in the sense that it employs similar exegetical principles to
midrash even though 'the material produced from the Palestinian midrashim was
written down later than the time of Philo, John and Paul' (Borgen, *Bread*, p. 54).

2. Borgen, *Bread*, p. 35.

3. Borgen, *Bread*, p. 35.

throughout the discourse and returned to at the very end.[1]

Borgen further suggests that John equates different terms within the discourse by means of the midrashic pattern 'A is B' so that 'it is said that a word or a phrase from the Old Testament is identical with another word or phrase'.[2] So the argument of the discourse develops as follows:

> He gave them bread from heaven to eat (v. 31)
> The bread = that which comes from heaven and gives life (v. 33)
> The bread which gives life = Jesus (v. 35)
> Jesus = the bread = that which comes down from heaven (v. 41)
> Jesus = that which comes down from heaven (v. 42)
> Jesus = the bread which gives life (vv. 48, 51)
> The bread = Jesus' flesh which he will give (v. 51)
> Flesh = food [blood = drink] (v. 55)
> The bread ≠ what the fathers ate but will give life to those who eat it
>   (v. 58).

So the words ἐγώ εἰμι are an integral part of the way in which Jesus reveals who he is and what that means in the discourse.

The characterization of Jesus in John 6 again enforces the narrator's conceptual point of view. Jesus is the dominant character in all three scenes.[3] He is the one who acts in word and deed. He knows what he will do to feed the multitude (v. 6). He tells the disciples to make the multitude sit down (v. 10). He distributes the bread and fish among the crowd (v. 11). He tells the disciples to pick up the fragments (v. 12). He withdraws before the crowd comes to try and make him king (v. 15). He walks on the sea and draws near to the disciples' boat (v. 19). He knows and alleviates the disciples' fear by declaring his identity in the words ἐγώ εἰμι· μὴ φοβεῖσθε (v. 20). Following this, it is Jesus who leads the discussion and explains to the crowd what his miracle really means (vv. 25-34). He then declares that it is he who is the true bread and that any one who comes to him will not hunger (v. 35). Jesus knows the secret words of the Jews (v. 52) and the thoughts of the disciples

---

1. For a fuller discussion of ἐγώ εἰμι's function in the exposition of Exod. 16.4 see the study of background material in Chapter 7.

2. Borgen, *Bread*, p. 89.

3. Cf. Crossan, *It is Written*, p. 9: 'The Discourse in 6.5 stresses, just as did the Narrative in 6.11, the complete dominance of Jesus over this entire event. Cf., in contrast, Mark 6.35, where the Disciples initiate the discourse.' Such dominance is partly achieved by the fact that the narrator shares Jesus' omniscient point of view with the reader (vv. 6, 15, 61).

(vv. 61, 64). The dominance of Jesus in all these things is enforced by the fact that he consistently speaks in the first person.[1] Everything is focused on him and this is epitomized in the 'I am' sayings of the discourse. It is this dominance that he displays in his words that causes offence among his audience (vv. 41, 42, 60).

Ironically Jesus' dominance is theologically based in his subservience to the Father. It is God who gives the true bread from heaven (v. 32). Jesus has been sent by him (vv. 39, 57). Jesus' claim to have come down from heaven is based in his obedience to the will of the Father (v. 39). He will raise the believer up at the last day but in this he is only doing his Father's will (v. 40). Thus Jesus' dominance goes hand in hand with the Father's action. Jesus only offers himself as the living bread (v. 51) inasmuch as the Father also gives that bread (v. 33).

In the light of Jesus' dominance, the other characters are portrayed in the way they react to his actions and words. While the narrator states that Jesus went (ἀπῆλθεν, v. 1), it is the role of the crowd to follow him (ἠκολούθει, v. 2) and the disciples are simply said to be 'with' Jesus (ἐκεῖ ἐκάθητο μετὰ τῶν μαθητῶν αὐτοῦ, v. 3).[2] After the sign, the crowd grasps something of Jesus' significance (v. 14). However, the narrator shows that even a correct title for Jesus can be misunderstood. Although Jesus is the king of Israel (1.49), it is wrong for the crowd to come and make him king by force (ἔρξεσθαι καὶ ἁρπάζειν, 6.15). The crowd's reaction to Jesus thus furthers the narrator's conceptual point of view because it explains to the reader that the kingship he attributes to Jesus is not the same as the kingship the crowd wish for him. In other words, the reaction of the crowd serves to make a distinction between the kingship that Jesus accepts (1.49; cf. 18.36) and the kingship that he rejects (6.15). So the characterization of others again functions to further the characterization of Jesus.

The walking on the water also emphasizes Jesus' dominance both through the action itself and through his words.[3] When the disciples first see Jesus walking on the water, they are afraid. 'But, once Jesus identifies himself, with his sea-walking revelation ('Εγώ εἰμι, 6.20) and comforts the fear of the disciples (μὴ φοβεῖσθε, 6.20), they are glad to

---

1.   Crossan (*It is Written*, p. 11) suggests that 'After the supreme and unqualified revelation of "I am" in 6.20, it is not very surprising that the "I" of Jesus should dominate the discourse... only Jesus uses "I" within the Discourse'.

2.   Cf. Crossan, *It is Written*, p. 7.

3.   Cf. Heil, *Walking on the Sea*, p. 79.

welcome (λαβεῖν) him into the boat (6.21a).'[1] Jesus' words not only
alleviate the disciples' fears but allow them to proceed to their destination at once (v. 21).

In the episode of the walking on the water the narrator's conceptual
point of view concerning Jesus' divine nature is reinforced. The reader
has already been told: 'In the beginning was the Word, and the Word
was with God, and the Word was God...all things were made through
him, and without him was not anything made that was made' (1.1, 3).
Now by walking on the water Jesus is seen to dominate that same creation in an act that begs questions concerning Jesus' identity. Who does
the narrator think Jesus is, if he can ascribe such actions to him?[2] It will
become apparent in the study of background material that Jesus' dominance over nature is both enhanced and given a foundation when
viewed in the light of Old Testament epiphanies.[3] Although his words on
one level should be taken simply as an identification to the disciples, they
may well identify him with the words of God, since they parallel the
epiphanic words of God in the Old Testament.[4] Certain indicators in the
text, such as the context and formulation of Jesus' words, may point the
implied reader to a deeper understanding of the walking on the water
which requires a knowledge of Old Testament epiphanies in order for
the narrator's conceptual point of view to be fully comprehended.

Just as the crowd acts as a foil to the person of Jesus in the feeding of
the five thousand, so this continues to be true in the discourse. In the
latter the crowd's reaction to Jesus' words offers the opportunity for
him to explain their meaning. They want an explanation for Jesus'
miraculous disappearance from the other side of the lake (v. 25).[5]

---

1.   Heil, *Walking on the Sea*, p. 148.

2.   The Matthean version of the walking on the water explicitly addresses the
question of Jesus' identity as those in the boat worship him, saying 'Truly, you are
the Son of God' (Mt. 14.33). Although there is no such declaration directly after the
walking on the water in John, Peter's confession at the end of the chapter (v. 68)
derives from how Jesus is perceived in both the discourse and the walking on the
water.

3.   The reasons for accepting this episode as such are discussed in the study of
background material below.

4.   Heil (*Walking on the Sea*, p. 80) is correct to see the primary function of the
ἐγώ εἰμι here as one of identification and not of revelation. Cf. also Barrett, *John*,
p. 281; Haenchen, *John*, I, p. 280. For the possibility of a double meaning to Jesus'
words see Chapter 6.

5.   Hinrichs (*Ich Bin*, p. 51) points out the connection between the walking on the

Instead, Jesus explains that they had not understood his miracle (vv. 26, 27). Thus their question becomes the starting point from which Jesus can explain what true bread is (vv. 27, 32, 33). The crowd's misunderstanding of Jesus' sign becomes the basis for his explanation of the true understanding of the miracle. Likewise, when the Jews murmur at him (v. 41), Jesus answers them (v. 43) and further explains himself. The questions of Jesus' narrative audience are written so that those readers with similar questions can hear the answer of Jesus to such objections. The interaction of Jesus with his narrative audience also allows the reader to interact with Jesus' (and the narrator's) conceptual point of view.

One important aspect of characterization concerns the reaction that Jesus' words cause among his hearers. The group which has up to this point in the Gospel acted together as 'the disciples' now splits into two groups: 'the many disciples' who no longer go about with Jesus (v. 66) and the Twelve who have nowhere else to go and who believe and have come to know that Jesus is the Holy One of God (vv. 68, 69). It is Jesus' words, including ἐγώ εἰμι, which cause a reaction in his audience. Even those who appear to be his disciples are divided in their rejection or acceptance of Jesus' claims. Heil suggests that Peter's words are in direct response to what has been revealed of Jesus through the 'I am' sayings:

> Peter's confession functions as the climactic response which concludes the paradigmatic series of revelatory words introduced by the self-identification formula ἐγώ εἰμι. Peter confirms these self-identifications of Jesus in 6.69b with the words 'You are (σὺ εἶ) the Holy one of Israel'.[1]

The fact that the disciples are not highly developed as individual characters in John 6, is not of great importance for the reader. Limited though it may be, the characterization which takes place is as a result of how they view Jesus' own character, especially through his claim to be the bread. Like the Samaritans of ch. 4 who believe because they have heard for themselves and know that Jesus is the saviour of the world (4.42), the Twelve realize that Jesus has the words of eternal life (6.68). However, unlike the Samaritans there is a division into those who accept Jesus' words (the Twelve) and those who find them offensive and withdraw from following Jesus. Here Jesus' claims have a negative as well as

---

water and the discourse in the crowd's wish for an explanation of how Jesus crossed the lake.

1. Heil, *Walking on the Sea*, p. 169.

a positive effect on the narrative audience. The characters in this latter part of the chapter (vv. 66-71) do not simply act as a foil to Jesus' own characterization but, through their reactions to his claims, also allow the reader to make a similar judgment about Jesus.

The crowd, described as 'a multitude' (v. 2) of five thousand men (v. 10), are an even less distinct group than the disciples. Their characterization proves of some interest, for the narrator seems to imply that the crowd, who start as neutral observers (v. 2), become more distinct as they listen to Jesus. This is achieved partly through the progression of terms the narrator uses for them and partly through their reactions to Jesus. As the crowd, they followed him because they saw him heal (v. 2). As the people, they are miraculously fed and acknowledge Jesus as 'the prophet who is to come into the world' (v. 14). They then follow Jesus because they have eaten their fill (v. 26). Through his provocative claims, which come to them in terms of ἐγώ εἰμι (v. 41), they become the Jews who murmur at Jesus. In this way it appears that the characters (both the disciples and the crowds) become more polarized in their views of Jesus as the chapter unfolds. It is also clear that the claims Jesus makes by means of ἐγώ εἰμι play a part in this, for it is the Jews' objection to such a claim that causes them to murmur at him (v. 41) and his offer based on the 'I am' saying of v. 51 that causes them to dispute among themselves (v. 52). Although it cannot be said that it is the words ἐγώ εἰμι alone which provoke the division among Jesus' narrative audience, it is the revelatory claim, of which ἐγώ εἰμι forms an essential part, that causes offence.

As with John 4, the dialogue in Jn 6.25-35 is conducted on two different levels. 'In John 6, by focussing on the difference between eating one's fill of bread and seeing a sign, Jesus indicates both the two levels of the feeding (and of the following dialogue) and the tension between the levels.'[1] The fact that there are two possible interpretations of Jesus' words would mean no more than that they were ambiguous. The tension between the two levels creates irony because the deeper (spiritual) meaning makes a nonsense of the crowd's literal (earthly) meaning.[2] Jesus instructs them not to work (ἐργάζομαι) 'for food which perishes, but for the food which endures to eternal life' (v. 27).

---

1. O'Day, *Revelation*, pp. 98, 99.

2. Cf. Duke, *Irony*, p. 17: 'Irony as a literary device is a double-levelled literary phenomenon in which two tiers of meaning stand in some opposition to each other and in which some degree of unawareness is expressed or implied'.

The crowd responds to the verb 'work' (*ergazomai*) but misunderstands Jesus' use of it. In v. 27 *ergazomai* implies 'earn by working,' 'work for,' but in v. 28 the crowd uses the same verb to mean 'perform,' 'work a work.' Jesus and the crowd are using the same words to mean different things.[1]

Jesus explains that the work they should do is to believe in the one God has sent (v. 29). The crowd ask Jesus for a sign to show that he is from God. They claim that they will then believe (v. 30). Ironically, this underlines the fact that they had not seen the significance of the feeding miracle of vv. 1-15, for it pointed to who Jesus is.[2]

Jesus tells the crowd that the Son of man will give them this bread. So in words similar to the Samaritan woman's they say 'Lord, give us this bread always' (v. 34; cf. 4.15). Here the full force of the irony strikes home. For when they ask for the bread they believe Jesus can give, he replies that he is what they want (v. 35). Earlier Jesus had said that 'the bread of God is that which/he who comes down from heaven, and gives life to the world' (v. 33). The ambiguity in the words ὁ καταβαίνων (that which comes down, or he who comes down) allows the crowd to ask Jesus to give them that bread. However, they had taken Jesus' words in the most obvious sense, when from Jesus' response the words should have been taken to refer to him. His response clears the misunderstanding: 'I am the bread of life'. In conjunction with the predicate, the words ἐγώ εἰμι reveal the irony of the crowd's misunderstanding. Jesus is what they seek but they were unaware (cf. 4.26). The words allow for no more misunderstanding, and the claim is offensive (v. 41).

Unlike the way he proceeds in the story of the Samaritan woman, the narrator does not divulge to the reader all the information at his disposal. The reader possesses more knowledge than the narrative audience about a second level to the concept of food (4.35) and so is not surprised when the crowds are told to work for food that endures to eternal life (6.27). It may not surprise readers either that Jesus offers such food, since they have heard Jesus offer living water to the Samaritan woman (4.13, 14). However, the character of Jesus surprises both the crowd and the

1.   O'Day, *Revelation*, p. 99.

2.   Borgen, *Bread*, p. 180: 'The works (5.36), exemplified with the feeding miracle (6.1ff.), and the scriptures (5.39-40), exemplified with the exposition of the quotation about the manna (6.31ff.), are two independent and parallel witnesses to the Son...the manna miracle and the feeding miracle are two independent and external types both of which are fulfilled in the spiritual sphere of the Son of God.'

readers by the response he gives to the request for such bread (v. 34). Unless readers pick up the possible double meaning in the immediately preceding statement, they are in danger of becoming the victims of irony, not knowing that Jesus is the bread of which he speaks (v. 35). As with the 'I am' saying to the Samaritan woman, the use of ἐγώ εἰμι here both reveals and resolves the irony. At the same time Jesus identifies himself with the true bread from heaven, which is not given by Moses but by God.

It is possible to detect irony in the context of ἐγώ εἰμι in 6.20 too. The narrator states that when the disciples 'had rowed about three or four miles, they saw Jesus walking on the sea and drawing near to the boat. They were frightened...' (v. 19). The reason given for the disciples' fear is that they saw Jesus coming to them. They are afraid because they do not know that it is Jesus. Ironically, Jesus, with the words ἐγώ εἰμι, shows that the person they fear is in fact the person they need.

Further irony in this chapter occurs on the part of the Jews. Duke points out the fact that the Jews claim that Jesus cannot be from God because they know his origin (vv. 41, 42).[1] Although they may know his earthly origin, unlike the reader they do not understand that 'the word became flesh' (1.14) and so cannot accept his claim to be that which comes down from heaven and gives life to the world. The fact is that Jesus actually knows their fathers (vv. 31, 49, 58) better than they know his (v. 43).

One of the characteristics of Johannine style is the interweaving of themes and phrases. John 6 is no exception to this rule and ἐγώ εἰμι plays a significant part in this. The theme of life, first mentioned in the prologue (1.4) and repeated in chs. 3 (vv. 15, 16) and 5 (vv. 39, 40), is taken up again in ch. 6 (vv. 27, 33, 35, 40, 47, 48, 51, 54, 58, 63). It is particularly significant for this study that life is explicitly linked to the predicate of the 'I am' saying (6.35, 48, 51). Jesus identifies himself with one of the main themes of the Gospel, a theme which the narrator depicts as the reason that the Gospel was written (20.31). The theme of Jesus' origin, which is taken up by the Jews in v. 42, has also been discussed in ch. 5. This too was first mentioned in the prologue (1.1-3, 9-11). In his claim to be the bread of life, Jesus also declares his origin, for he simultaneously identifies himself as the 'the bread of God...which comes down from heaven, and gives life to the world' (v. 33). The 'I

---

1. Duke, *Irony*, p. 64.

am' sayings also have a part in the theme of belief which grows in the chapter from Jesus' first mention that this is what God requires (v. 20), through Jesus' claims about belief in his discourse (v. 35, 36, 40, 64) to Peter's confession of v. 69, 'we have believed and have come to know that you are the Holy one of God'. Other themes could be added to these. Crossan emphasizes the themes of coming and going in John 6 and how these relate to the person of Jesus.[1] However, the writer does not simply return to these themes in vain repetition. The reader's concept of each theme is deepened as the themes return and are illustrated. The themes of the Gospel may be introduced early on but the content of those themes grows as the reader comes to understand what the narrator intends to convey by them.

This study of the function of ἐγώ εἰμι in John 6 has confirmed that the chapter should be viewed as a literary unit. Both the 'I am' saying on the lake and those of the discourse have shown the dominance of Jesus' character. Both types of saying have been linked with the Gospel's use of irony. The apparently deliberate echo of the 'I am' saying on the lake in the ἐγώ εἰμι of the discourse suggests that while they have different functions, it is correct to see an interaction between the different forms. The narrator's point of view concerning Jesus' divine origin is confirmed by Jesus' action of walking on the water as well as by his claim to be the bread come down from heaven. It is surely significant that by means of ἐγώ εἰμι Jesus again applies a thoroughly Jewish concept to himself. This time there is an explicit reference to the Jewish Scriptures which Jesus claims to fulfil. At the same time the 'I am' saying on the lake is enhanced when seen in the light of Old Testament epiphany formulae. This again suggests that the narrator intends Jesus to be understood in terms that are thoroughly Jewish.[2] Finally, there is the hint from the context of the ἐγώ εἰμι in Jn 6.20 that Jesus' words are said in the context of a divine action. The evidence for interpreting the words in this way must be discussed in the study of background material in Chapter 6 below.

---

1. Crossan, *It is Written*, p. 8.
2. Parallels that Borgen finds in Philo and Palestinian Midrash do not rule out considerable Hellenistic influence on John's conceptual point of view. Cf. Borgen, *Bread*, esp. p. 179.

3. John 8 : The Light of the World (8.12 [9.5]; 8.18, 24, 28, 58)

Within Jn 8.12-59, ἐγώ εἰμι occurs on the lips of Jesus five times and is used in a variety of contexts and forms. The similarity of form between Jesus' words 'I am the Bread of Life' (ἐγώ εἰμι ὁ ἄρτος τῆς ζωῆς, 6.35) and 'I am the Light of the World' (ἐγώ εἰμι τὸ φῶς τοῦ κόσμου, 8.12) is striking. So is the formal similarity between 4.26 (ἐγώ εἰμι, ὁ λαλῶν σοι) and 8.18 (ἐγώ εἰμι ὁ μαρτυρῶν περὶ ἐμαυτοῦ). These formal similarities act as a trigger for the reader to recall what has already been claimed by Jesus in the words ἐγώ εἰμι.

The conflict with the Jews in ch. 8 develops in the context of the discussion at the Feast of Tabernacles (7.2, 10, 14, 28, 37).[1] Debate about Jesus' authority and the origin of his teaching (7.16-19), judgment (7.24), Jesus' own origin (7.27-29) and destiny (7.33-36), whether he is the Christ (7.26-31; 40-44) and his claim to offer living water (7.37-39) precedes and prepares for his claim to be the Light of the World (8.12). Barrett aptly entitles his discussion of 8.12-59, 'Who is Jesus?',[2] for the question Jesus' opponents ask (v. 25; cf. v. 53) is the underlying theme of the chapter. As Jesus' identity is hotly debated, the words ἐγώ εἰμι appear frequently alongside the themes of witness and judgment (vv. 13-18), Jesus' origin and destiny (vv. 18-20), Jesus' relation to the Father and the Jews' relation to the devil (vv. 16-18; 30-47) and Jesus' and the Jews' relation to Abraham (vv. 39-58).[3] Significantly two narrative comments indicate that the controversy of ch. 8 takes place in the Temple, the centre of Jewish worship (vv. 20, 59).[4]

Jn 8.12-59 can be divided into three main sections. Each begins with Jesus speaking to his opponents. πάλιν οὖν...ἐλάλησεν (v. 12); εἶπεν οὖν πάλιν (v. 21); ἔλεγεν οὖν (v. 31). Each section also closes with a narrative comment. The first concludes by stating that Jesus' words had been spoken in the temple and that he had not been arrested

1. Barrett, *John*, p. 333; also Schnackenburg, *John*, II, p. 187.
2. Barrett, *John*, p. 359.
3. R.A. Whitacre (*Johannine Polemic: The Role of Tradition and Theology* [SBLDS, 67; Chico, CA: Scholars Press, 1982], p. 69) regards 8.31-59 as the 'Principal Text' in his discussion of the polemical nature of the Gospel.
4. Cf. C.L.B. Plumb, 'The ΕΓΩ EIMI sayings in John's Gospel' (MPhil thesis, Nottingham, 1990), p. 114. He argues from the Old Testament and Targums that the location of Jesus' 'I am' sayings in the Temple, where God's glory was to be expected, is paramount to their understanding as theophanies.

because his hour had not yet come (v. 21); the second with the statement that many believed because of Jesus' words (v. 30); and the final section with the comment that Jesus hid himself and went out from the temple (v. 59).

Kern suggests that these verses have a chiastic structure, centring around vv. 31-41.[1] Although this exaggerates the importance of certain issues (such as the truth of Jesus' judgment, vv. 21-30)[2] and rejects as secondary verses that do not fit into the schema (e.g. v. 25),[3] the words ἐγώ εἰμι certainly form an inclusio to the section and so confirm that it is to be regarded as a literary unit. Jesus' debate with the Jews begins with the words 'I am the Light of the world' (ἐγώ εἰμι τὸ φῶς τοῦ κόσμου, v. 12) and concludes with the words 'before Abraham was, I am' (πρὶν ᾿Αβρααμ γενέσθαι ἐγώ εἰμι, v. 58). Such an inclusio suggests that the different forms of 'I am' saying are meant to be seen in relation to one another.

Unlike that of ch. 6, the debate of ch. 8 centres on the authority for Jesus' self-revelation as the Light of the World rather than the meaning of it. Although the claim to be the Light of the World opens the chapter, the theme of light is not resumed until ch. 9. This does not necessarily mean that 8.12 has been displaced.[4] Although the debate may not be directly concerned with the content of Jesus' claim to be the Light of the World, his self-assertion by the words ἐγώ εἰμι in the opening verse

---

1. W. Kern, 'Die symmmetrische Gesamtaufbau von Joh.8,12-58', *ZKT* 78 (1956), pp. 451-54.

2. Cf. F.J. Moloney, *The Johannine Son of Man* (Rome: L.A.S., 1976), p. 126: 'While these ideas are present, they appear to be subordinated to other more important themes'.

3. Cf. Kern, *Die symmmetrische Gesamtaufbau*, p. 453. It seems better to accept the divisions suggested by the text, without rejecting the implications of Kern's analysis for the literary unity of the section.

4. Cf. Bultmann, *John*, pp. 329, 343; Barrett, *John*, p. 333. Rather than thinking of a displacement, Hinrichs (*Ich Bin*, p. 69) sees John 8 as primary and the influences of a redactor in Jn 9. He thinks the redactor's purpose was to provide a 'konkretion' of Jesus' light saying. It will be suggested below that the relationship between the themes of light, testimony and judgment derives from John's use of background material, where the same themes are also present. Moloney (*Son of Man*, p. 125) affirms that the theme of light fits into the context of ch. 8, but for a different reason: 'V.12 is not "out of place" merely because "light" is not mentioned again until 9.5. The whole of the first section of ch. 8 is concerned with Jesus' revelation of the Father, and there is every possibility that 'light' is used here in this sense.'

acts as its point of departure. As well as forming an inclusio, Jesus' claims made by means of the words ἐγώ εἰμι are central to the debate with the Jews. The first ἐγώ εἰμι (v. 12) sets out a claim of Jesus. The second (v. 18) concerns the validity of Jesus' testimony and his right to make such a claim. The third (v. 24) and fourth (v. 28) create an ambiguity concerning Jesus' identity (cf. v. 25). The final ἐγώ εἰμι removes that ambiguity in such a way as to anger Jesus' hearers and conclude the debate (v. 59). It is surely significant that a claim involving ἐγώ εἰμι both begins (v. 12) and ends (v. 58) a debate concerning Jesus' identity and authority and that claims involving ἐγώ εἰμι (vv. 18, 24, 28) also form an essential part of the development of this debate.[1]

The structural relationship in ch. 8 between the sign and a claim using ἐγώ εἰμι is the reverse of ch. 6, but in both cases a physical sign shows the validity of Jesus' revelation. Jesus' claim to be the Light of the World is shown to be valid by the sign which follows (9.5ff.) in the same way that the feeding of the five thousand was a sign to indicate Jesus' identity (cf. 6.26, 27). Both the ἐγώ εἰμι and accompanying theme of light are resumed in ch. 9 and thus draw the conclusions of ch. 8 into the sign of ch. 9. The same offer of light that the Jews in the temple rejected, because they claimed that Jesus' testimony was invalid (8.13), is accepted by the blind man outside the temple. People such as he are in turn put out of the synagogue for accepting the significance of both the sign and the claim (9.22). The conclusion of ch. 8 (i.e., Jesus' rejection in the temple) is paralleled in the subject matter of ch. 9 (i.e., the blind man's rejection by the leaders of the synagogue) and so leads into the next chapter thematically as well as structurally.

Jesus' audience in John 8 provides an interesting study in itself. The audience for his claim to be the Light of the World (8.12) is expressed in the third person masculine plural ('them', αὐτοῖς). The vagueness of this term is noted by commentators.[2] Those who respond to Jesus' claim are not 'the Jews' but 'the Pharisees' (8.13). They must be seen as at least part of the audience for the claim. It is logical to assume that the

---

1.   Commenting on 8.12-30, Moloney (*Son of Man*, p. 125) states 'The chapter is held together by the threefold repetition of ἐγώ εἰμι (vv. 12, 24, 28. Cf. also v. 18)'. It is unclear what Moloney means by 'held together' though it is in the context of arguing for the literary unity of the section. Certainly, the repetition of ἐγώ εἰμι (see also v. 23) provides support for keeping the passage in the form we now have it.

2.   Cf. e.g., B. Lindars, *The Gospel of John* (NCB; London: Marshall, Morgan & Scott, 1986 [1972]), p. 313; also Brown, *John*, I, p. 340.

next time 'they' are mentioned (v. 19) it refers again to the Pharisees. However, in v. 21, the audience are again referred to in the third person plural ('them', αὐτοῖς) but this time it is the more customary 'Jews' who respond to Jesus (v. 22). The audience is further complicated in v. 31 by the fact that Jesus speaks to 'the Jews who had believed in him'. Rather than being on Jesus' side, these 'believing' Jews seem to be the ones who seek to kill Jesus (v. 37). In v. 48 the audience return to being 'the Jews' (cf. vv. 52, 57). 'They' (v. 59) are the ones who pick up stones to throw at him.

The fact that Jesus' interlocutors are so ill-defined shows that the narrator is not primarily interested in the precise identification of Jesus' opponents. The opponents again act as a foil to Jesus. It does not matter who they are so much as what their objections and reactions to Jesus are. Jesus is the important character and the objections of his opponents serve as opportunities to explain, add to and re-emphasize his own claims. When he boldly announces that he is the Light of the World (v. 12), the Pharisees seek in vain to invalidate Jesus' claim (v. 13). This allows Jesus to show that his testimony is indeed true (v. 14).[1] He knows his origin and destiny (v. 14). His opponents are ignorant of these (vv. 14, 22), even though they claim to know them (vv. 41, 48). Likewise, when Jesus claims that the Father bears witness with him (v. 18), they ask him where his Father is (v. 19). This allows Jesus to explain that they know neither him nor his Father and to make the astonishing claim that if they knew him they would know his Father also (v. 19). Furthermore, the fact that the Jews misunderstand Jesus' statement that he is going away (vv. 21, 22), allows Jesus to explain that his audience are from below while he is from above, they are of this world while he is not of this world (v. 23).[2] The 'I am' sayings later in the chapter continue this pattern of response and explanation. In response to the 'I am' saying of

---

1. Schnackenburg, *John*, II, p. 194: 'If we bear in mind Jesus' status as representative, the dialectic and paradox of the whole narrative becomes apparent: as God's representative he himself gives totally adequate evidence because in him the Father speaks (v. 14). On the other hand, as God's representative he can be distinguished from the one who sent him, and so there are two witnesses.'

2. Brown, *John*, I, p. 347: 'The question may be asked if "I am [*ego eimi*] of what is above" is a special instance of *ego eimi*? On the one hand, the clear emphasis on *ego eimi* in verses 24 and 28 gives support to the suggestion; on the other hand, the contrast in 23 with "You are of what is below" makes any special emphasis on "I am" less likely.'

v. 24 the Jews want to know who Jesus really is (v. 25). This allows Jesus to explain that his role is to declare to the world what he has heard from the one who sent him (v. 26). Since the Jews do not understand that Jesus speaks to them of the Father (v. 27), he explicitly explains this in the following verse, in which he again takes the words ἐγώ εἰμι on his lips.

As in John 6, the dominance of Jesus' character is closely tied to his relationship with the Father. This is the case with two of the occurrences of ἐγώ εἰμι in John 8. In v. 18 Jesus declares, 'I am the one who bears witness about myself and the Father who sent me bears witness'.[1] The authority Jesus has to make such a claim as that in v. 12 comes from the Father. Only when the Jews have lifted up the Son of man will they know Jesus' true identity (ἐγώ εἰμι, v. 28). Only then will they know that his right to make such claims comes from his close co-operation with his Father. 'I do nothing on my own authority but speak thus as the Father has taught me' (v. 28). Through ἐγώ εἰμι Jesus is characterized as acting on his Father's authority (v. 28). Thus his Father is witness with him (v. 18) to the fact that he can make such claims as 'I am the Light of the World' (v. 12). The dominance of Jesus' character is again partly achieved by his use of the first person, which is epitomized by the words ἐγώ εἰμι. His self assertion through ἐγώ εἰμι is not limited to one form of the phrase. It is seen as much in his assertion that his audience will die in their sins unless they believe that 'I am' as in his claim to be the Light of the World (v. 12). It is also seen as much in his claim to be the one who witnesses (v. 18) as in the claim to exist before Abraham (v. 58).

Although the disciples are not part of the debate of ch. 8, the character of true disciples is alluded to. This begins with the offer made in the sub-clause of the 'I am' saying. 'He who follows me will not walk in darkness but will have the light of life' (v. 12b). The one who truly follows him is characterized as the one who continues in Jesus' word (v. 31). Such a person has been set free by knowing the truth (vv. 31, 32). Such a one will never see death (v. 51). At the same time, those who reject Jesus (false disciples/believers) do so because his word finds

---

1. Lindars, *John*, p. 318, suggests that 'This verse is the climax of the argument [of verses 12-20]... It almost amounts to a revelation.' He also points to the structure of the sentence to show the emphasis on Jesus and the Father: 'Notice the chiastic structure, the *ego eimi* of self revelation, and that the Father is held back to the very end'.

no place in them (v. 37) and they do not accept the truth (v. 40). The Jews who had believed do not find their way into the group of true disciples, for ultimately they reject Jesus' word. This is explicitly seen in their rejection of what he claims for himself through the ἐγώ εἰμι of v. 58.

In John 8 even the characterization of Jesus' opponents is pervaded by irony. Throughout the chapter they are the opposite of what they think: they think they are free (v. 33), while they are slaves to sin (v. 34); they think they are Abraham's children, and yet they do not have the characteristics of Abraham (v. 39);[1] they claim God as their only Father (v. 41), but their father is in fact the devil (v. 44); they claim that they are not born of fornication, while 'in essence the author is accusing them of being ἐκ πορνείας in its religious sense of idolatry';[2] and they seem to believe in him (v. 31), when they do not believe him (v. 45). The extent of irony in the characterization of the Jews is displayed in the statement, 'We have one father, even God' (v. 41). As Duke rightly asserts, 'these who charge Jesus with having a demon are the very children of the devil (8.38-45)'.[3]

The double meaning of the verb 'to lift up' (ὑψόω, 8.28; cf. 3.14; 12.32) is not in itself a further demonstration of Johannine irony. The verb could refer either to Jesus' exaltation or to his crucifixion and is thus ambiguous. Owing to the two possible levels of meaning, there is the potential for irony to take place. Duke points out that the Gospel as a whole makes use of this *double entendre*. Thus 'the dominant irony concerning Jesus' destiny is that his death is in fact an exaltation'.[4] Because the verb is in the second person plural it seems at first unlikely that it should refer to Jesus' exaltation. It appears improbable that the author would attribute Jesus' exaltation to the Jews. At the most obvious level Jesus is saying 'When you have lifted up the son of man in crucifixion, then you will know that ἐγώ εἰμι' (cf. 12.33 where ὑψόω is used

---

1.　Those who oppose Jesus are not even Abraham's children, for if they were they would do what Abraham did and would not be seeking to kill Jesus (vv. 39, 40). 'Thus the author may agree with his opponents concerning the characteristics of Abraham and his disciples, but it is these very characteristics which he finds lacking in his opponents' (Whitacre, *Polemic*, p. 71).

2.　Whitacre, *Polemic*, p. 76. Also Brown, *John*, I, p. 364; cf. Barrett, *John*, p. 348, who thinks that 'the implication (especially of the emphatic ἡμεῖς) is that Jesus was born of πορνεία'.

3.　Duke, *Irony*, p. 75.

4.　Duke, *Irony*, p. 113.

exclusively of crucifixion). Yet it is possible that irony operates at a deeper level in the use of ὑψόω in 8.28. Could it be that Jesus is saying that when the Jews lift him up in crucifixion they will actually be exalting him and achieving the opposite of what they intended? For the narrative audience of Jesus' words in 8.28, the use of ὑψόω is ambiguous, for he has neither been crucified nor exalted. It is only the informed reader who is able to detect such an irony in Jesus' statement.

Irony is not only at work here in the double meaning of ὑψόω. It can be seen in the use of ἐγώ εἰμι too. Unlike the ἐγώ εἰμι of Jn 6.35 and 4.26 where Jesus' use of the words takes away any ambiguity that may have been present, in 8.24 ἐγώ εἰμι is used in a new way in that it actually contributes to the ambiguity. Jesus' states: 'You will die in your sins unless you believe that I am'. The ambiguity of ἐγώ εἰμι is seen in the Jews' question 'Who are you?' (v. 25). The same ambiguous ἐγώ εἰμι is used again in 8.28. The fact that the Jews do not know Jesus' identity may allow readers, who know the implications of Jesus' ἐγώ εἰμι (i.e., the narrator's conceptual point of view), to take part in irony as the ignorance of the narrative audience is played off against the narrator's own point of view.[1]

From the first ambiguous ἐγώ εἰμι (v. 24) the question of Jesus' identity underlies the discussion and is expressly stated again in 8.53. There, 'Who do you claim to be?' is coupled with the ironic question 'Are you greater than our Father Abraham?'[2] Jesus claims that Abraham rejoiced to see his day (v. 56). The Jews' questions concerning Jesus' identity are then answered as Jesus removes any further possibility of misunderstanding his words. In a dramatic affirmation of a question that expected a negative response (8.58), Jesus claims 'Before Abraham was, ἐγώ εἰμί' (v. 58). The Jews' reaction shows a further twist in the irony, for although they now know the implications of Jesus' claims through the words ἐγώ εἰμι, they still think that such a point of view is invalid

---

1. See Chapters 6 and 7 below on the probable background to the use of ἐγώ εἰμι here and how that in itself contributes to the irony of the Jews' question 'Who are you?'

2. Brown, *John*, I, p. 367, recognizes that 'The Jews throw up the example of Abraham to Jesus much in the same way that the Samaritan woman (iv 12) had thrown up the example of Jacob to him: "Surely you don't pretend to be greater than our father Jacob who gave us this well?"' Cf. also Duke, *Irony*, p. 94, who suggests that 'The repetition of some of the ironies is so exact (cf. 4.12/8.53; 7.33-35/8.21-22) as to suggest "stock responses"'.

and so attempt to stone him. It is thus possible to understand the narrator's conceptual point of view about Jesus and yet still to reject it.

The use of irony in connection with ἐγώ εἰμι here can be seen to fit into Duke's pattern of misunderstanding: 'In this pattern (1) Jesus utters some ambiguity, (2) his interlocutor reveals confusion, and (3) usually either Jesus or the narrator explains'.[1] In John 8 ἐγώ εἰμι can be used to express both the ambiguity and the explanation. The fact that the narrator's use of ἐγώ εἰμι in irony is not restricted to any particular form of those words again points to the correlation in function between each type of 'I am' saying.

In the course of ch. 8, Jesus takes certain themes which are present in the Prologue and applies them to himself by means of the words ἐγώ εἰμι. The theme of light and darkness, so prominent there (1.5, 7, 8, 9), opens the discussion of ch. 8. Explicit mention of light is not made again until ch. 9 where it comes to the forefront of the discussion. There Jesus declares 'As long as I am in the world, I am the Light of the World' (9.5) and verifies the claims of ch. 8 by healing the man born blind. By means of the words ἐγώ εἰμι Jesus thus identifies himself as the light of the prologue and, in so doing, again confirms to the reader the narrator's conceptual point of view.

The theme of witness also first appeared in the prologue. There John the Baptist bore witness to the light that was coming into the world (1.7-9, 15). At Jesus' baptism, John again bore witness that Jesus is the Son of God (1.32, 34). Jesus too bore witness to Nicodemus of things that he knows and has seen (3.11, 32). The Samaritan woman also bears witness to Jesus and his words (4.39). Now Jesus takes this theme of witness upon himself, through the words ἐγώ εἰμι (8.18). The objection the Jews raise is that Jesus is bearing witness concerning himself and so his testimony cannot be true (v. 13). Jesus claims that it is not he alone but he and the Father (v. 16) who judge.[2]

---

1. Duke, *Irony*, p. 145. Cf. Culpepper, *Anatomy*, p. 152.
2. In Jn 5, Jesus states, 'If I bear witness to myself, my testimony is not true. There is another who bears witness to me, and I know that the testimony which he bears to me is true' (ἐὰν ἐγώ μαρτυρῶ περὶ ἐμαυτοῦ, ἡ μαρτυρία μου οὐκ ἔστιν ἀληθής, 5.31, 32). The theme of witness continues through the remainder of ch. 5 showing that Jesus' testimony is only the words his Father has given him (5.30-47). In 8.14 Jesus responds to the assertion that his testimony is invalid with the words, 'Even if I do bear witness to myself, my testimony is true' (κἂν ἐγώ μαρτυρῶ περὶ ἐμαυτοῦ, ἀληθής ἐστιν ἡ μαρτυρία μου...). This is followed in

In John 8 Jesus operates from a sphere which transcends narrative time. He knows the future consequences of his hearers' present actions. Jesus knows that his hearers' future destiny will be determined by how they regard his person now. They must believe now so that they will not die in their sins then (v. 24). He talks about both his origin and his destiny (vv. 14, 21, 23) and claims that those who keep his word will never see death (v. 51). Any difficulty in deciding the temporal point of view of Jesus' character in John 8 occurs because, while he operates within narrative time, his perspective transcends time. Jesus is from above and is not of this world (v. 23). For this reason he knows and is able to state what will happen in the future to those who do not believe. This is made even clearer when Jesus declares '*When* you have lifted up the son of man, *then* you will know that ἐγώ εἰμι, and that I do nothing on my own authority but speak thus as the Father taught me' (v. 28). It is only when Jesus is crucified/exalted that his hearers will understand who he really is and that he is what he claims to be.

In the contrast between the words Ἀβραὰμ γενέσθε and ἐγώ εἰμι in 8.58, Jesus claims this transcendent perspective for the past as well as the future. As Dodd asserts, 'He belongs to a different order of being. The verb γενέσθαι is not applicable to the Son of God at all. He stands outside the range of temporal relations. He can say ἐγώ εἰμι...'[1] This claim to pre-existence is offensive to Jesus' audience because of their differing points of view. They operate from a point of view within time, while Jesus operates from an 'omni-temporal' point of view. By their reaction the Jews show that they regard such a point of view as reserved for God.

The 'I am' sayings of John 8 present certain clues that must be taken into account when determining the meaning of these sayings. Once the

v. 18 by the words 'I am the one who bears witness to myself...' (ἐγώ εἰμι ὁ μαρτυρῶν περὶ ἐμαυτοῦ ...). The reader of Jn 8 has to grapple with the apparent contradiction that if Jesus was bearing testimony for himself, his witness would be invalid and yet, even when he does bear witness for himself his testimony is valid, because the Father testifies with him (8.18). According to 8.18, if Jesus were alone in his witness about himself that witness would be invalid, but his testimony is proved valid by the fact that the Father witnesses with him, thus he is not alone (ὅτι μόνος οὐκ εἰμί, 8.16). For an explanation of how the Jewish law about witness worked and how Jesus can be said to fulfil it, see J.P. Charlier, 'L'exégèse Johannique d'un précepte légal: Jean viii 17', *RB* 67 (1960), pp. 503-15.

1.   Dodd, *Interpretation*, pp. 261-62; Cf. also F. Kermode, 'John', in R. Alter and F. Kermode, *The Literary Guide to the Bible* (London: Collins, 1987), pp. 440-65.

implications of such clues have been considered, the task of determining the correct background by which these sayings should be understood can begin.

The structural importance of the 'I am' sayings in the development of the debate in John 8 is the first and most important clue to determining the meaning of the 'I am' sayings, for the similar function of different forms of ἐγώ εἰμι seem to imply a shared conceptual background. This is especially seen in the fact that both the first and the last uses of ἐγώ εἰμι in John 8 seem deliberately to point the reader to the words of the prologue for a correct understanding of their content (see above). As well as the theme of light, the 'I am' saying itself points back to the similar words in ch. 6. The peculiar use of ἐγώ εἰμι with a predicate in Johannine discourses, suggests that the reader is meant to compare such sayings. It may also suggest a similar conceptual background by which such sayings should be understood.

When Jesus claims that he is the one who bears witness about himself, with the Father, it is not only a development of the theme of witness in the Gospel but also forms a direct appeal to the Jewish law (8.17). As there is no explanation as to how the Jewish Law works apart from the need for two witnesses, it is assumed that the implied reader has an understanding of Jewish law and especially Deut. 19.15.

The words in 8.18 also seem to recall the similar words in John 4. There the most immediately plausible translation of Jesus' words ἐγώ εἰμι, ὁ λαλῶν σοι seemed to be 'I who speak to you am he.' It is possible that the words ἐγώ εἰμι ὁ μαρτυρῶν περὶ ἐμαυτοῦ should be similarly translated: 'I who witness about myself am he and the Father who sent me witnesses'.[1] In that case ἐγώ εἰμι would be truly absolute, without a predicate. It would then be necessary to supply a predicate from elsewhere to fully understand them.[2] Yet such a translation is unlikely since the phrase is paralleled by the words: 'And the Father who sent me bears witness' (v. 18b). This suggests that the whole phrase 'who witnesses about myself' should be taken as the predicate to Jesus' words. Nevertheless it may still be asked why Jesus' words are constructed in this periphrastic way.[3] If the words of Jesus were simply

---

1. F. Field (*Notes on the Translation of the New Testament* [Cambridge, 1889], p. 93) suggests that ἐγώ εἰμι here can be translated 'It is I'.

2. Dodd (*Interpretation*, pp. 94-96) suggests that 'I and He' is used in post-biblical Hebrew for 'I am [He]' (ἐγώ εἰμι) and thus its use here may be connected.

3. Cf. Charlier, 'L'exégèse Johannique', p. 513.

intended to emphasize that he was the witness with his Father, could the same sentiment not have been achieved through the words ἐγώ μαρτυρέω (with an emphatic εγώ)? This would exactly parallel the phrase μαρτυρεῖ...ὁ πέμψας με πατήρ. It will be argued below that the strange construction of Jesus' statement here and its similarity in form with 4.26 are clues which alert the reader to the background by which the phrase ἐγώ εἰμι may be fully understood.

Jesus' statement 'for you will die in your sins unless you believe that I am' (v. 24) begs the question which the Jews correctly ask, namely, 'Who?' As it stands the phrase is unintelligible. Furthermore it is questionable whether Jesus' answer to the Jews is sufficient explanation of this strange use of ἐγώ εἰμι. Although the readers have been given more clues to Jesus' true identity than the narrative audience, even they have not encountered Jesus' claim 'that I am' (as a predicateless statement) before this point.[1] It is significant for the question of background that the narrator does not explain the term.

Jesus' ἐγώ εἰμι here seems to raise more questions than it answers. It has no predicate. What could it mean to believe 'that I am'? The phrasing of Jesus' statement appears to be a hint to the reader, for 'I am' is expressly what Jesus' hearers should believe in order to rescue them from death in their sins. In such a context it is of utmost importance that the reader understand how to believe 'that I am' lest they too should die in their sins. What or who should the Jews believe that Jesus is to escape the same fate? A discussion of background material must address the question of whether the phrase ἐγώ εἰμι can itself be the content of belief (or even a title) that would be understood by the implied reader as a way to escape from death in their sins.

In form the 'I am' saying of 8.28 is very similar to that of 8.24. It is probable therefore that the use of ἐγώ εἰμι here should be linked to that verse. The reason the narrator gives for Jesus making this statement is that the Jews 'did not understand that he spoke of the Father' (v. 27). Jesus explains to his audience: 'When you have lifted up the Son of man, then you will know that ἐγώ εἰμι, and that I do nothing on my own authority but speak thus as the Father taught me'. Although the narrative audience do not ask, the same question of Jesus' identity is raised by this ἐγώ εἰμι as in the previous saying.

---

1.   Cf. Barrett, *John*, p. 343 and Schnackenburg, *John*, II, p. 200, for differing views on how to render Jesus' answer to the Jews in v. 25: τὴν ἀρχὴν ὅ τι καὶ λαλῶ ὑμῖν.

It is possible that the predicate for this 'I am' saying is the title Son of Man. Bultmann thinks that this is so: 'They will realise the meaning of the "I am" when they "have lifted up the Son of Man"; for then they will realise that he is the Son of Man'.[1] Such an interpretation would not necessarily imply a loss of meaning of ἐγώ εἰμι in either vv. 24 or 28, but would unite ἐγώ εἰμι with the other christological titles of the Gospel.[2] However, the reader who has just encountered two peculiar forms of 'I am' saying (vv. 18, 24), may not be satisfied. If all that is implied by the use ἐγώ εἰμι here is that Jesus is the Son of Man, why does he not say 'When you have lifted me up, then you will know that I am the Son of Man and that I do nothing on my own authority...'? Following so soon after that of v. 24, this ἐγώ εἰμι seems to point the reader away from simply supplying 'Son of Man' as its predicate.[3]

The ambiguity surrounding the use of ἐγώ εἰμι here does not remove the fact that it is set up as what the Jews will know, in the same way as it is what they should believe (v. 24). Along with the fact that they will know that Jesus does not act on his own authority, ἐγώ εἰμι is the content of what they will know when the Son of man is lifted up. Again a study of background must ask how 'I am' can be understood as a phrase that has content in itself and that can be said to be known and believed.

The ἐγώ εἰμι which occurs as the climax to ch. 8 raises different questions from those above. Jesus' argument with his opponents has reached its peak in discussion about origin and paternity. The Jews strengthen the question they raised in v. 25, saying 'Who do you claim to be?' (v. 53). Jesus' final statement is introduced with the solemn words ἀμὴν, ἀμὴν λέγω ὑμῖν. Such an introduction stresses the importance of Jesus' claim: πρὶν 'Αβραὰμ γενέσθαι ἐγώ εἰμί The contrast between the verbs in this sentence is not as vivid in the English

1. Bultmann, *John*, p. 349. Harner (*'I am'*, p. 44) also concedes that 'the mention of the Son of man in this verse allows a predicate to be supplied with *ego eimi*'. Cf. also, S.S. Smalley, 'The Johannine Son of Man Sayings', *NTS* 15 (1968–69), p. 295. Davies suggests that, rather than directly identifying himself with the Son of Man, 'he identifies himself as the one who declares to the world what he has heard from the Father, mentioned in 8.26...' (*Rhetoric*, p. 84). However, if a title is to be supplied as a predicate for Jesus' 'I am' saying in 8.28, it is better to agree with Bultmann and to make 'Son of Man' the predicate.

2. Against Moloney, *Son of Man*, p. 138.

3. Cf. Moloney, *Son of Man*, p. 138.

translation as in the Greek. γενέσθαι, the aorist infinitive[1] of γίνομαι, expresses the coming into existence of Abraham, maybe even his birth.[2] ἐγώ εἰμι is in stark contrast to that verb. Not only does the one verb express coming into existence while the other expresses existence itself, but the change in tense is evocative. Immediately 'there is a contrast between the created and the uncreated, and the temporal and the eternal'.[3] The omniscient narrator of the prologue is echoed by the omniscient, and 'omni-temporal' Jesus. The construction of Jesus' statement itself shows that his claim is not simply to pre-existence; for that, Jesus could have claimed that he was (ἤμην, imperfect of εἰμι), or even came into existence (ἐγενόμην) before Abraham. The reaction of the Jews emphasizes the significance of such a phrase to the reader. However, the narrator does not explain the reason that the Jews attempt to stone Jesus. It must be assumed that the implied reader knows why Jesus' audience reacts in the way that it does to his claim.

It should be noted here that Davies argues that the contrast in these verses does not refer to time, but concerns Jesus' superiority over Abraham. She thinks that the contrast between γενέσθαι and εἰμι is not significant because γενέσθαι may be 'an addition occasioned by later christological developments'.[4] She comments: 'The brief statement "Before Abraham, I am he" asserts that, in spite of Abrahams temporal priority, Jesus, as the light of the world, who fulfils God's promise, is superior to Abraham'.[5] She thus thinks that the Jews misunderstand Jesus' words, thinking that they refer to temporal precedence, when they do not. She thus thinks the words ἐγώ εἰμι are an identification formula, identifying Jesus as the Light of the World. However, considering the reaction of the Jews to Jesus' saying, which is similar to their reaction in Jn 10.31, it is clear that they interpret Jesus' words as more than a metaphoric reference to precedence.[6] It is clear, too, from the

---

1.   For the infinitive with πρίν see J.H. Moulton and N. Turner, *A Grammar of New Testament Greek*. III. *Syntax* (Edinburgh: T.& T. Clark, 1963), p. 140.

2.   Barrett, *John*, p. 352; L. Morris, *The Gospel according to John* (NICNT; Grand Rapids: Eerdmans, 1971), p. 473; Cf. NEB, ARV.

3.   B.F. Westcott, *The Gospel according to St John* (London: John Murray, 1882), p. 140. Cf. Kermode, 'John', p. 445.

4.   γενέσθαι is omitted by codex D and the old Latin versions. However, a stronger case needs to be made that γενέσθαι is not part of the original since all the other major manuscripts include it.

5.   Davies, *Rhetoric*, p. 86.

6.   Davies, *Rhetoric*, p. 86.

allusions to the prologue, which Davies rejects, that the narrator identifies Jesus with the Word, who was in the beginning with God. It is
surely part of John's irony that Jesus' narrative audience can correctly
interpret his words as a claim to a different nature, and yet at the same
time reject his claim as invalid.

An analysis of the literary function of ἐγώ εἰμι in John 8 has again
shown that the 'I am' sayings occur in the context of an ironic discussion about Jewish matters. There is a discussion about Jewish law in
which Jesus is a true witness. Jesus is greater than Abraham in a similar
manner to the way he was seen to be greater than Jacob (4.12).
However, the literary function of the 'I am' sayings here cannot be fully
understood without a knowledge of background material. The problem
remains that when the narrator does not explain a concept to the reader,
the text assumes that the reader understands. Having seen the clues that
the text gives the reader concerning each occurrence of ἐγώ εἰμι, it is
now possible to define the limits of any background material that the
text assumes in order to understand ἐγώ εἰμι of John 8. Any suggestions
for background should take into account that the 'I am' sayings of John
8 appear to function interdependently and therefore the meaning of one
ἐγώ εἰμι may affect how the reader views the meaning of another even
if they cannot be assigned to the same form. It will be argued below that
the striking similarities between John 8 and Isaiah 42–43 suggest that the
narrator expected the understanding reader to have a knowledge of the
same.

4. *John 10: The Gate (of the Sheep) (10.7, 9) and the Good Shepherd (10.11, 14)*

The following study will concentrate on the shepherd discourse in Jn
10.1-21. Although this passage is thematically linked with the discussion
in the Temple at the Feast of Tabernacles (vv. 24-39),[1] it is clear that it
takes place in the same geographical and temporal setting as the story of
the man born blind.[2] In fact, the words of the narrative audience

---

1. Cf. J.A. Du Rand, 'A Syntactical and Narratological Reading of John 10 in
Coherence with Chapter 9' in J. Beutler and R.T. Fortna (eds.), *The Shepherd
Discourse of John 10 and its context: Studies by members of the Johannine Writings
Seminar* (SNTSMS, 67; Cambridge: Cambridge University Press, 1991), pp. 94, 95.

2. Cf. Barrett, *John*, p. 367; Brown, *John*, I, p. 388; Du Rand, *John 10*, pp. 94,
95; and J. Painter, 'Tradition, History and Interpretation in John 10', in Beutler and

explicitly link the two passages: some ascribe Jesus' words to a demon (10.21), while others say, 'These are not the sayings of one who has a demon. Can a demon open the eyes of the blind?' (v. 22). Although the subject matter changes with the first verse of John 10, the context does not. Jesus' comment, that the Pharisees are guilty because they claim to see (9.41), leads directly in to his parable (παροιμία,[1] v. 6) about the sheep. The theme of sheep is resumed in the following paragraph (esp. vv. 26-29) and leads to Jesus' climactic claim of unity with the Father (v. 30).

Jn 10.1-21 divides into three parts.[2] Verses 1-6 introduce the new theme of sheep, shepherds and associated images by means of a parable (παροιμία, v. 6). Verses 7-18 explain and expand upon the parable. This section falls into a further three sub-sections: vv. 8-10 concern the door and the robbers; vv. 11-13 the Good Shepherd and the hirelings; and vv. 14-18 the character of the Good Shepherd in relation to his sheep.[3] Within this exposition of the parable (vv. 7-18), Jesus makes a fourfold claim through the words ἐγώ εἰμι. Twice he claims to be the door (vv. 7, 9) and twice the Good Shepherd (vv. 11, 14). Verses 19-21 show the reactions of the audience to Jesus' words.

Lindars suggests that the section beginning at v. 7, 'takes up features from the parable successively, expanding and developing them—the door (verses 7-9), the thief (10), the shepherd (11-13), the sheep (14-16)—and these have further developments in the sacrifice of the shepherd (17f.).'[4] The fourfold use of 'I am' is part of this process of explaining the parable in which the two images used with ἐγώ εἰμι run parallel.[5] In v. 7, Jesus claims to be the door of the sheep and goes on to

Fortna, *The Shepherd Discourse*, p. 54; Hinrichs (*Ich Bin*, p. 70) thinks that the abrupt change in subject indicates that the whole of 10.1-21 is redactional and has little connection with what has gone before.

1.   Cf. Barrett, *John*, p. 367: 'As it stands, it is neither parable nor allegory, though it is related to both forms of utterance. It is a symbolic discourse in which symbolism and straightforward statement alternate and stand side by side.' Cf. Beasley-Murray (*John*, p. 168) who sees it as fundamentally a parable but with Old Testament associations while Lindars (*John*, p. 354) sees it primarily as allegory.

2.   Cf. Beasley-Murray, *John*, p. 167; cf. also p. 166. Du Rand (*John 10*, p. 103) divides 10.1-21 into five parts, treating the narrative comment of v. 6 as a separate section, and dividing vv. 7-18 into two (vv. 7-10 and vv. 11-18).

3.   Cf. Lindars, *John*, p. 354.

4.   Lindars, *John*, p. 354.

5.   Schnackenburg, *John*, II, p. 288: 'The door-words and those about "the good

contrast himself with those who have gone before. In v. 11, Jesus claims to be the Good Shepherd and goes on to contrast himself with the hired hand. Thus the first occurrences of each 'I am' saying in John 10 contrast Jesus with impostors. When Jesus claims again to be the door (v. 9), it is in terms of the sheep and the benefit he gives them in his role as door ('if anyone enters by me, he will be saved and will go in and out and find pasture').[1] When Jesus claims a second time to be the Good Shepherd (v. 11), it is in terms of the benefits for the sheep from Jesus' role as the shepherd ('I know my own and my own know me, as the Father knows me and I know the Father; and I lay down my life for the sheep'). The second occurrence of each ἐγώ εἰμι saying is in terms of Jesus' relationship with his sheep and the benefits he gives them.

These parallel ἐγώ εἰμι sayings contribute to the structure of the whole discourse by the balanced way in which they develop Jesus' argument. For this reason Lindars thinks that 'the I am is...an explanatory statement, the first of a series of identifications which are made as the parable is taken point by point'.[2] For Lindars the structural function of ἐγώ εἰμι in Jesus' discourse is therefore to identify words from the parable with the person of Jesus.[3] Both the systematic exposition of the parable and the identification of Jesus with certain words in the parable create a formal correspondence with the use of ἐγώ εἰμι in John 6. There Jesus' discourse followed a midrashic pattern of exposition in which the words ἐγώ εἰμι systematically applied the concept of bread to the person of Jesus.[4]

Jesus is the dominant character of 10.1-21. Apart from a brief appearance of his audience in v. 6, when they are referred to in the third person plural, and again in vv. 19-21, when they are simply 'the Jews',

shepherd" have an identical structure (twice each)'. Cf. also, p. 294.

1. Hinrichs (*Ich Bin*, p. 71) points out the concept of the door shifts between the two 'I am' sayings so that in 10.9 'Gate no longer stands as the access of the legitimate shepherd to his flock, but as the saving access of the flock to the pasture'.

2. Lindars, *John*, p. 358.

3. Lindars (*John*, p. 358) is correct to say that 'I am' is used as a 'pointer to the interpretation of the parable' even if he may be incorrect in thinking that that necessarily rules out any further function of the phrase. The question of whether this use of ἐγώ εἰμι only identifies Jesus with the parable or whether it also identifies Jesus with Old Testament imagery will be discussed Chapter 7 below.

4. In both chapters a theme is introduced, interpreted and applied to Jesus by the words ηεγ΄ς εηιμι. In both cases the theme is further explained by Jesus and the 'I am' sayings are repeated. See discussion of Jn 6 above.

Jesus is the sole character in these verses.[1] It is Jesus' words which the
reader hears in vv. 1-18. The unspecified nature of Jesus' narrative
audience shows that their role is primarily as a foil to Jesus' words. They
are no more than types, whose misunderstanding and reaction to Jesus'
words further the plot of the narrative. The only characterization of
Jesus' audience that takes place within the narrative of John 10 is
actually within the discourse and then it is only by implication that Jesus'
words refer to the narrative audience.[2]

In a discourse again dominated by the 'I' of Jesus, he further explains
what his characteristics are. He offers life in contrast to those who come
only to destroy (v. 10). He lays down his life for his sheep (vv. 11, 15,
17, 18)[3] in contrast to those who care only for their own lives and safety
(vv. 12, 13). He knows his sheep and is known by them (v. 14) just as
he knows his Father and is known by Him (v. 15). The character of
Jesus is illustrated through both the parable and his explanation of it. His
'I am' sayings explain why he acts differently from others, for he is the
Good Shepherd as well as the Door of the sheep. Through such claims
to the narrative audience, he explains his character to the reader. The 'I
am' sayings of Jesus again show him to be dominant, for as the Good
Shepherd he lays down his life of his own accord, no one takes it from
him. He has power (ἐξουσία, v. 18) to lay it down and to take it up
again. Such power characterizes his unique role and his unique nature,
for only to the Good Shepherd who is willing to lay down his life for the
sheep and to no one else has the Father granted such power (v. 18).

When Jesus claims to be the Good Shepherd, he not only identifies
parts of the parable with himself by means of ἐγώ εἰμι, but also con-

---

1.   Schnackenburg, *John*, II, p. 288: 'neither the Pharisees (9.40) nor the Jews
(cf. 10.19) are expressly addressed'. Cf. Carson, *John*, p. 390.

2.   In fact, Jesus' words are often taken not to refer to the specific narrative
audience, but to 'embrace false messiahs within Judaism and redeemer gods of the
pagan world' as well as 'Pharisees who claimed to hold the keys of the kingdom (cf.
Mt. 21.13 = Luke 11.52) and in the perspective of the Gospel their successors in
contemporary Judaism' (Beasley-Murray, *John*, p. 170); also Hinrichs, *Ich Bin*, p. 71:
'The addressees of the discourse are in no way so clearly identifiable as the Jews'.
Instead, Hinrichs thinks (pp. 71, 72) that the addressees presupposed by the text are
post-Easter Christians. However, it is surely part of the Gospel's irony that Jesus'
words are obliquely addressed to those with whom he speaks, even if the reader is
meant to see echoes in them 'of their successors in contemporary Judaism'.

3.   This concept makes this portrait of a shepherd unique compared with Old
Testament portraits of a shepherd. Cf. Brown, *John*, I, p. 398; Lindars, *John*, p. 354.

trasts his own character with the character of his opponents.[1] Irony is
again at work in this characterization of Jesus' opponents, for those who
claim to be leaders and shepherds are no more than thieves and robbers
who come to steal, kill and destroy and do not care for the sheep at all
(v. 13). They ask 'Are we also blind?' (9.40) thinking that the answer is
'No',[2] but Jesus warns them that it is precisely because they claim to see
that they remain guilty. Since Jesus' parable follows directly on this
warning, it appears to be an ironic illustration of the Pharisees' blindness,
for it portrays Jesus as the one true leader (shepherd) and at the same
time pictures the Pharisees, who claim to be the leaders of Israel, as
impostors (thieves and robbers, vv. 1, 8, 10; strangers, v. 5; and hirelings,
v. 12). Jesus as the self-sacrificing shepherd is characterized in stark
contrast to the selfish hirelings.[3] They thus become the victims of Jesus'
ironic parable. The hostile reaction on the part of some of the Jews
(v. 20; cf. 8.48) suggests that they understood the implications of Jesus'
words.

Although there is no mention of disciples in 10.1-21, true discipleship
is clearly characterized in terms of the sheep. The sheep follow the
shepherd and are (willingly) led by him (vv. 3, 4). They also flee from
the hireling and the robber 'for they do not know the voice of strangers'
(v. 5). Because Jesus is the door, 'Anyone who enters' by Jesus 'will be
saved and will go in and out and find pasture' (v. 9). Thus the people
who wish to be saved are characterized as satisfied sheep because they
recognize the dual role Jesus claims for himself through the image of the
door as well as the shepherd. True discipleship recognizes the truth of
what Jesus claims for himself through the words ἐγώ εἰμι and requires
a response in terms of a relationship with the shepherd as well as a
proper use of the door. Such sheep know Jesus in the same way
that Jesus knows the Father (v. 14). These, along with some of
Jesus' narrative audience, are those who recognize that 'these are not

---

1. Cf. Brown, *John*, I, p. 388; cf. Schnackenburg, *John*, II, p. 294, also, p. 296.
Du Rand (*John 10*, p. 103) points out the importance of contrast in what he sees as
two mini-parables in vv. 1-5. Hinrichs (*Ich Bin*, p. 73) points out that the contrast
between the shepherd and the hireling brings about the application of the adjective
καλός to the shepherd and makes the shepherd's role specific. Below it will be seen
that a knowledge of certain background material heightens and confirms this contrast.

2. Barrett, *John*, p. 366.

3. Barrett, *John*, p. 374: 'The thief takes the life of the sheep; the good shepherd
gives his own life for the sheep'.

the sayings of one who has a demon' (v. 21).

The narrative comment in v. 6 presents a retrospective temporal point of view. The reader is presented with a discourse, which Jesus' narrative audience did not at first comprehend (v. 6). This narrative comment is given so that the reader does not misunderstand Jesus' parable in the way that the narrative audience did. His explanation (vv. 7-18) both corrects the misunderstanding of his narrative audience and explains to the reader how it should really be understood. The reader can thus adopt the narrator's conceptual point of view and see Jesus in the correct light.

Although the narrator does not give direct access to the thoughts of Jesus' audience here, the reader is able to understand their minds through their words. By showing the differing reactions of the audience to Jesus' words and so adopting an omniscient point of view, the narrator allows the reader to interact with the character of Jesus. The audience's reaction to Jesus' words (including his claims through ἐγώ εἰμι)[1] allows the reader either to accept that Jesus has a demon or (as the narrator hopes) to acknowledge that these are not the sayings of a demon (v. 21).[2] In this way Jesus' audience acts as a prompt for the reader to accept the narrator's conceptual point of view concerning Jesus and the words of the audience act as a foil to Jesus' own words.

Irony is expressed through Jesus' words in Jn 10.1-21 in the fact that he, as the Good Shepherd, willingly lays down his life for the sheep. While the Jews think that they are able to do away with Jesus when they want (cf. vv. 31, 39), his claim is that it is he who is in control. They cannot take his life from him because he is the one who lays it down of his own accord (v. 18).[3] Even when the Jews think that they have finally rid themselves of Jesus, the reader finds that it is in fact Jesus who gives 'up his spirit' (19.30). The irony does not end there, for Jesus claims not only to have the power to lay down his life, but the power to take it up

---

1. Painter, *Tradition and History*, p. 66 'It is the words of Jesus, explicitly Christological, which caused the schism'.

2. Du Rand (*John 10*, p. 99) makes a similar remark about the division and the reaction of Jesus' audience in Jn 9.16: 'among the Pharisees there is a division on the issue of Jesus' identity. The function of this is an implicit appeal to the reader to make his own decision'.

3. Schnackenburg, *John*, II, p. 301: 'the sovereignty of the Son manifests itself above all in this, that no one "takes from him" his life, despite every exertion that many people expend in that direction'. Cf. Morris, *John*, p. 498.

again.[1] The Father has given Jesus the power to take his life again, because he willingly gives it (vv. 17, 18). Thus, in his claim (through ἐγώ εἰμι) to be the Good Shepherd, Jesus shows that he is the one in control of his destiny. The fact that the same claim looks forward to the cross again shows that the character of Jesus operates from a perspective that transcends narrative time. By claiming to lay down his life and take it up at will (v. 18), Jesus contributes to the Gospel's dominant irony in which 'his death is in fact an exaltation'.[2] Because Jesus is in control of his own destiny and lays down his own life (v. 18), when those, who think they are in control, attempt to arrest him, 'he escaped from their hands' (v. 39). The irony is that the authorities (i.e., the Jews) have no authority over Jesus because he has been given authority by the Father (ἐξουσία, v. 18).

The main motif of the verses under review appears in the various pastoral images, some of which Jesus takes to himself by means of the words ἐγώ εἰμι. The images of sheep, thieves and robbers, hirelings and the shepherd are introduced in these verses for the first time, and it is clear even in the 'parable' (vv. 1-6) that the terms point to something deeper. Through these images some of the major themes of the Gospel are addressed. Jesus asserts that those who accept his claim made through ἐγώ εἰμι and enter through him as the gate 'will be saved' (σωθήσεται, v. 9). Because he is the door and the only legitimate entrance to the fold, he offers salvation. This salvation that Jesus offers also involves abundant life (v. 10). This is given because the Good Shepherd willingly gives his own life for the sheep (v. 11). As the Good Shepherd (vv. 11, 14), he knows his sheep in the same intimate relationship he has with his Father (vv. 14, 15). Thus the sheep/shepherd theme, exclusive to this chapter and applied to Jesus by means of ἐγώ εἰμι, is interwoven with themes which run through the whole Gospel, such as knowledge, life, salvation and Jesus' relationship with the Father (cf. vv. 17, 18).

The images which Jesus uses in the opening parable of John 10 suggest that the audience is expected not only to understand the images

---

1. Brown, *John*, I, p. 399: 'Many commentators have tried to weaken the telic force of v. 17, "I lay down my life in order to take it up again." (e.g. Lagrange, p. 283)... This is a failure to understand that in NT. thought the resurrection is not a circumstance that follows the death of Jesus but the essential completion of the death of Jesus.'

2. Duke, *Irony*, p. 113.

themselves, but also to understand to what (or to whom) his words were referring. The narrator explains that Jesus' own audience did not understand what he was saying (v. 6). For this reason Jesus explains his words to his hearers (and at the same time to the reader). It is legitimate to ask what the implied reader understands by the images in John 10 and, from that, what is implied when Jesus claims those images for himself.

It will be suggested below that the imagery of John 10 may allude to certain Old Testament passages. It should, however, be noted that such background material is only alluded to in John 10. Jesus' parable (vv. 1-6) is on one level self-explanatory, as is his exposition of it. Thus Lindars's comment concerning the door is right to warn against drawing too heavily upon external sources:

> It is unnecessary to go into the ramifications of the idea of the door in ancient mythology... because it is not allegorised as such. It is simply an item of the parable which John has used as a symbol of Jesus in terms of his own theology, and no other conceptions are either implied or required for the elucidation of the text as it stands.[1]

It is important nonetheless to ask whether the concepts presented to the reader have unseen implications for those who wish to 'join the authorial audience.'[2] Lindars is certainly correct in suggesting that the role of ἐγώ εἰμι is to apply the words of the parable to the person of Jesus. However, it must be doubted whether the words ἐγώ εἰμι function in this way only.[3] For this reason a literary study without reference to the cultural setting in which the text is written is incomplete. Although the study of background material contains the danger of reading into the text what may not be there, to limit the discussion to the surface level of the text is equally in danger of missing allusions and ironies that reside in and are implied by the text itself. A deeper level to the text of John 10 can only be discerned through a study of the conceptual background from which the Gospel was written. Although the images in John 10 are self-explanatory, they are also full of meaning in both Hellenism and Judaism.[4]

---

1. Lindars, *John*, p. 359.

2. Rabinowitz, *Truth in Fiction*, p. 127.

3. Against Lindars (*John*, p. 358); and Carson (*John*, p. 381) who thinks that the metaphors are 'all based on first century sheep farming', though he also sees Old Testament themes at work.

4. Cf. J.D. Turner, 'The History of Religions Background of John 10' in Beutler and Fortna, *The Shepherd Discourse*, pp. 33-52, for an overview of the

The study of the literary function of ἐγώ εἰμι in Jn 10.1-21 has pointed to a close link with John 9. A clear pattern has been seen in the way both 'I am' sayings apply concepts from the parable to the person of Jesus. In this the use of ἐγώ εἰμι shows similarities with John 6. However, in John 10 the exposition of the shepherd theme is not only in terms of Jesus himself but also in terms of those who oppose him, so there is a more starkly polemic tone in Jesus' words. Again this study has shown the irony at play in the use of ἐγώ εἰμι, yet it is a subtle irony which points a finger at Jesus' narrative opponents (i.e., the Jewish authorities) as the thieves and robbers of the parable without ever making this explicit. The wider irony of Jesus' claim to be the Good Shepherd is seen not in this chapter alone but in the Gospel as a whole. For in this 'I am' saying Jesus claims that he is the one who freely gives up his life. Such a claim has major implications for John's Christology and view of the cross, for it is clear that he sees Jesus' death neither as an accident nor an undesirable necessity but as the willing offering of Christ for his sheep. Furthermore, such a claim not only points to Jesus' role in laying down his life for the sheep, but also confirms the narrator's point of view about his divine nature. He is unique, for he knows and controls his own future even to the point of being able to take up his life again. His claim to be the gate also functions in the development of John's Christology, for those who enter by it find salvation and pasture. The focus of the discourse as a whole and of the ἐγώ εἰμι sayings in particular is again on the person and role of Jesus. Though the shepherd imagery is limited to this chapter (cf. 21.15-19), the discourse depicting Jesus as the shepherd and the gate is an integral part of the development of Johannine themes and Christology.

5. *John 11: The Resurrection and the Life (11.25)*

John 11 is set between the Feast of Dedication (10.22) and the week before the Passover (12.1). It comes in the watershed between Jesus' public ministry and the build-up to his death and so assumes a position of importance in the structure of the Gospel.[1] After the attempt on his life for blasphemy (10.33, 39) Jesus has withdrawn across the Jordan

diverse backgrounds suggested for the imagery in Jn 10.

1. Bultmann, *John*, p. 394: 'The crisis is coming on; the ὥρα of the passion is drawing near. The outward occasion of the fateful crisis is the raising of Lazarus'. Cf. Lindars, *John*, p. 378.

(10.40). There people come to him and accept the testimony that John the Baptist had given about him (10.41). In such a context the sisters, Mary and Martha, send to Jesus with the words 'Lord, he whom you love is ill' (v. 3).

Though the structure of John 11 may have a complex history,[1] in its present form it 'is clear and logical. It is a coherent narrative, though smaller units and individual scenes are recognizable in it.'[2] The passage may be divided as follows:

vv. 1-4	The illness of Lazarus: the sisters send for Jesus
vv. 5-16	The reaction of Jesus: delay and decision to go
vv. 17-27	Jesus meets with Martha: the *Resurrection and the Life*
vv. 28-37	Jesus meets with Mary: goes to the tomb
vv. 38-44	Jesus raises Lazarus
vv. 45-46	The reaction of the onlookers: link to what follows.[3]

Jesus' 'I am' saying is intricately linked with his sign. Previously John has linked the feeding of the five thousand to the claim to be the Bread of Life (6.35ff.) as well as linking the healing of the man born blind to Jesus' claim to be the Light of the World (8.12; 9.5). Now he links Jesus' claim to be the Resurrection and the Life (v. 25) to the raising of Lazarus. Here, however, the structure is different: 'instead of a narrative followed by a discourse on its meaning' (as in Jn 6) or a discourse followed by a narrative working it out (Jn 8; 9), 'we have a narrative interspersed with elements of dialogue that bring out its significance'.[4]

This whole episode is set up as a revelation of God's glory in Jesus. Jesus' first words are: 'This illness is not unto death; it is for the glory of God, so that the Son of God may be glorified by means of it' (v. 4). The theme of glory is resumed at the climax of the chapter when Jesus says to Martha, 'Did I not tell you that if you would believe you would see the glory of God?' (v. 40). Lindars correctly makes the connection between this verse and the 'I am' saying by stating that:

1.   Cf. Beasley-Murray, *John*, pp. 184-86; Brown, *John*, I, pp. 428-30; Lindars, *John*, pp. 383-86.

2.   Schnackenburg, *John*, II, p. 317; also C.H. Dodd, *Historical Tradition in the Fourth Gospel* (Cambridge: Cambridge University Press, 1963), pp. 228, 230.

3.   Cf. Bultmann, *John*, p. 396, for a similar structure. He ends the section at v. 44 and breaks vv. 28-44 into three sections (vv. 28-32, 33-40, 41-44) rather than two.

4.   Beasley-Murray, *John*, p. 184.

> The reference is to verse 23, interpreted in the light of the revelation saying of 25f... The miracle will prove that Lazarus' fatal illness was 'for the glory of God' because it will be a practical demonstration that Jesus is God's agent to give the Resurrection and the Life, the eternal salvation of mankind.[1]

Without the claim to be the Resurrection and the Life, the raising of Lazarus would be no more than a spectacular miracle (cf. 4.46-54). However, when combined with the claim that he is the Resurrection who offers ultimate victory over death (vv. 25b, 26), the miracle points to the far deeper truth of Jesus' words. The glory of God is revealed both in the raising of Lazarus and in the promise which stems from Jesus' claim to be the Resurrection and the Life: 'he who believes in me, though he die, yet shall he live, and whoever lives and believes in me shall never die' (vv. 25b, 26).[2] Such a promise is validated when Jesus restores physical life to a dead man. So, as an explanation of how God's glory is revealed through the raising of Lazarus, Jesus' 'I am' saying is central to the structuring of the whole episode.

Certain actions of Jesus in John 11 are both curious and difficult to interpret. At the beginning of the narrative, the reader is told that Jesus loved Lazarus (vv. 3, 5). Therefore Jesus' reaction to the sisters' message that Lazarus is ill is startling. He does not go to help his friend but stays where he is (v. 6), cryptically stating that this illness is for God's glory (v. 4). It would be understandable if Jesus did not want to return to Judea after the recent events in Jerusalem (10.31, 39). But,

---

1. Lindars, *John*, p. 400. The narrator does not actually tell us of Jesus making such a claim to Martha. The reader may legitimately be reminded of Jesus' words to the disciples in v. 4. However, the only claim made to Martha is the one through ἐγώ εἰμι in v. 25. The reader must either assume that the narrator has chosen not to relate part of Jesus' conversation with Martha because God's glory has already been promised in v. 4 or that the 'I am' saying (and accompanying promises) are to be taken as Jesus' claim that Martha will see God's glory. Cf. Beasley-Murray, *John*, p. 194.

2. E. Haenchen, *John*, II, p. 62: 'the really important thing for the Evangelist is that the bodily resurrection be taken as an intimation of the spiritual resurrection, and that becomes visible only in the incidental circumstance that Jesus brings Lazarus back to life here and now'. To say that the raising of Lazarus is incidental to the resurrection promised to whoever believes in Jesus (v. 25), is to limit the importance that John attaches to the sign. However, the sign does indeed point beyond itself to the end-time resurrection present in Jesus and which Jesus offers to those who believe in him.

unlike his disciples (v. 8), fear is not his reason for hesitating. After two days he decides to go to Bethany, explaining that he was glad he had not been there when Lazarus died (v. 15). This strange characterization of Jesus only makes sense in the light of three things. The first is the statement that this illness is for God's and Jesus' own glory (v. 4). The second is his claim through ἐγώ εἰμι to be the Resurrection and the Life and to offer life to those who believe in him (vv. 25, 26). The third is the outworking of that claim in the raising of Lazarus.

It may seem callous for Jesus to allow his friend to die simply in order to raise him. However, that is to see the episode from an earthly perspective. Through Jesus' 'I am' saying, the story is raised to a higher plane where the restoration of physical life is not as important as the promise of eternal life to all who believe that Jesus is the Resurrection and the Life. In other words, Jesus operates from a point of view in which the death of a friend can be for the glory of God. So Jesus' love for the two sisters extends beyond the physical help which they both know he would have offered if he had been there (Martha, v. 21; Mary, v. 32). Jesus did not simply allow Lazarus to die so that he could raise him again.[1] Rather, Lazarus' death was permitted so that Jesus' love could be seen to extend beyond the grave and offer life even 'though he die' (v. 25). Jesus' power over death also partly explains his strange prayer at Lazarus' tomb, where he prays more for his hearers' benefit than as a request to God (vv. 41, 42).[2] It is a prayer that is assured of a response, because Jesus has been sent by the Father. It is a prayer that his readers may come to know the same (v. 42). His prayer acknowledges that his power over death, and thus his claim to be the Resurrection and the Life, actually stems from the Father. Jesus' ability to raise Lazarus and his claim to be the Resurrection and the Life is based on the fact that he has been sent by the Father. It is because of his

---

1.   Haenchen (*John*, II, p. 60) is wrong to say that, 'The narrator is convinced that the eye-witness to a resurrection will come more readily to faith than the witness of a mere healing'. The unbelief and hostility of some of those who witnessed this miracle shows that the narrator does not have such a naive view of the miraculous in which the greater miracle is more likely to produce faith. In fact the opposite is the case as this spectacular miracle produces greater hostility ultimately resulting in the plot to kill Jesus.

2.   Jesus' words may also be explained by the fact that this prayer seems to be a deliberate allusion to the Old Testament. Cf. A.T. Hanson 'The Old Testament Background to the Raising of Lazarus', *SE*, VI, pp. 252-55.

divine mission that he operates from a divine perspective.

Even though the above shows that Jesus operates from a uniquely divine perspective in this story, he is also portrayed as very human. Jesus weeps (v. 35). He is moved in his spirit (whether to anger or to grief, vv. 33, 38).[1] His apparent helplessness is also pointed out by the onlookers: 'Could not he who opened the eyes of the blind man have kept this man from dying?' (v. 37). However, they do not yet know that as the Resurrection and the Life, the man Jesus transcends the human perspective and sees an opportunity for the glory of God in a human tragedy. Thus, in John 11, the narrator's perspective that the 'Word became flesh ($\sigma\grave{\alpha}\rho\xi$) and dwelt among us' (1.14) is shown in the characterization of Jesus as a character who possesses both a human and a divine perspective.

The characterization of Mary and her sister Martha has several points of interest for the present study. Initially they are introduced to explain the identity of Lazarus. Mary is apparently known to the reader as the one who anointed Jesus and wiped his feet with her hair (v. 2), even though this episode is not related until ch. 12.[2] Martha is the one who meets Jesus when he approaches Bethany (v. 20). Her faith in the person of Jesus is immediately revealed and also her hope that even now God will grant Jesus' request (vv. 21, 22).[3] When Jesus states that her brother

---

1.　Cf. Beasley-Murray, *John*, pp. 192-93, for a discussion of whether the verb ἐμβριμάομαι concerns Jesus' grief or anger as well as a discussion of what may have caused such an emotion. Against Beasley-Murray, see Lindars, who links the verb to the troubling of Jesus' spirit in 12.27 and concludes: 'We are thus driven back to the classic interpretation of this verse as a testimony to the human feelings of Jesus, who shares with all men in their pain and distress' (*John*, p. 339).

2.　This may suggest that Mary was (or had been) a member of the community for which the Gospel was written (cf. 19.25-27). It may alternatively be that such a community simply knew of the anointing from another tradition (such as the Synoptics). C.f. Beasley-Murray, *John*, p. 187; also, Barrett, *John*, p. 390. It is also possible that this is a literary device in which the narrator anticipates the story of the anointing by Mary at Bethany.

3.　Brown, *John*, I, p. 433, is wrong to say 'That she believes in Jesus but inadequately... 39 shows that she does not as yet believe in his power to give life'. Cf. Lindars, *John*, p. 394. Her belief is adequate, even though it may not be complete, because it is in Jesus' person (Schnackenburg, *John* [2], p. 329) and it is he who is the Resurrection. Thus the 'I am' saying 'signifies not so much a rejection of Martha's faith... as an extension of it and a setting of it on a sure foundation' (Beasley-Murray, *John*, p. 190). She may not know the implications of belief in Jesus' person, but that is different from inadequate belief. Cf. F.F. Bruce, *The Gospel*

will rise again (v. 23), she again shows her belief; she knows he will be raised at the end of time (v. 24), but this is little comfort to her now.[1] Her response to the 'I am' saying is a response of ideal belief, in which she bestows on Jesus' several titles common to the Gospel: 'Yes, Lord; I believe that you are the Christ, the Son of God, he who is coming into the world' (v. 27; cf. 20.31).[2] Her reaction to Jesus' 'I am' saying thus draws out his identity. The implications of belief in such a Jesus dawn on Martha, when Jesus says 'Take away the stone' (v. 39).[3] Jesus reminds her that she would see God's glory and proceeds to raise Lazarus, a remarkable visual-aid to what he had claimed through his 'I am' saying.

Mary plays a far smaller part in this episode than her sister. However, her part emphasizes that of her sister.[4] Although she is not present when Jesus makes his claim to be the Resurrection and the Life, Mary is a character in her own right. Jesus is moved by her weeping and he too weeps. The crowds are then forced to ask if this man who has opened the eyes of someone born blind is helpless in the face of a friend's death (v. 37). This in turn leads into the miracle which validates his claim to be the Resurrection and the Life. While Martha's role is to draw out the claim of Jesus concerning who he is, Mary's role is to draw out the implications of the claim in terms of this specific situation. Both characters are again a foil to the narrator's characterization of Jesus. The same is also true of Jesus' narrative audience. When Jesus demonstrates his 'I am' saying by raising Lazarus, they are divided. Many believe (v. 45).

---

of John (Basingstoke: Pickering and Inglis, 1983), p. 244; Bultmann, *John*, p. 401; also Westcott, *John*, p. 168.

1.   Westcott, *John*, p. 168: 'Martha acknowledges the doctrine of a resurrection, as an object of remote belief: as something of general but not of personal interest, and therefore powerless in the present bereavement'.

2.   Lindars (*John*, p. 396) points to the fact that these titles have all been used in the first chapter of the Gospel: 'the Christ (1.41), the Son of God (1.49; cf. 10.36), and he who is coming into the world (1.27, 30)'. Schnackenburg points to the end of the Gospel as a parallel with Martha's words: 'She declares her firm faith (πεπίστευκα), in the identical words the evangelist uses at the end of his book to sum up what he understands by Christian faith (20.31)' (*John*, II, p. 332).

3.   Martha's response to Jesus' words suggests that, while she may have a correct belief about Jesus (v. 27), she does not recognize the implications of such a belief, for she does not recognize that the one who claims to be the Resurrection and the Life can bring that resurrection to her brother who has been dead four days. Cf. Lindars, *John*, pp. 399-400.

4.   Cf. Haenchen, *John*, II, p. 65.

Some, however, tell the Pharisees what Jesus has done (v. 46). While it appears that these 'Jews' have not heard Jesus' words to Martha, their characterization acts as a foil to Jesus' words by prompting the reader to make a decision to accept or reject the narrator's conceptual point of view concerning Jesus.

The reader is explicitly notified by a narrative comment (v. 13) that the disciples misunderstand Jesus' use of the word 'sleep' (κεκοίμηται, vv. 11, 12) and so is alerted to the possibility of irony resulting from such a misunderstanding. Jesus has to explain that Lazarus' sleep is terminal; he has died (v. 14). The fact that the narrator plays upon the two possible meanings of the word 'sleep' (vv. 12, 13, 14) shows that the ambiguity here is deliberate.[1] 'There is thus a delicate irony', in the words of v. 12, 'whereby the disciples say what will actually happen, without realizing it'.[2] Neither do the disciples realize that the analogy with sleep is particularly apt, for, as the 'I am' saying will show, death is only as terminal as sleep for those who believe in Jesus (v. 25b).

There is further irony in Mary and Martha's greeting to Jesus. For them it is a tragic irony that the one person who could have helped them arrives too late to be of any use (vv. 21, 32). The deeper irony is that they do not realize that Jesus can help them even now. Martha expresses hope that Jesus can do something to alleviate her misery (v. 22). In response Jesus states: 'Your brother will rise again' (v. 23). The text makes clear that there is more than one level of meaning to Jesus' statement:

> (a) he could mean a miracle of return to life, like the Synoptic raising stories, such as Martha had just asked for, and, indeed, such as actually happens in the event; (b) he could be referring to the general resurrection, as understood by the Pharisees and popular Jewish belief at this time. This is how Martha actually takes it (see next verse); (c) he could be referring to a new quality of life beyond death, which is not tied to this eschatological and juridicial concept, and is not merely resuscitation to the present form of existence.[3]

The deliberately ambiguous nature of Jesus' words here sets the scene for irony to take place. Martha does not realize that all three levels of meaning are fulfilled in the person of Jesus.[4] Jesus is the Resurrection of

1. Cf. Lindars, *John*, p. 391.
2. Lindars, *John*, p. 391.
3. Lindars, *John*, p. 394.
4. Although Lindars's categorization of resurrection into three distinct concepts

which Martha speaks (v. 25). Thus the 'I am' saying here functions in a similar way to that in 4.26 where Jesus is the messiah of whom the Samaritan woman speaks (cf. 6.34, 35). At the same time the popular expectation revealed in Martha's words of v. 23 is also played off against the resurrection Jesus claims to be.[1] Therefore irony takes place in the fact that:

> The real resurrection takes place for the Evangelist at a time when the general expectation does not suppose it to take place, that is, in the here and now, and it consists of something that does not come into its own in the general expectation: in belief in the Son of God, who possesses the power to raise spiritually from the dead.[2]

It is Jesus' 'I am' saying which reveals this ironic and startling fact. It also resolves the tension between the different interpretations of Resurrection that lie within the passage.

As a result of this saying, the readers are placed in a privileged position with the narrator and character of Jesus so that they detect a final irony when they hear Jesus' narrative audience remark, 'Could not he who opened the eyes of the blind man have kept this man from dying?' (v. 37). By the claim that this episode will be for God's glory (v. 4, cf. v. 14), by the deliberate ambiguity between sleep and death (v. 13), and by Jesus' claim to be the Resurrection and the Life (v. 25) and to have power over death, the reader has been prepared for the raising of Lazarus. The narrative audience, however, still sees the help-lessness of the situation. Yet, unawares, its question says more than it could possibly imagine. By raising Lazarus, Jesus proves that he who opened the eyes of the blind man can do even more than keep him from dying. He can raise him from the dead and so prove the validity of his 'I am' saying.

Chapter 11 also displays several links with ch. 9. There is a definite theological purpose in both the blindness of the man (9.3) and the illness

---

is helpful, he is incorrect to say that Jesus' words in v. 23 refer only to the resurrection referred to in the 'I am' saying (*John*, p. 394).

1.   Schnackenburg, *John*, II, p. 330: 'Jesus replies with what the evangelist has deliberately phrased as an ambiguous remark (cf. v. 11), "Your brother will rise again"'. This deliberate ambiguity between the different understandings of resurrection provides the basis for irony to take place.

2.   Haenchen, *John*, II, pp. 62, 63; Hinrichs, *Ich Bin*, p. 83: 'The new life which Jesus gives and which he alone can give is in a different dimension than the earthly'.

of Lazarus (v. 4).[1] The connection between the two situations is mentioned specifically in the words of the Jews at Lazarus' tomb (v. 37). Yet there is another link in Jesus' words to his disciples: 'Are there not twelve hours in the day? If anyone walks in the day, he does not stumble, because he sees the light of this world. But if anyone walks in the night he stumbles because the light is not with him' (vv. 9, 10). The words 'light of this world' (v. 9) could refer to the sun if Jesus had not claimed the title for himself in both chs. 8 and 9. The reintroduction of the theme in ch. 11, however, points the reader back to Jesus' claim to be the Light of the World and especially to his words, 'We must work the works of him who sent me while it is day; night comes when no one can work. As long as I am in the world, I am (εἰμι) the light of the world' (9.4, 5). The reintroduction of the theme of light recalls all that Jesus previously claimed by the same theme. The words ἐγώ εἰμι also function in a similar way, reminding the reader of all that Jesus has already claimed for himself through these words.

For the implied reader, the narration of the raising of Lazarus not only points back to the healing of the blind man, but also points forward to Jesus' own death and resurrection. During the narration of the trial and passion of Jesus, the reader is aware of his claim to be the Resurrection and the Life, as well as the fact that he raised Lazarus. The implied reader then knows that Jesus' claim to be the Resurrection and the Life is ultimately shown to be true not in the raising of Lazarus but in his own resurrection which is far more than a physical resuscitation. In this way, the raising of Lazarus may be seen as an antetype of Jesus own death and resurrection.[2]

Within the narrative of John 11 Jesus clearly defines what he means by resurrection. However, his statement to Martha, that her brother will rise again (v. 23), draws a response from her which implies a common belief in the resurrection at the last day.[3] Jesus draws out Martha's traditional faith, before applying a modified concept of resurrection to himself by means of the words ἐγώ εἰμι. In his person Jesus brings the

1. Cf. Lindars, *John*, p. 379; Brown, *John*, I, p. 431.
2. Cf. Lindars, *John*, p. 399. Bultmann remarks 'doubtless there is more at issue here than simply a δοξασθῆναι through a miraculous act... the miraculous action of Jesus will bring him to the cross; that is... it will lead to his ultimate glorification' (*John*, p. 397). Cf. Beasley-Murray, *John*, p. 187.
3. Cf. Haenchen, *John*, II, p. 62; also Lindars, *John*, p. 394; Kundzins, *Die Ego-Eimi-Spruche,* p. 100.

future resurrection into the present and so fulfils and supersedes the
expectation expressed by Martha. Yet the text does not imply that the
resurrection Jesus offers completely replaces the general resurrection at
the last day (cf. 5.25-29; 6.39-40).[1] The promise of resurrection and life
to all who believe is not only a present reality but a future one too:
'even though he die, yet shall he live' (v. 25b).[2] Thus, as in 4.26 and
6.35, Jesus takes an expectation expressed by his narrative audience and
claims to be that of which his audience speaks.

The literary function of Jesus' ἐγώ εἰμι saying in Jn 11.25 is to take
an expectation expressed by Martha and to fulfil it in such a way that
the death and raising of Lazarus brings glory both to Jesus and the
Father.[3] By explaining the significance of the miracle, this ἐγώ εἰμι
saying forms an intricate part of the build-up to the raising of Lazarus.
Jesus' characterization is developed through the ironic interplay with
Martha. In this, the 'I am' saying both reveals and resolves the irony,
since Jesus is that of which Martha speaks. This irony, as well as the
characterization of Jesus' narrative audience, urges the reader to adopt
the narrator's point of view about Jesus as expressed through the 'I am'
saying. The raising of Lazarus both validates the claim Jesus makes
through the 'I am' saying and points to Jesus' own resurrection as the
ultimate guarantee of his words. In fact John portrays the raising of
Lazarus as the event which precipitates Jesus' trial and death (v. 53).
Thus this 'I am' saying is crucially placed at the beginning of the passion
story.

6. *John 13: The Betrayal (13.19)*

The build-up to the Passover in John begins after the raising of Lazarus,
as Jesus withdraws to a town in Ephraim (11.55). The events of ch. 12
take place in the week before this great feast (12.1). Now, as ch. 13
opens, the Passover is mentioned for the last time before Jesus' trial.[4] It

1.   Against Haenchen, *John*, II, p. 62.
2.   Dodd, *Interpretation*, p. 364: '*Prima facie*, all these passages [i.e. chs 5 and
11] affirm, first, that eternal life may be enjoyed here and now by those who respond
to the word of Christ, and, secondly, that the same power which assures eternal life to
believers during their earthly existence will, after the death of the body, raise the dead
to a renewed existence in a world beyond'.
3.   See discussion of background material in Chapter 7.
4.   The climax to the Passover theme is the citation of Scripture in 19.36 (cf.

is still before the feast and, although it is unclear whether the meal in which Jesus participates with his disciples is meant to be seen as the Passover meal,[1] the theological as well as chronological connection with that feast is explicit.[2] Even more important for the setting of this episode is the fact that 'Jesus knew his hour had come' (v. 1). From the first sign which Jesus accomplished at Cana (2.4), the concept of the hour has been developed (cf. 7.6, 8, 30; 12.27). Now it finally arrives (cf. also 17.1). The words of ch. 13 begin a new section of the Gospel.[3] Jesus' ministry among the people is complete. Chapters 13–17 occur in the company of the disciples alone ('his own', v. 1). Jesus' hour commences with his disciples and continues until his work is accomplished in the cross ('It is finished', 19.30) and the resurrection.

This study will concentrate on how the ἐγώ εἰμι of v. 19 functions in vv. 1-30. Most scholars see a major break at v. 20 and thus connect vv. 16-20 with the footwashing of vv. 1-15.[4] This does not account, however, for the obvious thematic link between the Old Testament prediction of the betrayal and accompanying ἐγώ εἰμι statement (vv. 18, 19) and the following discussion about the betrayer (vv. 21-30). The two enigmatic sayings which begin with 'Truly, truly' (vv. 16, 20) are also usually connected with the footwashing.[5] If, however, vv. 16-20

Exod. 12.46; Num. 9.12; Ps. 34.20) where Jesus is seen as the Passover Lamb. The connection of the Passover with Jesus' hour in 13.1 cannot be coincidental. Cf. R. Schnackenburg, *The Gospel according to St John* (trans D. Smith and G.A. Kong; London: Burns and Oates, 1982), III, p. 15.

1.   Barrett (*John*, p. 435) and Lindars (*John*, p. 444) do not think it is the Passover meal. Against this Morris (*John*, p. 611) implies that it is. Cf. Carson, *John*, p. 460.

2.   Cf. R.E. Brown, *The Gospel according to John* (2 vols.; AB, 29; London: Geoffrey Chapman, 1971), II, p. 549.

3.   For a discussion of the important position of this chapter in the structure of the Gospel, see J.C. Thomas, *Footwashing in John 13 and the Johannine Community* (JSNTSup, 61; Sheffield: JSOT Press, 1991), pp. 61-76.

4.   Beasley-Murray (*John*, p. 230) sees two major sections (1-20; 21-30); cf. also Brown, *John*, II, p. 549. J.D.G. Dunn ('The Washing of the Disciples' Feet in John 13.1-20', *ZNTW* 61 [1970], pp. 247-52), J.C. Thomas (*Footwashing*) and F.F. Segovia ('John 13.1-20, The Footwashing in the Johannine Tradition' *ZNTW* 73 [1982], pp. 31-51) all make a break at the end of v. 20; Westcott (*John*, p. 188) agrees with the above but notes the possibility of a break between v. 16 and v. 17 (though not between v. 15 and v. 16); Schnackenburg (*John*, III, p. 25) sees a break between v. 17 and v. 18; M.E. Boismard ('Le Lavement des Pieds [Jn, XIII, 1-17]', *RB* 71 [1964], pp. 5-24) also breaks at the end of v. 17.

5.   These two ἀμὴν, ἀμὴν sayings (vv. 16, 20) are generally seen to reflect an

are seen as a linking paragraph, their subject matter can be viewed in the light of both the footwashing and the betrayal without denying the break between vv. 20 and 21. If vv. 1-30 are thus seen as a unit,[1] the repeated mentions of Judas's presence in the footwashing scene (cf. vv. 2, 10, 11, 18) are not out of place but rather build up to the identification and expulsion of the betrayer in vv. 21-30. For these reasons, the following structure is suggested:

vv. 1-15: *The Footwashing* and its significance.
    vv. 1-5   Introduction to the footwashing
    vv. 6-11   Dialogue with Peter: the necessity of the footwashing
    vv. 12-15   The example of Jesus that should be obeyed

vv. 16-20: *Link* between the Footwashing and the Betrayal
    vv. 16,17   The role of the servant
    vv. 18,19   The prediction of the betrayer
    vv. 20   Jesus' identity with his disciples

vv. 21-30: *The Betrayal*: identification and expulsion of the betrayer
    vv. 21-25   The disciples want to know the identity of the betrayer
    vv. 26-30   Judas is identified and urged to leave

In this schema the ἐγώ εἰμι saying of v. 19 fits well. Rather than placing this saying about the betrayal exclusively into the footwashing scene, it is also seen in the context of Jesus' further prediction about his betrayal. The reader is not only told that Jesus will be betrayed but also reminded of the identity of the betrayer (cf. 6.71; 12.4). The reason that this information is given in advance is so that, when Jesus' words are fulfilled, faith will result rather than disbelief.[2] In such a structure, the 'I am' saying also fits neatly between the two ἀμὴν, ἀμὴν sayings and explains the reason why Jesus keeps warning the disciples of the impending betrayal. To place the two ἀμὴν sayings in a linking paragraph with the ἐγώ εἰμι saying also draws out their emphasis on the

early tradition parallel to that of the Synoptics; cf. Lindars, *John*, pp. 452, 455; Schnackenburg, *John*, III, p. 27; W.L. Knox, 'John 13.1-30', *HTR* 43 (1950), p. 162.

    1.   Schnackenburg, *John*, III, p. 7, regards vv. 1-30 as a larger unit; also Barrett, *John*, p. 435; Morris, *John*, p. 611.

    2.   Haenchen, *John*, II, p. 109: 'The purpose of the quotation—indicated in verse 19—is not merely to prepare the reader for the betrayal and to inform the reader that Jesus had exact foreknowledge of it; the quotation of Psalm 41.9 also provides the scriptural proof that this betrayal was prophesied in scripture and was therefore contained in God's plan of salvation'. Cf. 18.5, 6, 8 where the betrayal is accompanied by an ἐγώ εἰμι saying.

identification of true disciples with Jesus. The contrast with the one disciple who is not included in Jesus' words (i.e., Judas) becomes even more apparent because of this juxtapositioning.

The narrator in John 13 interprets the character of Jesus through his thoughts as well as his words. Both Jesus and the narrator are omniscient. The narrator knows Jesus' thoughts, just as Jesus himself knows that his hour has now come to depart this world (v. 1).[1] The narrator's knowledge of Jesus' thoughts displays an omniscient point of view. Because Jesus also operates from this perspective, he is able now to show his disciples the full extent of his love in the footwashing.[2]

Jesus' sovereignty is displayed by his interaction with the others at the table. His knowledge of the betrayer constantly comes to the fore (vv. 10, 11, 18, 19, 21). In the light of such sovereignty the disciples are correct to call Jesus their teacher and Lord (vv. 13, 14). Even in his betrayal, Jesus is sovereign. Because he is in control, the betrayal will bring about belief in the disciples rather than disillusionment (v. 19). The 'I am' saying thus contributes to the portrayal of Jesus' sovereignty. The final display of his control over events is the fact that, when Judas has succumbed to Satan (v. 27), Jesus actually sends him on his way to accomplish his deed.[3] Jesus knows that his hour has come and he knows that he is in control rather than Satan, for 'the Father had given all things into his hands' (v. 3).

The footwashing scene, placed as it is in the midst of this picture of sovereignty and omniscience, provides a stark contrast to the way in which such power is expected to be displayed. The disciples expect sovereignty to involve power and authority.[4] For that reason Peter's pride does not allow him to let Jesus wash his feet. Yet Jesus' sovereignty

---

1. Schnackenburg, *John*, III, p. 15: 'The date with which this text begins is closely related to the εἰδὼς, and further reinforces the frequently stressed prior knowledge that Jesus had of his death or his "hour"'.

2. Westcott, *John*, p. 189: 'This knowledge, which is spoken of as absolute (εἰδὼς), prompted the crowning display of love'.

3. Cf. Beasley-Murray, *John*, p. 231.

4. Haenchen, *John*, II, p. 107: 'The words "Lord" and "feet" come at the emphatic points of the sentence, at the beginning and the end, in tension with each other and thus depict the fundamental impossibility of the act: how can a teacher wash the feet of a student?' Thomas (*Footwashing*, p. 59) points out that the Johannine Jesus is the only 'superior' in ancient writings to willingly wash the feet of his inferiors.

displays itself in humble service.[1] Not only does the Lord and teacher perform the task of a servant by washing his disciples' feet, the narrator explains that it is precisely because he is sovereign, that he displays such humility and love. Verse 1 explains that because he knew his hour had come and that he was about to return to the Father, he showed them the full extent of his love. Verse 3 likewise shows that this is the reason that he rises from the table to serve his disciples. If it is correct to interpret the footwashing in the light of the cross, then the message of vv. 1 and 3 can be taken a stage further.[2] Because Jesus knows that he is sovereign and that his hour has come, he is able to show the disciples the full extent of his love by going to the cross. Precisely because of his sovereignty, he can undergo his greatest act of humility.[3] Simultaneous to the characterization of Jesus' sovereignty he is also characterized in his humanity, for it troubles even him that one of his disciples is to betray him (v. 21).[4]

The contrast in characterization between Jesus and the disciples is achieved in John 13 through the contrast in their points of view. Unlike the reader, the disciples do not know that Jesus' hour has now come. Because of this gap of information between Jesus' narrative audience and that given to the reader, an ironic tension is created. Peter's misunderstanding occurs because of his lack of knowledge. He does not know the future events of the death and resurrection of Jesus and, because he operates from a 'normal' point of view, he cannot understand why Jesus is washing his feet. Thus, while Peter is not characterized as stupid, he does become the victim of irony.[5] He has to undergo the footwashing

1.   This is the reason for the 'truly, truly' saying of v. 16. Just as Jesus' sovereignty does not involve 'lording it over' people, so his disciples must not 'lord it over' each other but follow his example of humble service.

2.   Lindars comments on v. 7 that 'the now/afterwards contrast alerts the reader to see in the act of washing the feet something to do with the meaning of the Passion' (*John*, p. 450). Cf. Schnackenburg, *John*, III, p. 16, on v. 1.

3.   The similar ἐγώ εἰμι saying of 8.28 points even more directly to the cross. There it shows that even when Jesus is crucified, he is sovereign and in fact it is there, where the world sees his shame, that he will be revealed in terms of 'I am'. Cf. J.E. Morgan-Wynne, 'The Cross and the Revelation of Jesus as ἐγώ εἰμι in the Fourth Gospel (John 8.28)', in E.A. Livingstone (ed.), *Studia Biblica 1978 II. Papers on the Gospels: Sixth International Congress on Biblical Studies: Oxford 3-7 April 1978* (Sheffield: JSOT Press, 1980), pp. 219-26.

4.   Cf. Morris, *John*, p. 624.

5.   Haenchen's comment on v. 9, that Peter's refusal to have his feet washed is

on faith, not yet knowing its meaning, but trusting that in the future he will understand (v. 7). The reader, however, shares the perspective of a narrator who knows the outcome of the story. Throughout ch. 13 the disciples are called to believe that Jesus is in control even though they do not yet share his viewpoint and will not understand the relevance of the present until some future time. This is especially true of the betrayal. The fact that Jesus has forewarned the disciples of this event will show that he operates from a divine, sovereign, omniscient perspective and is worthy of their faith (v. 19).

When Jesus talks of the character of true disciples, he is drawn again and again to mention that not all of the disciples are true. He assures Peter that he is clean and only needs his feet washed.[1] At the same time he declares that not everyone there is clean. He assures the whole company of his blessing if they are obedient to his exhortation to wash one another's feet,[2] while at the same time he insists that he does not refer to them all. In this worrying assertion, that among those so close to Jesus there is one who will betray him, Jesus offers the assurance that this will happen to fulfil Scripture. His prediction of it will bring the disciples to believe 'that I am'. The characterization of Judas is thus in stark contrast to the other disciples. Jesus is troubled by his very presence (v. 21). The height (or maybe the depth) of Judas's characterization is reached when the narrator comments, 'Satan entered him' (v. 27).

'in an absurd lack of understanding' (*John*, II, p. 108), shows that the reader, who has been supplied with knowledge by the omniscient narrator, may fall into the trap of ridiculing the characters who have no such inside knowledge.

1.　This interpretation takes the longer reading of the text of v. 10 (with Knox, and Thomas, *Footwashing*, pp. 19-25; also, J.C. Thomas, 'A Note on the text of John 13.10', *NovT* 29,1 [1987], pp. 46-52) in the full knowledge that most scholars prefer the shorter reading; e.g. Boismard, *Le lavement des pieds,* esp. pp. 10,11; Segovia, *Footwashing*, p. 43 n. 33, lists those scholars who prefer the shorter reading but himself opts for the longer reading.

2.　The discussion of what the disciples are exhorted to do depends on many and various interpretations of vv. 1-15. These do not fall within the scope of this study. For a fuller discussion of the footwashing in general see Boismard, Dunn, Knox, Segovia and Thomas (all cited above); also Schnackenburg, *John*, III, pp. 8-10. Both Richter and Lohse give a history of the interpretation of Jn 13. G. Richter, *Die Fusswachung im Johannesevangelium* (Biblische Untersuchungen, 1; Regensburg: Friedrich Pustet, 1967). W. Lohse, *Die Fusswaschung (Joh 13.1-20): Eine Geschicte ihrer Deutung* (dissertation, Friedrich-Alexander-Universität zu Erlangen-Nürnberg, 1967).

Despite this terrible assertion, all that this false disciple will achieve is to prove to the true disciples that Jesus' own word, expressed through the ἐγώ εἰμι saying, is true.

John 13 is overflowing with misunderstandings and tensions which can be seen clearly in the act of footwashing and its interpretation. Peter, characterized above, misunderstands the theological implications of what Jesus is doing when he washes the disciples' feet. He is shocked that his master should be serving him, so that, when he is told that it is a necessary part of his union with Jesus (v. 8), he asks for his hands and his head to be washed.[1] There is irony in the fact that Peter does not realize that he is already clean (v. 10), for if he had known this, he would not have asked for his hands and head to be washed. There is a constant play between the idea of physical washing (which Peter rightly interprets as a shocking act of humility on the part of Jesus) and what it points to theologically (which is a cleansing of the disciples who are clean [except for their feet]).[2] This tension also extends to the idea of Jesus the Lord and teacher (vv. 13, 14) who is willing to wash the feet of his disciples (see the deliberate reversal of these titles between vv. 13 and 14). Jesus, with every right to ask his disciples to serve him, is in fact the one who serves.

Lindars suggests that 'the juxtaposition of Jesus' love...and the devil's mastery over Judas...is the first hint of the irony which runs through the chapter'.[3] Lindars does not, however, elucidate how this

---

1. Thomas (*Footwashing*, p. 95) argues that Peter's request for his hands and head to be washed is significant and does not necessarily imply a complete washing.

2. The tension between the act of humility and a deeper interpretation of the footwashing, even in vv. 6-10 points to the unity of the passage as a whole. The repercussions of what Jesus has done (v. 12) reach beyond the act of footwashing to the laying down of his life on the cross. Just as the cross cannot be regarded simply as an act of humility (though it is this, for Jesus lays down his life for his sheep, 10.15) but is seen to be the completion of God's work of salvation in Jesus (19.30), so the footwashing must be seen in typically Johannine fashion as operating on two levels; both as an act of humility (vv. 13-16) and as an act which points to the cleansing Jesus offers his disciples (see esp. 15.3). The redaction-critical approach which separates the footwashing into two (apparently irreconcilable) interpretations is too simplistic in its view of a Johannine theology which cannot hold these two meanings of the footwashing in tension. E.g. Segovia, *Footwashing*. Schnackenburg, *John*, III, pp. 9, 10, gives a useful summary of various interpretations of the footwashing; cf. pp. 1-14, for his own view.

3. Lindars, *John*, p. 449.

irony works. The suggestion is presumably that the text deliberately plays off the tension between Judas and Jesus. Jesus has had everything given into his hands by the Father (v. 3) while Judas is in the hands of Satan (cf. vv. 2, 27). Yet this can hardly be said to be irony, for while there is a contrast between Judas and Jesus, there is no element of surprise in this. If there is any irony in the contrast between Judas and Jesus, it is in the fact that Jesus even has the betrayal under his control. Although he appears to lose control (in that one of his own disciples is to betray him), this is seen, by the fulfilment of Scripture and the accompanying ἐγώ εἰμι saying, to come under God's overarching plan. Thus ἐγώ εἰμι again has a role to play in Johannine irony.

Apart from the themes of betrayal and Jesus' knowledge of his destiny, which have been dealt with above, it is significant that the themes of light and darkness are again present in the context of an 'I am' saying. The concluding verse of this whole section states: 'So after receiving the morsel, he immediately went out; and it was night' (v. 30). In view of the theme of light and darkness, in which ἐγώ εἰμι has been used to portray Jesus as the light (see 8.12; 9.4, 5), the departure of Judas into the night is almost sinister.[1] Jesus had warned that he must work while it is day for the night was approaching 'when no one can work' (9.4). Now the narrator simply states 'and it was night'. Jesus who had claimed to be the light of the world, is now portrayed in contrast to Judas and the reader is drawn back to the words of John 3: 'the light has come into the world, and men loved darkness rather than light, because their deeds were evil. For everyone who does evil hates the light, and does not come to the light, lest his deeds should be exposed' (vv. 19, 20; cf. 1.5).

The question of what the reader should understand by the use of ἐγώ εἰμι in Jn 13.19 is a complex one. There is no explicit predicate to go with Jesus' words.[2] For this reason commentators fall into two camps concerning Jesus' use of ἐγώ εἰμι here. Beasley-Murray, for example, regards vv. 18-19 as 'a vague announcement of the impending betrayal

---

1. Cf. Lindars, *John*, p. 460.
2. Against this, see Davies (*Rhetoric*, p. 86) who suggests Jesus' claim to be Teacher and Lord (v. 13) as a predicate for the ἐγώ εἰμι in v. 19. While such an interpretation is possible, it hardly the only way to take these words. Considering the formal similarity of this saying with the sayings of 8.24, 28 and the link between this verse and Jesus' betrayal as well as the use of 'I am' in Isaiah (see Chapter 6 below), it is likely that there is a deeper meaning to Jesus' words here.

of Jesus'.[1] Other commentators, however, see this verse in the light of
8.28.[2] Although it will be argued below that 8.28 sheds light on the use
of ἐγώ εἰμι here, it must be noted that the narrative audiences are quite
different and the revelation of Jesus will have different consequences. In
8.28 Jesus' opponents are told that when he is lifted up, then they will
know that ἐγώ εἰμι; while in 13.19 the disciples are told that when
Jesus' prediction (particularly about his betrayal) occurs it is so they will
believe that ἐγώ εἰμι.[3] There is a distinction between the function of the
'I am' which will be revealed to Jesus' opponents when he is on the
cross and that of the 'I am' which will be revealed to his disciples when
his words come true. The former 'I am' has overtones of judgment (cf.
8.24); the latter encouragement to belief. Although the form of these
two sayings is similar and the content of what ἐγώ εἰμι means may be
the same, their function is different.

Having seen how the ἐγώ εἰμι of 13.19 functions, it is possible to ask
what the reader should understand through the phrase 'That when it
does take place you may believe that I am he'. The obvious question
that the reader may want to ask is the same as the Jews of 8.24: 'Who
are you?' The implied reader is left with a clue in the fact that the words
ἐγώ εἰμι do not make sense unless something is supplied to explain who
Jesus will be revealed to be. The fact that the narrator supplies no such
explanation means that 'the interpreter can assume that the intended
reader was capable of understanding them [i.e., characters, places,
customs and terms] without any explanation from the narrator'.[4]
However, the fact that the 'I am' saying will be fulfilled at the same time
as the fulfilment of Jewish Scripture may provide a clue for the correct
conceptual background by which the saying should be understood.

A study of the function of ἐγώ εἰμι in 13.19 has again shown that the
phrase occurs at an important point in the Gospel at the beginning of the

---

1.   Beasley-Murray, *John*, p. 237; Haenchen, *John*, II, p. 109, passes the phrase
by with no comment.

2.   Cf. Carson, *John*, p. 471; Lindars, *John*, p. 455; Schnackenburg, *John*, III,
p. 26; Brown, *John*, II, p. 571; Morris, *John*, p. 623.

3.   Is there a distinction here between knowledge and belief? The knowledge that
will be revealed to the Jews is a knowledge that is too late (almost a tragic vision).
When the disciples see the fulfilment of Jesus' words it will produce belief. The Jews,
who do not believe in what Jesus claims through ἐγώ εἰμι, will face an unenviable fate
when, at his death, they come to realize the truth of his claim (8.24).

4.   Culpepper, *Anatomy*, p. 8.

farewell discourses. Here Jesus predicts his betrayal and subsequent passion. The 'I am' saying itself also points forward to a future time when the disciples will believe ὅτι ἐγώ εἰμι. As such this saying also portrays Jesus' omniscient point of view and affirms to the disciples that he is sovereign, even in the apparently tragic events of the betrayal. At the same time Jesus' words are narrated in order to bring about belief on the part of the readers as well as the narrative audience.[1] In this there is also irony as Jesus' betrayal by one of his closest friends is seen not as a loss of sovereignty, nor even as an inevitable evil, but as an event which will bring about belief because of its fulfilment of Scripture. Jesus is thus characterized not as a tragic hero, who can do nothing about his impending doom, but as one who, knowing the future, has had everything given into his hands (v. 3). The discussion of background material in Chapter 6 must therefore ask how the words 'I am' may be the content of belief in such a context.

7. *John 14: The Way, the Truth and the Life (14.6)*

The temporal and geographical setting of John 14 remains the same as in the previous chapter. However, there is a significant theological change. During and after the meal of ch. 13, Jesus was troubled in spirit at his impending betrayal by Judas (v. 21), but, upon Judas's departure (v. 30), Jesus declares, 'Now is the Son of man glorified and in him God is glorified; if God is glorified in him, God will also glorify him in himself, and glorify him at once' (vv. 31, 32). These words of Jesus form the introduction to and so set the tone for a long discourse which continues through to Jesus' words, 'Rise let us go hence' (14.31).[2]

---

1. Cf. Carson, *John*, p. 471.

2. Cf. Beasley-Murray, *John*, p. 244; Brown, *John*, II, p. 623, regards 13.31-38 as introductory to this discourse. Cf. J.M. Reese, 'Literary structure of Jn 13.31-14.31; 16.5-6, 16-33', *CBQ* 34 (1972), pp. 321-31. Also, F.F. Segovia ('The Structure, Tendenz and *Sitz im Leben* of John 13.31-14.31', *JBL* 104 [1985], pp. 471-93) thinks (p. 477) that Judas's departure marks the start of Jesus' discourse. In contrast, Barrett (*John*, pp. 454-55), Haenchen (*John*, II, p. 124) and Lindars (*John*, p. 466) see the unit as starting at 14.1. Bultmann (*John*, p. 595) sees the unit as starting at 13.36 and places vv. 31-35 with 15.1-17 (p. 523). He also places the whole unit after ch. 16, but this does not account for the obvious link between Jesus' statement that he is going away (v. 33) and Peter's question in (v. 36); see also J. McCaffrey, *The House with Many Rooms: The Temple Theme of*

The discourse following Judas's departure can be divided into an introduction (13.31-38), the main discourse (14.1-27) and a conclusion (14.28-31).[1] The words 'Let not your hearts be troubled' which open the main discourse (14.1) are resumed towards the end (v. 27) and so form an inclusio.[2] This main section of discourse can be further divided at the end of v. 14 after which the new theme of the Paraclete is introduced.[3] The sub-section, which forms the subject of this study because it contains the words ἐγώ εἰμι, begins with Jesus' encouragement 'Let not your hearts be troubled' (14.1) and ends with his promise to do anything the disciples ask in his name (v. 14). De la Potterie divides this into two even smaller units (14.2-6, 7-14), in which the former develops the idea of 'the "place" where Jesus is going, and the "way" to get there' while the latter deals with present realities.[4]

De la Potterie's discussion of the structure of 14.1-14 is particularly important for the present study, since he thinks that:

> Within the section 14.2-11, verse 6 forms a genuine hinge between the two major subdivisions (vv. 2-6 and 6-11). At verse 6, in fact, the perspective changes sharply: One passes from the future tense to the present reality.[5]

If v. 6 does form such a 'hinge' in the development of the discourse, the ἐγώ εἰμι saying there would hold the key not only to how this section is structured but also to how it should be understood. Jesus claims to be the Way for the disciples to reach the Father not only in the future but

---

Jn 14.2-3 (AnBib, 114; Rome: Biblical Institute Press, 1988), p. 144, who sees the main body of the discourse starting at v. 36.

1. Segovia, *John 13.31–14.31*, p. 478.
2. Cf. I. de la Potterie, 'Je suis la voie, la vérité, et la vie (Jn 14.6)', in *idem, La Vérité Dans Saint Jean* (AnBib, 73; Rome: Biblical Institute Press, 1977), p. 250; also Segovia, *John 13.31–14.31*, p. 477.
3. Cf. Beasley-Murray, *John*, p. 244; Brown, *John*, II, p. 623: 'A point of demarcation seems to occur between 14 and 15, for in 15-16 the new theme of the paraclete is introduced. But even this break is not sharp; for the Paraclete comes at Jesus request (*erotan*), and vss 13-14 have been concerned with asking (*aitein*) in Jesus' name...Verses 13-14 are a problem: they are related to 12 and should probably be kept with that verse but they also offer a transition to 15.' Brown's hesitancy to propose a division of Jn 14.1-14 into subunits is wise and warns against imposing a complicated structure on the text. He tentatively suggests vv. 1-4; 6-11; 12-14 as subunits, with v. 5 serving to change the train of thought (*John*, II, p. 624).
4. De la Potterie, *La Vérité*, p. 250 and p. 264 respectively.
5. De la Potterie, *La Vérité*, p. 263.

also in the present.[1] De la Potterie's observation, that v. 6 marks a change from future promises to present realities, is significant in showing the change in perspective brought about through the 'I am' saying. However, such a shift in tenses may not be able to bear the structural weight that is required for it to be seen as a structural hinge of the whole section.[2]

A more solid basis for the structural pattern of John 14 may be seen in the questions of the disciples. Reese thus suggests a recurring threefold pattern which consists of:

(a)   a revelation by Jesus
(b)   a question by interlocutors who speak on a superficial level. Their intervention is purely formal, that is 'to give an opportunity for further elucidation'.
(c)   a response by Jesus to clarify his original revelation.[3]

Reese sees a recurrence of this pattern throughout the larger division (13.31–14.31) as well as in later parts of the farewell discourse (16.5-6, 16-33).[4] However, even within such a division of structure the 'I am' saying plays an important role as it forms the response by Jesus to clarify his original revelation.

As the discussion of structure suggests, Jesus' interaction with his disciples forms the basis for his discourse.[5] The disciples' questions are

1.   De la Potterie, *La Vérité*, p. 264.
2.   Others do not see the structural emphasis which De la Potterie places on v. 6. See the many divisions of structure outlined above, of which only Brown's places any significance on the words of v. 6. See also, J. Becker, 'Die Abschiedsreden Jesu im Johannesevangelium', *ZNTW* 61 (1970), pp. 215-46. Becker suggests that the chapter consists of a structure comprising various literary concepts (such as the inclusio—see above; and themes of departure and return) which are all found in vv. 1-3. His argument is neatly summarized by Segovia, *John 13.31–14.31*, p. 477, who concludes, 'vv. 1-3 ... thus become for Becker the key to both the structure and the fundamental meaning of the chapter and the discourse'.
3.   Cf. Reese, *Literary Structure*, pp. 321-22 (the words Reese quotes are from Dodd, *Interpretation*, p. 404). Reese's view of structure is very similar to Culpepper's pattern of misunderstanding (Culpepper, *Anatomy*, p. 152; cf. Duke, *Irony*, p. 145).
4.   Reese (*Literary Structure*, p. 323) thinks that the insertion of the vine discourse and its supplement (15.1-16.4) and of various individual sayings (13.34, 35; 14.13, 15b-17; 16.7-11, 12-15, 23b-24) has separated the exchanges between Jesus and his disciples which once formed a unit. However, even if this is not the case, it is common for John to use this pattern of misunderstanding as the basis for the structure of a passage (e.g. 3.3-5; 4.10-15, 31-34; 6.32-35). Cf. Culpepper, *Anatomy*, pp. 160-61.
5.   Cf. McCaffrey, *Many Rooms*, p. 144.

taken up and expounded by Jesus. Four different disciples (Peter, 13.36a-37; Thomas, 14.5; Philip, 14.8; the other Judas, 14.22) have the same function, namely, to draw from Jesus an explanation of concepts which they as the narrative audience do not understand. At the same time such terms are explained to the reader.[1] Jesus' 'I am' saying (v. 6), in response to Thomas's question, is just such an explanation. He states that the disciples know the way to where he is (ὅπου εἰμι ἐγώ, v. 3),[2] but Thomas protests that they cannot know the way if they do not even know the place to which he is going (v. 5).[3] Jesus replies with the unexpected statement that he himself is the Way (v. 6). Thus Thomas unwittingly draws a reply from Jesus far beyond what he expected (cf. 4.26; 6.35; 11.25). Through the characterization of Thomas, the character of Jesus is further enhanced. As with the other disciples, Thomas's characterization is not as an end in itself but instead further reveals the character of Jesus. In this way the disciples again act as a foil to the character of Jesus, asking him to explain his terms. This in turn enables the readers to avoid similar misunderstanding of Jesus' words and so to adopt the narrator's conceptual point of view.[4]

Jesus is again aware of his future destiny and operates from an omniscient point of view. He introduces the theme of his imminent departure with the words 'as I said to the Jews so now I say to you, "Where I am going you cannot come"' (13.33; cf. 7.33). Since Peter operates from a human point of view, it is understandable that he should

---

1.   Reese, *Literary Structure*, pp. 321-22. Cf. Segovia, *John 13.31–14.31*, p. 482, who suggests that this threefold structure is a 'series of parallel cycles' which are not merely 'cyclic in character but rather progressive: the christological statements are expanded and developed not only within each series but also from series to series'. Also Schnackenburg, *John*, III, p. 57.

2.   ἐγώ occurs in conjunction with εἰμι twice in these few verses. The first time Jesus states that he will come back to the disciples to take them where he is (ὅπου εἰμι ἐγώ, v. 3). Along with the phrase 'Where I am going' (ὅπου ἐγώ ὑπάγω, v. 4), the phrase 'where I am' causes Thomas to question where Jesus will be. Although the phrase 'where I am' cannot be directly linked to the ἐγώ εἰμι of v. 6, it may be that the reader is meant to see an interaction between these two uses of ἐγώ and εἰμι in such close proximity and to make a connection between the words ὅπου εἰμι ἐγώ and the absolute 'I am' used elsewhere. Cf. Schnackenburg, *John*, II, p. 81.

3.   Cf. Schnackenburg, *John*, III, p. 64.

4.   Culpepper (*Anatomy*, p. 152) suggests that the effect of such misunderstandings 'on the reader is greater than if the meaning had merely been stated simply from the beginning'.

ask Jesus to explain. He wants to know why he cannot accompany Jesus and understandably sees Jesus' words in purely material terms (v. 37). From his earthly perspective he boldly declares that he is willing to go with Jesus to death. However, Jesus points out that, even on a human plane, Peter is not able to go with him and will deny him that very night (v. 38). Although he operates from a higher plane than the disciples, Jesus realizes that they are disturbed by his words. He therefore explains his departure to them so that they may believe (14.29; cf.14.1, 10, 11; 13.19).[1] He also encourages them not to be worried but to to trust in God (14.1).

Even though Jesus is characterized as omniscient, he still sympathizes with the human perspective of the disciples, who do not know all that he does. So, by answering the disciples' questions, Jesus encourages them to join his conceptual point of view even though they do not possess the same advantageous knowledge as he. Jesus' claim, 'I am the way, the truth and the life' (v. 6), is just such an attempt to bring the disciples to his own perspective. Thomas, and the others, can know the way to the Father because they know Jesus who is the Way. Furthermore, the disciples do not need to see the Father, for they have seen Jesus (v. 9). Although Philip is correct to want a heavenly perspective, he does not need a direct view of the Father since that is provided in the person of Jesus. He is the only way to reach the Father to the extent that those who have seen him have seen the Father. Jesus is characterized as the means by which the disciples and, by implication, the readers are able to possess a divine point of view.[2] Ironically, the disciples who have been with him so long still have a restricted human point of view and do not really know Jesus (v. 9).

As the pattern of misunderstanding outlined above suggests, the disciples' questions in Jn 13.36–14.9 reveal certain ambiguities in Jesus' words. When Jesus speaks of the disciples knowing the way, Thomas protests that they do not even know where he is going (14.5). Jesus'

---

1. Culpepper, *Anatomy*, p. 36: 'In this discourse [John 13–17], as elsewhere, Jesus has a distinctive point of view from which he interprets his mission, his departure and return, and the disciples' relationship to him... In short the farewell discourse shows that Jesus knows the spiritual orientation of the disciples (15.19; 17.16) and the world, the hearts and minds of the disciples... and significant future events.'

2. Culpepper, *Anatomy*, p. 38: 'The implication is that unless the readers see Jesus in the light of the narrator's temporal and ideological point of view, they cannot understand who Jesus was'.

reply takes away any ambiguity about how they will get to where he is (ὅπου εἰμι ἐγώ, v. 3). He is the Way to the Father (ἐγώ εἰμι, v. 6). The reason the disciples know the way is that Jesus is the Way and they know Jesus. Thus the function of the 'I am' saying in Jn 14.6 is to remove the ambiguity involved in his statement about the way (v. 4).[1] Thomas's question 'How can we know the way?' only becomes ironic in the light of Jesus' revelation of himself as the Way, for while the 'I am' saying resolves the ambiguity in the use of the word 'way', it also reveals the extent of Thomas's ignorance. He does not know that the one to whom he speaks is also the one of whom he speaks (cf. 4.26; 6.35).

The ambiguity of Jesus' initial statements to the disciples (cf. 13.33; 14.5, 7, 19-21) allows irony to take place, 'for the first offer of saving truth by Jesus is always understood by the interlocutor on the surface level.'[2] Jesus clarifies his meaning to them (14.2, 6, 9, 22-23). At the same time this shows that they have not grasped the deeper meaning of what he has said. The use of irony here again furthers the revelation of the character of Jesus. If it was not for Thomas's inability to see who Jesus really is, there would be no need for such a clear explanation. Since Thomas does not understand, Jesus makes the emphatic declaration, 'I am the way and the truth and the life; no one comes to the Father but by me' (v. 6). The irony here is in the fact that 'this magnificent statement goes far beyond the scope of the question'.[3] Jesus' claim through an 'I am' saying thus functions as an indispensable part of the irony developed in this chapter as a result of the differing points of view between Jesus and his disciples.

The opening words of ch. 14 introduce the theme of belief which is reiterated throughout this section (cf. v. 29).[4] Even the declaration that

---

1. Lindars, *John*, p. 472: 'He [Thomas] takes Jesus' words and treats the two elements of them separately, first the destination and then the means of access. As the first is unknown, it follows that the second remains uncertain.'

2. Reese also states: 'The use of this pattern depends on the double level of meaning found throughout this gospel and exploits the possibilities of Johannine irony' (*Literary Structure*, p. 322).

3. Lindars, *John*, p. 472. Beasley-Murray, *John*, p. 252: 'The disciple's lack of understanding, as so often, provides opportunity for Jesus to clarify the revelation. The saying is commonly recognised as ranking with 3.16 as an outstanding expression of the Gospel.'

4. Bultmann, *John*, p. 600, states on v. 1: 'because faith in God can only be mediated by Jesus, the believer must realise that to give up faith in Jesus would also be to give up faith in God'. Brown, *John*, II, p. 624: 'The theme in vs 1 that faith in

Jesus goes to prepare a place for the disciples is intended to encourage them in their belief (v. 3). It may even be argued that this is the principal theme of the discourse.[1] Jesus calls the disciples to believe him that it is on his Father's authority that he speaks (v. 10). If they do not believe his words, he appeals to them to believe on account of his works (v. 11).[2] Anyone who has such a belief will actually be able to do greater works than Jesus (v. 12). All this is linked back to the theme of glory (vv. 13, 14) which opened this section of discourse (13.31, 32).

As so often in the Fourth Gospel, the theme of belief is accompanied by that of knowledge. Jesus claims that the disciples know the way where he is going (v. 4). Thomas claims that they do not (v. 5). The 'I am' saying of Jesus thus functions to remove the disciples' ignorance. Furthermore, Jesus claims that if the disciples had known him, they would know the Father. In fact, Jesus describes those who know him in this way as seeing the Father (vv. 7, 9).[3] From now on they do know the Father (v. 7). Now that Jesus has revealed himself as the Way to the Father, the disciples can no longer claim that they do not know the Father. In keeping with all Jesus' replies to the disciples questions, the 'I am' saying functions to remove any ignorance on the part of the disciples. Now that they know Jesus is the way to the Father Jesus is able to call them to believe that he is in the Father and the Father in Him (v. 11).

It has already been maintained that the cause of the disciples' consternation is the impending departure of Jesus.[4] His statement, that he is going away and that they will not be able to go with him, prompts Jesus to encourage them to believe. Jesus carefully explains that he is going to his Father so that the disciples will be able to join him there when he has made ready a place for them. In the face of this departure the disciples

God has its counterpart as faith in Jesus reappears in terms of knowing and seeing in vss 7 and 9'.

1. Cf. De la Potterie, *La Vérité*, p. 250. Also Segovia, *John 13.31–14.31*, p. 478; Beasley-Murray, *John*, p. 248; Schnackenburg, *John*, III, pp. 57, 64.

2. Brown points out that 'From Jesus' point of view both word and work are revelatory, but from the audience's point of view works have a greater confirmatory value than words' (*John*, II, p. 622).

3. Lindars, *John*, p. 474: 'Knowledge is replaced by sight. In religious language sight is the fullest and most direct form of knowledge'.

4. De la Potterie, *La Vérité*, p. 250: 'The profound disarray caused among the disciples by this announcement of Jesus' "departure" is the opportunity for chapter 14's speech of comfort'. Cf. Brown, *John*, II, p. 623; Schnackenburg, *John*, III, p. 58.

are to be encouraged because Jesus, whom they know, is the Way to the Father. Thus the 'I am' saying of Jn 14.6 can be seen to fit into the many themes of the chapter.

A study of the ἐγώ εἰμι saying of Jn 14.6 at once begs the question of how the three predicates of the words 'I am' relate to each other. Since the concepts of truth and life are so important to the Fourth Gospel there is a temptation to see these two concepts as more dominant than the context allows. This is all the more true in the light of parallels in thought in the ancient world. De la Potterie is correct to state 'the significant fact that, the authors who have analysed the passage on its own merits, without being preoccupied with its antecedents, have practically all arrived at the same conclusion: that it is ὁδός which is the most important word, the nouns ἀλήθεια and ζωή do no more than explain it; in other words, the words "the truth and the life" simply serve to make clear in what sense Jesus is "the way"'.[1]

The context of Jesus 'I am' saying here shows that the emphasis of the 'I am' saying is on 'the way' rather than 'the truth and the life'.[2] The discussion which precedes Jesus' declaration is concerned with the place to which Jesus is going. The concept of the 'way' is explicit both in Jesus' initial declaration (οἴδατε τὴν ὁδόν, v. 4) and in Thomas's reply (πῶς δυνάμεθα τὴν ὁδὸν εἰδέναι, v. 5). That Jesus then declares himself to be the Way, the Truth and the Life, must primarily be understood in the light of this discussion concerning where Jesus is going and the way to get there. This is confirmed by the lack of any explanation of the terms 'truth' and 'life' in the sub-clause to the 'I am' saying (v. 6b).[3] The second part of the verse simply explains in what sense Jesus is the Way. He is the Way in an exclusive sense which means that no one comes to the Father except through him. The words 'truth' and 'life' should be understood as another explanation of how Jesus is the Way.[4]

Once it has been established that the major concept in the 'I am'

---

1. De la Potterie, *La Vérité*, p. 249.

2. Cf. Schnackenburg, *John*, III, p. 64; also Beasley-Murray, *John*, p. 252.

3. De la Potterie explains how the verse is constructed in parallelism: 'It is composed of two parts, the one is positive, the other negative, following the law of antithetical parallelism' (*La Vérité*, p. 251). Also, he points out that the words ἡ ἀλήθεια καὶ ἡ ζωή 'hardly play any role in the literary structure: nothing corresponds to them in the negatively parallel section (v. 6b)...' (p. 252).

4. Cf. De la Potterie, *La Vérité*, p. 252.

saying of Jn 14.6 is that of 'the way', there remains the problem of how the reader should interpret this term when Jesus applies it to himself. Again the text itself provides the primary explanation of how Jesus is the Way. Lindars points out one of the ways the 'I am' saying functions here: 'it is...an explanatory statement, identifying a feature of the parabolic metaphor of the opening verses'.[1] Jesus has explained the place where he is going (i.e., the house with many rooms). He has explained why he is going there (i.e., to prepare a place for the disciples). Now he explains that he himself is the way to get there. He goes on to explain his role as the way (i.e., he and he alone is the access for people to reach the Father). Thus, at least on one level, the 'I am' saying of Jesus can be perfectly well understood without reference outside the text of John 14, for Jesus himself explains what he means by 'the Way'.

As the Way, Jesus adds that he is also the Truth and the Life. The reader cannot fail to remember that Jesus has, by means of ἐγώ εἰμι, already claimed to be the Life at the raising of Lazarus (11.25).[2] Indeed from the prologue the connection between the person of Jesus and life has been explicit (cf. 1.4). There the Life was described as being 'the light of men', a concept taken up in the 'I am' saying of 8.12. Jesus claims to be 'the bread of life' (6.35, 41, 48, 51) and life is mentioned in the context of his claim to be the Door and the Good Shepherd (cf. 10.9, 10). It is hardly surprising then that this theme of life is again linked with an ἐγώ εἰμι saying of Jesus. Life thus defines 'Way' in terms of John's whole theology about the person of Jesus. As the Way, Jesus is also the Life. In addition to this he is the Truth. This again was one of the characteristics of the Word of the prologue, who was described as 'full of grace and truth' (1.14). Truth, like life, is one of the major themes of the Gospel.[3] Jesus has declared to the Samaritan

1. Lindars, *John*, p. 472.

2. Brown, *John*, II, p. 630: 'Once again this is a description of Jesus in terms of his mission to men: "I have come that they might have life and have it to the full" (10.10)... this life the Father has given to the Son (5.26), and the Son alone can give it to men who believe in him (10.28).'

3. For a detailed discussion of truth in John see De La Potterie's extensive work, *La Vérité*; also Morris, *John*, pp. 293-96, who points out the emphasis on faithfulness; also Barrett, commenting on 1.14, *John*, p. 167. Brown (*John*, II, p. 628) and De la Potterie (*La Vérité*, p. 270) see truth here as synonymous with revelation. It may be true that Jesus claims to be the revelation of the Father (cf. v. 9). Whether the concept of the truth primarily conveys such an idea is doubtful. That Jesus claims to be faithful and reliable as 'the way' to the Father, is more plausible.

woman that the 'hour is coming, and now is, when true worshippers will worship the Father in spirit and truth' (4.24). He has claimed to be the 'true' bread (τὸν ἄρτον ...τὸν ἀληθινόν) from heaven (6.32-33). As the Light of the World he has claimed that his testimony and judgment are true (8.14, 16). He has also declared that if the Jews remain in his word they will know the truth and the truth will set them free (8.32). With such an emphasis on the concept of truth in the Gospel as a whole, it is highly significant that Jesus takes it and applies it to himself in the 'I am' saying of Jn 14.6. As a result of this ἐγώ εἰμι saying 'truth is not the teaching about God transmitted by Jesus but it is God's very reality revealing itself—occurring—in Jesus.'[1]

The study of the literary function of ἐγώ εἰμι in Jn 14.1-14 has been seen to fit into a clear pattern of misunderstanding which runs throughout the larger discourse. Because of its role in this pattern of misunderstanding the use of ἐγώ εἰμι is again part of John's use of irony. The narrator's conceptual point of view is played off against that of the narrative audience. The explanation which Jesus gives to the disciples' questions allows the reader to interact with Jesus and so adopt his point of view. Jesus' 'I am' saying has major implications for Johannine Christology as a whole for he does not only apply the immediate concept of the 'Way' to himself but also the Johannine themes of the Truth and the Life. Furthermore, as the Way, Jesus displays a unique role in providing access to the Father. The study of background material below must also bear in mind the significance given to the concept of the 'Way' by the context in which it occurs. The Johannine context demands that this term should not be taken to refer vaguely to Jesus as 'the Way in the sense that he is the whole background against which action must be performed, the atmosphere in which life must be lived.'[2] Rather, the term refers specifically to the Way by which the disciples may gain access to the Father. Due weight should therefore be given to the fact that, 'as an ego eimi saying, it is not a revelation-formula (i.e. You know the religious meaning of the way...this is what I am'), but an explanatory statement, identifying a feature of the parabolic metaphor of the opening verses'.[3]

---

1. R. Bultmann, *Theology of the New Testament* (London: SCM Press, 1955), II, p. 19.

2. E.M. Sidebottom, *The Christ of the Fourth Gospel* (London: SPCK, 1961), p. 146.

3. Lindars, *John*, p. 472.

8. *John 15: The (True) Vine (15.1, 5)*

The discourse of John 15 belongs to the same chronological setting as those which immediately precede and follow it. Even scholars who regard the chapter as misplaced[1] or as a later redaction[2] accept that John 15 must be understood as Jesus' final words to his disciples spoken in the light of his impending betrayal and death.[3] Following his claim to be the way to the Father (14.6), Jesus has told the disciples that he is the revelation of the Father (vv. 9, 10). He has promised not to leave them alone but to send the Holy Spirit to be with them (14.16, 17, 26). He has again encouraged them not to be worried (14.27). The motive for explaining all these things is that, when they take place, the disciples may believe (14.29). Jesus concludes his discourse with the words 'Rise, let us go hence' (14.31). The fact that he does not appear to depart but launches into another discourse, dramatically underlines that these are Jesus' final words. Although chs. 15–17 seem to be an interruption in the light of the finality of Jesus' words in Jn 14.31 and although the narrative comment which marks Jesus' actual departure (18.1) fits smoothly with the last words of ch. 14, the dramatic tension is heightened by the fact that Jesus, on the point of departure, delays in order to give his disciples some final teaching.

With the words ἐγώ εἰμι ἡ ἄμπελος ἡ ἀληθινή (v. 1), Jesus begins a new discourse which continues until the command to love one another (v. 17).[4] This discourse can be divided into two parts. The first of these parts concludes with the words 'These things I have spoken to you that my joy may be in you and that your joy may be full' (v. 11)[5] The

---

1. E.g. Bultmann (*John*, p. 529) places the discourse in the context of ch. 13.

2. E.g. Beasley-Murray, *John*, p. 269.

3. Cf. Schnackenburg, *John*, III, p. 95: 'The discourse in Chapter 15, then, clearly continues the farewell discourse, transfers it to the sphere of the community and applies it to that community by expressing openly the admonitions that are contained in Jesus' words of farewell'.

4. R. Borig, *Der Wahre Weinstock* (Münich: Kösel, 1967), p. 19: 'After the previous speech has been clearly concluded in 14.31 with the invitation to depart, 15.1 starts completely afresh and immediately introduces the image of the vine'. Also Schnackenburg, *John*, III, p. 96.

5. Schnackenburg (*John*, III, p. 92) argues that the phrase 'I have spoken these things to you' is a division marker throughout the farewell discourses (cf.14.25, 16.1, 4, 33). Borig (*Weinstock*, p. 19) sees v. 11 as introducing the next section.

second section, which explains the content of the commandments mentioned in v. 10, begins (v. 12) and concludes (v. 17) with the command to love one another. Although the deeper realities of the image of the vine are worked out in the teaching of vv. 12-17, this study will restrict itself to the first section since the use of ἐγώ εἰμι and the image of the vine occur in vv. 1-11. In this part, the image of the vine dominates vv. 1-6 but recedes so that the spiritual realities to which it points become dominant in vv. 7-11.

Brown suggests a major break in vv. 1-17 between vv. 6 and 7.[1] In vv. 1-6 he sees 'the figure of the vine and the branches' and in vv. 7-17 'an explanation of this figure in the context of Last Discourse themes'. He suggests that the 'I am' sayings (vv. 1, 5) form an inclusion for the figurative section of the discourse (vv. 1-6) and that 'in 7-17 there are inclusions between 8 and 16 (bearing fruit) and between 7 and 16 (asking and having it granted)'.[2] Verses 6-17 thus display a chiastic structure. Verse 11 is the turning point in the chiasm rather than a break in the discourse. However attractive this division of structure may seem for the significance of the 'I am' sayings, the theme of 'remaining in' (cf. vv. 4, 5, 6, 7, 9, 10) runs too strongly through vv. 1-10 for there to be a major break between vv. 6 and 7.[3] It is also hard to regard the second 'I am' saying as forming an inclusion since, rather than concluding what Jesus has to say concerning his role as the vine, it develops the idea further by explicitly introducing the idea that the disciples are the branches. Furthermore, the subtle change from the figurative to the real meaning of Jesus' words occurs as the idea of the disciples as the branches is expounded (vv. 6-8).[4]

Although the intricate structure of Jn 15.1-17 should be recognized, it seems best to see this in terms of the pattern which occurs in John 6 and

Whichever view is taken, the words ταῦτα λελάληκα act as marker for a break in the text. Against this see Carson, *John*, p. 511.

1.   Brown, *John*, II, p. 665.
2.   Brown, *John*, II, p. 667.
3.   Brown himself is aware that such an elaborate structure may 'reflect more the ingenuity of the investigator than any intention of the Johannine writer' (*John*, II, p. 668).
4.   While Brown (*John*, II, p. 665) sees the 'allegory' as ending in v. 6, for Lindars (*John*, p. 490) the image is not discarded until v. 9. Brown's suggestion that vv. 7-17 are an exposition of vv. 1-6 is better than seeing a complete abandonment of the image. However, it seems best to see the vine image as receding slowly but remaining in the background throughout the discourse.

10. According to this pattern, a theme is introduced and progressively developed in terms of Jesus' own role and mission. The first 'I am' saying introduces the theme of the vine, while the second re-introduces it in order to explain the implications of Jesus' claim for discipleship (v. 5b).[1] The importance of bearing fruit is emphasized in the first part of the discourse (vv. 1-11), while what it means to bear fruit is the subject of the second (vv. 12-17). Both 'I am' sayings therefore play an important role in the development of this discourse. This role is emphasized by the fact that the first saying opens this chapter.

Even though the vine discourse is addressed to the disciples in the context of Jesus' imminent departure, they have no active part to play. The narrator too is silent. Such silence on the part of both the narrator and the narrative audience therefore serves to emphasize the importance of Jesus' words.[2] It is Jesus who speaks. Any characterization is thus filtered through the words of Jesus. Because the conceptual point of view of the narrator coincides with the point of view of the character of Jesus, this discourse not only addresses the disciples but also the implied reader. Jesus' words thus show the conceptual point of view, which the reader, as well as the narrative audience, is encouraged to adopt.

In the image of the vine as well as in the use of the first person (as epitomized through ἐγώ εἰμι), the dominance of Jesus' character is again emphasized. He is the exclusive source of the disciples' fruitfulness (v. 4). Just as a branch cannot bear fruit on its own, neither can a disciple accomplish anything without Jesus (vv. 4, 5). Because Jesus is the vine, the person who remains in him is the one who will bear much fruit (v. 5). The call to remain in Jesus portrays him not only as the giver, but also as the sustainer of life.[3]

> The initiative always rests with Jesus himself. The disciples' part is that of response to a love already given, and as such entails submitting voluntarily to do his will in loving obedience.[4]

---

1. Lindars, *John*, p. 489: 'the new start, repeating v. 1a, indicates the introduction of a fresh theme, like the new start in 10.11. This is to be the exposition of the fruit.'

2. Hinrichs (*Ich Bin*, p. 76) puts the absence of the narrative audience down to the work of an ecclesiastical redactor, for whom the narrative audience holds little importance.

3. While the idea of Jesus as the sustainer of life is implied by the text it is not explicit (except at v. 13) and Lindars is correct to state that 'The allegory is entirely concerned with personal relationships, so that the categories of thought are moral, not Gnostic'. Against this cf. Bultmann, *John*, p. 530.

4. Lindars, *John*, p. 492. Cf. Beasley-Murray, *John*, p. 271.

As elsewhere the dominance of Jesus is expressed in his submission to the Father. In his dominance, Jesus is aware of his own unique dependence on the Father. The Father is the vinedresser (v. 1) who wishes the disciples to bear fruit (v. 8).[1] In loving the disciples Jesus is only imitating the love the Father has for him (v. 9). His command for obedience only reflects his own obedience to the Father (v. 10).

Although these verses focus on Jesus himself and his submission to the Father, in some ways they have more implications for his audience than they do for the characterization of Jesus. While Jesus' narrative audience is silent in these verses, his teaching concerns the characteristics of true disciples.[2] Jesus' identification of himself as the True Vine demands a response from those he portrays as branches. The constant command to abide in him 'goes beyond the allegory, because a branch has no moral power to abide in the vine'.[3] Yet it is through the analogy of the vine and branches that the dependence of the disciples upon Jesus is emphasized. They are to remain in him and in his love (vv. 4, 9). His word has cleansed them (v. 3) and now that word must remain in them (v. 7) for, by keeping Jesus' commandments, they abide in his love (v. 10). This has positive repercussions for those that remain in the vine (vv. 5, 7) as well as negative implications for those who do not (vv. 2, 6). The characterization of the disciples as branches that are wholly dependent on Jesus is a logical progression of Jesus' depiction of himself as the vine (v. 5). The 'I am' saying therefore sets the tone for the portrayal of the disciples in this discourse as well as the portrayal of Jesus himself.

In addition to 'remaining in' Jesus (μένειν ἐν, vv. 4, 5, 6, 7, 9), the emphasis of this discourse is on 'bearing fruit' (φέρειν καρπὸν, vv. 2, 4, 5, 8, 16).[4] The idea of pruning in order to bear more fruit comes directly from the vineyard imagery and yet its application to 'every

1. The connection with the Father is explicit in the 'I am' sayings of both chs. 14 and 15. While Jesus is the way to the Father in ch. 14, remaining in him enables the disciples to bear fruit which in turn glorifies the Father who is the vinedresser (vv. 1, 8).

2. Brown, *John*, II, p. 683, comments that 'it is...consonant with Johannine thought to present the Twelve who were the most intimate disciples of Jesus as the models of all Christians, both in their having been chosen and in their having been sent to bring the word to others'.

3. Lindars, *John*, p. 489.

4. Schnackenburg suggests that 'The bond between Jesus and his disciples... is given prominence by this image and further emphasised by the words μένειν ἐν' (*John*, III, p. 98).

branch of mine' (v. 2) already hints at a deeper meaning. This is confirmed by the word play between 'takes away' (αἴρει) and 'trims clean' or 'prunes' (καθαίρει, v. 2). For Brown 'it would seem that both verbs were chosen not because of their suitability for describing vineyard practices but for their applicability to Jesus and his followers'.[1] This word play has more to do with the Father's role as the vinedresser than Jesus' as the vine and yet, in the following verse, it is said to be Jesus' word that has made the disciples clean (καθαροί, v. 3). The reference to the word of Jesus recurs when he urges the disciples to 'remain in' his words (v. 8). In this context 'the word which I have spoken to you' (τὸν λόγον, v. 3) and 'my words' (τὰ ῥήματά, v. 7) must refer to living in obedience to what Jesus has said.[2] The idea of being made clean picks up on themes present in the footwashing scene (cf. 13.10, 11) and further shows that ch. 15 belongs in this context.[3]

The discourse of the True Vine is also linked to the latter part of ch. 13 through the command to love (15.10, 12, 17). This theme of love is developed in ch. 15 under the idea of bearing fruit. In ch. 14 Jesus says 'If you love me, you will keep my commandments' (v. 15). In ch. 15 Jesus reverses the same statement, 'If you keep my commandments, you will abide in my love' (v. 10).[4] The fact that the themes of love and obedience developed in ch. 14 occur again in the context of the vine, shows the continuity of thought between the farewell discourses. This continuity is strengthened by the repetition in the vine discourse (vv. 7, 16) of the promise that those who 'remain in' Jesus can ask whatever they wish and it will be done for them (14.13).

---

1. Brown, *John*, II, p. 660.

2. Although this occurrence of 'word' (τὸν λόγον, v. 3) is distinct from the λόγος of the Prologue, there is a connection. It is only because Jesus speaks what the Father speaks that he can declare the disciples clean (cf. v. 15). Brown (*John*, II, p. 660) regards Logos here as meaning 'the whole of Jesus' teaching'; also Lindars, *John*, pp. 488-89. Bultmann sees the disciples' purity as lying 'in the Revealer's word and in that alone' (*John*, p. 534); Schnackenburg correctly sees Logos here as defined by λελάληκα, 'through the discourse of Jesus, which contains life and spirit (6.63), the disciples, who have received it in faith into themselves, have been made clean' (*John*, III, p. 98).

3. Cf. D.J. Hawkins, 'Orthodoxy and Heresy in John 10.1-21 and 15.1-17', *EvQ* 47 (1975), p. 212.

4. Beasley-Murray, *John*, p. 274: 'The commands of Christ laid on those who would remain in his love (v. 10) are comprehended in the command to love one another'.

The reason that Jesus speaks these words to his disciples is given explicitly at the conclusion to the first section of the discourse: 'These things I have spoken to you, that my joy may be in you, and that your joy may be full' (v. 11). Just as the Gospel is written so that the readers may believe and that believing they may have life (20.31), so Jesus' words are spoken here that the narrative audience may have joy. In other words, Jesus speaks so that the disciples may join (or, more precisely, may receive) his conceptual point of view. Presumably they are written down so that the reader may do the same.[1] Jesus' point of view is one that is full of joy. If the disciples, and with them the readers, obey his commands just as he obeys the Father's commands, the joy which Jesus has will be in them. Such joy ultimately derives from the command to remain in Jesus who is the True Vine and the source of their fruitfulness. This same theme of joy is resumed later in the farewell discourse where Jesus again promises that anything they ask the Father in his name will be granted (16.22-24).

It was suggested above that the 'I am' sayings of John 15 function in a similar way to those of John 10.[2] There the first five verses consisted of a 'parable' ($\pi\alpha\rho\text{ο}\iota\mu\acute{\iota}\alpha$, 10.6), which was explained by Jesus as he applied certain concepts of the parable to himself. The similarities between the two chapters prompt Beasley-Murray, following Brown, to acknowledge that 'Vv. 1-6 consist of a *masal*, a kind of parable that finds exposition and application in vv. 7-17, much as the 'parable' of the Shepherd and his flock in 10.1-5 is developed in the discourse of 10.6-18.'[3] However, while accepting the similarities between the two discourses, it is not as easy in John 15 to separate the 'parable' from its interpretation.[4] Jesus already begins to explain and apply the image of

---

1. Cf. Hinrichs, *Ich Bin*, pp. 76, 77.

2. Hinrichs (*Ich Bin*, p. 78) suggests that the 'I am' sayings of Jn 10 and 15 show a further similarity in that they are the only truly 'allegorical' uses of ἐγώ εἰμι in John. For Hinrichs allegory is marked by the application of a parable ($\pi\alpha\rho\text{ο}\iota\mu\acute{\iota}\alpha$) to Jesus by means of ἐγώ εἰμι (cf. p. 77). Earlier (p. 52), he distinguishes between the 'tautegorical', the 'symbolical' and the 'allegorical' use of 'I am'. Thus the 'I am' saying on the lake is 'symbolical', the 'I am' in the bread of life discourse is 'tautegorical' (following Schweizer, *Ego Eimi*, p. 167, who regards all the 'I am' sayings with an image not as 'simile, nor allegory, nor symbolic speech' but as 'real speech').

3. Beasley-Murray, *John*, p. 269. This seems to contradict Beasley-Murray's preference for a break at v. 11. Brown, *John*, II, p. 668.

4. Cf. Carson, *John*, p. 510; also Hinrichs, *Ich Bin*, p. 78.

the vine in vv. 3 and 4 and, as has been argued above, the 'parable' does not completely end in v. 6. In ch. 15, Jesus opens the parable with the claim to be the Vine. In ch. 10, it is not until after the parable has been related that Jesus identifies himself with any aspect of it. Despite these differences, in both discourses the exposition of the image is developed further through the repetition of the 'I am' sayings. This leads the reader to compare the two sayings and to notice the similar way in which Jesus applies an image to himself by means of ἐγώ εἰμι.

The terms which Jesus uses within the parable of the vine are explained within the passage and the implications for the disciples are clear.[1] The image of the True Vine concerns both Jesus' relationship with his disciples and the consequences of that relationship in their lives.[2] Although it is implied that the vine gives life (for without it the branches wither, v. 6), the emphasis in this 'parable' is on fruit bearing.[3] Those branches that do not bear fruit are 'cast' out (v. 6). It is only then that they wither and are burned. Jesus as the Vine offers the disciples the ability to live a fruitful life which is in turn explained in terms of loving each other. The emphasis of this 'I am' saying is on Jesus as the one who enables the

---

1. Hinrichs, *Ich Bin*, p. 76: 'The image is interpreted in the context. It is a question of remaining in Jesus and the remaining of his word or his words in the audience (v. 7).'

2. Lindars (*John*, p. 488) suggests the Eucharistic words as the immediate setting for the allegory. Cf. A. Jaubert, 'L'image de la vigne (Jean 15)', in F. Christ, *Oikonomia: Festschrift O. Cullmann* (Hamburg: Reich, 1975), p. 99. The Eucharistic language does not, however, seem to match the allegory itself, in which 'there is no hint of believers drinking the fruit of the vine (cf. Mt. 26.29; Mk. 14.25; Lk. 22.18); indeed there is no mention of wine at all, still less a connection with Jesus' blood' (Carson, *John*, p. 511). Instead, Bultmann (*John*, p. 530) is correct to emphasize that the focus is on 'the tree itself with its shoots...' Besides, the Last Supper as described in John does not mention the institution of the Eucharist. For the reader to apply the concepts involved in the Lord's Supper to the Parable here is to read too much into the self-explanatory image that Jesus uses. Rather, as Barrett suggests, 'The truth is that John is speaking of the union of believers with Christ, apart from whom they can do nothing. This union, originating in his initiative and sealed by his death on their behalf, is completed by the believers' responsive love and obedience, and is the essence of Christianity' (*John*, p. 470).

3. Schnackenburg, *John*, III, p. 98, notes: 'It is...fully in accordance with Semitic and eastern thought, in that it is concerned with the utilitarian value of the vine (cf. the parable of the barren fig-tree, Lk 13.6-9). The vine therefore appears here above all as a fruit-producing plant and not—or at least not primarily—as a life-bearing one.'

disciples to glorify the Father by bearing fruit (v. 8) and not on the fact that he gives life. His role as life-giver is emphasized elsewhere (cf. 6.35-58; 10.9; 11.25; 14.6).

Even though the terms within the 'parable' of John 15 are to a large extent self-explanatory, the study of background material below must ask if any material is implied by the text which would help explain why this image is used of Jesus here. The above study has already set some criteria for deciding what material may be in view. The emphasis of the parable on fruit-bearing, rather than life, suggests that any background material should involve this concept. In addition, the application of the image of the vine to Jesus must make sense of the adjective accompanying it. When Jesus claims to be 'the true vine' (ἡ ἄμπελος ἡ ἀληθινὴ) the reader must at once decide the nuance of the word 'true'. This is particularly so, since 'the addition of the words ἡ ἀληθινὴ is striking, because they are emphasised by being placed after the noun'.[1] A study of background material must therefore ask in what way Jesus can claim to be the 'true' vine. Is Jesus contrasted 'with whatever also claims to be the "vine"'?[2] Or, do the words of Jesus suggest a particular vine, which is fulfilled or even replaced in him? While the rest of the discourse makes no reference to other claimants to this title (contrast Jn 10) but concerns the disciples' relationship to Jesus, the use of this adjective may suggest that Jesus' claim is in some way polemical, contrasting him with another vine.

In this study, the use of ἐγώ εἰμι in John 15 has been seen to draw attention to the dominant character of Jesus. The narrative audience is entirely absent from the text, merely listening, with the reader, to Jesus' words. These words, including the 'I am' sayings, are spoken to bring joy to Jesus' hearers. By obedience to Jesus' commands and by remaining in the Vine, the audience can participate in that joy which belongs to Jesus. As well as the dominant theme of the Vine which is directly linked with the use of ἐγώ εἰμι, the 'I am' saying is the source of Jesus' command to remain in him which, with the command to bear fruit, becomes another dominant theme of the discourse. The imagery that is applied to Jesus by means of 'I am' is therefore both the source and the foundation for the other themes of the discourse.

---

1.   Schnackenburg, *John*, III, p. 97.
2.   Bultmann, *John*, p. 530.

9. *John 18: The Arrest (18.5, 6)*

The opening words of ch. 18 make a clear and characteristic break from what has gone before.[1] Having finished praying, Jesus now crosses the Kidron valley with the disciples (v. 1). This narrative comment reminds the reader of Jesus' earlier invitation to depart (14.31) which now is finally realized.[2] The explanation that Jesus knows all that will befall him (v. 4) is also reminiscent of the similar comment before the footwashing scene (13.1, 3).[3] Immediately before Jesus' arrest, he has prayed for his glorification in his final hour (17.1, 4, 5) as well as for the protection of the disciples from evil (17.15). This chapter is therefore set in the context of the fulfilment of Jesus' hour.

Jn 18.1-27 can be broken down into three sections (vv. 1-11; vv. 12-18; vv. 19-27), each of which is concluded by a paragraph involving Simon Peter (vv. 10, 11; vv. 15-18; vv. 25-27).[4] It is clear that 18.1-11 forms a unit, though it is closely connected with the trial of Jesus that follows (vv. 12-27).[5] Verses 12-14 act as a transition to the trial before the high priest which ends in v. 27.[6] Though the present study is concerned with the function of ἐγώ εἰμι in Jesus' encounter with Judas and the authorities (vv. 1-9), it will also encompass Peter's attempt to

---

1. See the narrative comments in 13.21 and 17.1, as well as the way in which Jesus' own discourse is structured in 14.25; 16.1, 4b, 12, 25. Cf. Schnackenburg, *John*, III, p. 221; Barrett, *John*, p. 517.

2. There is no need here to discuss whether this opening phrase suggests that ch. 18 once immediately followed ch. 14. The fact that the content of ch. 18 fits well after the prayer of Jesus in ch. 17 (see below) suggests that if ch. 14 once immediately preceded ch. 18 without a break, chs. 15–17 must be seen as a redactional addition to the original form of the Gospel rather than a displacement from elsewhere. As it stands, however, the delay between Jesus' invitation to depart and his actual departure serves as a literary device which emphasizes the importance of Jesus' final words.

3. Cf. Lindars, *John*, p. 540.

4. Cf. Brown, *John*, II, p. 802; also C.H. Giblin, 'Confrontations in John 18.1-27' *Bib* 65 (2, 1984), pp. 220-29, who sees Peter's role in terms of confrontation.

5. Beasley-Murray, *John*, p. 321; Brown, *John*, II, p. 802; and Schnackenburg, *John*, III, p. 220. Giblin (*Confrontations*, pp. 211-12) sees the passion narrative in terms of 'movement in the narrative. Careful attention to entrances and exits distinguishes the staging of the Johannine passion narrative. John's use of them helps articulate a grouping of five scenes (18.1-11; 18.12-27; 18.28-19.6a; 19.6b-37; 19.38-42).' On this analysis the Passion narrative can be seen as a large unit, like an act of a play, where the action from one scene leads directly into the next.

6. So Brown, *John*, II, p. 813.

defend Jesus (vv. 10, 11). Reference will only be made where relevant to the rest of this larger unit.

The action of vv. 1-9 can be seen to centre around Jesus' self-declaration in vv. 5, 6 and 8.[1] The scene dramatically focuses on the encounter between Jesus and Judas.[2] Jesus commands the action in v. 1. Judas commands the action in vv. 2 and 3.[3] Jesus takes over again in verse 4.[4] Jesus declares himself in v. 5 at which Judas's presence is re-emphasized before Jesus' self-declaration is reiterated by the narrator (v. 6) and then repeated by Jesus himself (v. 8). The narrator's words 'Judas, who betrayed him, was standing there with him' are the last mention of Jesus' betrayer.

Thus the arrest scene can be divided in terms of Jesus' final encounter with Judas his betrayer. Jesus boldly confronts his adversaries in a section which is dominated by the phrase ἐγώ εἰμι.

v. 1	Jesus leads the disciples to the garden.
vv. 2, 3	Judas leads the soldiers to the garden.
vv. 4, 5a	Jesus confronts his captors and identifies himself: ἐγώ εἰμι.
[v. 5b	Judas is in their midst.
v. 6	The reaction to Jesus' self identification: ἐγώ εἰμι]
vv. 7, 8	Jesus again confronts his captors and identifies himself: ἐγώ εἰμι.
v. 9	Scripture is fulfilled

1. Beasley-Murray (*John*, p. 321), Brown (*John*, II, p. 813), Bultmann (*John*, p. 638), Schnackenburg (*John*, III, p. 220) and Giblin (*Confrontations*, p. 213) all regard vv. 1-3 as introductory to the main part of the section in which Jesus confronts his captors. It may be better to acknowledge that the action of these verses begins with Jesus' departure in v. 1 and Judas' initiative in v. 2 (see below) without denying that the main action takes place in vv. 4-9. Verses 1-3 are not merely introductory, nor merely a link to effect a change of geographical position on the part of Jesus, but, as will be seen below, they are an integral part of the build up to the confrontation between Jesus and Judas.

2. Giblin, *Confrontations*, p. 216: 'The whole ministry of Jesus seems to find its most critical moment in the passion narrative, beginning with this initial scene of confrontation'.

3. Note the emphatic repetition of Judas's name in v. 3 as well as his knowledge of where to find Jesus.

4. Note the similarity between the construction of vv. 3 and 4. 'So Judas, procuring a band ... [(ὁ οὖν Ἰούδας λαβὼν τὴν σπεῖραν ...)'; 'So Jesus, knowing all...('Ἰησοῦς οὖν εἰδὼς πάντα...).

Particular emphasis on the words ἐγώ εἰμι is provided by their three-fold repetition within the text as well as the peculiar reaction of the by-standers to Jesus' words.

An analysis of the structure of Jn 18.1-11 has shown that the scene of Jesus' arrest is dominated by his confrontation with Judas and the authorities. Judas is perhaps the most interesting character in these verses for it seems clear that he is deliberately compared and contrasted with the character of Jesus. In this dramatic scene Jesus is the leader of the disciples, while Judas is the leader of the band who come to arrest him.[1] Jesus goes forth across the Kidron valley leading his disciples (v. 1). Judas knows where Jesus would be (v. 2) and so he too leads the soldiers there (v. 3). The fact that Judas is the subject of the verb (ἔρχεται), while the band simply accompany him, suggests that Judas is the active leader of Jesus' opponents. Furthermore, it is Judas who procures (λαβών) this band of men to come and arrest Jesus.[2] Judas is thus perceived as the person who actively seeks to arrest Jesus. Of the disciples only Peter is named, as the one who tries to defend Jesus (v. 10). Of the captors only Malchus, Peter's victim, is identified. Thus there are two major characters, who dictate the action, Jesus and Judas; two minor characters, who are caught up in the action, Peter and Malchus; and two groups, the disciples and the 'band of soldiers and some officers from the chief priests and the Pharisees' (v. 3).

When the character of Jesus is examined in these verses, his authority becomes immediately apparent. Jesus does not passively accept his fate, but actively confronts his captors. He knows all that is to befall him (v. 4) and because of this omniscient perspective he takes the initiative.[3] While the first few verses depict Judas as the person in control of Jesus' arrest, in v. 4 Jesus takes the initiative away from the aggressors. He

---

1. Cf. Giblin, *Confrontations*, p. 216. Hinrichs (*Ich Bin*, p. 90) thinks that the emphasis is not on the encounter between Jesus and Judas, but between Jesus and the grouped representatives of the world.

2. Cf. Giblin, *Confrontations*, pp. 215-16.

3. Lindars, *John*, p. 540: '... the awe-inspiring effect of Jesus in what follows is prepared for by the note that he already knew what would result, so that he meets that situation with dignified calm'. Jesus' knowledge is contrasted with the knowledge of Judas which is temporal ('Judas knew the place', v. 2; Jesus knew 'all that was to befall him', v. 4). Jesus knows that the 'cup' which the Father has given him is the way of the cross and rebukes Peter for his rash action (v. 11). Because of this knowledge, Jesus confronts his aggressors and declares who he is (ἐγώ εἰμι, v. 4).

challenges them with the question 'Whom do you seek?'[1] When they reply that they are seeking Jesus of Nazareth he declares, through the words ἐγώ εἰμι, that he is the one whom they seek. In all this, Jesus is characterized as sovereign. His sovereignty in turn shows that the authority of Judas and his companions is ironically futile. These men came to Jesus with 'lanterns and torches and weapons' (v. 3), and by this thought that they were dictating the circumstances of his arrest. That Jesus himself, and not his captors, is in control becomes fully apparent by their reaction to his self-identification, 'I am he' (v. 6). This simple narrative comment, inserted after Jesus' first ἐγώ εἰμι, shows the irony of the situation.[2] Judas, who thought he was in control of Jesus' arrest, is overshadowed as Jesus confronts the group.[3] The active betrayer leaves the Gospel in a state of ignominy, powerless in the face of Jesus' sovereignty, standing passively among those who came to arrest Jesus. The rest of those who came to seek out Jesus 'drew back and fell to the ground' (v. 6).

While Jesus is characterized as sovereign, his sovereignty is again a submissive one. This is made clear in a comparison with Peter. Peter, like Judas, thinks that control is to be seized by force. Thus he reaches for his sword and strikes off Malchus's right ear. Jesus rebukes him, saying 'Put your sword into its sheath; shall I not drink the cup which the Father has given me?' (v. 11). Not only is Jesus submissive to his Father's will, but as a result he is also actively submissive to his captors (vv. 4, 8, 11) since this is his Father's will.[4]

---

1. Cf. Lindars, *John*, p. 540; Schnackenburg, *John*, III, p. 224; Barrett, *John*, p. 520; Brown, *John*, II, p. 809.

2. Lindars, *John*, p. 541: 'That John is building up to a climax is indicated by the words: Judas, who betrayed him, was standing with them. This is put in here specially to hold up the narrative, and make the repetition of v. 6 necessary. At the same time it is dramatically effective.'

3. Lindars, *John*, p. 541: 'Judas is confronted with the one whom he has betrayed, who foreknew that this would happen and told the disciples of it actually in his presence: "that when it does come to pass you may believe that I am he (*ego eimi*)." Thus the *ego eimi* here can be taken as a cross-reference to this verse in the Last Supper account, intended to call to mind the tragic irony of the situation.'

4. Schnackenburg, *John*, III, p. 227: 'The disciple lays about him violently, whereupon, Jesus, who possesses divine power and nevertheless gives himself up to his enemies, teaches Peter the lesson that God's will is supreme'. Brown, *John*, II, pp. 814, 818. See Jesus' comment in 10.17, 18: 'For this reason the Father loves me, because I lay down my life, that I may take it again. No one takes it from me, but I lay

The tension between Jesus' heavenly perspective and the earthly perspective of Peter creates further irony. In the light of his knowledge of events that are to befall him (v. 4), Jesus actively submits to the Father's will by declaring to his captors that he is the one they seek (vv. 5, 6, 8). Since Peter does not share this point of view, it appears to him that Jesus has lost control. Jesus' comment, 'Shall I not drink the cup which the Father has given me?' (v. 11), shows that his heavenly perspective is very different from Peter's worldly perspective. Peter's attempt to defend Jesus not only is ineffective, it also ironically shows that he does not share Jesus' heavenly perspective on events and so cannot see that his arrest is in accordance with the Father's will.[1]

Irony is also seen in the fact that Peter vainly tries to defend his master, while it is in fact his master who provides for Peter's safety (v. 8).[2] When Jesus repeats that he is Jesus of Nazareth (18.8), his ἐγώ εἰμι is adjoined to a request that the disciples should be allowed to go free. Thus, in declaring who he is, he partially fulfils his prayer to keep the disciples from the evil one (17.15; cf. 17.12; 6.39; 10.28).[3] The only person who has been lost to Jesus is the one of whom this had been foretold (17.12; cf. 13.18).

There could be no simpler nor more straightforward way for Jesus to identify himself to his captors than through the words 'I am'. Seldom are commentators so unanimous as to the fact that on one level these words of Jesus must be taken as a simple self-identification.[4] The text is clear: Jesus asks whom the band of men seek; they reply that it is Jesus

---

it down of my own accord. I have power to lay it down, and I have power to take it again; this charge I received from my Father.' Ironically, those who think they have come to take Jesus' life have no power, for it is he, himself, who lays it down.

1.   Giblin, *Confrontations*, p. 220: 'The rebuke to Peter serves to bring out not only Jesus' acceptance of the cup given him...but also Peter's lack of understanding regarding Jesus' messianic destiny.'

2.   Cf. Bultmann, *John*, p. 637; Barrett, *John*, pp. 520-21.

3.   Obviously this temporary safety from the authorities is not the entirety of what is involved in the disciples being kept. Ultimately this points to remaining in fellowship with him and with the Father and being raised up at the last day (6.39). However, the physical protection that Jesus offers the disciples at his arrest shows Jesus' concern for the well-being and protection of the disciples even at his darkest hour (cf. 19.25-27).

4.   Barrett, *John*, p. 520; Beasley-Murray, *John*, p. 322; Brown, *John*, II, p. 818; Bultmann, *John*, p. 639 n. 7; Lindars, *John*, p. 541; Schnackenburg, III, *John*, p. 224.

of Nazareth; and Jesus responds 'I am he' (v. 5).[1] On the level of v. 5, Jesus' declaration of who he is shows that he gives himself up to his captors out of his own volition. 'Jesus is not handed over powerless, but he is the one who surrenders himself and thereby proves his power.'[2] This deliberate action on the part of Jesus may well point the reader back to where he claimed (through the words ἐγώ εἰμι) to be the good shepherd and to lay down his life of his own accord (10.14, 15, 17, 18). However, the account of Jesus' arrest does not allow the reader to be fully satisfied with this definition of Jesus' 'I am'.

The narrator's repetition of ἐγώ εἰμι and the reaction of the onlookers to those words urges the reader to look for a double-meaning to the phrase 'I am'.[3] For, while it is clear that Jesus' words must be taken as self-identification, such a use in itself cannot explain the captors' peculiar reaction. Again the text may give an initial clue as to where the reader should look for information. The narrative comment at the end of v. 5 highlights the character of Judas and describes him as the one 'who

---

1.   The readings ὁ Ἰησοῦς ἐγώ εἰμι [א C L W] and ἐγώ εἰμι Ἰησοῦς [B(a)] should be rejected for the following reasons:

1.   Even when these words are to be taken as a simple self-identification on the part of Jesus, his name is superfluous since it has already been stated by the guards and would be understood.

2.   Neither of the two repeated occurrences of the words 'I am' have any manuscript support for the addition of 'Jesus'; this is especially relevant in the case of v. 6, where the narrative comment repeats Jesus' comment verbatim in order to explain the reaction of the onlookers.

3.   In the second variant, the addition of the word 'Jesus' can be explained either through dittography (where an abbreviation for 'Jesus' [IS] results from the first letters of the next word [εἰστήκει]) or through an attempt by a scribe to explain that Jesus was identifying himself in these words. Cf. Barrett, *John*, p. 520.

2.   Schnackenburg, *John*, III, p. 224; also Bultmann, *John*, p. 639.

3.   The deliberate repetition of the words ἐγώ εἰμι suggests that the emphasis should be on the words themselves. It is to the words ἐγώ εἰμι which Jesus' captors react and 'is not simply spontaneous astonishment' that Jesus should give himself up (Brown, *John*, II, p. 818). If the emphasis were on the reaction of the captors the narrator could have simply stated 'When Jesus said this...' Dodd likens this verse to the repetition of 'Your son will live' (ὁ υἱός σου ζῇ) in 4.50, 51, 53, saying 'In each place an expression entirely natural in the circumstances is given a special importance by a repetition which is sufficiently unnatural to draw the reader's attention' (*History*, p. 75 n. 2).

betrayed him'. The stark comment that Judas was among the captors when Jesus declared himself through the words ἐγώ εἰμι must surely point the reader back to Jesus' prediction of his betrayal in which he stated 'I tell you this now, before it takes place, that when it does take place you may believe that ἐγώ εἰμι' (13.19). Lindars comments that the narrative statement of v. 5 is 'dramatically effective' because:

> Judas is confronted with the one whom he has betrayed, who foreknew that this would happen and told the disciples of it in his presence...Thus the ego eimi here can be taken as a cross-reference to this verse in the Last Supper account [i.e.,13.19], intended to call to mind the tragic irony of the situation.[1]

This ἐγώ εἰμι therefore appears to be a reference to ch. 13 and shows that now is the time that Jesus' words there are to be fulfilled. As such this scene should lead the disciples to belief.

The use of ἐγώ εἰμι in Jesus' arrest scene may also point back to John 8. There Jesus claimed that his opponents would die in their sin unless they believed that ἐγώ εἰμι (8.24). Furthermore, it would be when they lifted up the Son of man that they would know that ἐγώ εἰμι (8.28). In ch. 18, Jesus identifies himself by the same words that had confused his opponents in the previous discussion about authority. Here too begins the Passion of Jesus, in which the Jewish authorities 'lift him up' on the cross. Although they attempt to do away with him, it is ironically his hour of glory (17.1-5). In this hour of glory Jesus' authority will be truly seen, for he has been given 'power over all flesh to give eternal life to all' whom God has given to him (17.2). The ἐγώ εἰμι in John 18 may therefore act as a cross-reference for the reader to its use in John 8 where Jesus claimed that he would be known in terms of ἐγώ εἰμι when he was exalted by his opponents but that would at the same time bring condemnation.

The phrase ἐγώ εἰμι has been used by Jesus in the Gospel on several occasions and has only once, in 8.58, provoked any surprising reaction on the part of his opponents. In ch. 8, Jesus' words provoked his opponents to anger and he was the one who 'drew back' ('Ιησοῦς δὲ ἐκρύβη καὶ ἐξῆλθεν ἐκ τοῦ ἱεροῦ, 8.59). In contrast, when Jesus utters the words 'I am' in 18.5-8, he deliberately makes himself known to his opponents and, rather than hiding himself from them, he hands himself over to them (vv. 8, 12). Here Jesus' words provoke his

---

1. Lindars, *John*, p. 541; also Schnackenburg, *John*, III, p. 224.

opponents to fear and they are the ones who 'draw back and fall to the ground' (ἀπῆλθον εἰς τὰ ὀπίσω καὶ ἔπεσαν χαμαί, v. 6). Despite the different reactions on the part of the narrative audience, in both instances it is precisely these surprising reactions to his utterance of the words ἐγώ εἰμι that alert the reader to look for a deeper meaning behind them. On at least one level it is clear that the use of ἐγώ εἰμι in John 18 draws the reader's attention to the other places where the phrase has been used, even though the previous occurrences may have been before a different narrative audience.

Although the above references to Jesus' 'I am' sayings elsewhere in John may help determine the force of the term for the reader, it is the soldiers and officers from the chief priests who react to Jesus' words here. The reader may well ask whether the words ἐγώ εἰμι would be understood by such people in a way that would explain their actions.[1] If the text of John 18 implies both a very simple and a very profound use of ἐγώ εἰμι when Jesus declares himself to his aggressors, the only clue the narrative gives to this double-meaning is the reaction of Jesus' narrative audience. The reader is expected to 'read between the lines' of the text and understand far more than is explicitly stated. It is significant that this final ἐγώ εἰμι alludes to several occurrences of the phrase elsewhere within the Gospel (8.24, 28, [58]; 10.14-18; 13.19). This occurrence, which in many ways fulfils the predictions of other occurrences of the term, takes the reader back to those occurrences to re-interpret them in the light of the reaction of the narrative audience to Jesus' words here. That the 'I am' is obviously here used to convey two meanings at one and the same time may also throw light on the earlier occurrences of the term. The way in which the self-declaration of Jesus in 18.5-8 is interpreted will automatically colour the use of ἐγώ εἰμι elsewhere in the Gospel, for it shows that the author of John can at one and the same time use 'I am' as a simple formula for identification and intend overtones of profound significance that are only explicit in this instance. It must be asked whether ἐγώ εἰμι is a term used with deliberate double-meaning as part of Johannine irony whereby a simple phrase can take on profound theological importance.[2]

1. It is possible, with Bultmann (*John*, p. 639) to regard this incident as miraculous, in which case it is not necessary for the band of men to understand why they fell back in this way (though it would still be comprehensible for the reader).

2. This occurs elsewhere on the lips of Jesus and on the lips of other characters. For example, the ironic questions of Nathanael (1.46); the Samaritan woman (4.12,

A literary study of the function of ἐγώ εἰμι in the arrest scene of Jesus has shown the important part the words play in the structure of this individual pericope. By the repetition of the words, attention is focused on Jesus and his self-identification. Furthermore, this scene occurs at an important point of the Gospel narrative. The arrest marks the beginning of Jesus' passion, and the words ἐγώ εἰμι show that Jesus willingly gives himself up to death. He, rather than the captors, is in control of his own destiny. Again the words ἐγώ εἰμι are accompanied by irony, for Judas thinks that he controls the arrest, but in fact Jesus does. The phrase ἐγώ εἰμι epitomizes the characterization of Jesus as the dominant character in this scene. Such dominance is due to the different perspective from which Jesus operates. Because he knows that this is his hour of glory, he goes to the cross willingly. Because Peter does not know this, he vainly tries to defend his master. Finally, it could be said that the words ἐγώ εἰμι actually function as a theme in these verses. Their threefold repetition at such a crucial stage of the Gospel and the mysterious reaction on the part of the narrative audience, forces the reader to ask whether the previous occurrences of the term were quite as straightforward as they first appeared. The questions raised by the reaction of Jesus' narrative audience to the words here encourages the reader to look for a deeper explanation to the simple words ἐγώ εἰμι.

cf. 4.25); the Jews (8.53); also Jesus' comment 'I and the Father are one' (10.30), where Jesus explains that his words are not blasphemous for the Scripture even regards the ones to whom God has spoken as gods (10.34-37). For a discussion of double-meaning within John, see W.D. Wead, 'The Johannine Double Meaning', *ResQ* 13 (1970), pp. 106-20.

Chapter 4

THE LITERARY FUNCTION OF ἐγώ εἰμι IN THE WHOLE GOSPEL:
SUMMARY AND IMPLICATIONS

1. *Summary*

Setting

The study of the literary function of ἐγώ εἰμι in the Gospel of John has
shown that the phrase is not restricted to any particular setting or
audience. It is common to the Book of Signs (Jn 1–11) as well as to the
Book of Glory (Jn 12–21). Nor can it be said that any particular form of
ἐγώ εἰμι saying is restricted to any particular setting. The 'I am' sayings
with a predicate are as characteristic of the Farewell discourses in the
presence of the disciples alone (14.6; 15.1, 5) as they are of Jesus' public
ministry (6.35-38; 8.12, [9.5]; 10.7, 9, 11, 14; 11.25). Likewise, the use
of ἐγώ εἰμι without an image is used in the presence of the disciples
alone (6.20; 13.19), in the presence of a complete stranger (4.26), in the
presence of Jesus' opponents (8.24, 28, 58) and in the presence of those
who come to arrest him (18.5-7). Sometimes the use of 'I am' is
specifically linked to a sign (6.35-58; 8.12; 11.25) and yet sometimes it is
hard to see any such link.[1] On occasions the use of the phrase may be
linked with a religious Feast (6.35-58; 8.12) while elsewhere such a link
is either tentative (ch. 10) or entirely lacking (11.25; 14.6; 15.1, 5).
Furthermore the use of 'I am' is not restricted to discourse (as in 6.35-
58; 10.7, 9, 11, 14; 15.1, 5). It may occur in debate with Jesus' opponents
(8.12, 18, 24, 58) or in private teaching (4.26; 11.25; 13.19) or in discussion with the disciples (14.6) or even as a declaration (6.20; 18.5-7).

The great variety of settings in which the words ἐγώ εἰμι are used by
the Johannine Jesus show that it is a phrase which pervades the whole
Gospel. It is restricted neither by audience nor by religious context.
Instead the words echo throughout the Gospel from Jesus' first

---

1.   Against Smalley, *Evangelist*, p. 91. See below.

declaration that he is the messiah of whom the Samaritan woman speaks to his dramatic arrest in which the utterance of the same words creates an astonishing response from Jesus' audience.

Structure

The use of ἐγώ εἰμι has been seen to be an integral part of the structure of many of the pericopes where the phrase appears. This occurs in various ways. The words may boldly introduce a section (8.12; 15.1) or form the climax and conclusion (4.26; 8.58); or a whole section of text may be formed around the words (ch. 8; 18.5, 6, 8); or it may be part of a structural link between two sections (13.19). Furthermore, a question or statement crucial to the debate is often resolved in a claim introduced by 'I am' (14.6 [answering v. 5]; also 4.26 [v. 10]; 8.58 [v. 53]; 11.25 [v. 24]). The ἐγώ εἰμι may in turn be linked with a sign in such a way that a miraculous work is re-interpreted in the light of what Jesus claims to be (6.35; 8.12 [9.5]; 11.25). As well as referring back (or forward) to one of Jesus' signs, ἐγώ εἰμι may apply to Jesus images that have already been mentioned in his teaching (6.35-38; 10.7, 9, 11, 14; 14.6) or entirely new images which are then further explained (15.1, 5). In all these occurrences 'I am' functions as an integral part of the unfolding narrative, sometimes in a very structured way (10.7, 9, 11, 14) and sometimes in a less obvious pattern (6.35, 48, 51). Although there is a place for distinguishing between occurrences of ἐγώ εἰμι in which a predicate is expressed and the other occurrences,[1] the use of ἐγώ εἰμι in chs. 6 and 8 suggests that there is a deliberate interaction between different forms of 'I am' sayings. In the past this interaction has easily been overlooked.[2]

Once the role played by ἐγώ εἰμι in individual pericopes has been studied, it may be asked whether the use of 'I am' forms a pattern in the Gospel as a whole. Such an attempt has been made by Smalley. Having discussed the 'I am' sayings which have a direct link with particular signs (6.35; 8.12; 11.25), he looks for links between the other ἐγώ εἰμι statements and the signs and discourses. He concludes that 'John's centre is to be found in seven signs, bound together with discourses and

---

1. See Chapter 5 §1 below.
2. Thus Schweizer, *Ego Eimi*, looks only at ἐγώ εἰμι with a predicate. J. Richter ('Ani Hu') and Harner (*'I am'*) only study ἐγώ εἰμι without. Brown (*John*, I, Appendix IV) and Zimmermann (*Das Absolute 'Ego Eimi'*) are rare in their acknowledgment of the interconnection of the different forms of 'I am'.

text-like sayings which expound various aspects of the theme of eternal life as that is to be found in and through Jesus Christ.'[1] He presents his readers with the following table, connecting each 'I am' saying with both a discourse and a sign:

Sign	Discourse	Saying 'I am'
1. Water into wine (2)	New life (3)	the true vine (15.1)
2. The official's son (4)	Water of life (4)	the way, and the truth, and the life (14.6)
3. The sick man (5)	Son, life-giver (6)	the door of the sheep (10.7)
4. The five thousand fed (6)	Bread of life (6) Spirit of life (7)	the bread of life(6.35)
5. The blind man (9)	Light of life (8)	the light of the world (8.12)
6. Lazarus (11)	Shepherd, life-giver (10)	the resurrection and the life (11.25)
7. The catch of fish (21)	Disciple life (14-16)	the good shepherd (10.11)[2]

Smalley is correct to see an overriding theme of life in the signs, discourses and 'I am' sayings. This is probably, however, more to do with the evangelist's purpose that the reader might find life in Jesus (20.31) than with a deliberate interdependence between them all. The unlikeliness of such an interdependence becomes apparent by Smalley's removal of the Shepherd discourse from the Shepherd saying in order to fit both into different parts of his schema. Life is one of the main themes (perhaps the theme) of the Gospel. As such it is not surprising that it is linked with John's characteristic features, since all of these are in accordance with the Gospel's overarching purpose to offer life to its readers. It may be tempting to seek a link between seven signs, seven discourses and seven 'I am' sayings, but such a temptation should be avoided except in the cases where such a link is explicit.[3]

Hinrichs approaches the question of structure in a different way. He thinks that the compositional principle on which John's Gospel is structured is a concentration on the word of Jesus.[4] In addition, he

1.   Smalley, *Evangelist*, p. 91. Brown (*John*, I, p. 534) also comments on the connection of the 'I am' sayings with the theme of eternal life.

2.   Smalley, *Evangelist*, pp. 91, 92.

3.   Painter (*Witness*, p. 38) is much more cautious in his view about whether the 'I am' sayings are to be linked with the signs in the structuring of the Gospel.

4.   Hinrichs, *Ich Bin*, pp. 16ff., 23ff.

thinks that the 'I am' sayings epitomize such a structural principle.[1] This means that the structural role of ἐγώ εἰμι is in the focus the words give to Jesus throughout the Gospel. Thus the statements of John the Baptist anticipate the 'I am' sayings of Jesus by their similar structure and yet the concentration remains on Jesus by the Gospel's reticence in applying the words ἐγώ εἰμι to anyone else.[2] For Hinrichs, the 'I am' sayings are therefore part of the Gospel's theological structuring principle which means that the traditional view of the Gospel as narrative should be called into question.[3] However, Hinrichs fails to work through exactly what this means in terms of the structure of the Gospel and how 'I am' may function in the Gospel as a whole.

How, then, do the 'I am' sayings fit into the structure of the Gospel? Like many of the major themes of John, they are interwoven in the fabric of the Gospel, gathering further meaning each time they occur. Because the 'I am' sayings also focus attention on the person of Jesus, each time the words occur they further reveal something of Jesus' role or identity so that the narrator's point of view first disclosed in the prologue is reinforced.

Though the first occurrence of ἐγώ εἰμι is strangely phrased, the reader may not see any hidden meaning in Jesus' words. However, as the words 'I am' become theologically loaded, especially when they provoke a strange reaction on the part of Jesus' narrative audience, the reader may be forced to ask whether that first occurrence was as straightforward as it initially appeared.[4] By the same words Jesus identifies himself on the lake and claims to be the Bread of Life. By the same words Jesus claims to be the Light of the World and then makes mysterious statements about his identity (8.24, 28) until the Jews finally take up stones to throw at him when he says 'Before Abraham was, I am' (8.58). At the same time the words ἐγώ εἰμι point forward to a future fulfilment (8.24, 28) and thus the reader is called to anticipate what it is about Jesus' exaltation on the cross which will reveal his identity in terms of ἐγώ εἰμι. The 'I am' of ch. 13 points forward to the

---

1.   Hinrichs, *Ich Bin*, p. 16.
2.   Hinrichs, *Ich Bin*, pp. 66, 67 sees 9.9 as redactional.
3.   Hinrichs, *Ich Bin*, p. 14.
4.   E.g. Carson (*John*, p. 276) who suggests that repeated reading of the Gospel by 'the thoughtful reader' may cause him or her to review the significance of 'I am' at 6.20, 'and wonder if this occurrence in v. 20 may not be an anticipation of a clearer self-disclosure by Jesus'.

betrayal and thereby simultaneously anticipates that of ch. 18. In this way the use of 'I am' in John 8 and 13 demands that the reader understand them in the context of the whole Gospel and especially of the betrayal and passion.

In addition, the very form of the 'I am' sayings calls for the reader to interpret them in the light of other similar sayings. Thus the words of 8.18 recall Jesus' words in 4.26. The ἐγώ εἰμι of ch. 14 is reminiscent in form to that of ch. 11, while the claim in ch. 15 occurs in the context of a parable and is thus reminiscent of ch. 10. The similarities between the different 'I am' sayings suggest that they should be interpreted in the light of one another and should perhaps be seen along the lines of the other christological themes of the Gospel. It is difficult, however, to determine a strict pattern to the way the 'I am' sayings develop in the Gospel as a whole, except that, by the time of Jesus' arrest the words have become a motif that the reader understands. The identity of Jesus revealed in this motif points forward to the cross and it is there that Jesus' opponents will ultimately see the significance of the words (8.28).

Characters and Characterization
Culpepper asserts that 'in John's narrative world the individuality of all the characters except Jesus is determined by their encounter with Jesus. The characters represent a continuum of responses to Jesus which exemplify misunderstandings the reader may share and responses one might make to the depiction of Jesus in the gospel.'[1] The use of ἐγώ εἰμι fits in with such a view of the characterization. By her questions, the Samaritan woman says more about Jesus than she imagines (vv. 12, 25). As her true character is revealed (vv. 16-18), so is that of Jesus (v. 19). In a statement containing ἐγώ εἰμι (4.26), Jesus reveals that the one with whom she speaks is the messiah of whom she speaks. Her characterization is a foil to the characterization of Jesus and draws out a declaration of his messiahship by means of ἐγώ εἰμι.[2]

In several other instances it is the response of characters to a statement by Jesus which prompts him to use the phrase ἐγώ εἰμι (6.33, 34; 11.23, 24; 14.4, 5).[3] By the words ἐγώ εἰμι ὁ ἄρτος τῆς ζωῆς, Jesus is

1. Culpepper, *Anatomy*, p. 104.
2. Cf. O'Day, *Revelation*, pp. 93-96, for the way that the text reveals the character of Jesus.
3. Cf. 8.24, 25 where it is the reverse; an ἐγώ εἰμι prompts a question from the Jews for it seems to veil the true identity of Jesus.

seen to be that bread which the crowd seeks (6.35). With these words Jesus switches the focus of the discussion from the bread which God gave through Moses to a revelation of himself. Jesus' person is characterized not only by the image of bread but by all the other images which he takes upon himself through the words ἐγώ εἰμι. 'Each serves in one way or another to enrich the disclosure of Jesus' identity.'[1] The centre of attention focuses on Jesus as he makes remarkable claims about himself and his mission.

It may justifiably be asked whether there is any development of the character of Jesus in the Gospel by the use of ἐγώ εἰμι. Culpepper states: 'In John the character of Jesus is static; it does not change. He only emerges more clearly as what he is from the beginning'.[2] To the extent that the identity of Jesus is revealed in ch. 1, how far can it be claimed that there is a true development of Jesus' character in the rest of the Gospel? Does the Gospel not simply reinforce what has already been introduced? Here a distinction needs to be made between characterization and identification/revelation. Just because Jesus' identity is revealed as early as ch. 1, this does not mean that there is no further characterization of the person of Jesus. It may be true that who Jesus is is encapsulated early in the Gospel. However, it is only in the outworking of the Gospel that Jesus' characterization is developed, albeit in accordance with the titles already revealed. Jesus could be identified as the Word (1.14), the Christ (1.17), the Lamb of God (1.29), the one who baptizes with the Holy Spirit (1.33) the king of Israel (1.49) and the Son of Man (1.51) and yet remain no more than a 'flat' character.[3] It is in interaction and discourse that Jesus' characterization is developed. Since 'characters are defined and shaped for the reader by what they do (action) and what they say (dialogue) as well as what is said about them by the narrator or other characters',[4] it is correct to talk about a development of Jesus' characterization even though this is also a reinforcement of what has already been stated about him.[5] After all 'virtually the whole

---

1. Culpepper, *Anatomy*, p. 109.
2. Culpepper, *Anatomy*, p. 103.
3. Forster (*Aspects*, p. 75) divides characters into 'flat' and 'round'. See below.
4. Culpepper, *Anatomy*, p. 7.
5. Thus Culpepper, *Anatomy*, p. 108: 'What Jesus says about himself and his mission progressively defines his relationship to the Father and exposes the blindness of others.'

gospel is devoted to what he says and how others react to him'.[1]

If it is correct to see a development of the characterization of Jesus in John's Gospel, it also correct to see the use of ἐγώ εἰμι as having a role in that development. Concerning flat characters, Forster states:

> In their purest form, they are constructed round a single idea or quality: when there is more than one factor in them, we get the beginning of the curve towards the round.[2]

From this point of view, as long as Jesus remains no more than a list of titles, his characterization remains incomplete and unconvincing. Yet 'the test of a round character is whether it is capable of surprising in a convincing way'.[3] In several of the occurrences of ἐγώ εἰμι Jesus surprises the narrative audience by claiming to be what they are looking for. Although the readers already know that Jesus is the Christ (1.17) when he encounters the Samaritan woman (4.26), they cannot fail to be surprised with the narrative audience when Jesus claims to be the bread which the crowd seeks (6.35; cf. 14.6). Likewise, readers are surprised with the disciples when Jesus states that he will be betrayed by one of them (13.18, 20) and yet they should not be surprised when it happens because both Scripture (v. 18) and he (v. 19) have predicted that it would happen. Even more surprising is his assertion that in this betrayal the disciples will come to know that ἐγώ εἰμι. Thus, the 'I am' sayings in John help in achieving a roundness in Jesus' character.

Irony

The use of ἐγώ εἰμι in the irony of John's Gospel has shown itself time and time again. The Samaritan woman expects a negative answer to her question 'Are you greater than our father Jacob?'(4.12). The Jews expect a negative answer to their question 'Are you greater than our father Abraham?' (8.54). To the former Jesus replies that he is the messiah (4.26), to the latter he answers the statement directly. 'Before Abraham was, I am' (8.58). The Samaritan woman does not realise that when she speaks of the messiah, she speaks to the messiah. The crowd do not realize that when they ask for the bread (6.34), that they are speaking with the one who is that bread (6.35). When Martha talks of the resurrection at the last day, she does not realize that she is speaking

---

1. Culpepper, *Anatomy*, p. 106.
2. Forster, *Aspects*, p. 75.
3. Forster, *Aspects*, p. 85.

with the one who can bring that resurrection into the present (11.24, 25). On the use of such irony in ch. 4, O'Day goes so far as to say that:

> As a result of John's use of irony to communicate the dynamics of revelation, the narrative does not mediate the revelation but is the revelation.[1]

The potential for irony reaches its peak in the 'I am' sayings without a predicate. The Jews do not understand who Jesus is when he claims that they will die in their sins unless they believe that ἐγώ εἰμι (8.24, 25). Here the potential for misunderstanding the term makes irony possible. The astute reader must recognize both the senselessness of the term when taken the way the Jews do and also the deeper meaning that the term may have in and of itself, in order to appreciate any irony.[2] The *double entendre* conveyed by the absolute use of 'I am' comes to its greatest expression in the arrest of Jesus when it is obvious that a mundane meaning is being played off against a far deeper meaning. It is only those who see both meanings who can appreciate the irony. A study of background material must attempt to define exactly what this deeper meaning may be.

Point of View

Culpepper argues that the narrator's point of view coincides with that of the character of Jesus.[3] He concludes that:

> The consonance between Jesus and the narrator is a result of the author's expression of his point of view through both his central character and his narrator.[4]

The point of view expressed through the ἐγώ εἰμι sayings has been seen to be closely linked with the characterization of Jesus. In connection with his 'I am' sayings, Jesus knows the future outcome of present actions (6.35; 8.12, 24, 28; 10.9; 11.25, 26; 13.19), and is also seen as pre-existent (8.58). He stands over the natural order when he appears to the disciples on the lake (6.20), when he heals the man born blind (9.5,

---

1. O'Day, *Revelation*, p. 92.
2. This observation has implications when looking for the potential background to understand the phrase ἐγώ εἰμι, for it can neither be taken in such a profound way as to eliminate the Jews' comment, nor in such a mundane way as to make Jesus' words in both vv. 24 and 28 meaningless.
3. Cf. Culpepper, *Anatomy*, p. 36. Cf. Davies, *Rhetoric*, pp. 38-39, for a similar discussion of Jesus' omniscient point of view.
4. Culpepper, *Anatomy*, p. 43.

6) and when he raises Lazarus (11.25). By the authority of what Jesus claims through ἐγώ εἰμι, he offers benefits which extend to eternal life (6.35; 8.12; 10.9, 14; 11.25, 26; 14.6; 15.5). The point of view expressed by the 'I am' sayings thus places Jesus beyond narrative time and space. When Jesus proclaims ἐγώ εἰμι he adopts a divine perspective.

The Implied Reader
To a certain extent all the above categories have shown the significance of ἐγώ εἰμι for the implied reader. This is particularly true of the use of irony in which one meaning is played off against another.[1] In this the reader is urged to adopt the heavenly point of view which is that of both the narrator and Jesus. In addition the use of ἐγώ εἰμι has often pointed beyond itself in order to be understood. This is especially seen in the two enigmatic sayings in John 8 and the one in 13.19 in which Jesus presents ἐγώ εἰμι as the content of knowledge or belief. The lack of predicate makes nonsense of a surface reading of the text and suggests that the implied reader knows the meaning of ἐγώ εἰμι as the content of belief. It must be the task of the background study in Chapters 6 and 7 below to determine exactly how this takes place and what precisely is implied by Jesus' words. At the same time the background study of 'I am' must explain the strange reactions that Jesus' words can cause on the part of his narrative audience but which the implied reader must understand. In such a study it may prove significant that Jesus' words are often stated in discussion with 'the Jews' and sometimes in the particular context of discussions about Jewish themes (Jacob in Jn 4; Moses in Jn 6; Abrahamic descent in Jn 8).[2] It may also prove significant that on certain occasions, Jesus specifically takes an Old Testament or Jewish concept upon himself by means of ἐγώ εἰμι (Jn 6.35-58 and Jn 11.25 respectively).

Links with Other Johannine Themes and Titles
As well as applying an Old Testament concept or a current Jewish expectation to Jesus, the ἐγώ εἰμι of John also takes some of the main themes of the Gospel and explicitly shows that Jesus is both the fulfilment and the embodiment of those themes. This is particularly seen in

---

1. Cf. Davies, *Rhetoric*, pp. 363-67, who deals with 'Irony' in her discussion of the 'Implied Readers'.
2. Davies (*Rhetoric*, pp. 354-57) argues that a knowledge of Scripture (and Jewish terms) is essential to understand the Fourth Gospel. She thus includes a discussion of Scripture under her discussion of the Implied Reader.

three of the 'I am' sayings which are predicated by themes that are introduced in the prologue of the Gospel.

John 8.12. In Jn 8.12, Jesus explicitly applies to himself the theme of light which applied to the Word of the prologue (1.4, 5, 9, 10). It is thus made clear to the reader that Jesus is the Word of which the prologue spoke. He is to be identified with the 'light of men' (1.4), 'the light that shines in the darkness' (1.5), and 'the true light that enlightens every man' (1.9). As such he is associated with the work of creation and yet rejected by it (1.10). Thus the 'I am' saying of 8.12 deliberately points the reader back to the prologue of the Gospel. The function of the 'I am' saying is to show that Jesus embodies and fulfils all that has been said of the Light (cf. Jn 3.16-21) as well as all that is yet to be said (cf. 12.34-36).

John 11.25. As well as applying to Jesus the current expectation of Martha concerning the resurrection, the 'I am' saying of 11.25 is also predicated by the term 'life'. This again is a theme first introduced in the prologue. As with 'light', so the concept of 'life' is explicitly linked with the Word (1.4). In an excursus on the concept of life in the Fourth Gospel Schnackenburg comments:

> The idea of life belongs indisputably to the core of John's theology and Gospel. The word field (ζωή, ζ. αἰώνιος, ζῆν, ζωοποιεῖν) is richly represented in the gospel and in 1 John, and is spread fairly evenly over chapters. The idea itself spreads into every area of Johannine theology and a comprehensive description would require a whole book.[1]

By combining the concept of life with the predicate 'resurrection', the type of resurrection to which Jesus' 'I am' saying ultimately points is defined. That Jesus is the Resurrection and the Life takes up the claim that he is 'the life that was the light of men' (1.5). He also embodies the 'eternal life' (3.15, 16, 36; 4.14; 5.24, 40 etc.) which he offers to others. The fact that Jesus claims to be the life also points forward to the summary of the Evangelist's purpose in writing (20.31). It is because Jesus is the Life that the readers of the Gospel are able to 'have life in his name'. It is because Jesus is the Life that he can claim that the reason he came is, 'that they may have life and have it abundantly' (10.10b).

---

1.   Schnackenburg, *John*, II, p. 352.

> This life of God which Christ embodies in his person, reveals and imparts
> in his words (6.63, 68) and manifests and symbolically transfers in his
> signs (healings, feedings, raising), is given to all who accept his revelation
> and believe in him.[1]

The same theme is again applied to Jesus in the saying of 14.6. Although
not every 'I am' saying can be linked directly with this theme of life,
Smalley is correct to draw attention to this theme in connection with
John's use of 'I am' (See 'Structure' above).

John 14.6. In addition to the theme of 'life' in John 14.6, the idea of
truth is applied to Jesus. This again was one of the characteristics of the
Word in the Prologue, who was described as 'full of grace and truth'
(1.14). Truth, like Life, is one of the major themes of the Gospel.

> He [the writer] uses ἀλήθεια 25 times, over against once in Matthew and
> 3 times each in Mark and Luke (47 times in Paul, and 20 times in the
> Johannine Epistles). There is a similar disparity with the adjectives
> ἀληθής (14 times in John, once each in Matthew and Mark, not in Luke,
> 4 times in Paul), and ἀληθινός (9 times in John, not in Matthew or Mark,
> once each in Luke and Paul). The concept plainly matters to John.[2]

With such an emphasis on the concept of truth within the Gospel as a
whole, it is significant that Jesus takes this concept and applies it to
himself in the 'I am' saying of 14.6. The character of Jesus portrayed
through the 'I am' sayings thus identifies himself with three of the major
themes of the Gospel. As a result, truth, life and light are not simply
transmitted by Jesus but are embodied by him.[3]

Other 'I Am' Sayings. The Johannine themes of life and truth are closely
connected with 'I am' elsewhere in John. The former is seen in the 'the
Bread of Life' (6.35ff.) and 'the Light of life' (8.12b). It is also implicit in
the sayings of John 10, in which salvation is offered (10.9) and Jesus'
purpose is seen to be to give life to his sheep (10.10, 11, 15). The latter
is connected with the 'true vine' (15.1; cf. 10.11, 14) as well as with the
'true bread' (6.32).

Above it was noted that all of the 'I am' sayings with a predicate in
some way expressed the theme of life. However, it has also been observed

---

1. Schnackenburg, *John*, II, p. 355.
2. Morris, *John*, p. 294. For a brief discussion of John's use of 'truth' see
Morris, *John*, pp. 293-296. For a detailed discussion see De La Potterie, *La Vérité*.
3. Cf. Bultmann, *Theology*, p. 19.

from the above studies that ἐγώ εἰμι is used in the context of many of the other major themes of the Gospel as well. Below is an attempt to list how extensive this interaction is.

Themes linked directly with 'I am'

'I am' and belief	6.35; 8.24; 11.25; 13.19
'I am' and knowledge	8.28; 10.14; (14.6, 7)
'I am' and witness	(8.12, 13), 8.18
'I am' and truth	(4.24, 26); (8.17, 18); 14.6
'I am' and origin/destiny	6.40, 51; [7.34]; (8.23, 24)
'I am' and time: past and future	8.58; 13.19; [7.34]
'I am' and the Father	8.18; 8.28; 10.14; 14.6; 15.1
'I am' and Titles	4.26; 8.28
'I am' and Authority	(6.20); 8.28; (18.5, 6)[1]

The above table confirms the suggestion that ἐγώ εἰμι is interwoven into the main themes of the Gospel, and should be treated in a similar way to some of those themes. The different themes permeate the different forms of 'I am' saying and further suggest the interaction of each saying, not only with the other sayings but also with the main fabric of the Gospel.

2. *Conclusion and Implications*

At the conclusion of these literary studies, it may be asked how such an investigation relates to previous studies of ἐγώ εἰμι. First of all, it should be noted that these studies confirm the conclusions of Schweizer about the essential unity of the Gospel.[2] Both the interaction between the different 'I am' sayings and the similarities in form and function suggest that it is right to treat the Gospel as a literary unity.[3] This also confirms that Hinrichs is right to see the 'I am' sayings as part of the theological construction of the book.[4] 'I am' is an essential part of the Gospel,

---

1.   The references with square brackets indicate an εἰμὶ ἐγώ and have not been studied above. The references in normal brackets are those in which there is a link in the context of the 'I am' saying, but not in the saying itself.

2.   Schweizer, *Ego Eimi*, p. 108.

3.   This is not to say that the Evangelist did not use sources, nor even that there have been no redactions in the history of the text as it now stands, but simply that the final form of the text makes sense in its own right and that the way that ἐγώ εἰμι is interwoven into the various themes of this text has created a literary unity in which the 'I am' sayings play an important role. Cf. Schweizer, *Ego Eimi*, pp. 108-109.

4.   Hinrichs, *Ich Bin*, pp. 16ff. Whether as a result he is correct to suggest that

interacting with other christological themes.

Secondly, this approach has confirmed Zimmermann's view[1] that there is a closer interaction between the predicated and the unpredicated sayings than has been granted in studies which have created a strict separation based on form.[2] Thus the 'I am' saying of Jn 6.20 is still reverberating in the reader's mind when Jesus pronounces that he is the bread from heaven (6.35).[3] Likewise, the ἐγώ εἰμι which opens the sharp debate of ch. 8 returns in different forms and with ever increasing implications until the climax of 8.58.[4] The interaction of the different sayings is shown through the structuring of individual pericopes as well as in the interweaving of the 'I am' sayings with various Johannine themes. Such interaction can only be seen when ἐγώ εἰμι is studied in the context of the Gospel as a whole and so underlines the strength of an approach which begins an investigation of ἐγώ εἰμι in John's Gospel with a literary analysis of how the words function. The interaction among different uses of ἐγώ εἰμι does not rule out the importance of form in the study of 'I am' but stresses that differences in form should not become the basis for a strict segregation of the sayings. Zimmermann also suggests that the interaction of these sayings is such that, if the background to the ἐγώ εἰμι sayings with a predicate is in Mandaism, the background to the ἐγώ εἰμι without a predicate should be seen there too.[5]

the Gospel should no longer be regarded as determined by narrative is not so clear. To suggest that John is structured by theological concerns does not of itself rule out a narrative form.

1. Zimmermann, *Das Absolute 'Ego Eimi'*, pp. 271-72. Whether this takes the form of an 'outworking' of the unpredicated sayings in the sayings with an image as Zimmermann suggests (p. 273) will be addressed below. Cf. also Brown (*John*, I, Appendix IV, pp. 534-38) who suggests, 'the absolute use of 'I am' in John is the basis for the other uses, in particular for the use... with a nominal predicate' (p. 537).

2. Cf. Schweizer, *Ego Eimi*, does not even address the 'I am' sayings without an image; Harner's study, 'I am', does the reverse.

3. Cf. Schnackenburg, *John*, II, p. 11.

4. This is confirmed by Davies (*Rhetoric*, pp. 82-87) who links the 'I am' saying of 8.58 with Jesus' claim to be the Light of the World. However, her sugges-tion that 'the Light of the World' should be taken as the predicate to the 'I am' saying in 8.58 is surely taking this link too far.

5. Zimmermann, *Das Absolute 'Ego Eimi'*, p. 58. Also Brown, *John*, I, p. 537: 'If the background of the use in class (1) [i.e., the absolute use] is the OT and Palestinian Judaism, we may well suspect the same for class (3) [i.e., the use with a predicate nominative/image]'. Against this Schulz argues that a similarity in form

These literary studies have shown the dominance of Jesus as the main character of the Gospel. The 'I am' sayings are an integral part of the characterization of the Johannine Jesus and thus confirm the work of Hinrichs which emphasizes the concentration on Jesus' words which is brought about by the use of ἐγώ εἰμι.[1] Jesus interacts with the reader, as with the narrative audience, through the 'I am' sayings, and so his true character is made known in a deeper way than can be done by the initial list of titles in ch. 1. By the ἐγώ εἰμι of Jesus the reader is helped to come to a correct belief about who he is as well as a correct belief about what he does. In this way the 'I am' sayings are seen to be essential to the purpose of the Gospel. The 'I am' sayings also reflect a point of view which goes beyond the narrative time (cf. esp. 8.58) and thus imply a divine perspective. It is therefore important to seek a background which further explains the dominance that ἐγώ εἰμι gives to the Johannine Jesus as well as to ask what audience such a use of 'I am' assumes. This is especially true since there is an enigma surrounding the absolute ἐγώ εἰμι which urges the reader to look beyond the text of John in order to understand the term. Furthermore the only explicit indicators of the author's conceptual/theological world view in the context of ἐγώ εἰμι are Jewish ones: our father Jacob (4.12), discussion about Jerusalem (4.20ff.); the Passover, the Feast of the Jews (6.4) our fathers (6.31), Scripture quotation and Moses (6.31, 32); Abraham (ch. 8), your law and Scripture quotation (8.17). This suggests that it makes sense to look to this Jewish milieu for understanding of ἐγώ εἰμι.

Finally, the important role that the Johannine 'I am' sayings play in John's use of irony should be noted. While Harner has noted the possible double-meaning in some of the 'I am' sayings without a predicate,[2] no one seems to have raised the role of ἐγώ εἰμι in John's use of irony.[3] It would be expected that the constant use of irony in connection with the

does not necessarily imply a similarity in background. Therefore he is able to see different backgrounds at play even with the 'I am' sayings with a predicate (*Komposition*, p. 92; cf. pp. 93, 128-31). See Chapter 5 §1 below.

1. Hinrichs, *Ich Bin*, esp. p. 16.
2. Harner, *'I am'*, pp. 43, 44 (on 8.24, 28); p. 45 (on 18.5, 6, 8), p. 47 (on 4.26). Cf. also Brown, *John*, I, p. 534, on 18.5, 6, 8.
3. Though Duke comes close in his discussion of the metaphorical nature of the 'I am' sayings: 'Metaphor is like irony in that it says one thing and means another, presenting two levels of meaning which the reader must entertain at once. In metaphor, however, the two levels are deeply identified; in irony they are in opposition' (*Irony*, pp. 143-44; cf. also pp. 139-42).

use of ἐγώ εἰμι may be reflected in the function of the background material for these sayings. All the above points concerning the literary function of ἐγώ εἰμι will help the critic delimit a correct background for understanding the words. In this way the text itself becomes the judge of what may or may not be seen as a legitimate parallel.

Part III

THE WORLD BEHIND THE TEXT:
THE HISTORICAL BACKGROUND TO 'I AM'

Chapter 5

DELIMITING THE SOURCES

1. *Implications of Form:*
Predicated and Unpredicated 'I Am' Sayings

The preceding literary studies have emphasized the similarities in literary
function among all the occurrences of ἐγώ εἰμι in John's Gospel. It is,
however, clear that there are different forms of 'I am' saying which
have distinct functions. An immediate distinction can be made between
those 'I am' sayings with an image (e.g. 'I am the bread of life/the light
of the world/the good shepherd' etc.) and the rest (e.g. 'I who speak to
you am he'/'Before Abraham was I am'). The former type of saying can
be easily recognized by its formulaic structure as well as by the similarity
of function in all the sayings where Jesus applies an image or concept to
himself as a predicate to the words 'I am.' The other 'I am' sayings have
generally been regarded as 'absolute' or 'predicateless' occurrences of 'I
am' in which Jesus' words have no grammatical predicate (even though
a predicate may be implied from the wider context). It will be argued
below that such a simple formal categorization of John's 'I am' sayings
into those with a predicate and those without may in fact be misleading.
A new categorization of those 'I am' sayings without an image is needed
before the question of background material can be addressed.

'I am' Sayings with an Image
The ἐγώ εἰμι statements with an image all have a similar structure. This
structure is so formulaic that each saying can be divided into several
constitutive parts. In this, Schulz's observations are helpful:

> The Johannine *Ego eimi* saying falls
> A. into the 'self-predication', the 'revelation word' or the 'predication of
> ontological nature', and
> B. into the 'soteriological sub-clause' or the 'word of promise'.[1]

---

1. Schulz, *Komposition*, p. 86.

In other words, Schulz sees two main parts to such 'I am' sayings: the saying itself and a sub-clause which shows the soteriological implications of Jesus' claim. According to Schulz, there is an additional subdivision of the sayings in which:

> A breaks down further into:
>   i. the presentation (ἐγώ and εἰμί) and
>   ii. the 'image-word' with the article.
> B can be divided into:
>   i. the 'invitation' or 'call to decision' and
>   ii. the promise for the believers as the assurance of salvation or the 'threat against unbelievers.'[1]

Although not every ἐγώ εἰμι saying with an image has all these characteristics, their formulaic structure identifies them as a peculiar Johannine feature.[2] Schulz cites 10.11, 14 and 15.1 as examples of ἐγώ εἰμι where there is a self-predication but no invitation, promise or threat, and 14.6 as an example of self-predication with a threat. The rest of the 'I am' sayings with an image (6.35, 51; 8.12; 11.25; 15.5) fall into his category of invitation and promise.[3] This remarkably formulaic construction has led these statements to be studied separately from the other occurrences of ἐγώ εἰμι in John and has led scholars to search in different spheres of thought to explain the meaning and background of each type of saying. Yet it will be argued below that, despite the difference in form, the 'I am' sayings with an image share the same conceptual background as those without.

The formulaic nature of the 'I am' sayings with an image in John and those in Mandaism has led scholars to ask whether the Mandaean sayings aid a correct understanding of the sayings in John.[4] However,

1. Schulz, *Komposition*, p. 87. Schulz is following the works of Schweizer, *Ego Eimi*, p. 33; Kundzins, *Die Ego-Eimi-Spruche*, pp. 192, 221; H. Becker, *Die Reden des Johannesevangeliums und der Stil der gnostischen Offenbarungsrede* (FRLANT, 68; Göttingen: Vandenhoeck & Ruprecht, 1956), pp. 54, 56; and H. Blauert, 'Die Bedeutung der Zeit in der johanneischen Theologie. Eine Untersuchung an Hand von Joh 1-17 unter besonderer Berücksichtigung des literarkritischen Problems' (dissertation, Tübingen, 1953).

2. Cf. Schweizer, *Ego Eimi*, p. 9.

3. Schulz, *Komposition*, p. 88. Though the predicateless ἐγώ εἰμι of 8.24 does not belong to these 'I am' sayings with an image, it also fits into the category of self-predication with a threat. This further confirms an interaction should be seen between the forms.

4. This does not necessarily mean that John was dependent on the sayings of

such formal similarities may prove deceptive and must be balanced against the dissimilarity in function between the sayings of John and those of Mandaism. On the one hand, the Mandaean texts are a monologue in which the revealer remains unchallenged.[1] On the other hand, the 'I am' sayings in John often occur in dialogue where they can be challenged by the narrative audience (6.41, 52; 8.13, 19, 25, 59; [10.19]; 14.8). While the 'I am' sayings of Mandaism are spoken in a universal context, the ἐγώ εἰμι sayings in John are spoken by a narrative character with a specific narrative audience in view.[2] The Gospel form, in which ἐγώ εἰμι is spoken by one of the main characters, gives the words a provocative function which is lacking in the Gnostic/Mandaean parallels.[3]

John 8 is a particularly good example of the fact that, despite formal similarities with the claim to be the Light of the World (v. 12), the 'I am' sayings of Mandaism do not fit well with the ἐγώ εἰμι of John. The Mandaean sayings do not possess a form without a predicate. They could therefore only be in mind for the saying in 8.12 and not for the related use of ἐγώ εἰμι in the rest of the chapter. This point is confirmed by the fact that Schweizer does not take sufficient account of the context of Jn 8.12, preferring to see it in the context of the other

Mandaism as such. It could be that John was only indirectly dependent on such sayings (i.e., they both drew on a common source) or that any interdependence is from John to Mandaism and not vice verse. The 'I am' sayings of Mandaism would then still be the closest formal parallels to John and would imply a common heritage. This would in turn mean that the sayings of Mandaism may helpfully be used to help the interpretation of John. Thus Schweizer thinks that 'a religious-historical relationship especially with the Mandaean sources is in fact conceivable and makes many concepts of our "image-sayings" understandable so that Mandaean texts closely related to our image-sayings are apparently based on ancient tradition' (*Ego Eimi*, pp. 111-12).

1. Cf. eg., the 'light' sayings in Lidzbarski, *Ginza*, pp. 58ff.

2. Against this see Hinrichs, *Ich Bin*, pp. 76-77, on the unspecific nature of the narrative audience in the farewell discourses.

3. The Gospel genre, which relates the 'I am' sayings in the context of Jesus' earthly ministry means that they function in a very different way even to such 'I am' sayings as occur in Revelation where Jesus' authority to speak in this way is never challenged by the narrative audience. If the Mandaean sayings are to be ruled out as background material for the Johannine sayings on the basis of this different function, the sayings of Revelation should be ruled out on the same basis. Cf. Kundzins (*Die Ego-Eimi-Spruche*, pp. 105-106) who is nevertheless correct to point out the similar soteriological function of the sayings in John and Revelation which is lacking in many of the Mandaean parallels.

'light-sayings' of the Gospel.[1] Bultmann, too, cannot fit the saying with its context and thus places it with 12.44ff. where the theme of light is taken up again.[2] The literary study of ἐγώ εἰμι in John 8 showed that this separation is unjustified, and that the saying of 8.12 does indeed fit its context. Only if a separation of the saying of 8.12 from its context in John 8 is allowed can the formal parallels from Mandaism be brought into consideration. The immediate debate on a matter of Jewish law also raises doubts about looking to non-Jewish parallels to explain the opening 'I am' saying. If Mandaism is still to be maintained as a possible source of the background to the 'I am' saying in 8.12, then it must be allowed that it has been so adapted to fit into the context of the debate and of the other 'I am' sayings that the function it possesses in John is vastly different from that in Mandaism.

Furthermore, Kundzins argues that the form of the 'I am' sayings with an image in John itself suggests that they are earlier than those of Mandaism. Although some Mandaean sayings contain a soteriological sub-clause, he points out that such 'I am' sayings in Mandaism are 'long-winded'. Combined with uncertainty of the existence of a pre-Johannine Mandaism,[3] the succinctness of the Johannine ἐγώ εἰμι formulae[4] also favours the priority of the Johannine sayings. Thus Kundzins argues that the subordinate clause of the Johannine sayings which offers eternal life displays original thought and is not dependent on the 'long-winded' clauses of Mandaism.[5]

It may be concluded that the Johannine 'I am' sayings with an image are constructed in a strictly formulaic way. However, the context, function and interaction with the other ἐγώ εἰμι sayings of the Gospel suggest that the correct background by which they should be interpreted is not that of Mandaism. Furthermore, they display signs of priority over the Mandaean sayings. It will be argued below that the rigid formulation

---

1. Schweizer, *Ego Eimi*, p. 164. Schweizer is right to point out that the theme of light is 'scattered' throughout the Gospel (p. 163) and its use elsewhere in the Gospel should be taken into account when interpreting the saying of Jn 8. Yet to ignore the immediate context of the saying is even more culpable than to ignore those sayings.

2. Bultmann, *John*, p. 342. In his statement that 'Jesus describes himself as the Revealer' in this saying, there is a hint that Bultmann also has the Gnostic/Mandaean revealers in mind as the background to the saying. He certainly thinks that the term 'light of life' (v. 12b) has such an origin.

3. See Chapter 1, Section 1b on Gnosticism and Mandaism above.

4. Kundzins, *Die Ego-Eimi-Spruche*, p. 104.

5. Kundzins, *Die Ego-Eimi-Spruche*, p. 102.

of John's saying directs the implied reader to the correct background of the 'I am' sayings. However, rather than pointing the reader to formal parallels (i.e., parallel uses of 'I am'), it will be argued that John's use of 'I am' with an image points to conceptual parallels. This means that it is parallels to the images accompanying ἐγώ εἰμι which provide the key to the correct background and not the words 'I am' themselves.

'I Am' Sayings without an Image
In previous studies of 'I am' it has been argued that those sayings without an image also display the features of a fixed formula. Wetter believes that these 'I am' sayings should be seen in a strictly formulaic way. He points out that within the Gospel are certain things that were expected to be understood by the first readers, the meaning of which is only hinted at.[1] He believes that this is in fact deliberate, and that only the 'initiated' can fully understand these expressions. It must be an old formula which was comprehensible to the initiates but is unclear and perhaps insoluble to the 'uninitiated'. He concludes that

> we are concerned here with a stereotyped expression which has been used with an apparently technical meaning by the author of the Gospel; a meaning which also appears to be so familiar to his readers that he does not even need to elucidate it.[2]

The literary studies above have confirmed that Wetter is correct in the fact that the 'I am' sayings appear to have a meaning so familiar to the implied reader that the author does not need to elucidate it.[3] He is also correct to emphasize that it is only when the Son of man has been

1. Wetter, 'Ich bin es', p. 224.
2. Wetter, 'Ich bin es', p. 226; J. Richter (*Ani Hu*, p. 17) uses this belief that ἐγώ εἰμι has a technical meaning in the New Testament as justification for seeking a parallel in the 'Ani Hu' of the Old Testament.
3. Whether this was intended only to be understood by initiates within John's community (Wetter ['Ich bin es', pp. 225-26; cf. pp. 233-34] seems to have the idea of Gnostic initiates) or whether it would have been understood by the first century world at large is a matter that cannot be so easily concluded. The study of background material below will seek to determine what conceptual point of view the readers were expected to share with the author so that they could share his/her understanding of the words ἐγώ εἰμι. Cf. Duke, *Irony*, p. 147, who suggests that some forms of irony would be more effective if they were only understood by insiders. Cf. also W.A. Meeks, 'The Man from Heaven in Johannine Sectarianism' *JBL* 91 (1972), pp. 69-70. See also discussion of John's possible audience below.

exalted that the true meaning of the phrase will become apparent to the Jews.[1] However, the weakness in Wetter's argument is in the fact that he assigns ἐγώ εἰμι to a 'stereotyped expression', a fixed formula.[2] The danger of thinking of ἐγώ εἰμι as a single formula, is that, either those occurrences of 'I am' which do not fit in with a specific formula are dismissed, or else the meaning of the formula is imposed upon every occurrence of the phrase irrespective of whether it fits.[3] For Wetter, the only certain occurrences of this secret formula in John are those found in 8.24, 28 and 13.19.[4] Thus the sayings of 8.58 and 18.5, 6, 8, which demand an explanation because of the narrative audience's reaction, are not considered as part of his formula.

In maintaining that ἐγώ εἰμι is the New Testament revelation formula, Zimmermann comes to a similar conclusion concerning the formulaic nature of the words. He states that:

> The places in the N.T. in which it [i.e. the formula] is encountered with certainty (Jn. 8.24, 28; 13.19; Mk 13.6) show that it only occurs as the saying of Christ, or, in Mk 13.6 is placed by him in the mouth of the ψευδόχριστοι.[5]

By regarding only these limited occurrences of ἐγώ εἰμι as definite encounters with the revelation formula, Zimmermann also by-passes the uses of 'I am' that do not fit into his formal categorization. To regard the absolute ἐγώ εἰμι as the New Testament revelation-formula is therefore misleading since Zimmermann ignores the occurrences of ἐγώ εἰμι that do not fit his pattern. While it may be true that ἐγώ εἰμι is sometimes used as a revelation-formula in the New Testament, John's use of ἐγώ εἰμι is itself so varied that only three out of the ten occurrences without an image actually accord with Zimmermann's formula.

Although the 'I am' sayings with an image seem to suggest a fixed formula is being used, it has already been intimated that those without

---

1. Wetter, 'Ich bin es', p. 226.

2. Cf. Wetter, 'Ich bin es', p. 224.

3. C.L.B. Plumb (*ΕΓΩ ΕΙΜΙ*) comes remarkably close to this in thinking that every time ἐγώ εἰμι occurs in the Gospel of John it represents a theophany. Despite the many parallels that Plumb brings from the Old Testament and the Targums to support his case, it is far from certain that this is so in every occurrence of the phrase in John. Stauffer (*Jesus*, pp. 142-59) may also be accused of imposing similar meaning on every occurrence of ἐγώ εἰμι.

4. Cf. Wetter, 'Ich bin es', pp. 228-29.

5. Zimmermann, *Das Absolute 'Ego Eimi'*, p. 54.

such an image are by no means so clear. This is further shown by the fact that there is no consensus on which occurrences of ἐγώ εἰμι should be regarded as 'absolute' sayings. Thus Brown sees 8.24, 28, 58 and 13.19 as the absolute use with no predicate and 6.20 as a use where the predicate is implied but not expressed, while 18.5ff. is a use with a double meaning and 4.26 is excluded.[1] Schnackenburg regards 6.20; 8.24, 28, 58; 13.19 and 18.5, 6, 8 as absolute occurrences, yet he sees 6.20 and 18.5, 6, 8 as essentially different since they are primarily identifying formulae (and therefore imply a predicate).[2] Harner argues that, while 8.58 and 13.19 are absolute, the occurrences in 8.24 and 28, along with 18.5, 6, 8; 4.26 and 6.20, contain a double meaning in which a predicate is implied on at least one level.[3]

In view of the somewhat confusing criteria that have been used to determine whether ἐγώ εἰμι should be regarded as 'absolute' or not, it may be helpful to categorise these 'I am' sayings strictly in terms of their form. Once this has been done it will be possible to determine whether there is a correlation between function and form.

These 'I am' sayings without an image fit into three main categories of form:

1.   Those sayings combined with the definite article and a present participle:
4.26:   ἐγώ εἰμι, ὁ **λαλῶν** σοι
8.18:   ἐγώ εἰμι, ὁ **μαρτυρῶν** περὶ ἐμαυτοῦ...

2.   Those sayings which are grammatically absolute and in which the words ἐγώ εἰμι stand alone:
a.   8.58   πρὶν Ἀβραὰμ γενέσθαι **ἐγώ εἰμι**.
b.   6.20   **ἐγώ εἰμι**· μὴ φοβεῖσθε
18.4-8   Ἰησοῦς...λέγει αὐτοῖς· Τίνα ζητεῖτε; ἀπεκρίθησαν αὐτῷ· Ἰησοῦν τὸν Ναζωραῖον. λεγει αὐτοῖς, **Ἐγώ εἰμι**...ὡς οὖν εἶπεν αὐτοῖς· **Ἐγώ εἰμι**, ἀπῆλθον εἰς τὰ ὀπίσω καὶ ἔπεσαν χαμαί. πάλιν οὖν ἐπηρώτησεν αὐτούς· τίνα ζητεῖτε; οἱ δὲ εἶπαν·

---

1.   Brown, *John*, I, pp. 533-34. Here Brown does not include 8.18, though he refers to Charlier's interpretation of it as a reference to divinity in his comments, *John*, I, p. 341. For a reference to 4.26 see his comment, *John*, I, p. 172.

2.   Schnackenburg, *John*, II, p. 80.

3.   Harner, *'I am'*, pp. 37-48. Harner follows Bultmann in suggesting that Son of man may be the predicate for 8.28, but wishes to see an absolute use at the same time.

Ἰησοῦν τὸν Ναζωραῖον. ἀπεκρίθη Ἰησοῦς εἶπον ὑμῖν ὅτι ἐγώ εἰμι[1]

3. Those sayings which are grammatically absolute and which stand in a ὅτι clause to express future fulfilment:

8.24 ἐὰν γὰρ μὴ πιστεύσητε **ὅτι ἐγώ εἰμι**, ἀποθανεῖσθε ἐν ταῖς ἁμαρτίαις ὑμῶν.

8.28 ὅταν ὑψώσητε τὸν υἱὸν τοῦ ἀνθρώπου, τότε γνώσεσθε **ὅτι ἐγώ εἰμι**...

13.19 ἀπ᾽ ἄρτι λέγω ὑμῖν πρὸ τοῦ γενέσθαι, ἵνα πιστεύσητε ὅταν γένηται ὅτι ἐγώ εἰμι..

These three formal distinctions may prove more helpful in the categorization of the 'I am' sayings without a predicate nominative than the traditional discussion of whether they have a predicate (explicit or implied).

By comparing the form of these sayings it becomes clear that there is not one fixed formula. Rather there are three formal variations. By the fact that the participial clause acts as a predicate, the first category of sayings, to which 4.26 and 8.18 belong, seems to create a formal link between the 'I am' sayings with a predicate nominative (image) and those without. On the other hand, the second and third categories of 'I am' sayings are grammatically absolute (whether a predicate can be implied from the context or not).[2] Even within the second category,

---

1. Ὅτι ἐγώ εἰμι here differs formally from those instances above where it occurs in a phrase regarding the future. Here it is simply reporting what has happened and is a result clause rather than a purpose clause. This does not rule out the fact that the reader may be meant to call to mind the other 'I am' sayings at this point of the narrative, and indeed even to see a beginning of the fulfilment of these sayings in 8.24, 28; 13.19.

2. To the second and third categories of form (i.e. those ἐγώ εἰμι sayings without any predicate), it may be possible to add another. This is the reversed use of the words ἐγώ and εἰμι in conjunction with ὅπου. These sayings are seldom placed among the 'I am' sayings but, in the light of the diversity of form seen in the above sayings may not be out of place here (cf. Brown, *John*, I, p. 314). If the ἐγώ εἰμι sayings without a predicate are not so formulaic as has often been assumed, then it may be that the occurrences where the words are inverted because of an accompanying ὅπου should also be included. These sayings occur at 7.34, 36; 12.26; 14.3; 17.24. Further study is needed to determine whether such sayings should be included among the Johannine ἐγώ εἰμι sayings. However, if this form is accepted as one of John's ἐγώ εἰμι sayings, it would also be necessary to ask whether every occurrence of ἐγώ in the vicinity of εἰμι should also be included among the 'I am' sayings. This

where the words ἐγώ εἰμι stand alone, it is possible to see a distinction between the saying of 8.58 and the other two. In 8.58 ἐγώ εἰμι is in formal contrast to the verb γενέσθαι, while in 6.20 and 18.5, 6, 8 the words stand as a phrase in their own right. In the third category ἐγώ εἰμι stands within a ὅτι clause which points to future fulfilment. It is this category which Wetter and Zimmermann regard as a formula. However, the variation in the presentation of 'I am' when not accompanied by an image suggests that to designate the words ἐγώ εἰμι on their own as a 'revelation-formula' may be too simplistic, since it is clear that the 'formula' has several distinct forms.

While John's use of ἐγώ εἰμι without a predicate is very varied in form, this does not of itself rule out a background which understood ἐγώ εἰμι as a fixed formula. The literary study of 'I am' in John showed time and again that it was being used on more than one level. It may be therefore that a background, where the mere utterance of the words ἐγώ εἰμι had great significance, is deliberately played off against a less loaded use of the term. However, the Rabbinic interpretation, where *'ani hu'* (אני הוא) has become such a fixed formula that the mere utterance of it would represent blasphemy,[1] does not easily fit the way 'I am' without a predicate is used in John. If a rabbinic interpretation is meant to be seen behind Jesus' words in Jn 8.24 and 28, it is surprising that it is the Jews who then ask 'Who are you?' (8.25). They would be the ones most likely to understand the rabbinic implications. If the words ἐγώ εἰμι were to be understood as a name for God here, then the reaction of v. 59 would be expected here. Instead, the Jews simply ask 'Who are you?' A hostile reaction would be expected again in v. 28, but there the reaction is positive to the extent that many of these Jews put their faith in Jesus. Thus, although such an interpretation is possible, it seems that it could only be brought into play on the two occasions where there is an explicit reaction to the words of Jesus (8.58 and 18.5-8), but not in the highly problematic sayings of 8.24, 28 and 13.19.[2] It

is highly unlikely and would surely lessen the significance of the phrase ἐγώ εἰμι. However, see Freed, *1.20 and 4.25*, who regards John the Baptist's words in Jn 1.20 as an occurrence of the formula.

1. See Dodd and Stauffer [ch. 1.2]. Cf. also Zimmermann's quotation of a rabbinic story in which a rabbi gets upset at his student who introduces himself as 'I' (*Das Absolute 'Ego Eimi'*, p. 269). Cf. J. Ashton, *Understanding the Fourth Gospel* (Oxford: Oxford University Press, 1990), pp. 141-47.

2. It is these sayings, which provoke no hostile reaction on the part of Jesus'

should also be noted here that even the reaction of the Jews to the ἐγώ εἰμι in Jn 8.58 cannot simply be explained as a reaction to the Hebrew term *'ani hu'* as a name for God. Even if such an interpretation is implicit, the emphasis in this verse is on the difference between the verb γενεεσθαι and the verb εἰμί. The tension between the tense of the two verbs would be lost if the reader was only meant to see the utterance of a divine name here.

It would therefore be better to look for a background for these sayings which also contains the variations of form which occur in John. It may be that in finding such a background, further light will be shed on both the function and meaning of the sayings in John. It will be argued below that such a background is found in the Isaianic use of *'ani hu'* which parallels the Johannine use of ἐγώ εἰμι both in its function and in its formulation.

Conclusion

It may be concluded that there is a clear distinction between the formulaic 'I am' sayings with an image and the varying forms of the other 'I am' sayings. However, the distinction between those 'I am' sayings with an image and those without is not so rigid as to deny the interaction which occurs between them in the Gospel. This interaction is such that it suggests a similar conceptual background by which the different sayings may be understood. Although the 'I am' sayings with a predicate nominative are formulaic, they do not function in the same way as the formally similar Mandaean sayings. Besides, if the different 'I am' sayings in John share the same conceptual background, Mandaism is ruled out as a possibility since it does not possess an absolute 'I am'. Finally, it has been argued that a background which demands that the 'I am' sayings without an image be understood in a strictly formulaic way is in danger of excluding those sayings that do not fit such a formula. It would therefore be best to look for a background which can accommodate the images which accompany ἐγώ εἰμι as well as the different forms of 'I am' sayings without an image. It will be argued below that the Old Testament provides just such a background.

narrative audience, which Zimmermann wishes to regard as definite (i.e., unambiguous) uses of the revelation formula (p. 171, above).

2. *Implications of Function: The Characterization of Jesus*

Bultmann attempted to define the 'I am' sayings in John according to their function within the text rather than their form. He suggested that the 'I am' sayings could be assigned four functions, all of which answered different questions about the person of Jesus:

1. The 'presentation formula', which replies to the question: 'Who are you?' By the use of ἐγώ εἰμι the speaker introduces himself as so and so; here ἐγώ is the subject...It is used as a sacred formula in the ancient Orient: the God who appears introduces himself by it, cp. Gen. 17.1: 'The Lord appeared to Abram and said to him, 'I am El Shaddai...'

2. The 'qualificatory formula', which answers the question: 'What are you?', to which the answer is 'I am that and that', or 'I am the sort of man who...' Here too ἐγώ is subject...Isa. 44.6: 'I am the first and the last, and apart from me there is no God'; 44.24: 'I am Jahweh, who made all things'.

3. The 'identification formula', in which the speaker identifies himself with another person or object. Here too ἐγώ is the subject...

4. The 'recognition formula', which is to be distinguished from the others in the fact that ἐγώ is the predicate. For it answers the question: 'Who is the one who is expected, asked for, spoken to?' to which the reply is 'I am he'.[1]

At a first glance this appears to be a very useful way of distinguishing the various 'I am' sayings in the Gospel and the different roles they play. However, the fact that Bultmann assigns 6.35, 41, 48, 51; 8.12; 10.7, 9, 11, 14; 15.1, 5 to the recognition formula, on the grounds that 'in the context of the Gospel the ἐγώ is strongly stressed and is always

---

1. Bultmann, *John*, pp. 225-26 n. 3. Bultmann's definitions have been very influential. J. Richter takes them on board for his study of the absolute ἐγώ εἰμι in the New Testament, adding John 9.9 and 18.5ff. as identification formulae ('Ani Hu', pp. 64, 65) while he regards 8.24, 28, 58 and 13.19 as proclamation formulae (pp. 68-74). Beasley-Murray, too (*John*, p. 89) seems to regard Bultmann's definitions as the best way of looking at ἐγώ εἰμι when he refers his readers without further comment to the footnote already cited. See Ashton, *Understanding*, p. 184 n. 50, who rightly comments: 'By classing most of the "I am" sayings as "recognition formulae"...he [Bultmann] empties them of any real content'.

contrasted with a false or pretended revelation', shows the weakness of his distinctions.[1] For it can hardly be the case that ἐγώ is the predicate in all of these, unless the term 'predicate' loses all its grammatical meaning.[2] For Bultmann the other two 'I am' sayings with an image (11.25; 14.6) are 'probably identification formulae', although it is uncertain precisely with whom or with what Jesus is identifying himself.[3] Since 8.24 provokes the question 'Who are you?', it seems that Bultmann would assign this to 'presentation'. At the same time, he wishes the ἐγώ εἰμι to mean 'that he is everything which he claimed to be',[4] which would seem to make it more of a recognition formula. He takes 8.28 as an identification of Jesus with the title Son of Man, while at the same time reflecting the saying of 8.24. For Bultmann, the use of ἐγώ εἰμι in 8.58 appears to be a special instance of the phrase, which is in no way connected with 'the ἐγώ εἰμι statements of the revelation discourses'.[5] Rather, 'the ἐγώ which Jesus speaks as the Revealer is the "I" of the eternal Logos, which was in the beginning, the "I" of the eternal God himself'.[6] This seems to imply that Bultmann regards this saying as an identification formula, which identifies Jesus with the Logos and with God. However, he seems to dismiss such a suggestion, saying, 'we should...reject the view that ἐγώ εἰμι means "I (Jesus) am God" i.e., that the sentence identifies Jesus with God'.[7] It appears therefore that Bultmann sees the use of ἐγώ εἰμι in 8.58 as a unique instance of the phrase which does not fit with his categories of function.[8] The occurrences of ἐγώ εἰμι in

1. Bultmann, *John*, pp. 225-26 n. 3.

2. Surely it is not the Johannine context, but Bultmann's disposition to see such Mandaean sayings as 'the Ambassador of Light am I' [*R. Ginza* II, pp. 64, 17ff.] as background, which leads him to see ἐγώ as the predicate in the majority of the Johannine 'I am' sayings. See the 'light' sayings in Lidzbarski, *Ginza*, pp. 58ff.

3. Bultmann, *John*, p. 226.

4. Bultmann, *John*, p. 349.

5. Bultmann, *John*, p. 327 n. 4.

6. Bultmann, *John*, p. 327.

7. Bultmann, *John*, p. 327 n. 5.

8. Bultmann (*John*, pp. 327-28 n. 5) is wrong to suggest that 'after πρὶν Ἀβρ.[αάμ]γενέσθαι the stress must be on the subject ἐγώ', for it is surely not the contrast between Jesus and Abraham, but the contrast between Abraham 'having become' and Jesus 'being' that is the primary emphasis of this verse. It is not just a contrast between two people but a contrast in natures which is important. However, against this, see Davies, *Rhetoric*, p. 86.

4.26; 8.18, 23 and 18.5-6, 8 are dismissed because they are profane uses of the term.[1]

Bultmann's belief, that the majority of the 'I am' sayings with a predicate should be seen in contrast to other claimants, is rightly questioned by Kundzins who asks whether an 'I am' saying in John *always* implies such a contrast. He also asks whether even the presence of ἀληθινός necessarily implies a contrast.[2] He points to the examples of 4.26 and 14.6 where Jesus uses ἐγώ εἰμι in such a way that the primary reference of Jesus' words is certainly not one of contrast. In the first instance, Jesus claims to be the messiah of whom the Samaritan woman speaks. In the second he takes up Thomas's objection: πῶς οἴδαμεν τήν ὁδόν (14.5);[3] Jesus *is* the way of which Thomas speaks. Although there is a contrast between Jesus and the bread that came down from heaven at the time of Moses (6.49, 50), it is clear that the function of the 'I am' sayings in Jn 6.35, 41, 48, 51 is to identify Jesus with that bread of which the Jews spoke (cf. 6.34). Likewise, while there is a contrast with the thieves and robbers who have come before (10.1, 8), one of the functions in the text of the ἐγώ εἰμι sayings in John 10 is to identify Jesus with certain features of the parable which opens the chapter.

Therefore the implications of the function of the various ἐγώ εἰμι sayings in John need to be redefined in a way which allows each saying to perform more than one function. In order to achieve this, I propose that the 'I am' sayings with an image should be seen as emphasizing Jesus' identity in relation to his *role* (for others), while the other 'I am' sayings should be seen as emphasizing Jesus' *identity* in itself. In other

1. Bultmann, *John*, p. 226. This is particularly surprising since Bultmann is at pains to show the many profane parallels of the formula when citing background material. The idea that these sayings should be dismissed as profane when dealing with John's use of ἐγώ εἰμι seems to make no sense in the light of their contexts: 4.26 at the very least identifies Jesus as the messiah; 8.18 could easily be seen in terms of qualification: 'I am the one who witnesses about myself'; and 18.5-6 cannot be dismissed as a profane formula without first explaining why such a formula should provoke such a response.

2. Kundzins, *Die Ego-Eimi-Spruche*, p. 99.

3. Kundzins, *Die Ego-Eimi-Spruche*, p. 100. Cf. also Brown, who thinks that since Bultmann regards 11.25 and 14.6 as identification formulae, they cannot be 'primarily a contrast with another's claim to be the resurrection, the life, the way and the truth' (*John*, I, p. 534). Brown continues 'it is also probable that the five statements that Bultmann attributes to (d) [*recognition formulae*] have features that belong to (c) [*identification formulae*] as well'.

words, while the 'I am' sayings without a predicate are primarily concerned with *who Jesus is*, those with a predicate are primarily concerned
with what Jesus does. At the same time the Gospel displays a relationship between who Jesus is and what he does so that what he does also
reveals his identity, his essential character. Conversely who Jesus is is
revealed in what he does. It is only because of who Jesus is that he is
able to fulfil the role which he has.

It is clear that the 'I am' sayings with a predicate focus on Jesus' role.
As Brown comments:

> The stress in all these 'I am' statements is not exclusively on the 'I', for
> Jesus also wishes to give emphasis to the predicate which tells something
> of his role. The predicate is not an essential definition or description of
> Jesus in himself; it is more a description of what he is in relation to man.[1]

Just as Jesus is the Bread of Life (6.35, 41, 48, 51) because he offers
nourishment (cf. 6.51), so he is the Light of the world (8.12) because he
brings light. Jesus is the Good Shepherd (10.7, 9) in as much as he does
not act like those who have come before, but instead cares for his
disciples. It is because these 'I am' sayings with a predicate concern
Jesus' role, that they are accompanied by a sub-clause which offers life.
Jesus' role as the Resurrection and the Life (11.25) means that those
who come to him will not perish. Jesus' role as the Vine means that
those who remain in him will bear fruit (15.5). Jesus' role as the Way
has an exclusive emphasis, which means that no one can come to the
Father except through Jesus (14.6).

On the other hand, the 'I am' sayings without a predicate seem to
emphasize Jesus' identity. These sayings are therefore primarily in terms
of who Jesus is, rather than what he does. Jesus is the messiah whom the
Samaritan woman expects (4.26). It is he who walks to the disciples on
the water (6.20). The literary study of ch. 8 emphasized that there too, it
is the question of Jesus' identity which is at issue. The Jews will know
who Jesus is when it is too late (8.24, 28). When the soldiers come to

---

1. Brown, *John*, I, p. 534. Brown's wording suggests that he is deliberately
rejecting Bultmann's assertion that 'ἐγώ is strongly stressed' (Bultmann, *John*,
pp. 225-26 n. 3). Brown, *John*, I, p. 534, continues 'In his mission Jesus is the source
of eternal life for men ("vine", "life", "resurrection"); he is the means through
whom men find life ("way", "gate"); he leads men to life ("shepherd"); he reveals
to men the truth ("truth") which nourishes their life ("bread")'. Cf. also Brown,
John, I, p. 269. Schnackenburg, *John*, II, p. 80: 'All the images, in other words, are
interpreted as referring to the significance of Jesus Christ for believers'.

arrest Jesus, he again declares his identity with the words ἐγώ εἰμι (18.5, 6, 8). In these passages the emphasis is on the 'I', and Jesus does reveal something about his essence. As Schnackenburg states: 'All these passages are linked by Jesus' claim to a totally unique mode of being which transcends human categories'.[1] The idea that the absolute ἐγώ εἰμι concerns Jesus' identity will be further elucidated below in the light of the Old Testament parallels to the term and the way those parallels are used in John.

Zimmermann seems to take a similar point of view concerning the function of the different 'I am' sayings. He argues that the predicated 'I am' sayings are an unfolding of the absolute ἐγώ εἰμι.[2] He thinks that the absolute 'I am' is an extension of the Old Testament revelation formula in which God is made known. For Zimmermann, Jesus is the revealer of God.[3] In other words, the absolute ἐγώ εἰμι talks of Jesus' identity. The 'I am' sayings with a predicate, on the other hand, display what Jesus is in regard to humanity (i.e., his role).[4] Yet the two are intimately related: 'Not only is his gift inseparable from him, the giver, it is identical with him. He gives the living bread by giving himself (6.35); he not only brings the light, he is it (8.12).'[5] The following may be concluded from this brief study of the function of ἐγώ εἰμι in John's Gospel: if the predicated ἐγώ εἰμι of John emphasizes the role of Jesus, while the unpredicated ἐγώ εἰμι emphasizes his identity, there are obvious implications when the background of the sayings are taken into account. It would be expected that the use of background material would bear this observation out. In other words, the background for the ἐγώ εἰμι sayings with a predicate should explain what he does and what the significance of that is for those who believe in him, while the background for the ἐγώ εἰμι without a predicate should convey who he really is.

---

1. Schnackenburg, *John*, II, p. 80.
2. Cf. Zimmermann, *Das Absolute 'Ego Eimi'*, p. 273.
3. Zimmermann, *Das Absolute 'Ego Eimi'*, p. 271.
4. Zimmermann, *Das Absolute 'Ego Eimi'*, p. 272: 'Bread, Light, Life, Truth... the intention of all these concepts is to paraphrase what Jesus himself offers to human beings, to set forth what he has to give them'.
5. Zimmermann, *Das Absolute 'Ego Eimi'*, p. 272.

Chapter 6

JESUS' IDENTITY: UNPREDICATED 'I AM' SAYINGS

Many have pointed to the *'ani hu'* of Isaiah as a parallel to the ἐγώ εἰμι of John.[1] The absolute use of 'I am' in the Old Testament is striking as the only conclusive parallel to the use in the New Testament. However, it will be argued below that it is not only in the words ἐγώ εἰμι that John points back to Isaiah, but also in the way that those words are presented. It has been seen that the use of 'I am' without a predicate does not easily fit into a formulaic pattern unless many of the sayings are discarded. Yet the occurrences of a phrase which includes ἐγώ εἰμι often seem to act as a key to point the alert reader back to the Old Testament and especially to Isaiah in order to interpret Jesus' sayings on a far deeper level. The single phrase containing ἐγώ εἰμι may alert the implied reader to an entire thought world, which is shared with the implied author. Those within the same cultural framework as the implied author would automatically understand the implications of the words ἐγώ εἰμι.[2] The fact that the narrator does not need to explain the words implies that the intended audience shared the author's conceptual point of view in this matter.[3]

It will therefore be argued that, when Jesus takes an Old Testament phrase which involves the words ἐγώ εἰμι, it is not only these words themselves that are important, but it is also the *thought world* to which

1. See Chapter 1: 'Possible Parallels: The Old Testament' - above.

2. For my understanding of how ἐγώ εἰμι may work in John's Gospel, I am indebted to a paper given by R.Watts which argued that a single phrase may alert the reader of a text to an entire thought world that those within the same conceptual framework would automatically understand. The reader within such a framework would correctly interpret the implications of the phrase in the light of the shared thought world (Watts, 'Camelot, Eskimos and the Grand Piano: The History of Hermeneutics in Biblical Studies: the role of Ideology in New Testament Social Backgrounds' [A paper given at the 1990 Tyndale New Testament Study Group in Cambridge]).

3. Cf. Culpepper, *Anatomy*, p. 8.

Jesus' words point, which helps explain what he means when he utters the phrase. As a result there is every possibility of seeing a reference to the Old Testament even in those sayings which have not usually been regarded as 'absolute' occurrences of 'I am' (e.g. 4.26; 8.18). The best way to show how this happens is to look at each occurrence of unpredicated ἐγώ εἰμι in turn, to see the way John may be using the Old Testament.

While not exactly the same, a similar phenomenon to that outlined above occurs in midrashic exegesis. The Talmud attributes seven basic rules of exegesis to Rabbi Hillel, who lived in the first century BCE.[1] One of Hillel's laws of exegesis was that of Gezerah Shawah: 'Verbal analogy from one verse to another; where the same words are applied to two separate cases it follows that the same considerations apply to both.'[2] What this parallel shows is that there is tradition which claims to go back to the first century BCE in which a mere verbal analogy is sufficient for a verse to be used in interpreting the same words elsewhere. It is therefore entirely plausible that the verbal analogy of the 'I am' sayings with certain verses of the Old Testament means that Jesus' words are to be interpreted in the light of the words which they parallel. Furthermore, Barrett has adequately shown John's evocative handling of the Old Testament and this evocative treatment suggests that such a use of ἐγώ εἰμι would concur with the Gospel's style and conceptual viewpoint.[3]

1. *John 4.26*

It is clear that when the reader first encounters ἐγώ εἰμι in the Gospel of John it is in terms of Jesus' identity.[4] The Samaritan woman's

1. Harner, *'I am'*, p. 18, suggests Hillel was active about 25 BCE, while Doeve seems to place his work some time after 30 BCE. Cf. J.W. Doeve, *Jewish Hermeneutics in the Synoptic Gospels and Acts* (Assen: Koninlijke, 1954), p. 63. Longenecker points to the theories that Hillel may have been Gemaliel's father or grandfather: cf. R. Longenecker, *Biblical Exegesis in the Apostolic Period* (Grand Rapids: Eerdmans, 1975), p. 33.

2. This is a translation of the middoth of Hillel (Aboth de Rabbi Nathan 37; Introduction to Sifra 3a; Tosefta Sanhedrin 7.11) by J. Bowker, *The Targums and Rabbinic Literature* (Cambridge: Cambridge University Press, 1969), p. 315.

3. C.K. Barrett, 'The Old Testament in the Fourth Gospel', *JTS* 48 (1947), pp. 155-69.

4. Brown, *John*, I, p. 177, comments that in vv. 25, 26 the 'woman finally RECOGNISES WHO JESUS IS...' (his emphasis).

perception of who Jesus is has grown from 'a Jew' (v. 9), through 'sir' (vv. 11, 15) to 'a prophet' (v. 19). When offered living water by Jesus (v. 10), she has asked an ironic question about his identity: 'Are you greater than our father Jacob?' (v. 12). Now she asserts that when the Messiah comes, he will explain everything to her. Through ἐγώ εἰμι Jesus declares that he is the messiah for whom she waits. Thus Jesus makes a claim about his identity; he is the messiah. But is this all that this 'I am' saying signifies for Jesus' identity?

The literary study of ἐγώ εἰμι in Jn 4.26 asked why Jesus' words were formulated in such a strange way. Why did he not say simply ἐγώ εἰμι ὁ χριστός (cf. 1.20)? The answer may lie in John's use of background material, for the words of 4.26 are almost a direct parallel to words in Isa. 52.6:

Jn 4.26: λέγει αὐτῇ ὁ Ἰησοῦς· **ἐγώ εἰμι, ὁ λαλῶν σοι.**
Isa. 52.6: διὰ τοῦτο γνώσεται ὁ λαός μου τὸ ὄνομά μου ἐν τῇ
ἡμέρα ἐκείνῃ, **ὅτι ἐγώ εἰμι αὐτὸς ὁ λαλῶν·** πάρειμι[1]

For the alert reader both the words ἐγώ εἰμι and the phrase which accompanies them point to these words in Isaiah. From this it follows that the phrasing of Jesus' words itself may say more than that he is messiah. It may point the reader back to these words in Isaiah, even if the Samaritan woman herself would not have seen such implications in Jesus' words.

If the phrasing of Jesus' words is meant to direct the reader to Isaiah, then Jesus' claim to messiahship should be interpreted not only in the context of a debate with the Samaritan woman, but also in the context of Isaiah 52. In Isaiah the LORD had said that in *that day* the people would *know* that it is he who speaks. Now, when the woman says that she *knows* that messiah is coming (4.25), Jesus claims to be the one who speaks. By Jesus' 'I am' saying the woman is given the opportunity of becoming one of the people who *know* that it is Jesus who is the one who speaks in that day.[2] When Jesus says 'I am he who speaks,' he thus

---

1. It is surprising that, in the light of the work J. Richter undertakes on the LXX of Isaiah, including Isa. 52.6 ('Ani Hu', pp. 33-34) he does not even mention the ἐγώ εἰμι of Jn 4.26 in his study of the New Testament occurrences of the term. F.W. Young does link Jesus'words in 4.26 with those of Isaiah 52.5, though he makes no reference to the 'I am' saying ('A Study on the Relationship of Isaiah to the Fourth Gospel', *ZNW* 46 [1955], pp. 225-26).

2. If Hinrichs (*Ich Bin*, p. 16) is correct that the concentration on the word of Jesus is the essence of John's Christology, this 'I am' saying must have a significant

takes the words of Yahweh and applies them to himself. The day of which Isaiah speaks is also parallelled in Jesus' discussion about *the day* when true worshippers will worship in spirit and in truth. If the Isaiah passage is in mind, Jesus' claim is not only in the light of the messiah's coming (v. 25), but in the light of the LORD's coming in redemption to Zion (Isa. 52.8, 9).[1] Through the ἐγώ εἰμι of 4.26, Jesus' identity as messiah is therefore qualified by the phrase in which it is uttered. It is the whole phrase, and not only the words ἐγώ εἰμι (*ani hu*), which points the reader to the Isaianic passage, which in turn defines what is meant by messiahship.

If it is correct to see in Jesus' words a reference to the similar words of Isaiah, then it would mean that this verse operates on two levels. The first level is there for all to see. Jesus claims to be the messiah of whom the Samaritan woman speaks. It is the phrasing of Jesus' words, which provides the key to interpreting them on a far deeper level. On this second level, Jesus' words make him out to be the fulfilment of the LORD's promise that the people would know his name, and also know that it is he who speaks. Jesus' identity as messiah is therefore an identity which includes an identification with Yahweh.[2] Thus the verbal analogy of Jesus' words with the words of Yahweh in Isaiah calls for a radical re-interpretation of the first 'surface' level of meaning in Jesus' words.

There are also two levels of irony at work in Jesus' words to the Samaritan woman in v. 10. On the first level, outlined in the literary study above, the Samaritan woman is the victim of the irony, for she

part to play in John's thought. In claiming to be the one who speaks, Jesus takes the words of Yahweh upon himself. Such a claim by Jesus offers theological justification for the fact that the title of the Word (λόγος) is applied to Jesus in the Prologue. It also explains how Jesus can claim that he speaks the very words of God (3.34; 14.10, 24; 17.8) as well as the reason that Jesus' words can offer life (6.63, 68). Cf. Lincoln, *Trials*, pp. 21ff.

1.   Stauffer also suggests that the word 'show' (ἀναγγελεῖ) in 4.25 'is a favourite expression of Deutero-Isaiah often combined with the theophanic formula ANI HU' (*Jesus*, p. 152). Stauffer cites 14 occurrences of the verb, ἀναγγελεῖ, in Second Isaiah (40.21; 41.22-23, 26; 42.9 × 2; 43.9, 12; 44.7 × 2; 46.10; 48.3, 14). This further confirms that John is not concerned simply with the words ἐγώ εἰμι ('ani hu') but the whole context in which they occur in the Old Testament.

2.   Such a point of view is supported by John's theology in which Jesus only acts in unison with his Father (e.g. 8.28). It also concurs with the Johannine Christology as a whole where Jesus is the sort of messiah who is also 'Son of God' (20.31).

does not know that Jesus really is the messiah. On the second level of irony, readers who do not correctly understand the 'clue' within the text which points to a deeper understanding of Jesus' words become the victims. They do not know that the reason Jesus can offer living water is his close identification with God and not only the fact that he is messiah. When Jesus' claim is seen in this way, the shortcomings of Bultmann's attempt to categorise the 'I am' sayings strictly in terms of their function become evident.[1] On one level Jesus' 'I am' saying answers the question 'Who are you?' and therefore fits into Bultmann's 'presentation' formula as well as into his 'recognition' formula showing that Jesus is the one expected (even though this was an unexpected revelation for the Samaritan woman!). A second level explains what sort of messiah and therefore fits into Bultmann's 'qualification' formula. To suggest that the function of the 'I am' saying is to explain Jesus' identity, allows a broader view of how 'I am' may be operating, while trying to keep the importance of that function in view.

2. *John 6.20*

The 'I am' saying of 6.20, unlike that of 4.26, does not disclose any explicit christological content. Jesus does not declare to the disciples that he is the messiah, or the Son of God, but simply that it is he who walks on the water. It is true that this ἐγώ εἰμι saying concerns Jesus' identity in as much as the disciples do not recognize that it is Jesus who is approaching them.[2] However, this does not initially appear to be a question of theological or christological identity but of human identity. The function of the ἐγώ εἰμι saying here is one of reassurance, and so is inextricably linked with the command not to fear. On this level, Jesus' saying is a recognition formula, making known to the disciples that it is he, their friend, whom they know.[3]

However, for the reader familiar with the Old Testament, the command not to fear may be associated with the assurance of the LORD. The verb 'to fear' (φοβεῖσθαι) is preceded by the negative word of command μὴ 80 times in the LXX. Of the 66 occurrences in the Old Testament

---

1. See discussion in Chapter 5: 'Delimiting the Sources', above.

2. Cf. Barrett, *John*, p. 279; Heil, *Walking on the Sea*, p. 79 also recognizes its role in terms of Jesus' identity.

3. Cf. Barrett, *John*, p. 281; Bruce, *John*, p. 148; Haenchen, *John*, I, p. 280; Morris, *John*, p. 350.

(not including the Apocrypha), 36 occur in the mouth of God or of an angel; in a further twelve, the reason given not to fear is the presence of God.[1] For the reader of Jn 6.20, the most striking of these occurrences are those in which the command not to fear is accompanied by the words ἐγώ εἰμι. In all these occurrences the phrase occurs in the mouth of God.

> Gen. 26.24: **Ἐγώ εἰμι** ὁ θεὸς ᾿Αβραὰμ τοῦ πατρός σου· **μὴ φοβοῦ**· μετὰ σοῦ γάρ εἰμι...
>
> Gen. 46.3: **Ἐγώ εἰμι** ὁ θεὸς τῶν πατέρων σου· **μὴ φοβοῦ** καταβῆναι εἰς Αἴγυπον·
>
> Jer. 1.8: **μὴ φοβηθῇς** ἀπὸ προσώπου αὐτῶν, ὅτι μετὰ σοῦ **ἐγώ εἰμι** τοῦ ἐξαιρεῖσθαί σε, λεγει Κύριος.
>
> Jer. 1.17:[2] **μὴ φοβηθῇς** ἀπὸ προσώπου αὐτῶν μηδὲ πτοηθῇς ἐναντίον αὐτῶν, ὅτι μετὰ σοῦ **ἐγώ εἰμι** τοῦ ἐξαιρεῖσθαί σε, λέγει κύριος.
>
> Jer. 46.28:[3] **μὴ φοβοῦ**, παῖς μου ᾿Ιακώβ, λέγει Κύριος, ὅτι μετὰ σοῦ **ἐγώ εἰμι**·...
>
> Jer. 42.11:[4] **μὴ φοβηθῆτε** ἀπὸ προσώπου βασιλέως Βαβυλῶνος, οὗ ὑμεῖς φοβεῖσθε ἀπὸ προσώπου αὐτοῦ· **μὴ φοβηθῆτε**, φησὶ Κύριος, ὅτι μεθ' ὑμῶν ἐγώ εἰμι τοῦ ἐξαιρεῖσθαι ὑμᾶς καὶ σώζειν ὑμᾶς ἐκ χειρὸς αὐτοῦ·

The frequency with which the command not to fear occurs in the mouth of God in the Old Testament, may not in itself indicate to the reader of John's Gospel that Jesus' words on the lake are anything more than a simple reassurance that the disciples need not be afraid. However, since the occurrences of the phrase in the Old Testament cited above are accompanied by the words ἐγώ εἰμι in the LXX, and the instances in Jeremiah occur in the context of deliverance, it is most likely that the reader familiar with the Old Testament would find Jesus' simple words on the lake to be pregnant with meaning.

It may be argued that, since none of the ἐγώ εἰμι sayings cited above can be regarded as absolute sayings, Jesus' words are not close enough to them in form to suggest a conscious use of Old Testament language. However, in addition to those occurrences in Genesis and

---

1. Figures compiled with the aid of E. Hatch and H. Redpath, *Concordance to the Septuagint* (3 vols.; Oxford: Clarendon Press, 1897).

2. LXX; Hebrew says 'Do not be dismayed by them, lest I dismay you before them' (אל־תחת מפניהם פן־אחתך לפניהם).

3. Chapter 26 in the LXX.

4. Chapter 49 in the LXX.

Jeremiah, the command not to fear occurs in the mouth of God in Isaiah 43. The reader, who has seen the striking similarity in the Greek of Isa. 52.6 to the ἐγώ εἰμι of Jn 4.26, may also be alert to the fact that Jesus' words in Jn 6.20 are reminiscent of Isaiah's vocabulary. In the first verse of Isaiah 43, Israel is commanded not to fear, because the LORD, her Creator, has redeemed her:

> Isa. 43.1: **μὴ φοβοῦ**, ὅτι ἐλυτρωσάμεν σε· ...[1]

The LORD then tells Israel that he will be with her even when she passes through the waters:

> Isa. 43.2a: καὶ ἐὰν διαβαίνῃς δι' **ὕδατος**, μετὰ σοῦ **εἰμι**.

Again the LORD portrays himself as the Saviour of Israel:

> Isa. 43.3a: ὅτι **ἐγώ** κύριος ὁ θεός σου ὁ ἅγιος Ἰσραὴλ ὁ **σώζων**
> **σε**· ...

In such a context the similarity between the words of Jn 6.20 and Isa. 43.5 take on greater significance:

> Jn 6.20: **ἐγώ εἰμι· μὴ φοβεῖσθε**
> Isa. 43.5: **μὴ φοβοῦ**, ὅτι μετὰ σοῦ **εἰμι**.[2]

To this can be added the fact that a few verses after this call from the LORD that Israel should not be afraid, there is the occurrence of a very significant ἐγώ εἰμι saying (see 8.18, 24, 28 below):

> Isa. 43.10: γένεσθέ μοι μάρτυρες... ἵνα γνῶτε καὶ πιστεύσητε καὶ
> συνῆτε ὅτι **ἐγώ εἰμι**...

The command of the LORD for Israel not to fear is accompanied in both Isaiah and Jeremiah by the idea that he is Saviour. It is also in this capacity that Jesus comes to the disciples on the lake and commands them not to fear. Thus it can be said that 'In uttering Ἐγώ εἰμι Jesus identifies himself with the performance of the properly divine action of dominating a chaotic sea and rescuing people from its distress. Thus the Ἐγώ εἰμι identifies Jesus as the one acting on behalf of Yahweh in this situation.'[3]

Again, it is not only the words ἐγώ εἰμι which point the reader to the

---

1. The significance of Isa. 43 for the walking on the water is emphasized by Heil, *Walking on the Sea*, p. 59, in his discussion of Matthew's version of the story.

2. Cf. Isa. 41.10 where there is a similar phrase in the LXX: **μὴ φοβοῦ**, μετὰ σοῦ γάρ **εἰμι**, μὴ πλανῶ· ἐγώ γάρ **εἰμι** ὁ θεός σου...

3. Heil, *Walking on the Sea*, p. 79.

Old Testament when Jesus speaks to the disciples on the lake. Rather it is the combination of these words with the command not to fear, as well as the miraculous context of the saying, that point to the words of Yahweh, the saviour of Israel. Heil correctly points out that 'Jesus reveals Yahweh's saving will by the very action of walking on the sea, not merely by the statement "It is I"'.[1] He is also correct to suggest that ἐγώ εἰμι 'derives its significance from Jesus' epiphanic action of walking on the sea'.[2] In addition, ἐγώ εἰμι also derives its significance from the accompanying command not to fear.[3] Again, the verbal analogy between Jesus' words and those in Isaiah radically alters the meaning of those words.

Abbott questions whether ἐγώ εἰμι can ever actually be used to mean 'It is I myself'. He agrees that this interpretation is usually assumed to be correct[4] and that this would agree with the Matthean and Marcan accounts 'namely, that the disciples "thought they saw a phantasm". In opposition to this, Christ might naturally be supposed to say "*I am [not a phantasm but] I [myself]*"' (his italics).[5] Yet Abbott argues:

> There is no proof that the Greek words can mean this. And there is proof that, in the Discourse on the Last Days, Mark uses ἐγώ εἰμι to mean 'I am [*the Saviour, Deliverer*, or *Christ*].' Moreover in that Discourse Luke (who omits the Walking on the Waters) agrees with Mark in the use of ἐγώ εἰμι, and Matthew shews that he understood the phrase thus by supplying the ellipsis, 'I am *the Christ*'. Lastly, Luke indicates that he would not have agreed in rendering ἐγώ εἰμι 'I am my very self' by the fact that elsewhere, when he actually attributes a meaning of this kind to our Lord, he adds αὐτός.[6]

Thus Abbott regards the ἐγώ εἰμι of this verse as an idiomatic ellipsis in which a word or phrase is left out but would be understood by the audience because of its acceptance as an idiom.[7] Although the words ἐγώ εἰμι mean 'I am he' when they are uttered by Jesus at his arrest (18.5, 6, 8) and by the blind man (9.9), there is a predicate (i.e. Jesus of

---

1. Heil, *Walking on the Sea*, p. 80.
2. Heil, *Walking on the Sea*, p. 79.
3. Heil is proved further correct when he states: 'OT background for both the comfort-bringing μὴ φοβεῖσθε and the identifying ἐγώ εἰμι is found in Isaiah 43.1-13' (*Walking on the Sea*, p. 59).
4. E.g., Barrett, *John*, p. 281; Carson, *John*, p. 275; Lindars, *John*, p. 247.
5. E.A. Abbott, *Johannine Grammar* (London: A. & C. Black, 1906), p. 182.
6. Abbott, *Grammar*, p. 182.
7. See Abbott, *Grammar*, pp. 172, 178 for an explanation of ellipsis.

Nazareth) in the context of the arrest and in the account of the man born blind, while no predicate can be supplied from the context of Jn 6.20.

Against Abbott, the Synoptics took Jesus' words to mean 'It is I myself and not a ghost' (Mk 6.49 50). This is evidence that the words ἐγώ εἰμι could mean 'It is I myself' and do not necessarily imply an ellipsis. It seems better therefore to allow for the possibility that the words here have a double meaning. On one level they identify Jesus to the disciples in a purely human way. At the same time *their formulation* points to a deeper meaning. Jesus identifies himself with the saving act and words of Yahweh and so this saying too speaks of Jesus' identity, an identity which involves intimate identification with the words and deeds of God (cf. 4.34; 5.36). When Jesus calls out to his disciples, ἐγώ εἰμι· μὴ φοβεῖσθε, he speaks not just as their friend but also speaks the words of the LORD. The Old Testament background to Jesus' assertion gives a theological explanation for his ability to walk on the water. It is because of his intimate identification with God that he is able to draw near on the sea and to declare 'It is I; do not be afraid'. Unless the reader sees both levels to Jesus' words, he/she may become the victim of irony, recognizing that it is Jesus who walks on the water, but failing to recognize who Jesus really is.

3. *John 8*

Verse 18

The ἐγώ εἰμι of 8.18 operates as a half-way house between those 'I am' sayings with an image and those without.[1] It is formally very similar to Jn 4.26. However, there is no predicate to be supplied from the context and so it is most natural to take the whole phrase ὁ μαρτυρῶν περὶ ἐμαυτοῦ as the predicate. Thus, rather than meaning, 'I who witness about myself am he' (cf. 4.26), the words seem to mean 'I am the one who witnesses about myself.' Unlike the other 'I am' sayings without an image, the words ἐγώ εἰμι refer more to Jesus' role than to his identity. In this respect the words of 8.18 are like the 'I am' sayings with an image. Just as he can only be described as the 'Good Shepherd' because

---

1. This is affirmed by J.A.T. Robinson, *The Priority of John* (ed. J.F. Coakley; London: SCM Press, 1985) p. 385 n. 124: 'There is not even a clear division between the two classes [of I am sayings]. Thus 8.18, "I am the one who witnesses about myself", is rightly rendered by the NEB, "Here I am, a witness in my own cause." It is a reminder too of how precarious it is to count up seven "I ams" (cf. also 8.23).'

that is the role he fulfils, Jesus can only be described as the 'witness' because that is his role. He identifies himself with one of the two witnesses required by Jewish law (cf. v. 17);[1] his Father is the other.

Charlier rightly points out that 'The periphrastic construction cannot be preferred without reason to the straightforward ἐγὼ μαρτυρῶ which one would be correct to expect.'[2] However, unlike the words ἐγώ εἰμι ὁ λαλῶν σοι (4.26), the words ἐγώ εἰμι ὁ μαρτυρῶν περὶ ἐμαυτοῦ (8.18) are not directly parallelled in the LXX. Even so, the phrase seems to take its content from the opening words of Isa. 43.10 (LXX):[3]

> Isa. 43.10: γένεσθέ μοι μάρτυρες, καὶ ἐγώ μάρτυς, λέγει Κύριος ὁ θεὸς, καὶ ὁ παῖς μου ὃν ἐξελεξάμην...

Having summoned the nations to bring their own witnesses (43.9), the LORD now calls on Israel to be his witnesses. According to the LXX, he too is to be a witness, and also the servant whom he has chosen. This servant has been chosen 'as a covenant to the people, a light to the nations, to open the eyes that are blind, to bring out the prisoners from the dungeon, from the prison those who sit in darkness...' (42.6, 7).[4] It is Jesus' claim to be that light to the world and to offer light to those who follow him which prompts the discussion of his validity as a witness (8.12, 13).[5] In his role as a light to the nations, the servant of the LORD is also called upon to bear witness to the LORD (43.10). Thus when Jesus claims to be the one who bears witness, he seems to be taking on the role which was to be accomplished by the 'servant of the LORD' in Isaiah. Jesus' witness is valid because he identifies himself with the role of the servant, as well as because the Father bears witness with

---

1.   Cf. Charlier, *L'Exégèse Johannique*, esp. pp. 505-509, for a discussion of John's use of Jewish law.

2.   Charlier, *L'Exégèse Johannique*, p. 513.

3.   The similarities between Isa. 42–43 and Jn 8 are helpfully laid out in the form of a synopsis by Coetzee (*Ego Eimi*, p. 171), who points out six major points of contact. These suggest, in his view, that 'Jesus' absolute EGO EIMI utterances in Jn 8 deliberately refer to the prophecies of Is[aiah] 42-43...'

4.   Cf. Hoskyns, *John*, II, p. 377.

5.   The Jews' charge against Jesus is that his witness is not true (οὐκ ἐστιν ἀληθής, v. 14). In Isaiah the LORD calls upon the world to hear and say 'It is true' (ἀληθῆ, v. 9). E.J. Young comments on Isa. 43.9, 'If the nations cannot produce their own witnesses, let them hear what God is saying and let them acknowledge that God's witness is true'. The same sentiment holds for Jesus' statement in 8.18 (*The Book of Isaiah* [NICOT; Grand Rapids: Eerdmanns, 1972], III, p. 148).

him.[1] The fact that Jesus points to the Father's role in witnessing seems to indicate dependence on the LXX rather than the MT, for it is only in the LXX that the LORD witnesses alongside his servant.[2]

Freed points out that there is a similar passage in I Samuel in which the LXX follows the Hebrew text. There Samuel says to the people:

1 Sam. 12.5: Μάρτυς κύριος ἐν ὑμῖν καὶ μάρτυς χριστὸς αὐτοῦ...

From this, Freed argues that in Jn 8.18, Jesus is seen as 'the anointed' (χριστὸς) and so bears witness with God, just as 'the anointed' was called to bear witness in defence of Samuel. Freed goes on to argue that 'as messiah, Jesus can witness for himself'—the implication of which seems to be that Jesus does not need to call on two witnesses as Samuel had done.[3] Whether the similarity of these two texts can be taken to prove that Jesus is here seen as the messiah is far from certain, yet Freed's observation does lend weight to the suggestion that Jesus' claim to be the one who witnesses could derive from the Old Testament. However, because of the similarities between the rest of John 8 and Isaiah 42–43, it seems more likely that the Isaianic passage should be seen as the main Old Testament influence on Jesus' claim here.

If Jesus' claim to be the one who witnesses alludes to Isa. 43.10, it is again the words that accompany Jesus' ἐγώ εἰμι that provide the key to a correct understanding of them. By means of ἐγώ εἰμι, Jesus takes the role of the witness from the passage in Isaiah and applies it to himself.[4]

1.   That Jesus 'has been sent' by the Father may also parallel the idea in Isaiah of the servant who 'has been chosen' by the LORD. Cf. Freed, *8:24*, p. 167.

2.   The MT text of this verse does not include the LORD as a witness, nor is it likely that Israel should be seen separately from the Servant of the LORD. Thus it is translated ' "You are my witnesses," says the LORD, "and my servant whom I have chosen..." '. In the Hebrew there appears to be only one witness who is both Israel and the Servant of the LORD. It could be argued that the servant of the LORD should be seen as a separate witness, since the servant is singular, while Israel is plural. However, in the light of the identification of 'my servant' with Israel elsewhere this is unlikely (cf. 44.1). Freed points out that in the LXX there seem to be three witnesses: 'the people addressed, God himself, and his servant are three witnesses to the uniqueness of the Hebrew deity' (*8.24*, p. 167).

3.   Freed, *8.24*, p. 167.

4.   Such a use of the Old Testament is more in line with the way the 'I am' sayings with an image function than with the unpredicated sayings. See my discussion on the bread of life (pp. 67-80). The fact that John explicitly uses ἐγώ εἰμι in the Bread of life discourse (6.35, 41, 48, 51) to take a concept from the Old Testament (where there is no 'I am' saying in the context) and apply it to the person of Jesus (by means of

In his role as the one who witnesses as well as in his role as the light of the world, Jesus takes on the same role as the servant whom the LORD has chosen, and as such is identified with him. Thus the description of Jesus as the one who witnesses speaks not only of his role but, by implication, of his identity.

Verses 24 and 28

Unlike the 'I am' saying of v. 18, neither that of 8.24 nor that of 8.28 speak primarily of Jesus' role. Here it is a question of believing that or knowing that ἐγώ εἰμι. Thus the sayings of 8.24 and 28 both concern Jesus' identity. The Jews' question ('Who are you?', v. 25) in response to Jesus' ἐγώ εἰμι statement (v. 24) shows that even they have grasped this point. They need to know Jesus' identity to be saved from dying in their sins. While the first of these two ἐγώ εἰμι sayings concerns the consequence of not believing who Jesus is, the second concerns the time when his identity will be revealed. The problem raised by Jesus' use of 'I am' here is that there is no predicate in the context with which Jesus can be identified.[1] In this sense they are truly absolute. Since the verb 'to be' usually requires a predicate, these words make little sense in their context.[2] So, in this sense too, the Jews are correct to want to supply a predicate to Jesus' words. The reader too may be left with the Jews to ask 'Who are you?', unless an investigation of the background material can bring to light a knowledge assumed by Jesus' words.

Again the Septuagint translation of Isaiah appears to provide the key to a correct understanding of both these 'I am' sayings, as well as to the saying of 13.19. Combined with ἐγώ εἰμι, the two phrases to *know that* and to *believe that* in such close succession reflect one 'I am' saying in Isaiah which combines both ideas in one phrase:

the words ἐγώ εἰμι), is a precedent for such a use of the expression in 8.18. Borgen (*Bread*, p. 78) suggests this is an accepted midrashic form of exegesis.

1.   Bultmann's suggestion (*John*, p. 349) that Jesus is to be identified with 'Son of man' is rightly rejected by Schnackenburg (*John*, II, p. 202) 'for the following reasons: (1) It would obscure the connection with v. 24, and v. 28 must be a deliberate echo of that. (2) Jesus never says directly, "I am the Son of man". In 9.35-37 this self-testimony is implied, but the ἐγώ εἰμι is avoided. Perhaps John too preserves the knowledge that Jesus only used the title "Son of man" in the third person. (3) The title "Son of man" is associated with a particular complex of ideas, especially "exaltation" and "glorification", and is introduced here in the wake of the word ὑφοῦν. The statement of the main clause stands on its own.'

2.   Barrett, *John*, p. 342.

Jn 8.24: ἐὰν γὰρ μὴ **πιστεύσητε ὅτι ἐγώ εἰμι**, ἀποθανεῖσθε ἐν ταῖς ἁμαρτίαις ὑμῶν

Jn 8.28: ὅταν ὑψώσητε τὸν υἱὸν τοῦ ἀνθρώπου, τότε **γνώσεσθε ὅτι ἐγώ εἰμι**...

Isa. 43.10: γένεσθέ μοι μάρτυρες...ἵνα **γνῶτε καὶ πιστεύσητε** καὶ συνῆτε **ὅτι ἐγώ εἰμι.**[1]

The similarity between the words of Jesus in John and those of the LORD in Isaiah appears to be deliberate, so that the words in John can by implication be interpreted in the light of the passage in Isaiah. Those readers who have already seen the similarity in vocabulary between the first half of this verse and Jesus' words in 8.18 have their view confirmed that Jesus is referring back to this passage in Isaiah when debating with the Jews in John 8. The reader who has also seen the connection between Jesus' words in 4.26 and the words of Isa. 52.6 may again see a reference to that verse in the combination of the verb 'to know' and the phrase ἐγώ εἰμι:

Isa. 52.6: διὰ τοῦτο **γνώσεται** ὁ λαός μου τὸ ὄνομά μου ἐν τῇ ἡμέρᾳ ἐκείνῃ, **ὅτι ἐγώ εἰμι** αὐτὸς ὁ λαλῶν· πάρειμι...

However, while there may be an indirect allusion to this verse, it seems that the main reference in John 8 is to the saying of Isa. 43.10.

The claim of the LORD in Isaiah 43 comes in the midst of his defence as the only God. YHWH calls Israel to witness that he alone is the saviour of Israel.[2] In v. 8, this very same Israel has been described as blind and deaf[3] and yet they are now called to be witnesses in order that they may know and believe and understand (v. 10). Whybray points out that 'the usual function of a witness is to enlighten others rather than himself'. However, 'in defiance of contextual appropriateness he [Second Isaiah] here states what is the real aim of this oracle and indeed of his whole work, that the exiles, his audience, should be convinced of

---

1. Unlike the first half of Isa. 43.10 (see above), the LXX follows the Hebrew fairly closely for the second part of the verse. It should be noted that the Hebrew has 'know and believe me (ותדעו והאמינו לי) and understand that I am he' which suggests that the LXX is being followed by John.

2. C. Westermann suggests that 'In the trial speech, v. 10 represents the endorsement of a testimony in court.' (*Isaiah 40–66* [OTL; trans. D.M.G. Stalker; London: SCM Press, 1966], p. 122).

3. If Isa. 42 and 43 provides the background to John 8, it is surely not by chance that both the sign and the debate, which follow, take up this theme of spiritual blindness which is also a theme in Isa. 42.18-20 (cf. Jn 9.39-41).

Yahweh's unique power'.[1] Westermann points out that, like the Greek phrase ἐγώ εἰμι, the words *ani hu* do not make sense on their own as the object of belief or knowledge:

> We are told in terse words that defy translation, but which may be approximately rendered as, 'that it is I.' If we made this into a main clause, it would run, 'I am he'—a cry used in personal encounter, whose significance depends in each case on the circumstances.[2]

In the case of this verse it is the clauses following the expression *ani hu* which determine its significance. There Yahweh speaks of his exclusive claim to be the saviour of Israel, for:

> Before me no god was formed,
> > nor shall there be any after me.
> I, I am the LORD,
> > and beside me there is no saviour (vv. 10b, 11).

The claim to be the only God, the claim to be the only saviour of Israel and the claim to be Yahweh, all determine the meaning and significance of the words *ani hu*.

The use of *ani hu* in Isaiah is suggestive for the use of ἐγώ εἰμι in Jesus' mouth. The Isaianic context speaks of Yahweh as the only saviour because he is the only God. *Ani hu* speaks of the exclusive divinity of Yahweh as is confirmed by the repetition of the phrase in Isa. 43.13: 'I am God, and also henceforth I am He...' Thus the Johannine Jesus takes words which, in the context of Isaiah, expressed the exclusive claim of Yahweh to be the Saviour of Israel. The clause '*to know and believe that I am*' thus carries with it an exclusive soteriological function which explain why Jesus can say that those who do not 'believe that I am' will die in their sins (8.24). In John Jesus has been given this exclusive soteriological function that in Isaiah was reserved for God alone (cf. Jn 3.17; 4.42; 10.9). Jesus can use the words ἐγώ εἰμι for himself in this way, because of his close identification with the Father; he does nothing on his own authority but speaks only as the Father has taught him (8.24). It is Jesus' exclusive role as the only begotten from the Father (1.14), the Logos who was in the beginning with God and was identified as God/god (1.1), the only one who has seen God (1.18) that allows him

---

1. R.N. Whybray, *Isaiah 40–66* (New Century Bible; London: Oliphants, 1975), p. 84.
2. Westermann (*Isaiah*, p. 122) says much the same of the Hebrew as Barrett (*John*, p. 342) does of the Greek.

to use these words of himself. In other words 'he whom God has sent utters the words of God' (3.34) to such an extent that he can use words reserved for God and apply them to himself. Again the phrase which contains ἐγώ εἰμι speaks of an intimate identification of Jesus with the exclusive God of Isaiah.

Although these two 'I am' sayings in John 8 appear to be directly dependent upon Isa. 43.10, they may be indirectly influenced by a phrase more common to the rest of the Old Testament. If John's use of the term ἐγώ εἰμι is interpreted in the light of the LXX, the combination of the phrase 'to know that' with ἐγώ εἰμι in 8.28 may also point the reader back to the phrase 'to know that I am Yahweh'. While this phrase occurs elsewhere in the Old Testament,[1] it takes on particular significance in the book of Ezekiel. A full study of this 'Statement of Recognition' (i.e. the phrase 'to know that I am Yahweh') in Ezekiel was carried out by W. Zimmerli.[2] He concludes that

> the statement of recognition is not concerned with that part of Yahweh's being that transcends the world, though a superficial look at the strict formulation, 'know that I am Yahweh,' may tempt us to this conclusion. Such a knowledge always takes place within the context of a very concrete history, a history embodied in concrete emissaries and coming to resolution in them.[3]

This has a parallel in the 'I am' saying in Jn 8.28, where it is the concrete action of the lifting up of the Son of man which will bring about the knowledge on the part of Jesus' hearers. Could it not also be that just as 'the strict formulation of the recognition formula has become a tool with which one can assimilate the comprehensive process of recognition of Yahweh that is so significant for Israel's faith',[4] so too the 'I am' saying in Jn 8.28 has become a tool for the recognition of Jesus that is so significant for the Gospel reader's faith?

The importance of the formulation 'to know that' in the understanding of the absolute 'I am' sayings of the Old Testament is acknowledged by J. Richter, who devotes a section of his dissertation to the study of this phrase.[5] As well as examining the use of the term in Ezekiel, Richter

1.　See W. Zimmerli, 'Knowledge of God According to the Book of Ezekiel' in W. Zimmerli, *I am Yahweh*, pp. 39-63, for a full account of the use of this formula in the Old Testament.

2.　Zimmerli, *I am Yahweh*, pp. 29-98.

3.　Zimmerli, *I am Yahweh*, p. 63.

4.　Zimmerli, *I am Yahweh*, p. 91.

5.　J. Richter, 'Ani Hu', pp. 47-58.

looks at the use of the formulation 'to know that I am Yahweh' in Exodus, where the phrase occurs nine times.[1] Five of these occurrences refer to the people of Israel (6.7; 10.2; 16.12; 29.46; 31.13) while four refer to the Egyptians (7.5; 14.4) or Pharaoh (7.17; 8.22). He concludes that the function of the phrase in Exodus concerns the area of history: 'In the sphere of history—by the fact that God shows himself to be powerful in history—Israel, like the Egyptians, recognise that he is Yahweh'.[2] This corresponds to the Johannine idea that the recognition of Jesus will also occur in an historical event ('When you have lifted up the Son of man, then you will know that I am', 8.28; cf. 13.19). In Ezekiel (25–32)[3] as well as in Exodus, the opponents of Yahweh are the object of this knowledge when the LORD rescues his people, just as in John it is the opponents of Jesus who will know that ἐγώ εἰμι. This knowledge is also combined with a threat in many cases, just as there is a threat that the Jews will die in their sins unless they believe that ἐγώ εἰμι (8.24). For example:

> Ezek. 25.7 ... I will cut you off from the peoples and will make you perish out of the countries; I will destroy you. Then you will know that I am the LORD.[4]

Both Richter[5] and Zimmerli[6] point out the use of this 'recognition statement' in Deutero-Isaiah. In Isa. 49.23 and 26, the full form of the 'recognition statement' occurs. The second of these two occurrences concerns Yahweh's role in salvation and would therefore be in line with the meaning of the 'I am' statement in 43.10:

> Isa. 49.26: Then all flesh shall know that I am Yahweh, your Saviour, and your Redeemer, the Mighty one of Jacob.

It seems that the use of the phrase 'to know that I am he' (43.10; 52.6) is synonymous with the recognition statement 'to know that I am Yahweh' (45.3, 6, 7). This is confirmed by Westermann, who comments on 43.11a: 'The first clause, "I, I, Yahweh" corresponds to the words of

---

1. J. Richter ('Ani Hu', p. 52) excludes Exod. 31.13 as secondary on the grounds that it is used in a formulaic sense in connection with a command to keep the Sabbath and has little to do with the context.
2. J. Richter, 'Ani Hu', p. 52.
3. J. Richter, 'Ani Hu', p. 53.
4. See also Ezekiel 25.11, (14), 17; 26.6; 28.23, 24; 29.9.
5. J. Richter, 'Ani Hu', pp. 55-57.
6. Zimmerli, *I am Yahweh*, pp. 53-56.

v. 10b just discussed "that I am he"'.[1] This observation (i.e. that the term 'I am he' in 43.10 corresponds to the phrase 'I am Yahweh') adds weight to the idea that the phrase 'then you will know that ἐγώ εἰμι' (8.28) may be influenced not only by Isaiah 43 but also by the Old Testament use of the self-introductory formula 'I am Yahweh'. If this is so, then Zimmermann is justified to see a link between this Old Testament revelation formula and the ἐγώ εἰμι in John.[2] However, this link between the phrases 'I am he' and 'I am Yahweh' occurs in Isaiah, and it would be wrong to view the use of ἐγώ εἰμι in John 8 as an ellipsis in which the name of God is understood. For John, the use of ἐγώ εἰμι points back to the whole context of the use of the words 'I am' in Isaiah 43.10 and not simply to the fact that *ani hu* may sometimes stand in the place of the formula 'I am Yahweh'.

To interpret Jesus' words in Jn 8.24, 28 in the light of such a background confirms that these words have to do with Jesus' identity. They are concerned with Jesus' identification with the Father. That Jesus is to be closely identified with the Father is completely consistent with Johannine Christology (cf. 1.1; 10.30). Ἐγώ εἰμι identifies Jesus with Yahweh's saving action and even with Yahweh himself. By the formulation of Jesus' ἐγώ εἰμι statements, the reader is pointed back once more to the words of the LORD in Isaiah, which then determine the meaning and significance of Jesus' own words. The Son's identification with the Father is so close that he can even take words from Isaiah concerning the LORD's role as the only God, and use them of himself. Just as knowledge of Yahweh's identity will be revealed in an act of history, so will knowledge of the Son's identification with the Father. Just as this will be revealed to Yahweh's opponents as well as his followers, so will it be revealed to his opponents as well as to his followers (cf. 13.19). In John this revelation will take place when Jesus is 'lifted up' by the Jews. It should at the same time be noted that the Son is always in submission to the Father, a fact emphasized in the second half of v. 28 (cf. 5.19-24).[3]

By implication Jesus' 'I am' sayings also occur in the context of the forgiveness of sins, for, if an unwillingness to believe that ἐγώ εἰμι will

1. Westermann, *Isaiah*, p. 123.
2. Zimmermann, *Das Absolute 'Ego Eimi'*, p. 64-65.
3. Zimmerli (*I am Yahweh*, pp. 12-13) points out the fact that the mediator of the LORD in the Old Testament is able to use the words 'I am Yahweh' when mediating the words of the LORD to his people. However, the mediator did not take these words to apply to himself.

result in the Jews dying in their sins, it must be assumed that the opposite is true: belief would result in them being saved from such a death. The combination of ἐγώ εἰμι with the question of sin suggests that there may be an allusion to Isaiah 43.25 in the 'I am' saying of 8.24.[1] In the LXX there is a double ἐγώ εἰμι as the LORD claims:

> Isa. 43.25: ἀλλὰ **ἐν ταῖς ἁμαρτίαις σου** προέστης μου καὶ **ἐν ταῖς ἀδικίαις σου. ἐγώ εἰμι ἐγώ εἰμι** ὁ ἐξαλείφων τὰς ἀνομίας σου ἕνεκεν ἐμου, καὶ **τὰς ἁμαρτίας σου** καὶ οὐ μὴ μνησθήσομαι.

In the verses that follow the LORD calls upon the people to remember him (v. 26) and reminds them of the punishment he brought upon those who transgressed previously. This 'I am' saying from Isaiah makes sense of the warning that the Jews will die in their sins, for in Isaiah the saying occurs in the context of the burden of sin which the people have placed on the LORD. However, it is he in whom they must believe because it is he who blots out sins and does not remember transgressions. If Jesus' 'I am' saying of 8.24 alludes to these verses from Isaiah as well as to 43.10, then the implications of that must carry over to the 'I am' saying of 8.28. By means of ἐγώ εἰμι Jesus identifies himself with the forgiving action of Yahweh. In other words, when Jesus is lifted up by the Jews, it will be revealed that he is the one who blots out transgressions and remembers sin no more.[2] However, for those who do not believe, the result will be that they die in their sins.[3]

---

1.   Lindars thinks that a more general form of salvation is implied by the background to Jesus' words here. He thinks of the salvation connected with all the 'I am' sayings (Isa. 41.4; 43.10, 13, 25; 46.4; 48.12; cf. Deut. 32.39) in which 'Yahweh is the one who created all things, who raised up Cyrus to conquer Babylon, and who will restore Israel. All his power is concentrated on this one fact, that he is the one who saves his people. Now we have the same phrase on the lips of Jesus in a parallel situation - that God, who created all things through the Word, is the one who saves mankind through him in the events of the incarnate life; cf. 3.16. We may, then, fill out the saying thus: "I am the one through whom salvation is accomplished"' (*John*, p. 320).

2.   The suggestion that Jesus' 'I am' saying here implies that the cross involves the blotting out of sin runs contrary to both Bultmann and Forestell. Cf. R. Bultmann, *Theology*, II, p. 54; J. Forestell, *The Word of the Cross: Salvation as Revelation in the Fourth Gospel* (Rome: Pontifical Biblical Institute, 1974), p. 2. For a critique of both Bultmann and Forestell, see M. Turner, 'Atonement and the Death of Jesus in John: Some questions to Bultmann and Forestell' *EvQ* 42 (2. 1990), pp. 99-122.

3.   There is a correspondence between the comment in Isaiah that their first father sinned (43.27) and the parallel theme in Jn 8 where Jesus claims 'You do

Verse 58

Because of the contrast between γενέσθαι and εἰμι in this 'I am' saying, the emphasis here is on the verb (εἰμι) rather than on the pronoun (ἐγώ). Jesus not only claims that he existed before Abraham but speaks of this existence in the present tense. By implication this 'I am' saying refers to Jesus' essential nature. Furthermore, this saying comes as the climax of a discussion about Jesus' identity and is the answer to earlier questions on this subject: 'Are you greater than our father Abraham, who died?' (8.53; cf. 4.12); and: 'Who is it that you claim to be?' (v. 53). The issue of Jesus' identity also lies behind the question that prompts this climactic 'I am' saying (v. 57).

The literary analysis of John 8 showed that the reader should see an interaction between all the occurrences of ἐγώ εἰμι in this debate with the Jews.[1] This interaction in itself suggests that the same background should be seen for this 'I am' saying as for the rest of the chapter. Even though Isaiah 42 and 43 do not provide such a close verbal parallel to this verse, there are certain elements within the passage from Isaiah which may indicate that the 'I am' sayings there are still in mind in the final ἐγώ εἰμι of John 8. Isa. 43.10, alluded to by the ἐγώ εἰμι of vv. 24 and 28, is of interest since the absolute 'I am' saying is followed immediately by the phrase 'Before me no god was formed.' In the LXX the Hebrew נוֹצַר (was formed) is translated ἐγένετο so that in the Greek there is a verbal link between this verse and Jn 8.58:

> Isa. 43.10: ... καὶ συνῆτε ὅτι **ἐγώ εἰμι**· ἔμπροσθέν μου οὐκ
> **ἐγένετο** ἄλλος θεὸς ...
> Jn 8.58   πρὶν Ἀβραὰμ γενέσθαι ἐγώ εἰμι.

Not only do both passages show a contrast between the verb 'to be' (εἰμί) and the verb 'to come to be' (γίνομαι), even the contrast in tenses between the aorist and the present occurs in both. Just as God's

---

what you have heard from your father' (v. 38, cf. vv. 41, 44).

1.   This is a point emphasized by R. Robert who suggests that this interaction calls for a consistent translation of ἐγώ εἰμι in 8.24, 28 and 58 ('Le malentendu sur le nom divin au chapitre VIII du quatrième Évangile', *Revue Thomiste* 88,2 [1988], pp. 278-87). Robert suggests that, if all three occurrences of ἐγώ εἰμι are absolute, which he thinks they are, they should be translated uniformly. It follows that they should take the form of the last ἐγώ εἰμι rather than the first two which are often translated ambiguously. Admittedly, Robert regards ἐγώ εἰμι from the start as an utterance of the divine name which assumes a consistent use of the term.

very nature is contrasted with the temporal existence of the gods of the nations, so Jesus' nature is contrasted with that of Abraham. It is also possible that John picks up on the temporal meaning of the LXX's use of ἐμπροσθέν ('before') in his own use of πρὶν.

This temporal contrast may provide a further link between John and Isaiah. In Isa. 43.13 the LORD says 'Even from the day I am he' (Heb: גם־מיום אני הוא). This is translated by the LXX as ἔτι ἀπ' ἀρχῆς ('Even from the beginning'—taking מיום to refer to the past).[1] Guilding seems to favour such an interpretation by placing v. 13 alongside Jn 8.58 in her synopsis of the two passages.[2] If this is the correct way to take the Hebrew, a stronger case could be made for the fact that a temporal contrast occurs in the context of an absolute 'I am' saying in both John and Isaiah. Just as Jn 8.58 provides a contrast between the time of Abraham and the ἐγώ εἰμι of Jesus, so Isaiah's use of *ani hu* creates a contrast between the 'I am' of God and the beginning of time. However, Pieper argues that the Hebrew cannot support such a meaning and that מיום 'never means "from the first day onward," ...There is not a single example in the Old Testament for that translation.'[3] Thus he suggests that מיום means מן־היום הזה and that such a translation as: 'Also henceforth I am he' (RSV, taking מיום to refer to the present and the phrase to refer to the future time starting now) is correct. Furthermore, since the LXX does not translate *ani hu* as ἐγώ εἰμι in this instance but seems to subsume the absolute 'I am' in the previous phrase καὶ ἐγώ Κύριος ὁ θεὸς, a link with Jn 8.58 cannot be made from the LXX.

A particularly interesting parallel to Jn 8.58 occurs in the Targum of Isaiah 43.[4] What is most striking is the reference to Abraham, who is nowhere mentioned in the text of Isaiah itself:

> I am he that is from the beginning, yea the everlasting ages are mine, and beside me there is no god. I, even I, am the Lord; and beside me there is no

---

1. See J.L. McKenzie, *Second Isaiah* (AB, 20; New York, Doubleday:1968), p. 53, who favours this translation. This rendition is supported by the Vulgate (*ab initio*) and the Syriac (*mn ywmm qdmy'*) translations of this verse, but these may themselves be dependent on the LXX rather than the Hebrew.

2. A. Guilding, *The Fourth Gospel and Jewish Worship: A Study of the Relation of St John's Gospel to the Ancient Jewish Lectionary System*. (Oxford: Clarendon Press, 1960), p. 108.

3. A. Pieper, *Isaiah II* (trans. E.E. Kowalke; Milwaukee, WI: Northwestern Publishing House, 1979), p. 222.

4. This link is suggested by Guilding, *Jewish Worship*, p. 109.

saviour. I declared to Abraham your father what was about to come; I delivered you from Egypt... Yea from everlasting I am He, and there is none that delivereth from my hand (Targum of 43.10-13).[1]

The mention of Abraham in the Targum of Isaiah is particularly attractive for the study of Jn 8.58. The tradition that Abraham was given a view of the future could plausibly be alluded to in 8.56 where Jesus says 'Your father Abraham rejoiced to see my day; he saw it and was glad'.[2] In both cases Abraham has a knowledge of the future. There is also a parallel between 'Abraham your father' in the Targum and 'Your father Abraham' in John. Moreover, the Targum translation supports a link between Jn 8.58 and Isa 43.13 since, like the LXX, the targum seems to take מיום as a reference to the beginning of time. The problem of dating how early this tradition may be, means that it can only be regarded as a possibility that John knew and referred to the Targumic tradition.[3]

Maybe the best way to see the 'I am' saying of 8.58 is as a special development of the allusions made so explicitly by the other sayings in John 8. Surely it is this ἐγώ εἰμι more than any other which forces the reader to see Jesus' words as a claim to divinity. It is the reaction of the Jews to these words which confirm that the reader was correct to think that Jesus was equating himself with the words of Yahweh in the earlier uses of the phrase. Thus the fact that this 'I am' saying is formulated slightly differently from the other sayings in the same chapter actually helps to draw out their previous significance. The reader who has seen an allusion to the exclusive claims of Yahweh in 8.24 and 28 now knows that such a formulation on Jesus' lips was no mistake, for, by means of

1.   J.F. Stenning, *The Targum of Isaiah* (Oxford: Clarendon Press, 1953), pp. 144, 146.

2.   Cf. Guilding, *Jewish Worship*, p. 109.

3.   Guilding, *Jewish Worship*, p. 109, comments that 'in view of the very close dependence of John 8 on Isaiah 43 it seems by no means impossible that the tradition is an early one'. However, there is a need to demonstrate that John used such targumic traditions elsewhere before it can be certain that he is doing so here. B. Chilton presents a strong case for a knowledge of traditions contained in the Isaiah Targum on the part of the Synoptic Jesus (*A Galilean Rabbi and his Bible* [London: SPCK, 1984], pp. 57-147). Cf. also B. Chilton, *The Isaiah Targum* (The Aramaic Bible, 11; Edinburgh: T. & T. Clark, 1987). More work is necessary on the relationship between the Johannine Jesus and the Targums. See C.L.B. Plumb, *EGW EIMI*, and C. Williams (PhD thesis, Cambridge University, forthcoming), who both study the connection between the targums and John's use of ἐγώ εἰμι. The dissertation of Plumb works on the basis that John was acquainted with targumic tradition.

the very same words, he claims to have existed before Abraham and thus claims for himself not only the words of God but the very nature of the God who claimed 'I am he: before me no god was formed.' The Jews correctly interpret Jesus' words as an identification with the nature of God (cf. 10.33). They are, however, unwilling to accept that his witness is true. For this reason they pick up stones in order to kill Jesus.

4. *John 13.19*

Jesus' statement to the disciples in 13.19 echoes his words in 8.24 and 28 and is surely meant to be interpreted in the light of those verses. In both 8.28 and 13.19 the 'I am' saying is formulated as a prediction of future events. When these events happen, Jesus' identity will be revealed. Yet it is at the most unlikely times that this fulfilment takes place. The fulfilment of the first saying is at Jesus' death; the fulfilment of the second is at his betrayal. In addition, the fulfilment of the ἐγώ εἰμι of 13.19 will take place at the same time that Scripture is fulfilled concerning Jesus (13.18).

The study of structure in John 13 suggested a close link between the 'I am' saying of 13.19 and the quotation from Ps. 41.9 in v. 18. If such a link is correct, it may be that the belief in v. 19 will be accomplished when the disciples see that Scripture is being fulfilled in Jesus' words.[1] In that case, it is not so much the betrayal itself which will bring the disciples to believe, but the fact that in that betrayal the words of Scripture are fulfilled. The text which is quoted in 13.18 may also point beyond Jesus' betrayal itself to the events of his Passion and Resurrection. Just as his use of ἐγώ εἰμι points beyond the words *ani hu* to their original context, so this quotation, which appears to refer exclusively to Jesus' betrayal, may also point beyond the words of the quotation itself. Dodd suggests that:

> The taunt of the enemy [in Psalm 41], 'Now that he lieth he shall rise up no more,' and the sufferer's appeal, 'O Lord, raise me up' (ἀνάστησόν με), would in this connection naturally suggest the resurrection of Christ.'[2]

---

1. In the light of rabbinic interpretation of Ps. 41, Brown (*John*, II, p. 555) raises the possibility of supplying 'the messiah' as an implicit predicate to Jesus' 'I am' saying in 13.19. However, since Jn 13 does not hint at such a Messianic interpretation of the Psalm he correctly dismisses such a possibility as unlikely.

2. C.H. Dodd, *According to the Scriptures: The Sub-structure of New Testament Theology* (London: Nisbet, 1952), p. 100. Cf. M.J.J. Menken, 'The Translation of Psalm 41.10 in John 12.18', *JSNT* 40 (1990) pp. 61-79, who argues that John uses the Hebrew version of Ps. 41 here rather than the LXX.

The following verses of the Psalm also suggest that such an interpretation may be in mind; even though the Psalmist is betrayed by his friend, he is raised up again:

'By this I know that thou art pleased with me, in that my enemy has not triumphed over me. But thou hast upheld me because of my integrity, and set me in thy presence for ever' (vv. 11, 12).

When Jesus is betrayed by his friend, the disciples (and the readers) should perhaps see that God's word is being fulfilled and at the same time should believe, because through its original context the quotation points beyond itself to Jesus' vindication.[1] All this will occur in order that the disciples may believe that ἐγώ εἰμι.

As well as an allusion to the words of Jn 8.24, 28, where Isa. 43.10 is the most likely background, there are several points of contact between Jn 13.16-19 and the words of Yahweh in the same verse from Isaiah. The parallels between the two passages are laid out as follows:

Isa. 43.10	Jn 13.16-19
...λέγει Κύριος ὁ θεὸς	ἀμήν ἀμήν λέγω ὑμῖν,
καὶ ὁ παῖς	οὐκ ἔστιν δοῦλος μείζων τοῦ
	κυρίου αὐτοῦ οὐδὲ ἀπόστολος
	μείζων τοῦ πέμψαντος αὐτόν.
	εἰ ταῦτα οἴδατε, μακάριοί ἐστε ἐὰν
	ποιῆτε αὐτά. οὐ περὶ πάντων ὑμῶν
	λέγω· ἐγώ οἶδα τίνας
ὃν ἐξελεξάμην	ἐξελεξάμην· ἀλλ᾽ ἵνα ἡ γραφὴ
	πληρωθῇ, ὁ τρώγων μου τὸν ἄρτον
	ἐπῆρεν ἐπ᾽ ἐμὲ τὴν πτέρναν αὐτοῦ.
	ἀπ᾽ ἄρτι λέγω ὑμῖν πρὸ τοῦ
	γενέσθαι,[2]
ἵνα γνῶτε καὶ πιστεύσητε καὶ συνῆτε	ἵνα πιστεύσητε ὅταν γένηται
ὅτι ἐγώ εἰμι,...	ὅτι ἐγώ εἰμι,...

---

1. It may be contested that the original context of the quotation from Psalm 41 is not necessary to understand the words of Jesus in Jn 13.18. However, since the reason Jesus tells the disciples of his imminent betrayal is to solicit belief, an implicit allusion to Jesus' vindication in words predicting his betrayal would provide a basis for the disciples to believe that Jesus was still in control.

2. F.W. Young (*Relationship*, p. 227) suggests that the articular infinitive πρὸ τοῦ γενέσθαι is a peculiarly Isaianic construction, which is characteristically used by Isaiah in the context of the verb ἀναγγέλειν. He suggests therefore that Jesus is functioning in this passage as ὁ ἀναγγέλων ἅπαντα (the one who reveals all things).

Just as it is Yahweh who has chosen Israel to be his witnesses, so Jesus has chosen the disciples (v. 18). In Isaiah, Israel is seen as the servant of the Lord. In John, the disciples are called to follow Jesus' example (v. 15) and to do what he has done because they are servants while he is the master (v. 16). In addition, Jesus tells the disciples that they are correct to call him 'Lord' (ὁ κύριος, vv. 13, 14) as well as teacher. An allusion to this passage of Isaiah would be highly significant for John's Christology, for here Jesus takes on a role which parallels that of Yahweh (including the title 'Lord'). Jesus no longer plays the role of Yahweh's servant (cf. 8.18) but of the LORD himself. Like Yahweh in the face of his enemies (43.13), he is sovereign in the face of his betrayal, a fact which is emphasized over and over again as an assurance to the disciples (vv. 1, 3, 11, 18, 19, 27).[1]

As with that of 8.58, this 'I am' saying alludes to all that has already been claimed by the term earlier in the Gospel. As such the allusion to Isa. 43.10 may be indirect and apply more to the 'I am' saying itself than to the earlier discussion in ch. 13 about the role of a servant. However, even if it is only in the phrase ἐγώ εἰμι that Jesus alludes to Isa. 43.10, it must still be significant that Jesus who is 'Lord' (Jn 13.14) takes the words of the 'Lord' and applies them to himself when he uses the words ἐγώ εἰμι.[2] Thus, in the fulfilment of the Scripture about betrayal, Jesus will be seen to be identified with the 'Lord' of the Old Testament. It is for this reason that, in the most unlikely of situations of betrayal and crucifixion, Jesus' sovereignty will be seen and his identity revealed. This saying concerning Jesus' identity is also seen to be an identification formula, identifying him with the saving words and deeds of Yahweh.

---

1. It is possible that there is an allusion in 13.19 to the 'I am' saying of Isaiah 48.12. In Isa. 48.12, the LORD declares 'For I knew you would deal very treache-rously, and that from birth you were called a rebel' (NRSV). The LORD goes on to state that it is for the sake of his name and his glory (vv. 9, 11; cf. Jn 13.31) that he restrains his anger. Then he says: 'Listen to me, O Jacob, and Israel, whom I called: I am He (אני הוא); I am the first, and I am the last...' (NRSV). As with Isa. 43, there is a link in this passage between the 'chosenness' of Israel and the 'chosenness' of the disciples in 13.17.

2. Morris comments that the term 'Lord' 'expresses a very high reverence, perhaps even having overtones of divinity. Jesus proceeds to endorse this way of speaking. He commends the disciples, for these expressions point to His true position' (*John*, p. 620).

5. *John 18.5, 6, 8*

The strange use of the words 'I am' in Jn 18.5, 6 and 8 clearly show that, while ἐγώ εἰμι is used as a simple identification formula,[1] the two words may simultaneously have a far deeper meaning. The reason that the soldiers fall down when Jesus utters the words ἐγώ εἰμι is not stated. It is assumed that the reader will know. While accepting the fact that Jesus identifies himself to the soldiers with these words, the reader must look for something that would explain their strange reaction. The words here act as a trigger to point the reader to the other occurrences of the term in the Gospel to explain Jesus' words. The threefold repetition of ἐγώ εἰμι emphasizes the importance of the expression. That this saying occurs at the moment of betrayal particularly points back to 13.19 where the fulfilment of Scripture and of Jesus' own words was linked to the betrayal in order that the disciples might believe.[2] Thus a simple recognition formula in which Jesus states that he is the person whom the soldiers seek is given a double meaning by the reaction of those same soldiers to his words as well as by the previous use of ἐγώ εἰμι in the Gospel. Although it is correct to talk of Jesus' identity in terms of Jesus of Nazareth on one level, on another level there is something that cannot be explained without looking into the environment in which the Gospel was first written. In that environment, the Gospel writer can take simple words and, by the way they are formulated (8.24, 28; 13.19) as well as by the reactions to them (8.58; 18.5, 6, 8), allude to a background where Yahweh alone is God and Saviour. In the Gospel, these words are taken up by Jesus and applied to himself.

6. *Summary*

This study of background material has shown that the words of Jesus are to be interpreted in the light of similar phrases in Isaiah. Like the

1. Davies (*Rhetoric*, p. 83) correctly recognizes that the 'I am' sayings in this chapter function as a means of self-identification. However, she fails to make any comment about the strange reaction on the part of Jesus' narrative audience.

2. While the 'I am' saying of 13.19 is surely recalled in 18.5, 6, 8, the disciples do not believe 'that I am' at this point in the narrative. In fact, although Jesus had warned them about his imminent betrayal so that they would believe, Peter's reaction shows how unexpected the betrayal was and how he had not grasped that Jesus was still in control. It is not until after the resurrection that the disciples recognize who Jesus really is (cf. 20.28).

midrashic form of interpretation Gezerah Shawah, 'the same considerations apply to both' Isaiah and John.[1] In other words when Jesus uses the words 'I am' he alludes not only to the *ani hu* of Isaiah but also to the context in which those words occur. From the above study it seems not only plausible but probable that John is pointing his readers to the use of 'I am' in the Old Testament and in particular to the *ani hu* of Second Isaiah. If this is the case, the six distinctives of *ani hu* which are laid out by Harner must have implications for the use of ἐγώ εἰμι in John. These six distinctives can be summarized as follows:

1. '*'Ani hu'* in Second Isaiah is always attributed to Yahweh. It is a solemn statement or assertion that only he can properly make. If anyone else spoke these words, it would be a sign of presumptuous pride, an attempt to claim equality with Yahweh or displace him. This is very nearly the case in 47.8, 10, in which Babylon makes the presumptuous statement, "I am, and there is no one besides me". In these verses it is interesting that Second Isaiah uses the single word 'I' (*'ani*) to express the idea "I am". He is evidently contrasting Babylon's claims with the *'ani hu'* of Yahweh. Yet even here he refrains from attributing the phrase *'ani hu'* to anyone other than Yahweh.'[2]

2. 'The phrase *'ani hu'* signifies that Yahweh alone is God, in contrast to the so-called "gods" of the various peoples of the world. This assertion of exclusive monotheism is a major theme for Second Isaiah which he expresses in a variety of ways...he makes the explicit assertion that there is no god besides Yahweh (44.6, 8; 45.5, 6, 18, 21, 22; 46.9).'[3]

3. ' ...For Second Isaiah the belief in Yahweh as Lord of history is closely related to the assertion that he alone is God. This belief in Yahweh's sovereignty over history finds particular expression in the prophet's conviction that he is about to redeem the people of Israel by restoring them to their homeland. In a number of passages Second Isaiah weaves these ideas together (44.6-8; 45.1-8; 46.5-13).'[4]

4. For Second Isaiah the belief in Yahweh as redeemer of Israel was closely related to the belief that he is also the creator of the world... It is significant to note here that Second Isaiah associates the phrase *'ani hu'* with creation faith. In this way he indicates that this phrase of self-predication, in addition to its other meanings, also presents Yahweh as creator of the world.'[5]

5. 'One of Second Isaiah's main tasks was to awaken faith on the part of his fellow exiles in Babylon and reassure them that Yahweh was indeed about

1. Bowker, *The Targums*, p. 315. See above.
2. Harner, *'I am'*, p. 7.
3. Harner, *'I am'*, p. 8.
4. Harner, *'I am'*, p. 9.
5. Harner, *'I am'*, pp. 10, 11.

to restore them to their homeland. Many of the people, he realised, were inclined to believe that Yahweh was powerless because the Babylonians had destroyed their temple in Jerusalem and taken a large number of Israelites into exile. In the context of this need for renewed faith, Second Isaiah represents Yahweh as using the self-predication "I am He".[1]

6. 'Second Isaiah regarded the phrase "I am he" as an abbreviated form of other expressions, especially "I am Yahweh," summing up in concise terms everything represented by the longer terms.'[2]

Harner's observations about the use of *ani hu* in Second Isaiah have specific implications for the use of such a phrase in John. By using the words ἐγώ εἰμι, Jesus takes upon himself a phrase that speaks of the fact that Yahweh, the one true creator God will come to his people and save them. As such the phrase is eschatological, expressing the time when the LORD will come to Zion and when the messenger will proclaim 'The LORD reigns' (52.6, 7). This phrase is also soteriological, for the purpose of his coming is to save his people (52.7). However, most striking of all is the fact that Jesus takes on himself a phrase that is reserved for Yahweh alone and thus intimately identifies himself with God's acts of creation and salvation. This is in fact no different from the rest of John's high Christology in which Jesus is identified with the Logos who has been active with the Father in creation (1.2, 3).[3]

While the words 'I am' may not be profound in themselves, *the way that they are formulated* in John points the reader to these words in Isaiah for a correct understanding of who Jesus is. The use of the phrase in Isaiah fits in very well with John's own Christology and suggests that John saw the events and words of Jesus' life as a fulfilment of that day when Israel would see the salvation of Yahweh. By the way he uses ἐγώ εἰμι he wishes his readers to see the same.

1.   Harner, *'I am'*, p. 12.
2.   Harner, *'I am'*, p. 14.
3.   See ch. 9.3: 'The "I am" sayings and Christology'.

Chapter 7

JESUS' ROLE: 'I AM' WITH ITS ACCOMPANYING IMAGES

The Old Testament (particularly the LXX) immediately commends itself as a possible source of material for the predicated 'I am' sayings in John, because it provides parallels for many (perhaps all) of the Johannine images, as well as for the absolute use of ἐγώ εἰμι. Such a background proves a problem to those who seek formal rather than thematic parallels, since those predicates which frequently show the nature and acts of God in the Old Testament are absent in John.[1] However, it will be argued that the Old Testament is indeed the conceptual background by which the 'I am' sayings with an image should be understood. Following the suggestion of Borgen, it will further be proposed that a primary function of ἐγώ εἰμι in John is to take an Old Testament image and apply it to the person of Jesus.[2] Thus the function of ἐγώ εἰμι is not as a formal parallel to the predicated 'I am' sayings of the Old Testament but a conceptual one; a means of taking Old Testament (and other) concepts and applying them to the person of Jesus. It may even be that when the words 'I am' occur with an image as a predicate the reader is meant to understand 'I am' as a pointer to the Old Testament. Jesus' words would thus mean 'I am the Bread/the Light/the Vine etc. of which the Scriptures speak'. The Bread of Life discourse acts as the starting point for such an understanding of the function of the predicated ἐγώ εἰμι in John. It will be argued that the images of Light, Shepherd (in association with the image of the door) and Vine all allude in a similar fashion to the Old Testament and portray Jesus as the fulfilment of these Old Testament images. These images are therefore seen to define Jesus' role and mission as a fulfilment of Old Testament ideas.

---

1. See Schweizer, *Ego Eimi*, pp. 37, 38, who suggests that of the predicates in the OT referring to the 'nature and acts of God', only 'shepherd' occurs in John.
2. Borgen, *Bread*, pp. 72, 78.

As well as taking up ideas from the Old Testament and applying them to Jesus it will also be suggested that ἐγώ εἰμι can be used to take up current Jewish expectations for the same purpose. Such is the case in John 11.25 when Jesus calls himself 'the Resurrection and the Life'.[1] The same happens in John 6 where the Jews appear to expect Jesus to give them manna from heaven to eat (v. 31). The concepts of truth and life may originally take their meaning from the Old Testament, but, as the literary studies have shown, they have been transformed in the context of John's Gospel so that, when Jesus claims these titles for himself, the reader is to see Jesus as the fulfilment of all that has been asserted by these terms throughout the Gospel. This is also true of Jesus' claim to be the light of the world (8.12).

1. *Fulfilment of Old Testament Expectations*

John 6

Following Borgen, the literary study of the function of ἐγώ εἰμι in John 6 suggested that John's use of the Old Testament in this chapter fits into an accepted midrashic form of interpretation.[2] Borgen further suggests that the words of the Old Testament quoted by the crowd (v. 31) are introduced by a fragment of the haggadah in much the same way as happens in *Exod. R.* 25, 2.6:

> ...and made manna [which is bread] come down to Israel from heaven,
> for it says: 'Behold I will cause to rain down bread from heaven for you'
> (Exod. 16.4).[3]

However, Jesus' discussion with the crowds about bread from heaven is an exposition of the miracle of the feeding of the five thousand (vv. 1-15) as well as an application of the Old Testament to himself.[4] Jesus perceives that the crowd have misunderstood the miracle and have

---

1. Cf. Kundzins, *Die Ego-Eimi-Spruche*, p. 100.
2. See the literary study of Jn 6 above (pp. 67-80). The warning given by Brown (*John*, I, pp. 265-66) about the date of midrashic texts referring to manna should be heeded here, since the midrashic exegesis upon which Borgen's thesis (below) depends is drawn from later texts than John's Gospel.
3. Borgen, *Bread*, pp. 61-62. Borgen also points to Philo, *Legum Allegoria* 3.162a, where words from the Old Testament are introduced by haggadic material. Cf. Philo in Ten Volumes, *Philo I* (LCL; F.H. Colson and G.H. Whitaker; London: Heinnemann, 1981).
4. Against Lindars, *John*, p. 256.

therefore followed him for the wrong reasons (v. 26).[1] In view of this misunderstanding he encourages them to seek what is really important; 'the food which endures to eternal life' (v. 28). Jesus expounds the meaning of the miracle in terms of his own mission and role, for he explains that the work of God is to believe in the one whom he has sent (v. 29). As the Son of man, he is the one who can give such food because God has set his seal on him (v. 27). The crowd, however, want him to perform another sign to show that he really is from God (v. 30). The definitive sign for them is the one they cite from the Old Testament: 'He gave them bread from heaven to eat' (v. 31). In demanding such a sign they display an expectation that Jesus should be able to perform the same signs as Moses if he truly is from God (v. 31).[2]

Jesus re-interprets the words which the Jews quote from the Old Testament in three ways in order to show that he himself, rather than any sign, is the 'true' fulfilment of their expectations:

> Jesus presents his new interpretation, following precisely the order of the quotation. His interpretation adds three new statements to the quotation: (1) 'Not Moses but my Father'; (2) 'not "he gave" but "he is giving"'; (3) The 'bread from heaven' which Jesus' Father gives is the true, the real (ἀληθινόν) bread.[3]

By pointing out the real author of the signs which Moses performed, Jesus implies that he is not the one whom the crowd should be asking for a sign. Instead they should look to the Father to give them an authentic sign from heaven. It is the Father who is the ultimate author

1. Though it was earlier said that they 'saw the sign which he had done' (v. 14), it is revealed that they had not really seen the significance of the miracle. Cf. Carson, *John*, p. 283; also Lindars, *John*, p. 254.

2. Brown quotes examples of such an expectation in Jewish writings: 'The 2nd-century A.D. apocryphon II Bar 29.8 says: "The treasury of manna shall again descend from on high, and they will eat of it in those years." The Midrash Melkilta on Exod 16.25 says: "You will not find it [manna] in this age, but you shall find it in the age that is coming." The Midrash Rabbah on Eccles. 1.9 says: "As the first redeemer caused manna to descend, as it is stated, "Because I shall cause to rain bread from heaven for you (Exod. 16.4)," so will the latter redeemer cause manna to descend.' However, if there was such an expectation at the time of writing it is only alluded to in John. Thus Brown is right to warn that, 'Although all these passages illumine the passage in John, we must stress that the rabbinic references come from a later period, and we cannot be certain how important the manna theme was in Jesus' time' (*John*, I, p. 265).

3. Schnackenburg, *John*, II, p. 42.

of bread from heaven (v. 32a). It is he who will give the sign which they seek (v. 32). In fact he is giving them such a sign at the moment Jesus speaks. The crowd are mistaken to think that the 'true' or 'authentic' sign that Jesus was from God would be for him to give them manna like Moses had done (v. 31). Although this would be 'real' bread for them, for Jesus it is not so. He categorizes manna along with the loaves and fishes as 'food which perishes' (v. 27). The 'true' bread is of a different category. It is defined as ὁ καταβαίνων ἐκ τοῦ οὐρανοῦ καὶ ζωὴν διδοὺς τῷ κόσμῳ (v. 33). Rather than perishing, it offers life. The past tense also gives way to the present.[1] In the light of such a re-interpretation of their quotation, the crowd ask Jesus to give them such bread (v. 34). With the words ἐγώ εἰμι Jesus claims that the 'authentic' sign which they seek is actually fulfilled in him (v. 35).[2]

Borgen suggests that Jesus' re-interpretation of the Old Testament quotation is remarkable in its similarities to midrashic form and method. The similarity to midrashic method occurs particularly in the contrast made between the words of the quotation and the re-interpretation by Jesus. Borgen points out three similarities:

1. In Palestinian midrash, Philo and John the Old Testament passage 'is followed by an exegetical pattern of contrast' using the terms 'not...but'.
2. 'To this pattern of contrast an explicative statement can be added, as is done... in John 6.33.
3. The determining agreement is, however, that John 6.32 gives a different reading of the Old Testament quotation cited in v. 31b, in accordance with this midrashic pattern for correcting the Hebrew text.'[3]

---

1. Carson, *John*, p. 286: 'Present tenses, especially in John, are often past-referring (the so-called "historic present"), but if this one is present-referring, then Jesus is not only saying that his Father has been ignored while Moses has gained centre stage in the thought of his opponents, but that the true bread is in any case not the manna in the wilderness but what the Father is now giving.'

2. It could almost be said that Jesus is the sign which the Father gives. On the signs in general, F.W. Young, , comments: 'it is clear that while the miracles are the σημεῖα, Jesus himself is the σημεῖον of the only "true God"' (*Relationship*, p. 224). However, Jesus is not only a sign from the Father but also the fulfilment of all that is indicated by the sign.

3. Borgen, *Bread*, p. 63. The passage that Borgen cites as an example of this pattern of correction is Midrash Mekilta on Exod. 16.15: '"Man did eat the bread of strong horses" (Ps. 78.25). Do not read (אל תקרי) "of strong horses" (אבירים), but (אלא) "of the limbs" (איברים), that is, bread that is absorbed by the limbs.' Borgen also cites Philo, *Det. Pot. Ins.* 47-48, in *Philo II* (LCL; F.H. Colson and G.H. Whitaker; London: Heinnemann, 1979).

It may be concluded that the way the Old Testament is used in John 6 in conjunction with ἐγώ εἰμι is thoroughly Jewish.[1]

For two reasons Borgen suggests that even the words ἐγώ εἰμι are themselves a midrashic formula:

1.   The function of ἐγώ εἰμι within John 6 is to take something from the Old Testament and apply it to someone in the first person singular. In other words ἐγώ εἰμι here functions as an identification formula, identifying Jesus with the words of the Old Testament quotation.[2]

2.   There are examples in other midrashic literature in which the Old Testament is applied to people by means of the first person pronoun.

While it is true that the function of ἐγώ εἰμι in John 6 is to take something from the Old Testament and to apply it to someone in the first person singular, this does not prove that the words ἐγώ εἰμι constitute a midrashic formula. Such a suggestion must be demonstrated by the evidence Borgen cites from Midrashic sources and not from John itself. Since two of Borgen's examples of the midrashic use of 'I am' come from John's Gospel itself (and thus cannot be regarded as independent evidence for a midrashic formula), his second point is far from convincing.[3] Thus he only cites *Lam. R.* I, 16 §45 as an independent

---

1.   Since the 'I am' saying is clearly a re-interpretation of the Old Testament quotation, it is unlikely that the reader should see such parallels as those found in the Mandaean literature and proposed by Schweizer, *Ego Eimi*, p. 73 and Schulz, *Komposition*, pp. 96, 97. Such parallels seem to have little to do with the passage of Scripture that is cited by the crowd. They also have little to do with the context in which the Bread of life discourse occurs. Cf. Schnackenburg, *John*, II, p. 44. The texts cited by Schweizer and Schulz are found in Lidzbarski, *Ginza*, p. 557, and E.S. Drower, *The Canonical Prayerbook of the Mandaeans* (Leiden: Brill, 1959), nos 352-55, pp. 243-50 respectively.

2.   Borgen (*Bread*, p. 73) mentions an unpublished dissertation by Schaedel, who 'classifies "Ego eimi" as a formula of identification, where well known eschatological terms and metaphors are being connected with Jesus' (K. Schaedel, 'Das Johannesevangelium und "Die Kinder des Lichtes". Untersuchungen zu den Selbstzeugnissen Jesu im 4. Ev. und zur Heilsterminologie der "Ēn-Fesha-Sekte"' [unpublished dissertation, Vienna: 1953], p. 15 and pp. 232-46).

3.   Borgen, *Bread*, pp. 72. Borgen points to two other instances in John's Gospel where he sees a similar use of the Old Testament. The first is John the Baptist's application of an Old Testament quotation to himself by means of כֹּה in 1.23. The other also concerns John the Baptist where 'the lamp' is applied to him in

example of such a use of 'I am'. Even Borgen admits that this example is of uncertain date.[1] Furthermore, the passage does not necessarily show an accepted midrashic formula since it is not a respected Rabbi but the hated Trajan who uses 'I am' to apply Deut. 28.49 to himself:

> On his arrival he found the Jews occupied with this verse:
> 'The Lord will bring a nation against thee from far, from the end of the earth, as the vulture (הַנֶּשֶׁר) swoopeth down' (Deut. 28.49).
> He said to them: 'I am the vulture (אֲנָא הוּא נִשְׁרָא) who planned to come to you in ten days, but the wind brought me in five.'[2]

Although Borgen has legitimately asked whether the words ἐγώ εἰμι are themselves part of a midrashic formula, he has brought no firm evidence to support this possibility. However, he has rightly pointed out that the use of ἐγώ εἰμι with a predicate in John 6 does act as a formula to identify Jesus with the concept of bread in the Old Testament. At the same time he has raised the issue of whether the other predicated 'I am' sayings function in a similar way. Since the concern of this study is to see how John uses ἐγώ εἰμι in conjunction with the Old Testament, it must be left to others to investigate whether there is further evidence to suggest that this was an accepted midrashic formula or whether *Lam. R.* 1, 16 §45 is an isolated example of such a use of 'I am'.

While the words ἐγώ εἰμι may not in themselves be part of a midrashic formula, Borgen has convincingly demonstrated that their repeated use in the discourse of John 6 continues the midrashic exposition of the theme of manna. He argues that the significance of John's midrashic treatment of the Old Testament in conjunction with ἐγώ εἰμι becomes apparent when the parallel 'I am' statements are placed together:

5.35 by means of the verb ἦν. Both these references suggest that, even if John was using a formula, he was reticent to use the words heg'w ehimi when applying the words of the Old Testament to John the Baptist and wished to reserve those for Jesus alone. However, these examples can only be used to show how John's Gospel uses the Old Testament and not as evidence that John was using a midrashic formula. Thus Borgen has only one example outside John of 'I am' being used as a midrashic formula for taking words from the Old Testament and applying them to someone in the first person singular.

   1. Borgen, *Bread*, p. 73.
   2. Borgen, *Bread*, p. 73 (Heb. emphasis Borgen's).

v. 35:   ἐγώ εἰμι ὁ ἄρτος τῆς ζωῆς
v. 41:   ἐγώ εἰμι ὁ ἄρτος ὁ καταβὰς ἐκ τοῦ οὐρανοῦ
v. 48:   ἐγώ εἰμι ὁ ἄρτος τῆς ζωῆς
v. 51:   ἐγώ εἰμι ὁ ἄρτος ὁ ζῶν ὁ ἐκ τοῦ οὐρανοῦ καταβὰς
           (Following Borgen's emphasis)[1]

In each instance Jesus' words refer back to the quotation from the Old Testament and proceed to explain further what that verse means when applied to his mission and role. Borgen may also be correct to suggest that 'The supplement "of life" which is attached to the word "the bread" in v. 35, is probably a new and fresh exegetical combination and is hardly due to the adaptation of a fixed and traditional phrase "the bread of life" to the word "bread" in the Old Testament quotation cited in v. 31b. The lack of relevant parallels outside John supports this interpretation.'[2]

It follows from the above that this midrashic exegesis of the 'true' meaning of the Old Testament quotation continues throughout the Bread of life discourse. Once Jesus has claimed that he is the bread from heaven, he goes on to explain in more detail what this means in terms of his own ministry and role. This explanation continues to re-interpret the meaning of the Old Testament quotation and shows exactly how the manna can be seen as a type for Jesus' own ministry. Just as the bread was given 'to eat', so too Jesus as the bread of life satisfies people's hunger (vv. 35b, 48-51). Jesus is the bread of life inasmuch as 'those who come to him shall not hunger, and those who believe in him shall never thirst' (v. 35b). Just as the Old Testament quotation did not (in Jesus' re-interpretation) refer to literal bread, so too this hunger is not literal hunger. This hunger involves coming to Jesus and receiving the benefits which that affords (vv. 35b, 37), including life and resurrection at the last day (v. 40). Jesus himself, like the bread, 'has come down from heaven' (v. 38). When Jesus uses the words ἐγώ εἰμι in conjunction with the term 'the bread of life', he can be seen to be taking the Old Testament and applying it in a typological way to his own role.[3] The bread from heaven points to the fact that

---

1.   Borgen, *Bread*, p. 72.
2.   Borgen, *Bread*, p. 73.
3.   Cf. Carson, *John*, pp. 286. I take my definition of typology as 'the study which traces parallels or correspondences between incidents recorded in the OT and their counterparts in the N.T. such that the latter can be seen to resemble the former in notable respects and yet to go beyond them' (I.H. Marshall, 'An

Jesus himself has come down from heaven, and thus the incarnation is seen as a fulfilment of the words 'he gave them bread from heaven to eat' (v. 31).

In establishing John's midrashic use of the Old Testament, it is necessary to ask from which Old Testament passage the quotation referred to in 6.31 comes. This may in turn show more precisely how Jesus is to be seen as the fulfilment of these words. It is here that the 'I am' sayings of John 6 may present a model for the reader's understanding of the rest of the 'I am' sayings with a predicate. For the quotation by the Jews seems to take more than one Old Testament passage as its source of reference. This suggests that John is not only concerned here with the fulfilment of a particular passage but also (and perhaps more importantly) with the fulfilment of the whole concept of manna.[1] The two most pertinent Old Testament parallels are found in Exodus 16 and Psalm 78:

Exod. 16.4 (LXX): ἐγώ ὕω ὑμῖν ἄρτους ἐκ τοῦ οὐρανοῦ
Ps. 78.24 (77.24 LXX): καὶ ἔβρεξεν αὐτοῖς μάννα φαγεῖν, καὶ ἄρτον οὐρανοῦ ἔδωκεν αὐτοῖς·

However, to these two passages can be added the following, which also display certain similarities with Jn 6.31:

Exod. 16.15 (LXX): ὁ ἄρτος ὃν ἔδωκε Κʹυριος ὑμῖν φαγεῖν[2]
Neh. 9.15 (LXX, Cf. also v. 20): καὶ ἄρτον ἐξ οὐρανοῦ ἔδωκας αὐτοῖς

Assessment of recent developments' in D.A. Carson and H.G. Williamson [eds.], *It is Written: Scripture Citing Scripture. Essays in honour of Barnabas Lindars SSF.* [Cambridge: Cambridge University Press, 1988], p. 16).

1. E.D. Freed agrees that 'there is no one passage from the O.T. which completely satisfies this quotation...' (*Old Testament Quotations in the Gospel of John* [SNT, 11I; Leiden: Brill, 1965], p. 12).

2. There are several parallels between the story of the manna in Exod. 16 and Jn 6. The people in Exodus are told to gather (συλλέξουσι, v. 4b) while at the feeding of the five thousand the disciples are told to do the same (συναγάγετε, v. 12). In Exod. 16 the people murmur (διεγόγγυζε, v. 2) while in Jn 6 the Jews murmur at Jesus (ἐγόγγυζον, v. 41). The Lord offers the people of Israel both flesh and bread to eat (κρέα φαγεῖν καὶ ἄρτους, v. 8) while Jesus equates the bread with his flesh (ἡ σάφξ μού, v. 51). It is possible that these parallel themes are further meant to draw the reader's attention to the fact that the words of Jn 6 are to be seen in the light of this passage (see also Num. 11; Guilding, *Jewish Worship*, p. 62)

Ps. 105.40 (104.40 LXX): καὶ ἄρτον ἐξ οὐρανοῦ ἐνέπλησεν αὐτούς
Wis. 16.20: ἄνθ᾽ ὧν ἀγγέλων τροφὴν ἐψώμισας τὸν λαόν σου, καὶ
ἕτοιμον ἄρτον ἀπ᾽ οὐρανοῦ παρέσχες αὐτοῖς ἀκοπιάτως... [1]

Freed thinks that 'this quotation can best be explained by saying that John had in mind Exod. 16.4 and Ps. 78.24 and probably was familiar with both the Hebrew and Greek texts. He may have quoted his texts from memory or deliberately invented a quotation to suit his theological purpose for including the quotation in the first place.'[2] The reference to the grumbling of the Jews in v. 41 probably suggests that the Exodus passage is the primary allusion, while the passage from Psalm 78 is secondary but still important. However, Freed does not elucidate why John should use a quotation which combines more than one Old Testament reference.[3]

1. Freed (*Old Testament Quotations*, p. 12) also points to similarities in Exod. 16.35; Num. 11.6-9; Deut. 8.3, 16; Josh. 5.12; Prov. 9.5; *2 Bar.* 29.8. The Midrashic character of John's exegesis of the Old Testament passage is picked up by M. Hengel in an article concerning John's use of the Old Testament. ('Die Schriftauslegung des 4. Evangeliums auf dem Hintergrund der urchristlichen Exegese', *JBTh* 4 [1989], pp. 249-88). Like Freed, he suggests that the Old Testament quotation is a 'mixed citation, in which the Evangelist, as elsewhere, combines different verses with one another (Ex.16.4; 16.15; Ps.24; cf. Neh.9.15), in which he knows both the LXX and the Hebrew text...' (p. 267).

2. Freed, *Old Testament Quotations*, p. 15. Cf.also Lindars, *John*, p. 257

3. The first two verses of Isa. 55 may be in view in the sub-clause of the 'I am' saying in 6.35, which offers satisfaction for thirst as well as for hunger. Isa. 55.1 (LXX):Οἱ διψῶντες πορεύεσθε ἐφ᾽ ὕδωρ, καὶ ὅσοι μὴ ἔχετε ἀργύριον βαδίσαντες ἀγοράσατε, καὶ πίετε ἄνευ ἀργυρίου καὶ τιμῆς οἶνον καὶ στέαρ. Cf. Carson, *John*, p. 289. Attractive as the similarity of ideas may be, there are few linguistic parallels to suggest that John was alluding to these verses. Verbal similarities are restricted to διψάω (Jn 6.35) and possibly φαγεῖν (some manuscripts of the LXX [Vaticanus, Marchalianus (margin)] attest φάγετε rather than πίετε. This is accepted by Nestlé and Tischendorf but is rejected by both Rahlfs and Göttingen). Bernard saw an allusion in v. 28 to the Hebrew of Isaiah 55.2a 'Why do you spend your money for that which is not bread, and your labour for that which does not satisfy?' (*John*, I, p. 191). Cf. Guilding, *Jewish Worship*, p. 63. For 'labour' John uses ἐργάζεσθε (v. 27) and τὰ ἔργα (v. 28), while the LXX of Isa. 55 uses τὸν μόχθον (v. 2). The LXX also omits the concept of bread in v. 2 so that a link with the bread of John 6 or even with the 'food' (τήν βρῶσιν) of 6.27 is improbable. It is only by analogy that the labour that does not satisfy (τὸν μόχθον ὑμῶν οὐκ εἰς πλησμονήν, Isa. 55.2) becomes the bread for which those who come to Jesus will not hunger (οὐ μὴ πεινάσῃ, v. 35). A closer parallel to John's phrase exists in Isa. 49.10 where 'in a day of salvation' (v. 8) it is said of the prisoners whom God has

If the idea of manna is seen as a *type*, which points to Jesus' role among humanity, the reason that John includes concepts from more than one Old Testament passage in his quotation becomes clear: Jesus' claim to be the true bread from heaven alludes not only to a particular Old Testament passage cited by the crowd (whichever passage that may be) but includes all that would be implied in the Old Testament concept of bread from heaven.[1] This means that John 6 takes up not only particular passages that speak of bread but also ideas associated with the concept of bread. Thus Pancaro probably is right to point out that the idea of bread is associated with the Law, and that, in calling Jesus the 'bread from heaven', John has consciously transferred attributes from Torah to Jesus.[2] He states:

> Of greatest importance, in this respect, are those texts which speak of the 'word of God' as food and identify the 'word' or 'wisdom' explicitly with the Law (the precepts), so that the Law is itself viewed as 'food'. Such is the case in Deut. 8.2, 3; Sir 24.21-23 and Wisd. 16.26 (comp. also. Ps. 19.11f; 119.103).[3]

Pancaro supports his argument by discussing those passages he lists above. In addition he refers to the thought of Torah as Bread in Rabbinic texts, such as *Gen. R.* 70.5 where Rabbi Joshua (whom Pancaro dates at about 80 CE) is recorded as declaring to Akilas the proselyte '"Bread" refers to the Torah, as it says, Come eat of my bread (Prov. 9.5)'.[4]

F.W. Young suggests that the portrayal of Jesus in John 6 depends

---

called forth 'they shall not hunger or thirst' (οὐ πεινάσουσιν οὐδὲ διψήσουσιν); cf. Brown, *John*, I, pp. 247, 269. However, since the reference to thirst both recalls Jesus' similar claim to the Samaritan woman (4.13, 14) and anticipates the exposition of vv. 53ff., it is better to see the sub-clause of the 'I am' saying as a further exposition of Jesus' claim to be the bread of life rather than a specific allusion to another Old Testament passage.

1. The parallel between Jesus' role and the reason given in Deut. 8.3, 16 for the provision of manna may also be alluded to. There it was stated that 'he humbled you and let you hunger and fed you with manna , which you did not know, nor did your fathers know; that he might make you know that man does not live by bread alone, but that man lives by everything that proceeds out of the mouth of the LORD.'

2. Pancaro, *Law in the Fourth Gospel*, p. 452.

3. Pancaro, *Law in the Fourth Gospel*, p. 455.

4. Pancaro, *Law in the Fourth Gospel*, p. 457, refers to H.L. Strack and P. Billerbeck, *Kommentar zum Neuen Testament aus Talmuc und Midrasch* (7 vols.; trans. H. Freedman; London: Soncino, 1922–1961), II, p. 638.

considerably on the thought-world of Isaiah. He singles out two passages in Second Isaiah which seem to throw light on John:

Isa. 40.6:   ἐξηράνθη ὁ χόρτος, καὶ τὸ ἄνθος ἐξέπεσεν, τὸ δὲ ῥῆμα τοῦ θεοῦ ἡμῶν μένει εἰς τὸν αἰῶνα.

Isa. 55.10, 11:   ὡς γὰρ καταβῇ ὑετὸς ἢ χιὼν ἐκ τοῦ οὐρανοῦ καὶ οὐ μὴ ἀποστράφῃ ἕως ἂν μεθύσῃ τὴν γῆν, καὶ ἐκβλαστήσῃ καὶ δῷ σπέρμα τῷ σπείροντι καὶ ἄρτον εἰς βρῶσιν, οὕτως ἔσται τὸ ῥῆμα μου, ὃ ἐὰν ἐξ'ελθῃ ἐκ τοῦ στόματός μου, οὐ μὴ ἀποστράφῃ, ἕως ἂν συντελεσθῇ ὅσα ἠθέλησα καὶ εὐοδώσω τὰς ὁδούς σου καὶ ἐντάλματά μου.[1]

Young argues that the contrast in Isaiah between humanity, which perishes as the grass, and the word of God, which lasts forever, may have influenced John's mention that there was much grass in that place (v. 10).[2] Be that as it may, the passage from Isaiah 55 is suggestive, not only for Jesus' portrayal in John 6, but also for John's Christology as a whole. Young comments:

> Here the ῥῆμα τοῦ θεοῦ is compared to the rain or snow which comes down (καταβαίνειν) from heaven, waters the thirsty earth and eventually provides the bread (ἄρτος) for food (βρῶσις). The ῥῆμα goes forth from God to return only after it has provided bread for food, the bread or food being the accomplishment of God's will, His commands and the making of straight ways for His people.[3]

However, while John may be indebted to Isaiah for his understanding of Jesus' mission and role in general, the specific reference in John 6 is the bread from heaven which was given in Old Testament times through Moses. Any allusion to these words from Isaiah in connection with Jesus as the Bread of life are therefore best regarded as secondary.

When applied to the person of Jesus by means of ἐγώ εἰμι, the exposition of the bread from heaven in John 6 concerns his role. The bread from heaven is a *type* which points to Jesus' role as the one who satisfies 'true' hunger by giving life to those who come to him (v. 51). Just as the words that accompanied the predicateless ἐγώ εἰμι acted as a pointer to a whole thought world in which the 'I am' saying should be interpreted, so it is the accompanying phrase here that points the reader to the background by which the ἐγώ εἰμι saying should be understood.

---

1.   Cf. F.W. Young, *Relationship*, pp. 227-28.

2.   F.W. Young, *Relationship*, pp. 229-30.

3.   F.W. Young, *Relationship*, p. 228. Young even hints that there is a relationship between John's doctrine of the incarnate logos and the book of Isaiah (p. 229).

However, because the manna is only a *type* and the feeding of the five thousand is only a *sign*, there is a contrast between them and the 'true' bread. Those who eat them will die. Those who eat the 'true' bread will live forever (v. 51). Thus, when Jesus claims to be the bread of the Old Testament quotation, he also claims to be superior to that bread which could be eaten and still afforded no security against death. By so doing, he both fulfils and exceeds the Old Testament concept of bread. If Pancaro is right that the concept of bread also concerns the law, Jesus' role is seen both to fulfil and exceed the role of the law. The law was intended to nourish the Jewish people. By the 'I am' sayings of John 6, it is now Jesus who fulfils that role. While this certainly implies that the role of the law within Judaism is now obsolete, John does not focus on this negative aspect but on the positive nourishment that Jesus affords to humanity.[1]

John 8.12 (9.5)

Unlike the 'I am' saying of Jn 6.35, Jesus' claim to be the light of the world does not immediately follow an Old Testament quotation and so it may at first appear to be an entirely different use of the phrase. However, it will be shown below that this claim alludes directly to the prophecies of Deutero-Isaiah concerning a light for the Gentiles (Isa. 42.6; 49.6; 51.4) as well as to the prophecy in the early part of Isaiah that a light shall dawn in the region of Galilee (Isa. 9.1, 2). The phrase may also call to mind all that is encompassed in the Old Testament concept of light. In addition, the theme of light is one of the major symbols of the Fourth Gospel, which is first introduced in connection with the pre-existent Christ in the prologue (1.4, 5, 9) and has also been developed within the Gospel at the conclusion of Jesus' discourse with Nicodemus (3.16-21; cf. also 12.35, 36).

In discussing the absolute 'I am' sayings of John 8 above, the parallels between Isaiah 42, 43 and John 8 were indicated time and again. These parallels are not limited to the occurrences of the absolute ἐγώ εἰμι. The theme of light, which is the predicate of Jn 8.12, is also present in Isaiah 42.[2] Here Yahweh declares to his chosen servant:

Isa. 42.6b, 7 καὶ ἔδωκά σε εἰς διαθήκην γένους, εἰς φῶς ἐθνῶν, ἀνοῖξαι ὀφθαλμοὺς τυφῶν, ἐξαγαγεῖν ἐκ δεσμῶν δεδεμένους καὶ ἐξ οἴκου φυλακῆς καθημένους ἐν σκότει.

1. See discussion of Purpose and Audience below in Chapter 9.
2. Cf. Coetzee, *Ego Eimi*, p. 171.

In these verses the identity of the servant seems to be the people of Israel.[1] Yahweh has chosen them to bring justice/judgment (κρίσιν, 42.1, 3, 4) to the nations (τοῖς ἔθνεσιν, v. 1; ἐπὶ τῆς γῆς, v. 4). It is in this task that the people of Israel become a light to the nations, though they themselves are blind (42.18, 19; 43.8).[2] In ch. 43 this judgment is brought to the nations through the chosen servant's witness to Yahweh. The result of Israel's witness is 'that you may know and believe and understand that I am he. Before me no god was formed, nor shall there be any after me...' (43.10). In the same way, Israel's role as a light to the nations reveals the exclusivity of Yahweh's divinity so that its culmination is Yahweh's claim: 'I am the LORD, that is my name; my glory I give to no other, nor my praise to graven images' (42.8).[3] For this reason, the nations who have gathered before Yahweh are obliged to admit that Israel's witness to him is true (43.9).

In view of all the other parallels between John 8 and Isaiah 42, 43, it becomes highly likely that Jesus' claim to be the light of the world derives primarily from the Isaianic concept of the servant of the LORD, Israel, being a light to the nations.[4] If this is so, Jesus' claim to be the

---

1.   Westermann regards 42.5ff. as an interpolation so that it cannot be assumed that Yahweh is addressing the same person as vv. 1-4 (*Isaiah*, p. 99). However, Israel can still be seen to be the addressee by analogy with 41.9, where the same words are used of Israel's calling as the servant. Cf. Westermann, *Isaiah*, p. 99. Besides, the Johannine use of Isa. 42, 43 is not bound by such considerations; for, if the Johannine concept of Light of the world derives from Isa. 42, it derives from the final form of the text in which it is Israel's role, as servant of Yahweh, to be a light to the nations. Although Cyrus is later seen to be the LORD's anointed (45.1), it is surely Israel who is the LORD's servant in Isa. 42, 43. Explicit reference to Israel as Yahweh's servant in 41.8, 9 and 44.1 makes it clear that Israel is being addressed in 43.1, 14, 15, 22, 28. Moreover, the servant is addressed in the plural in 43.10 and by inference in 42.18, 19.

2.   Westermann suggests that 'judgment' in these verses concerns the claim to divinity: 'If we examine Deutero-Isaiah for instances of *mispat* with reference to the Gentiles, we shall at once find them in the "trial speeches" which present a legal process between Yahweh and the Gentile nations. They all turn upon justice, *mispat*, and result in the Gentiles' gods' claim to divinity being declared to be nothing: Yahweh alone is God' (*Isaiah*, p. 95).

3.   Whybray, *Isaiah*, p. 76, rightly argues that 'These verses are not...an independent piece but the culmination of the argument.'

4.   Schnackenburg observes that the Gnostic idea of light 'in which the Gnostic redeemer frees people from darkness and brings them into the light is something totally different from the believing discipleship which Jesus asks for.' He suggests

Light of the World should be seen in the same way as his claim to be the Bread of Life. By means of the words ἐγώ εἰμι Jesus takes an Old Testament concept and applies it to himself. He is the light of which Isaiah spoke. By implication he also takes on the role of the servant of Yahweh in his task of bringing light to the nations and simultaneously fulfils the role which Israel was supposed to accomplish.

As with bread in John 6, the Old Testament concept of light is the *type* which points ultimately to Jesus. Jesus fulfils the role which Israel was supposed to play, but he also exceeds it, for in Isaiah even the servant was blind (42.19). In John, Jesus has no such disability and therefore promises that, 'he who follows me will not walk in darkness, but will have the light of life' (8.12b). Just as in Isaiah, the role of being a light to the nations results in Israel's witness to Yahweh as the one true God (42.8; 43.10), so for Jesus the role of being the light of the world also results in his role as witness (8.14, 18). In this, Isaiah 42, 43 further commends itself as the correct background for John 8, since it makes sense of the apparently sudden change from the theme of light to the theme of witness. It is in his role as witness that Jesus performs his role as light of the world. In the same way, the people of Israel perform their role as a light to the nations by their witness to Yahweh as the one true God.

Furthermore, it is not only Jesus' 'I am' saying which points to a fulfilment of this passage from Isaiah. His actions also show that he fulfils the role of light to the nations. Israel's task as a light to the nations is to open the eyes of those who are blind (42.7). When Jesus repeats his claim to be the light of the world (9.5), it is in just such a context.[1] Jesus demonstrates his right to claim to be the light of the world by fulfilling the requirements of such a claim. Thus the healing of the blind man shows that Jesus has a right to claim to be the light of

---

that the closest parallel to the Johannine dualism is found at Qumran but that 'the idea of universal salvation, which was unknown to the particularist Qumran sect, is foreshadowed in Second-Isaiah. Here the "Servant of Yahweh" is already called "light of the pagans" or "of the nations" (Is 42.6; 49.6; 51.4)...' (*John*, II, p. 190). Cf. Carson, *John*, p. 338.

1.   The opening of eyes that are blind is in the context of God's glory being made known, as Whybray comments on 42.8: 'Yahweh now addresses the exiles, giving a reason for his action. As in some other passages (e.g. 48.9-11) this is not primarily his love for his people Israel, but his glory' (*Isaiah*, p. 76). This is also the case in Jn 9.3, 'that the works of God might be made manifest in him'.

the world precisely because the sign fulfils the Old Testament expectations associated with such a claim.

If Jesus takes the Isaianic phrase 'a light to the nations' from Isaiah 42.6 and applies it to himself by means of ἐγώ εἰμι, it is likely that there is also an allusion to the other passages in Deutero-Isaiah in which the same phrase is used. This is confirmed by the fact that in Isa. 49.6 Yahweh again speaks of the role of his servant as the bringer of light to the nations:

Isa. 49.6   καὶ εἶπέ μοι, Μέγα σοί ἐστι τοῦ κληθῆναί σε παῖδά μου, τοῦ στῆσαι τὰς φυλὰς Ἰακώβ καὶ τὴν διασπορὰν τοῦ Ἰσραὴλ ἐπιστρέψαι· ἰδοὺ τέθεικά σε εἰς φῶς ἐθνῶν, τοῦ εἶναί σε εἰς σωτηρίαν ἕως ἐσχάτου τῆς γῆς.

That the theme of this verse concerns universal salvation makes it very suggestive in the Johannine context where Jesus describes himself as the light of the world and not just as a light to the nations. It may also be significant that here it appears to be an individual who is the servant of Yahweh. The servant here could also be an embodiment of Israel (49.3).[1] If the concept of 'a light for the nations' in Isaiah 49 contains a precedent for an individual taking on the role of Israel at the same time as restoring the people (49.5), then it is possible that Jesus' role as the light of the world implies that he has taken on the 'true' role of Israel at the same time as being the one who has been chosen to restore the people by offering light to those who follow him. Such an implication would be no different from his claim to be the true vine (15.1, 5), where Jesus himself seems to embody the true role of Israel while at the same time being the source of life (see below).

The final occurrence of the phrase 'light to the nations' accords with the context of Jesus' claim to be 'the light of the world' in John 8. In Isa. 51.4 the phrase is juxtaposed with the idea of judgment/justice which further suggests that Jesus' claim is perfectly at home in the context of a debate about witness and judgment and that the exposition of Jesus' claim to be the light of the world is not in fact deferred until ch. 9.[2] It is interesting that here it is neither the servant nor the people

1. For a short discussion of the problems associated with the word 'Israel' in 49.3, cf. Whybray, *Isaiah*, p. 137-38; For a fuller discussion cf. Westermann, *Isaiah*, pp. 208-10. Whatever may be the history of the formation of the text, it is likely that in this place it is the prophet who is seen to be the servant of the LORD.

2. Hoskyns's belief (*John*, p. 379; cf. also Brown, *John*, I, p. 343) that the exposition of 8.12 does not take place until ch. 9 is only half true. For, in the light

of Israel, but Yahweh's justice/judgment itself which is to be a light to the peoples:

Isa. 51.4, 5   ἀκούσατέ μου, ἀκούσατέ μου λαός μου, καὶ οἱ βασιλεῖς πρὸς μὲ ἐνωτίσασθε· ὅτι νόμος παρ᾽ ἐμοῦ ἐξελεύσεται, καὶ ἡ κρίσις μου εἰς φως ἐθνῶν. ἐγγίζει ταχὺ ἡ δικαιοσύνην μου, καὶ ἐξελεύσεται ὡς φῶς τὸ σωτήριόν μου...[1]

If such a phrase lies behind John's use of the term 'light', it follows that when John talks of the 'true light that enlightens every man' (1.9) and 'the light of the world' (8.12; 9.5), it refers not so much to an inner existential enlightenment[2] but to the enlightenment of justice/judgment which shows up humanity's acts for what they really are (9.40, 41).[3] That the Johannine concept of light concerns judgment rather than inner enlightenment is confirmed by the use of the term in Jn 3.19, 20. There the parallels between the use of 'light' in both Isa. 51.4 and Jn 8.12 are remarkable, for in the context of condemnation it is said:

of Isa. 42, 43 (which Hoskyns himself suggests as the likely background for Jn 8 [p. 377]), the role of the light to the nations is seen in terms of witness and judgment (42.1-4) and this is precisely the theme of Jn 8. Hoskyns is however correct to see the more direct outworking of such a claim in the sign of ch. 9. Bultmann (*John*, p. 342) also removes Jn 8.12 from its present context in an attempt to find a more suitable context and places it after 9.1-41 and in the context of 12.44-50. Schweizer too (*Ego Eimi*, pp. 163-66) takes the 'light-sayings' out of their context in the Gospel because they do not fit in with his proposed background material. Such shuffling of the text may be symptomatic of an attempt to bring the Gospel material in line with supposed background material rather than seeing whether any background material actually functions in the same way as the Gospel. For a discussion of Isa. 40–55 as a background to the 'trial motif' in John, see Lincoln, *Trials*, pp. 18-24.

1.   The addition of 'light of my salvation has gone forth' (φῶς τὸ σωτήριόν) in certain Greek manuscripts (including Sinaiticus) to the Hebrew 'my salvation has gone forth' (יָשַׁע אצי, v. 5) may suggest that John was dependent on the LXX rather than the Hebrew, for in John anyone who comes to the light is offered 'the light of life' (8.12b). However, the soteriological sub-clause could just as easily derive from the sub-clause of Isa. 49.6 where the light will bring salvation to the ends of the earth.

2.   Against Bultmann, *John*, p. 342.

3.   In a context, where Jesus' claim to be the light of the world concerns judgment as well as the offer of life, the warning that the Jews will die in their sins unless they believe that ἐγώ εἰμι makes sense. It is only by believing in the light that they will be rescued from the judgment of the light (5.24).

And this is the judgment (ἡ κρίσις) that the light (τὸ φῶς) has come into the world (τὸν κόσμου), and men loved darkness rather than light, because their deeds were evil. For everyone who does evil hates the light, and does not come (ἔρχεται[1]) to the light, lest his deeds should be exposed (3.19, 20).

All this confirms that the Isaianic concept of 'a light to the nations' is the Old Testament term which Jesus takes upon himself by means of ἐγώ εἰμι in Jn 8.12. As in the case of the claim to be the bread of life, it can be said that John uses the Old Testament in a typological way when he applies it to Jesus by means of ἐγώ εἰμι. The light to the nations is a type for the role of Jesus. By means of the phrase 'light of the world' Jesus identifies himself with the role of the servant of the Lord who may also be seen in the Isaianic context as an embodiment of the role of Israel.

In the same way that other occurrences of ἐγώ εἰμι in John bring with them the implications of the context in which they occur in the Old Testament, so too the claim to be the light of the world brings with it many of the implications associated with the 'light to the nations'. However, as with the claim to be the bread of life, the words of the Old Testament have been reinterpreted in reference to Jesus. Jesus is not just 'a light to the nations' but is in fact 'the light of the world'. This change may be partly accounted for by the fact that, while the LXX renders all three occurrences of 'a light to the nations' as εἰς φῶς ἐθνῶν (42.6; 49.6; 51.4), the Hebrew of Isa. 51.4 (לאור עמים) differs from the other two occurrences (לאור גוים). The Johannine choice of the expression 'light of the world' (τοῦ κόσμου) would then encompass both expressions just as the quotation in John 6 encompassed more than one Old Testament reference. However, since John has already developed the theme of light in terms of Jesus' coming into the world (3.19; 1.9) it is probable that his choice of τοῦ κόσμου is to link Jesus' claim in with those passages where Jesus has already been referred to as the light as well as those passages which refer to the world (cf. 1.9, 10; 3.16-19; 7.6).

When seen in its context, Jesus' claim to be the light of the world probably also alludes to Isa. 9.1, 2 which contains references both to

---

1. In Jn 8.12 it is the one who follows (ὁ ἀκολουθῶν) Jesus as the light of the world who receives the light of life. This is parallel to the one who comes (ὁ ἐρχόμενος) to Jesus as the bread of life (6.35) and expresses the same idea as 3.20.

'light' and 'the Gentiles'. The argument for such an allusion is clearly spelled out by Lindars:

> It was suggested in the notes on 7.41 that John may well be darkly alluding to the messianic text Isa. 9.1f. Now the juxtaposition of a depreciatory comment on Galilee in 7.52, and of Jesus' announcement of himself as the light in the verse immediately following, even more strongly suggests that this text is in mind. This becomes even more probable when we turn our attention to the rest of the verse, and compare it with Isa. 9.2: 'The people who walked in darkness have seen a great light; those who dwelt in a land of deep darkness on them a light has shined.'[1]

In other words Jesus' claim to be the light of the world should be seen as an ironic reply to the Jews declaration 'Search and you will see that no prophet is to rise from Galilee' (7.52). If the Jews themselves had searched they would have seen that Galilee is mentioned in their Scriptures and, while there may not be a reference to a prophet from Galilee, there is a reference to a light that will arise from Galilee:

Isa. 9.1, 2 (LXX):[2] Τοῦτο πρῶτον ποίει, ταχὺ χώρα Ζαβουλὼν, ἡ γῆ Νεφθαλὶμ ὁδὸν θαλάσσης, καὶ οἱ λοιποὶ οἱ τὴν παραλίαν κατοικοῦντες καὶ πέραν τοῦ Ἰορδάνου, Γαλιλαία τῶν ἐθνῶν, τὰ μέρη τῆς Ἰουδαίας. ὁ λαὸς ὁ πορευόμενος ἐν σκότει, ἴδετε φῶς μεγα· οἱ κατοικοῦντες ἐν χώρᾳ καὶ οκιᾷ θανάτου, φῶς λάμψει ἐφ᾽ ὑμᾶς.

Such an allusion would again show that Jesus' claim to be the light of the world fits into the context of the Gospel. Jesus takes the idea of light from Isaiah 9 and applies it to himself. Thus he claims to be the light that was to arise in Galilee of the Gentiles. At the same time he claims to be the light for the Gentiles referred to in the second part of Isaiah.

As Lindars has hinted, the reference to Isa. 9.1, 2 also illuminates the contrast between light and darkness in the sub-clause connected with the 'I am' saying.[3] While it is true that John's language is similar here to the language of Qumran,[4] there is an even closer parallel between the followers of Jesus who will not 'walk in darkness' (περιπατήσῃ ἐν τῇ σκοτίᾳ, v. 12b) and the people who 'walk in darkness' (πορευόμενος

1. Lindars, *John*, p. 315.
2. In the Hebrew, the chapter division comes between these two verses.
3. Lindars, *John*, p. 316.
4. See 1 QS 3.1-9, where the phrase 'light of life' (3.7) occurs as well as a contrast between people of light and darkness (3.3) and the importance of walking 'perfectly in all the ways of God' (3.10). Dupont-Sommer, *Essene Writings*, pp. 76-77.

ἐν σκότει) in Isa. 9.1, 2. Just as the light has shined on those who dwelt in the land and the darkness of death (ἐν χώρᾳ καὶ σκιᾷ θανάτου), so, as the light of the world, Jesus offers the light of life (τὸ φῶς τῆς ζωῆς).[1]

The allusion to Isa. 9.1-2 is further confirmed by Jn 7.41, for the ironic statement of the Jews concerning Galilee (7.52) follows on the similar question of the people: 'Is the Christ to come from Galilee? Has not the Scripture said that the Christ is descended from David, and comes from Bethlehem, the village where David was?' Such a reference would concur with the Johannine use of irony which is so often present in the context of the 'I am' sayings. On the one hand, the Gospel may assume that the reader has knowledge of the story of Jesus' birth in Bethlehem and would thus see the irony in the ignorance of the crowd about Jesus' earthly origin.[2] On the other hand, if Jesus' claim to be the Light of the World alludes to Isa. 9.1-2, it is ironic that both the crowd and the Jews have not understood the reference in their Scriptures to the light that was to shine in Galilee of the Gentiles. While the Jews' and some of the crowd reject the idea that Jesus could be the messiah because he does not fulfil their Scriptures, they are blind to the fact that he fulfils the Old Testament far more fully than they had imagined.

Pancaro suggests the possibility that in the symbolism of light John contrasts Jesus to the Torah. However, he concedes that this is far from certain:

> The uncertainty stems from the fact that, whereas the 'living water' and the 'bread of life' in the Fourth Gospel have counterparts... in which one may find a symbolic reference to the Law, 'light' has no such counterpart.[3]

Part of the problem for Pancaro is that he is uncertain about whether the Johannine concept of light stems from Judaism or the Old Testament rather than Hellenism. If a Jewish source could be ascertained, 'the possibility of such a contrast would be greater.'[4] He tentatively suggests that, in the wisdom literature of the Old Testament, light did become equated with the Law. In defence of this he refers to the following:

---

1. For John, Jesus has come into the world for those who dwell (κατοικοῦντες, Isa. 9.1, 2) in darkness, 'that whoever believes in him may not remain (μὴ μείνῃ) in darkness' (12.46).

2. Cf. Barrett, *John*, pp. 330-31.

3. Pancaro, *Law in the Fourth Gospel*, p. 485.

4. Pancaro, *Law in the Fourth Gospel*, p. 485.

Prov. 6.23:   For the commandment (מצוה) is a lamp and the teaching (תורה) is a
              light
Wis. 18.4:   For their enemies deserved to be deprived of light and imprisoned in
              darkness, those who had kept your children imprisoned, through
              whom the imperishable light of the law (τὸ ἄφθαρτον νόμου φῶς)
              was to be given to the world (NRSV).
Sir. 24.27 (LXX):[1] It makes instruction shine forth like light.

Pancaro also refers to Ps. 119.105, where 'word' (ὁ λόγος) is equated
with light and suggests that 'the representation of the Torah as light is
frequent' in the Rabbinic writings.[2] This would be particularly relevant
for John 8 since the ensuing discussion with the Pharisees concerns
'your law' (v. 17). It is possible, then, that Jesus' 'I am' saying here not
only points to the fulfilment in himself of various Old Testament
passages about light, but also to the fulfilment of what the concept of
light had come to embody (including the concept of Law). If this is the
case, Jesus would, as the Light of the World, take on the role that was
played by the Torah in Judaism. However, this should not primarily be
seen as a contrast with the Law (against Pancaro), but as a typological
fulfilment of what the Law pointed to (cf. 5.46, 47). As in John 6, the 'I
am' saying of Jesus concentrates on the positive side of what he offers
to humanity, rather than the obsolescence of what has gone before.[3]
While Pancaro is correct to draw attention to the possible equation of
the Law with light, the above evidence suggests that this is a secondary
reference. The primary background to Jesus' claim to be the light of the

1.   The Syriac renders this verse quite differently: 'It pours forth instruction
like the Nile...'
2.   Pancaro, *Law in the Fourth Gospel*, p. 485. Pancaro refers to the work of
Strack–Billerbeck (*Kommentar*, II, p. 357) who point to such passages as *Apoc.
Bar.* 77.16: 'If you regard the law and act carefully in wisdom, the light will not fail
you'; and *Apoc. Bar.* 59.2: 'In that time the light of the Law lightened all those who
sat in the darkness'.
3.   See Carson's exegesis of 1.16, 17 (*John*, pp. 131-34) who rightly agrees
with Westcott (*John*, p. 14) that grace and truth was 'the natural issue of all that had
gone before'. Carson continues: 'This cannot mean that there is no contrast between
law and Jesus Christ: that contrast is explicit, on the surface of the text. But the law
that was given through Moses, and the grace and truth that came through Jesus
Christ (v. 17), alike sprang from the fulness of the Word (v. 16), whether in his pre-
existent oneness with the Father, or in his status as the Word-made-flesh. It is from
that "fulness" that we have received "one grace replacing another".' Cf. N.A. Dahl,
'The Johannine Church and History', in J. Ashton, *The Interpretation of John*
(Issues in Religion and Theology, 9; London: SPCK, 1986), pp. 129-30.

world is the Old Testament passages (particularly in Isaiah) which Jesus takes and applies to himself by means of ἐγώ εἰμι.

Thus ἐγώ εἰμι in Jn 8.12 functions in a very similar way to John 6.35. In both places Jesus takes an Old Testament concept and applies it to himself. In both places the claim alludes to more than one Old Testament passage while at the same time drawing on one passage in particular. In both places Jesus re-interprets the Old Testament reference in terms of his own role and mission so that in John 6 he does not claim that he is simply the bread from heaven but is the bread of life and in John 8 he is not just a light to the nations but the light of the world. In both places his role is explained in terms of what he offers to others.

John 10

The primary reference of the 'I am' sayings in John 10 is clearly to the parable (παροιμία) which opens the chapter. Jesus does not merely claim to be the Door (vv. 7, 9; cf. vv. 1, 2), but the door of which the parable spoke.[1] Likewise, Jesus claims to be the shepherd of whom the parable spoke (vv. 11, 14; cf. vv. 2-5). In John 10 there is neither a specific Old Testament quotation, as in John 6, nor a particular Old Testament phrase, as in John 8, which Jesus takes on himself by the words ἐγώ εἰμι. However, the passage is full of Old Testament allusions which demonstrate John's complex but subtle use of the Old Testament.[2] Just as the claims to be the Bread of Life and the Light of the World allude to more than one Old Testament passage, so the twofold claim of ch. 10 appears to allude to several Old Testament images.[3]

Perhaps the main Old Testament allusion in John 10 is to the prophecy of Ezekiel 34.[4] There Ezekiel is told to prophesy against the

---

1. Lindars (*John*, p. 358) correctly states that to follow Bultmann (*John*, p. 377 n. 7) in regarding v. 9 as the original form 'would mean "You know what 'the door' means as a religious symbol (the way of escape from the prison, the gate into heaven, etc.). Well, that is what I am!"' However, since that would allow for 'only the slightest connection with the parable, which has supplied the vocabulary, but not the meaning . . . the primary reference of the door, and for that matter of the sheep is to specific words in the parable, i.e. verses 1 and 2.' Cf. Carson, *John*, p. 385.

2. Cf. esp. C.K. Barrett, 'The Old Testament in the Fourth Gospel', *JTS* 48 (1947), p. 163.

3. Cf. Barrett, 'Old Testament', p. 162.

4. Cf. Brown, *John*, I, pp. 389, 397; Carson, *John*, pp. 381-82. Guilding (*Jewish Worship*, p. 130) observes that Ezek. 37.16ff., which itself provides parallels with John 10, was the haphtarah for the time around Dedication in the first

'shepherds of Israel' (προφήτευσον ἐπὶ τοὺς ποιμένας τοῦ Ἰσραήλ, v. 1), who are the leaders of God's chosen people:

> The prophet begins by denouncing the corrupt rulers of Israel as false shepherds of God's flock. Instead of feeding the sheep, they prey upon them; instead of protecting them they allow them to wander unheeded, with the result that the flock is scattered and devoured by wild beasts (vv. 1-6). The shepherds therefore are to be deposed from their office (v. 10), and God himself will seek out His sheep as a shepherd seeks out his flock in the dark and cloudy day (vv. 11, 12). He will lead them out (ἐξάγειν - v. 13) from their place of exile, collect (συνάγειν, v. 13) the scattered flock, and lead them into (εἰσάγειν - v. 13) the land where they will find good pasture (νομῇ - v. 14). God will feed His sheep and give them rest and they shall know Him (γνώσονται ὅτι ἐγώ Κύριος ὁ θεὸς αὐτῶν - v. 30)...He will save His sheep (σώσω τὰ πρόβατά μου - v. 22), and will set over them one shepherd (ἀναστήσω ἐπ' αὐτοὺς ποιμένα ἕτερον - v. 23), namely David (i.e. the Messiah of David's line). God will then eliminate the evil beasts and give peace to the flock. The prophecy ends with the emphatic proclamation, πρόβατά μου καὶ πρόβατα ποιμνίου μου ἐστὲ, καὶ ἐγώ Κύριος ὁ θεὸς ὑμῶν (v. 31).[1]

The conceptual similarities between Ezekiel 34 and John 10 are immediately apparent. The false shepherds in Ezekiel (vv. 1-7) are paralleled by the hireling, thieves and robbers in Jesus' parable, where the thief comes to steal, kill and destroy (v. 10). The hireling cares only for himself and abandons the flock to wild beasts (vv. 12, 13). Likewise the shepherds of Ezekiel are charged with putting their own interests before the care of God's flock and leaving the sheep to the wild beasts (vv. 2, 6). This is in contrast with the care that God will show to his flock (vv. 11-16, 25-30; cf. Isa. 40.11). These similarities between Ezekiel 34 and John 10 suggest that the concept of the false shepherd as well as that of the Good Shepherd is drawn from such a background.

In the Ezekiel passage God states that he will be the shepherd (34.15) of his sheep. At the same time he will set up his servant David (v. 23) as shepherd. By the words ἐγώ εἰμι in John 10, Jesus identifies himself with the role which God would accomplish as the promised Good Shepherd. At the same time Jesus fulfils the role of God's servant David. Jesus' close relationship with the Father (Jn 10.14, 15) is thus parallelled in Ezekiel by the thought that both God (vv. 11-16) and his

year of the cycle, while Ezek. 34 was the second-year haphtarah.

1. Dodd, *Interpretation*, pp. 358-59. I have added the verse references for the sake of convenience. Cf. Lindars, *John*, p. 353.

servant David (vv. 23, 24) are to be the shepherd of the flock. In Ezekiel the relationship between God and his servant is so close that God speaks of there being only one Shepherd (Ezek. 34.23; cf. 37.24), a fact also emphasized in John (10.16; cf. v. 30).[1] The concept of salvation mentioned in connection with Jesus as the gate (v. 9) is present also in Ezekiel (34.22). The conceptual similarities between Ezekiel's shepherd imagery and that of John are so close that Jesus' parable seems deliberately to allude to the ideas in Ezekiel. By claiming to be the Good Shepherd and by his care for the sheep, Jesus does the work that God promised he would do in Ezekiel.[2]

John's use of the Old Testament with the unpredicated 'I am' sayings showed how the context of the Old Testament has a bearing on the meaning of the text in John. The same is true of the context in which the shepherd/sheep imagery occurs, for the parable which begins John 10 immediately follows Jesus' discussion with the Pharisees about their blindness. By claiming to be the Door of the sheep, he implies that they have been attempting to enter the sheepfold by climbing in over the wall. They are the thieves and robbers of whom he speaks, while he is both the gate and the shepherd. His bold declaration that all who came before him were thieves and robbers suggests that he is equating them with those shepherds described by Ezekiel who did not care for the sheep. At the same time, by contrasting himself with such shepherds, Jesus equates himself with the activity of YHWH. Jesus is the Good Shepherd that YHWH had promised. In fact it was the LORD himself who was to care for his sheep. Jesus' identity with the Father is to be likened to the identity of David, the LORD's servant, with YHWH in Ezekiel. Whether Jesus is to be identified with God through his claim to be the shepherd or with his servant David is of little importance, for they both perform the same task. This is true to such an extent that Jesus can claim 'I and the Father are one' (v. 30).

In addition to Ezekiel 34, many Old Testament references seem to be reflected in vocabulary which is used in John 10. The theme first appears in Num. 27.17 where Moses asks for a successor 'who

---

1. G. Reim, *Studien zum alttestamentlichen Hintergrund des Johannes-evangeliums* (SNTSMS, 22; Cambridge: Cambridge University Press, 1974) p. 184, states: 'If one compares John 10 with Ezekiel 34, it is striking that both speak of the shepherd and in fact of the "one shepherd". This concept is found only in Ezekiel in the O.T. and only in John in the N.T.'

2. Cf. Lindars, *John*, p. 353.

shall go out before them (ἐξελεύσεται) and come in before them (εἰσελεύσεται), who shall lead them out (ἐξάξει) and bring them in (εἰσάξει); that the congregation of the LORD may not be as sheep without a shepherd (ὡσεὶ πρόβατα, οἷς οὐκ ἔστιν ποιμήν)'. The parallel between this call of Joshua and the image of the shepherd in John 10 is again apparent. In John the shepherd leads out the sheep (ἐξάγει, v. 3)[1] and the sheep go in (εἰσελεύσεται) and go out (ἐξελεύσεται) through the gate and find pasture (v. 9). The fact that the later shepherds of Israel fail to live up to the ideal set out in Numbers is one which runs through the book of Jeremiah. The theme is particularly similar to that of Ezekiel in Jer. 23.1-6, where the LORD condemns the shepherds for failing to attend to his sheep (vv. 1, 2). He promises to 'gather the remnant' of his people from the nations and bring them back to their own fold (v. 3),[2] and to 'raise up for David a righteous Branch who shall reign as king and deal wisely, and shall execute justice and righteousness in the land' (v. 5).[3]

While the idea that there will be one shepherd is present in Ezek. 34.23 and 37.24, in Jer. 23.3 the LORD promises that he will gather the scattered Israel again (cf. 31.10; Zeph. 3.10). The fact that the sheep will be gathered into one flock is even more explicit in Mic. 2.12. There the LORD declares:

Mic. 2.12

I will surely gather all of you, O Jacob, I will gather the remnant of Israel; I will set them together like sheep in a fold, like a flock in its pasture, a noisy multitude of men.	συναγόμενος συναχθήσεται Ἰακὼβ σὺν πᾶσιν· ἐκδεχόμενος ἐκδέξομαι τοὺς καταλοίπους τοῦ Ἰσραήλ, ἐπὶ τὸ αὐτὸ θήσομαι τὴν ἀποστροφὴν αὐτῶν· ὡς πρόβατα ἐν φλίψει,,[4] ὡς ποίμνιον ἐν μέσῳ κοίτης αὐτῶν ἐξαλοῦνται ἐξ ἀνθρώπων.

1. ἐξάγειν ('to lead out') is also used in Ezek. 34.13; see above.
2. The Hebrew נוה ('fold') is rendered νομή ('pasture') by the LXX; cf. Jn 10.9.
3. Other references in Jeremiah to the leaders as shepherds occur at 2.8 (RSV 'rulers'); 3.15; 10.21; 12.10; 22.22; 25.34, 35, 36 (LXX 32.34, 35, 36); 49.19 (LXX 29.19); 50.6 (LXX 27.6); 50.44 (LXX 27.44); 51.23 (LXX 28.23). The LXX seems to have translated the Hebrew for 'lover' (רעה) as 'shepherd' (רעה) at 3.1 and 3.3. However, the proximity of 'shepherd' in 3.15, may suggest that it is the Hebrew that is mispointed.
4. Instead of ἐν φλίψει ('in trouble') the Hebrew talks of sheep in a 'fold' (בצרה, *bosrah*). There is great disagreement over the translation of this word. While the MT reads *bosrah*, (lit. 'stronghold') and refers to a Moabite town (cf. Jer.

As in Ezekiel, God here 'promises to perform the work of gathering which belongs to his role as the shepherd of Israel. The title "shepherd" belongs to Yahweh's identity as ruler of his people.'[1]

The attraction of this passage in Micah for John 10 is that the image of sheep also occurs in the context of a 'gate' which the sheep are to pass through:

Mic. 2.13

He who opens the breach will go up	διὰ τῆς διακοπῆς πρὸ προσώπου αὐτῶν
before them; they will break through	διέκοψαν, καὶ διῆλθον πύλην καὶ
and pass the gate, going out by it.	ἐξῆλθον δι' αὐτῆς, καὶ ἐξῆλθεν ὁ
Their king will pass on before them,	βασιλεὺς αὐτῶν πρὸ προσώπου αὐτῶν,
the LORD at their head.	ὁ δὲ Κύριος ἡγήσεται αὐτῶν.

Although θύρα is generally used to render the Hebrew words for 'door' (mostly דלת or פתח), there are a handful of Old Testament passages where it is used by the LXX to render 'gate' (שער).[2] Just as the LORD leads the sheep out through the gate (v. 13), so the shepherd in John leads out the sheep from the fold (vv. 3, 4). While the meaning of the Micah passage is much disputed,[3] just as in Ezekiel and Jeremiah, the 'shepherd/sheep' imagery again occurs in the context of the LORD's condemnation of those who are meant to be the shepherds of his flock (3.1ff.). However, despite the attractiveness of a background where the sheep imagery occurs in the same context as a gate, it is quite clear that the imagery in John differs greatly from that in Micah. The idea of the shepherd breaking out of the fold and leading his sheep is entirely absent in John where the role of the gate is one of protection from

48.24), the word is rendered as 'fold' by the Targum (בנו חוטרא) and the Vulgate (*in ovili*). This has caused scholars to repoint the Hebrew so that it reads *basira* which is taken to mean 'in the fold/encampment'. J.D.M. Derrett ('The Good Shepherd: St John's use of Jewish Halakah and Haggadah', *ST* 27 [1973], pp. 25-50) suggests that this hypothetical reconstruction would not have been known 'to the contemporaries of Jesus' (p. 38) and thus suggests that either the MT should be taken as it is or that the LXX (ἐν φλίψει) correctly translates the Hebrew *besarah*. However, he still finds enough parallels to think that Micah (among other passages) is in view when Jesus claims to be the 'gate' of the sheep.

1. J.L. Mays, *Micah* (London: SCM Press, 1976), pp. 75, 76.
2. E.g. Exod. 39.40 (LXX 39.20); Job 5.4; Prov. 14.19; Ezek. 46.12 (46.13).
3. For the different interpretations of this passage cf. Mays, *Micah*, p. 75; L.C. Allen, *Joel, Obadiah, Jonah and Micah* (NICOT; Grand Rapids: Eerdmans, 1976), pp. 300-303; also R.L. Smith, *Micah–Malachi* (WBC; Waco, TX: Word Books, 1984), pp. 28-30.

thieves and robbers. In John the function of the gate concerns the legitimate access to the fold which is used by both shepherd (v. 2) and sheep (v. 9). It is thus unlikely that the Micah passage should be seen as background material for John 10.

The Johannine concept of the gate finds a closer parallel in Psalm 118.20 (LXX 117),[1] although this does not occur in the context of shepherd imagery. As in Micah the word used in the LXX to translate the Hebrew שער is πύλη. However, there are certain conceptual parallels with John 10 that are worth noting:

Ps. 118.19-21 (LXX 117.18-21): ἀνοίξατέ μοι **πύλας** δικαιοσύνης· **εἰσελθὼν** ἐν αὐταῖς ἐξομολογήσομαι τῷ Κυρίῳ. αὕτη ἡ **πύλη** τοῦ Κυρίου, δίκαιοι **εἰσελεύσονται** ἐν αὐτῇ. ἐξομολογήσομαί σοι, ὅτι ἐπήκουσάς μου καὶ ἐγένου μοι εἰς **σωτηρίαν**.

The Psalmist requests to be able to enter through the gate (v. 19), just as in John the sheep enter by Jesus (εἰσέλθη, v. 9). Likewise the sheep are to go in (εἰσελεύσεται, v. 9) and come out and find pasture. While these parallels may be explained simply on the grounds that they consist of vocabulary which is necessary to the concept of any gate, it is significant that the Psalmist declares that, by answering his prayer (i.e. by letting him go through the gate), the LORD has become his salvation. In John 10 anyone who enters by Jesus will also experience salvation (σωθήσεται, v. 9).

Despite this parallel in Psalm 118, it may be better to regard Jesus' claim to be the Door simply in terms of the parable which itself is steeped in the Old Testament sheep/shepherd imagery. John is not stringently bound by concepts that occur in the Old Testament, but develops that imagery to suit his Christological purpose. Jesus not only takes on himself the image of the promised shepherd, but also stresses the exclusivity and legitimacy of his role, by claiming to be the gate of the sheep.[2]

On several occasions in the Psalms the LORD is portrayed as the shepherd of Israel. This image is perhaps most developed in Psalm 23 (LXX 22), which Barrett thinks is equal in importance to Ezekiel 34 for the understanding of John 10. In it 'there is a shepherd who leads and pastures his flock, defends it in time of danger, and supplies it with all

---

1. Cf. Carson, *John*, p. 385.

2. Cf. Lindars, who suggests (against Bultmann) that 'The special features in John's allegory are not derived from extraneous sources... The door and the thieves belong to the underlying parable...' (*John*, p. 353).

things necessary for life'.[1] However, this Psalm does not provide a very close parallel either to the vocabulary or to the imagery of John 10 which suggests that it is not primary background material for John's use of the sheep/shepherd imagery. What is confirmed by the Psalm's use of this imagery is the fact that the Old Testament as a whole regarded YHWH as the ideal shepherd who cared for his sheep.[2] Ps. 78.70-72 also shows that David was in some way regarded as the ideal shepherd of the people of Israel. It is these two themes that are present in Ezekiel 34, where they are combined.

Beutler raises the possibility that John 10 may allude to Zech. 13.7.[3] However, the picture of the Good Shepherd in John 10 is not concerned with the passive striking of the shepherd nor yet with the scattering of the flock. In fact the reverse is the case. The emphasis of John 10 is on the fact that the shepherd gives himself willingly for the sheep (esp. v. 18) and on the gathering rather than the scattering of the sheep (v. 16). While 'it is at least possible that the verse in Zechariah already has a positive sense, in which the death of the shepherd opens the way for a new gathering of the flock',[4] there is no suggestion that the striking of the shepherd is voluntary. There also needs to be more evidence that the striking of the shepherd is to be compared with 'one whom they have pierced' in 12.10.[5] That such a comparison is implicit in John 10 is far too speculative. Beutler is thus correct to conclude that it is unlikely that Zech. 13.7 has directly influenced the shepherd imagery in John 10.[6]

1. Barrett, 'Old Testament', p. 163.

2. Other Psalms which use the shepherd/sheep imagery in various ways are: 44.11, 22 (LXX 43) ; 49.14 (48); 74.1 (73); 76.20 (75); 78.52, 70-72 (77); 79.13 (78); 80.1 (79); 95.7 (94); 100.3 (99); 107.41 (106); 114.4, 6 (113); 119.176 (118).

3. J. Beutler, 'Der alttestamentliche-judische Hintergrund der Hirtenrede in Johannes 10', in J. Beutler and R.T. Fortna (eds.), *The Shepherd Discourse of John 10 and its Context: Studies by Members of the Johannine Writings Seminar* (SNTSMS, 67; Cambridge: Cambridge University Press, 1991) pp. 18-32.

4. Beutler, *Hintergrund der Hirtenrede*, p. 30.

5. See Beutler, *Hintergrund der Hirtenrede*, p. 30.

6. Beutler, *Hintergrund der Hirtenrede*, p. 31. It is possible that the idea of the shepherd being willing to die for his sheep, stems from Isa. 53.6-9, in which the iniquity of the sheep is taken by the servant of the LORD. Lindars suggests that 'the chief influence has been the Church's use of Isa. 53 to expound the crucifixion, a passage which at least includes mention of the sheep as those who benefit from the Servant's sacrificial death' (*John*, p. 361). However, the willingness of the Shepherd to die for his sheep is primarily a Johannine feature. In the light of Jesus'

Barrett is correct to conclude his discussion of the Old Testament background to John 10 in the following way:

> The allegory of the Shepherd is an O.T. construction...But it is not based on any single O.T. text or passage. There are real shepherds and real flocks, and there are symbolical shepherds and symbolical flocks in nearly every part of the O.T. The Evangelist has made up not a mosaic of fragments but a unitary picture, the separate features of which can for the most part be recognized in the O.T., though they are fitted into a quite distinctly Christian framework.[1]

What Barrett describes as 'a distinctly Christian framework' occurs in the application and exposition of the features within the παροιμία to the person and mission of Jesus. Even with all the Old Testament allusions outlined above, John's concept of the Good Shepherd is unique. The ideas that occur in the Old Testament are developed in a peculiarly Johannine way.[2]

As with the bread which came down from heaven, the consequences of Jesus' claim for the believer are expounded in terms of the life which he gives (v. 10; cf. 6.51). The mutual knowledge between the shepherd and his sheep (v. 14) is typically Johannine and even goes beyond the care that YHWH shows for his sheep in Ezekiel. The recognition formula of Ezekiel is seen in an expanded form in Ezek. 34.30, 31 where YHWH declares:

> 'And they shall know that I, the LORD their God, am with them, and that they, the house of Israel are my people, says the Lord GOD. And you are my sheep, the sheep of my pasture, and I am your God, says the Lord GOD.'[3]

impending death, Jesus' willingness to give himself up for the sheep shows that the crucifixion is in his control (see literary study above). Thus the crucifixion is the primary reference in Jesus' words. If Isa. 53 is in mind it has been thoroughly transformed in the light of the crucifixion.

1. Barrett, 'Old Testament', p. 164.

2. Derrett (*The Good Shepherd*) attempts to show how Jn 10 is a midrashic exposition of several Old Testament passages, namely Exod. 22.1, Isa. 56.1–57.19 and Mic. 2.12, 13. While it is likely that Jn 10 does show signs of midrashic exposition of certain Old Testament passages, Derrett's work is not as thorough nor as plausible as Borgen's work on Jn 6. Derrett's attempt to reconstruct the 'original' parable behind Jn 10 is at best conjectural. What Derrett's work does show is that John's use of the Old Testament is both subtle and in line with Jewish exegesis.

3. Cf. W. Zimmerli, 'Knowledge of God According to the Book of Ezekiel', in Zimmerli, *I am Yahweh*, pp. 29-98.

Yet even this does not go as far as the mutual knowledge shown between shepherd and sheep in John 10, a knowledge that is further developed in John's Gospel so that to know Jesus is also to know the Father (14.7). Perhaps influenced by the Isaianic servant, John also develops the Old Testament concept of the Good Shepherd to such an extent that Jesus is willing to lay down his life for the sheep.[1]

John 14.6
In Jn 14.4 Jesus asserts that the disciples already know the way where he is going (v. 4). On this verse Lindars comments:

> Apart from an allusion to Isa. 40.3 in 1.23, **way** (*hodos*) occurs only in this and the next two verses in the Fourth Gospel, and never in the Johannine Epistles. This is surprising, considering the wide range of meaning of this word in general and the importance of the idea of 'going' in John's presentation of the Passion...But the fact that the word here comes as a non-Johannine intruder suggests that we should look for a specific saying in the underlying tradition to account for it.[2]

Lindars himself suggests that this 'non-Johannine intruder' is parallel to Jesus' claim to be the door in John 10 and may also derive from a Synoptic saying of Jesus such as that in Mt. 7.14: 'For the gate (πύλη) is narrow and the way (ὁδὸς) is hard, that leads to life (εἰς τὴν ζωὴν)'.[3] However, it may be that this 'non-Johannine intruder' is not to be accounted for 'in the underlying tradition' of the Synoptics but instead in a specific concept in the Old Testament. Such a suggestion may be reinforced by the only other use of 'the way' in Jn 1.23.[4]

On the surface John the Baptist's quotation from Isa. 40.3 seems to refer to his own role, for it is in response to the demand from those sent on behalf of the Pharisees: 'What do you say about yourself?' (1.22).

---

1. Bultmann goes so far as to say that the differences between the shepherd/ sheep imagery of John and that of the Old Testament 'show that the Johannine shepherd is either an original conception, or else that it stands in another tradition' (*John*, p. 367).

2. Lindars, *John*, p. 471.

3. Lindars, *John*, p. 472. Lindars also draws parallels with the 'moral sense' in which the way is used in the Old Testament and particularly in Wisdom's appeal that men should keep her ways in order that they might find life (Prov. 8.32, 35).

4. Lindars (*John*, p. 471) points to the fact that the quotation from Isaiah is the only other place where John uses ὁδὸς, but no one suggests that its meaning there may have a bearing on its meaning in Jn 14.

However, in John's Gospel, the Baptist always points away from himself to the person of Jesus (cf. vv. 7, 8, 26, 27, 29-34). This is true even of the quotation which John applies to himself. For although his role fulfils the Old Testament, it is only as the voice which points to something greater. John's role is as the voice who cries in the wilderness. Unlike in the Synoptics, there is neither an emphasis on a moral preparation of the people nor even a call to repentance (Mk 1.2-5), instead John points to the one whom his audience do not know (v. 26) and whose sandals John is unworthy to untie (v. 27): the 'Lamb of God' (v. 29). Thus it is likely that the words which John quotes from Isaiah also point to Jesus. The manner in which John the Baptist makes 'straight the way of the Lord' (v. 23) is in his witness to Jesus as the voice calling in the wilderness. The question pertinent to the use of ὁδός in John 14 is whether the whole phrase 'the way of the Lord' may refer to Jesus rather than (or as well as) the traditional interpretation in which it refers to John the Baptist's ministry of preparation for the work of Jesus. In other words, what is the 'way of the LORD' for which John prepares by his witness?

When the concept of 'the way of the Lord' in Isaiah is studied in more detail various links with John's Gospel become apparent. The first point of significance for both John 1 and John 14 is that the preparation of 'the way of the LORD' in Isa. 40.3 has the result that, 'the glory of the LORD shall be revealed, and all flesh shall see it together, for the mouth of the LORD has spoken' (καὶ ὀφθήσεται ἡ δόξα Κυρίου, καὶ ὄψεται πᾶσα σὰρξ τὸ σωτήριον τοῦ θεοῦ· ὅτι Κύριος ἐλάλησε, v. 5).[1] Jn 1.14 claims explicitly: 'We have beheld his glory, glory as of the only Son from the Father'. So the glory that Jesus reveals is connected at the outset of John's Gospel with the glory of the Father. In the context of John 14 this connection is even more explicit. For, at the departure of Judas in Jn 13.31, Jesus declares: 'Now is the Son of man glorified, and in him God is glorified'. Just as the glory of the LORD is

---

1. Westermann comments that in the idea of preparing a way in Isa. 40.3, 'we have...the first instance of a special feature which constantly recurs in what Deutero-Isaiah has to say' (*Isaiah*, p. 38). A little later, in discussing the Babylonian use of the term, Westermann adds that in Isaiah 'It is, however, designated a highway "for Yahweh our God", just as the magnificent highways of Babylon were strictly highways for her gods. Its designation as the highway for Yahweh is more precisely explained in v. 5, "And the glory of Yahweh shall be revealed".'

mentioned in the context of 'preparing the way of the LORD' in Isa.
40.5, so glory occurs in the context of both the occasions that John uses
the term 'way'. In addition, following the 'I am' saying of 14.6, Jesus
says 'He who has seen me has seen the Father' (ὁ ἑωρακὼς ἐμὲ
ἑωρακεν τὸν πατέρα, v. 9). Thus Jesus' claim to be the Way is
followed by a claim that God is seen in him. This corresponds to the
revelation of God in Isaiah that was to follow the prophet's
proclamation 'Prepare the way of the LORD'.

Both Carson and Barrett point to Isa. 49.3 as a more direct link with
Jn 13.31.[1] There the LORD says 'You are my servant, Israel, in whom I
will be glorified'. Starting from 13.31, Proctor tentatively suggests that
the same background may carry over into John 14 where Jesus claims
to be the Way, the Truth and the Life. Such a suggestion is strengthened
in that the reference to Isa. 49.3 is echoed in the repetition of Jesus'
claim that God will be glorified in the Son (14.13). Proctor himself
comments:

> Strikingly, as we read through the following chapter of Isaiah we find,
> successively, proclamation of a way of redemption from exile (49.8-13),
> affirmation of the covenant faithfulness of God to Israel (vv. 14-18), and
> the emergence of new life out of barrenness and death within the
> covenant community (vv. 19-23). On that basis 'all flesh shall know that
> I am Yahweh your Saviour' (v. 26). Way, truth and life, given by
> Yahweh to Israel, make Yahweh known in the world, as God majestic
> and unrivalled. We should at least consider the possibility that some
> influence from this chapter in Isaiah has emerged in the Johannine
> saying.[2]

It is difficult to ascertain whether the terms 'truth and life' derive from
Isaiah 49, since the parallels are conceptual rather than verbal. However,
there is a stronger connection with the term 'way' since the LORD
declares that the mountains shall be made a 'way' for the people
(v. 11). There is a further similarity between John and Isaiah in Jesus'
words in Jn 14.2, 3 where he claims that he goes away to prepare a

---

1.   Carson, *John*, p. 482; Barrett, *John*, p. 450.

2.   J. Proctor, 'The Way the Truth and the Life: Interfaith Dialogue and the
Fourth Gospel' (1991), p. 19 n. 25 (an article submitted to the Epworth Review as
a response to K. Cracknell, *Towards a New Relationship* [London: Epworth,
1986]). For his understanding of 'truth' in Jn 14.6 Proctor points to D.C.C. Braine,
'The Inner Jewishness of John's Gospel as a clue to the Inner Jewishness of Jesus',
SNTU 13 (1988), pp. 101-55.

place for his disciples. A few verses later Isaiah also declares: 'The children born in the time of your bereavement will yet say in your ears: "The place is too narrow for me; make room for me to dwell in"' (Στενός μοι ὁ τόπος, ποίησόν μοι τόπον ἵνα κατοικήσω, v. 20). However, at best Jesus' words only form a tentative verbal allusion to these words in Isaiah, since in one the people ask for a place but in the other Jesus prepares a place unsolicited.

In the light of the tentative link that has been drawn between the concept of the way in John 14 and the use of the term in both Isaiah 40 and 49, it is necessary to look at how Second Isaiah uses the term elsewhere. By so doing it will be easier to ascertain whether Jesus' self-attribution of the term ὁδός in John alludes to Isaiah's use of 'Way'.

There is a further possible link between John 1 and John 14 in the words of Isa. 42.16. There the LORD declares: 'I will lead the people in a way that they know not, in paths they have not known I will guide them' (καὶ ἄξω τυφλοὺς ἐν ὁδῷ ᾗ οὐκ ἔγνωσαν, καὶ τρίβους, οὓς οὐκ ᾔδεισαν).[1] A similar lack of knowledge also characterizes the crowd to whom John the Baptist declares that he is 'the voice of one crying in the wilderness, "Make straight the way of the Lord"' (1.23). Immediately after this quotation from Isaiah, John the Baptist announces, 'among you stands one whom you do not know' (μέσος ὑμῶν ἔστηκεν ὃν ὑμεῖς οὐκ οἴδατε, 1.26). If the previous declaration about 'the way of the LORD' is part of John's testimony to Jesus, it is ironic that among the crowd stands one who (later in the Gospel) claims to be the Way and yet they do not know it. A lack of knowledge is also explicit in the context of Jesus' claim to be the Way in John 14. There Thomas asks 'Lord, we do not know where you are going; how can we know the way?' (κύριε, οὐκ οἴδαμεν ποῦ ὑπάγεις· πῶς δυνάμεθα τὴν ὁδὸν εἰδέναι, 14.5). By his words Thomas explicitly links the disciples' lack of knowledge with the term 'way'. Thus in the context of both occurrences of ὁδός in John, there is, in the ignorance on the part of the narrative audience, an analogy with Isa. 42.16 where the LORD declares that he will lead the people in a way that they do not know.

The occurrence of the term 'way' in Isa. 43.19 simply states that YHWH is doing a new thing by making a way in the wilderness.[2] Isa.

---

1. That this verse continues, 'I will turn the darkness before them into light,' is also consistent with John's presentation of Jesus. See discussion on Jn 8.
2. Though linked to the other occurrences of 'way' in Deutero-Isaiah, 45.13

48.17 repeats the fact that it is the LORD who leads his people in the way they should go. As in the other occurrences of the 'way' in Isaiah, 'the way the people should go' concerns the journey out from exile in Babylon. In this instance the declaration of the LORD is followed by the exclamation, 'O that you would hearken to my commandments!'. In the LXX of Isaiah 48 these words also occur in the context of an ἐγώ εἰμι saying:

Isa. 48.17:   Ἐγώ εἰμι ὁ θεός σου, δέδειχά σοι τοῦ εὑρεῖν σε τὴν ὁδόν, ἐν ᾗ πορεύσῃ ἐν αὐτῇ. καὶ εἰ ἤκουσας τῶν ἐντολῶν μου, ἐγένετο ἂν ὡσεὶ ποταμὸς ἡ εἰρήνη σου...

The LXX combines two parallel Hebrew phrases in one Greek one. By so doing, it makes the 'way' the object of the sentence. Of more pertinence to John 14 is the link between 'being taught to find the way to go' and obedience to the commandments of the LORD. Not only has Jesus just given the disciples a new commandment (13.34, 35), but, in the discourse which follows this 'I am' saying, he also goes on to assert, 'If you love me, you will keep my commandments' (Ἐαν ἀγαπᾶτέ με, τὰς ἐντολὰς τὰς ἐμὰς τηρσετε, 14.15). This emphasis on keeping the commandments of Jesus is taken up again (v. 21), before Jesus promises the disciples that he leaves peace with them (εἰρήνη, v. 27). The concept of peace is also present in the use of 'Way' in Isa. 59.8, where the prophet declares that the people do not know the way of peace.

Isaiah's call to prepare a way is repeated in 57.15 and 62.10. In this last verse, all that is encompassed in the idea of the 'way of the LORD' is expressed. It is interesting that what began as 'the way of the LORD' in Isa. 40.3 has here become 'the way for the people'. The two phrases are synonymous in the sense that both speak of the way of redemption from exile. The way of the LORD in Isaiah is also the way that the people will pass on their journey from exile back to Jerusalem. If, by his ἐγώ εἰμι saying in John 14, Jesus applies to himself the concept of the Way of the LORD from Isaiah, it could express the twofold idea of the way by which the LORD passes in the redemption of his people as well as the way by which the people must pass in their return from Exile.

In the light of a comparison between Isaiah's use of the phrase 'way

concerns aligning the ways of humanity with the purposes of God, rather than preparing a way for his people to walk in.

of the LORD' and Jesus' claim in John to be the Way, it is necessary to draw some conclusions about the probability that Jesus' words in John actually allude to the term in Isaiah. It is certain that the links between John and Isaiah are by no means as strong as the links between John and the Old Testament in the previously studied 'I am' sayings. Furthermore, unlike the sayings of John 6 and John 8, there is no direct reference by Jesus' audience to the Scriptures. Neither is there the sort of Old Testament imagery so important to the 'parable' of John 10. Nor would any of the Isaianic passages which speak of 'the way of the LORD' provide sufficient basis on its own to argue that John was referring to that particular passage. However, if, as before, the concept of the 'way' is regarded as a *type*, it is possible that all the uses in Isaiah provide a sufficient basis for thinking that Jesus' claim to be the way to the Father at least alludes in part to Isaiah' use of the term.

The possibility that Jesus' claim to be the way is based on Isaiah's concept of the 'way of the LORD' is strengthened by the fact that the community at Qumran called themselves the 'Way'. As Brown points out, 'Those who entered the community were "those who have chosen the Way" (1 QS ix 17-18), while those who apostatized were "those who turn aside from the Way" (CD i 3). The regulations of community life were "regulations of the Way" (1 QS ix 21).'[1] Their reason for naming themselves thus is explicitly based on Isa. 40.3. This is seen in 1 QS 8.12-16:

> When men [who have been tested] become members of the community in Israel according to all these rules, they shall separate themselves from the places where wicked men dwell in order to go into the desert to prepare the way of Him, as it is written, 'Prepare the way of the Lord in the desert; make straight a highway for our God in the wilderness.' This (way) is the study of the Law which He commanded through Moses, that they may act according to all that has been revealed from age to age, and as the prophets have revealed through His holy spirit.[2]

The fact that the community at Qumran closely associated the concept of the 'way' with the Law strengthens the suggestion that Jesus' words should also be linked with the concept of the Law. What is more interesting for the above study is the fact that Qumran provides an example in which the 'way of the LORD' as expressed in Isaiah can be abbreviated to 'the way' and can be applied to a specific community.

---

1. Brown, *John*, II, p. 629.
2. This version is that of Brown, *John*, II, p. 629.

Such an application of 'the way' to a community also seems to have occurred within the early church (Acts 9.2; 19.9, 23; 22.4; 24.14, 22). If, by claiming to be the Way, such groups (i.e., Qumran and the early church) took their point of reference from the concept of the 'way of the LORD' in Isaiah, it is not unlikely that the words of Jesus allude to the same passages of Scripture.[1]

The theme of the way of the LORD is also prominent in Malachi. A bridge between the use of 'way' on the lips of Jesus (in a grammatically absolute form) and the Isaianic phrase 'the way of the LORD' may be provided in Malachi's use of the term, for the Isaianic cry to prepare the way occurs in Mal. 3.1. There the LORD declares:

> Behold, I send my messenger to prepare the way before me, and the Lord whom you seek will suddenly come to his temple; the messenger of the covenant in whom you delight, behold, he is coming, says the LORD of hosts.[2]

A few verses earlier, in Mal. 2.8, the LORD declares that the priests have turned aside from the way:

> ὑμεῖς δὲ ἐξεκλίνατε ἐκ τῆς ὁδοῦ
> καὶ ἠσθενήσατε πολλοὺς ἐν νόμῳ.

---

1.   Brown, *John*, II, p. 629, suggests that the allusion to the Old Testament in Jn 14.6 is one mediated both through Judaism and through the Christian community's adoption of the term as a self-designation (cf. Acts 9.2; 19.9; 22.4; 24.14, 22). Using the temple imagery of 2.21 as another example, Brown also suggests that 'it is not unusual for the Johannine Jesus to take terminology once applied to Israel (and subsequently adopted by the Christian community) and apply it to himself'. While such a concept may reflect 'this whole chain of usage of the imagery of "the way"', it seems from the discussion above that John's ultimate point of reference is the Old Testament itself and not the subsequent development of the concept within Judaism (or within the church).

2.   Here, by the parallelism of the verse, the messenger of the covenant is intimately connected with the LORD 'so that "the Angel" is associated or identified with "the Lord"' in much the same way that the Son is associated or identified with the Father in John (P.A. Verhoef, *The Books of Haggai and Malachi* [NICOT; Grand Rapids: Eerdmans, 1987], p. 289). This Malachi passage, which refers to the LORD's appearance in his Temple, may take on greater significance in the light of McCaffrey's study on Jn 14.2, 3, *Many Rooms*, which argues that 'this text states in equivalent Johannine terms that the New Temple of the risen Jesus is the way of access to the heavenly temple of the Father's house' (p. 21).

Although 'way' is paralleled here by 'instruction' (LXX: 'law'), it is grammatically absolute.[1] As such it is nearer in form to the words of Jesus in Jn 14.6 than the whole phrase 'way of the LORD' used in Isaiah.

In Malachi 2 the LORD also speaks of his covenant of 'life and peace' (τῆς ζωῆς καὶ τῆς εἰρήνης, v. 5). Levi is presented as an example in whose mouth 'true instruction' (νόμος ἀληθείας) was present (v. 6). Thus the concepts of life, true instruction and way occur within four verses of each other. As in Isaiah, the concept of the 'way' is accompanied in Malachi by the theme of glory. In God's call to give glory to his name (δοῦναι δόξαν τῷ ὀνόματί μου, 2.2) there is a verbal link with Jn 14.13 where Jesus promises 'Whatever you ask in my name (ἐν τῷ ὀνόματί μου), I will do it, that the Father may be glorified (ἵνα δοξασθῇ ὁ πατὴρ) in the Son'.[2]

It should be noted in conclusion that Pancaro sees in the concept of the 'way' a reference to the Law. He suggests that:

> In the OT (especially in Dt) the 'way of the Lord' is the path marked out for man by the will of God. So much so, that ἐντολὴ may be used as a synonym for the 'way'.[3]

In this Pancaro is dependent on Michaelis who suggests that 'the way of the Lord is the walk which God requires of man'.[4] Michaelis cites the example of Ps. 119.15, 'I will meditate on thy precepts (ἐν ταῖς ἐντολαῖς σου) and fix my eyes on thy ways (τὰς ὁδούς σου)', and

1. Pancaro (*Law in the Fourth Gospel*, p. 270) is thus wrong to agree with Michaelis that ὁδός is not found absolutely in theOld Testament. Cf. W. Michaelis, 'ὁδός' *TDNT*, pp. 48-96.

2. Is it possible that these words in Malachi explain the significance of the sub-clause of Jesus' 'I am' saying in which he asserts that 'no one comes to the Father, but by me' (14.6b)? Since Mal. 2.5-9 portrays Levi as the ideal priest, who provides true instruction to God's people, it is conceivable that Jesus' 'I am' saying alludes to the role of the priest. As mediator between God and humanity, the priest would provide access to God. For such an allusion to take place it would have to be established that John saw Jesus in this manner.

3. Pancaro, *Law in the Fourth Gospel*, p. 270.

4. Michaelis, 'ὁδός', p. 51. Michaelis, however, does not think that the 'way' in Jn 14.6 refers to the Old Testament usage of the term, 'for ὁδός is not used there in the absolute, and expressions like ὁδὸς ἀληθείας and ὁδοὶ ζωῆς are not direct parallels...A more likely suggestion is that in Jn 14.6 there is antithesis to the Torah, the more so as statements about the Torah are transferred to Jesus elsewhere in John' (p. 82).

Deut. 8.6, 'So you shall keep the commandments of the LORD your God, by walking in his ways and fearing him'.[1] It has already been indicated that Jesus' claim to be the Way, the Truth and the Life also occurs in the context of giving a new commandment (ἐντολὴν καινὴν, 13.34). The concept of law (instruction) is also paralleled with the way in Mal. 2.8 (see above). Since the law can also be linked with the ideas of truth and life (cf. Ps. 119.30, 37), it is probably correct to link Jesus' claim to be the Way, the Truth and the Life closely with the concept of the law. In addition the law provides the way to God as well as making known the way of God to humanity. In Jesus' claim to be the Way, the Truth and the Life, he also makes known the way of God to his disciples and provides exclusive access to God.

From this study it again becomes clear that Jesus' 'I am' saying alludes to more than one Old Testament passage.[2] It is again best to see the 'I am' saying in a typological manner. Jesus takes up the ideas that had been conveyed through the term in the Old Testament and applies them to himself in a way which goes beyond the original ideas. It was suggested in the literary study that the predicates 'Truth' and 'Life' which accompany Jesus' claim to be the Way in this 'I am' saying should be seen as further defining that term. In addition it was seen how, by taking the concepts of 'Truth' and 'Life' upon himself Jesus fulfilled two of the main themes of the Gospel in himself. These two themes are probably therefore a development of the theme of the way in John 14 and so probably do not derive independently from the Old Testament.

---

1.   Michaelis, 'ὁδός', p. 51, also refers to Deut. 10.12-13; 11.22; 19.9; 30.16; Josh. 22.5; 1 Kgs 2.3; 3.14; 2 Chron. 17.4, 6; Ps. 119.3-4; Zech. 3.7.

2.   The Old Testament (especially in the so-called wisdom literature) speaks on several occasions of the 'way of truth' as well as the 'way of life'. See De La Potterie, *La Vérité*, pp. 254-55, who thinks that these should not be seen as a primary source of background for Jn 14 since they concern a moral 'rectitude' not present in John (e.g. Ps. 119.30; Prov. 5.5, 6). However, he does think that it is significant that several of these passages (e.g. Prov.15.24; 21.21) do have an eschatological perspective. Brown agrees, saying, 'In John there is no stress on the moral aspect of the way such as is found in the OT concept of the "way of truth"; rather, for John, Jesus is the way because he is the revelation of the Father' (*John*, II, p. 628). However, following McCasland, Brown warns against drawing too sharp a distinction between the revelatory and the moral idea of 'way' in Jn 14. Cf. S.V. McCasland, 'The Way' *JBL* 77 (1958), pp. 222-30.

John 15.1, 5

The way in which the ἐγώ εἰμι of John 15 uses the Old Testament is similar to and yet more complicated than that of John 10. While there is no παροιμία which introduces the words of Jesus in ch. 15, the concept of the vine, like that of the shepherd, runs through much of the Old Testament. However, unlike ch. 10, it is difficult to determine which particular passage, among many, is the primary source of reference for the Johannine concept of the vine.

Perhaps the best starting point for an investigation into the background material for the vine imagery in John 15 is Psalm 80 (LXX 79), where God is described as the shepherd of Israel (v. 1 [Hebrew: v. 2]). There the Psalmist also talks of Israel as a vine and at the same time he portrays God as the gardener:[1]

Ps. 80.8 (LXX 79.8): ἄμπελοω ἐξ Ἀιγύπτου μετῆρας, ἐξέβαλες ἔθνη καὶ κατεφύτευσας αὐτήν. ὡδοποίησας ἔμπροσθεν αὐτῆς, καὶ κατεφύτευσας τὰς ῥίζας αὐτῆς, καὶ ἐπλήσθη ἡ γῆ.

The Psalmist goes on to describe how the walls that protected this vine have been broken down (vv. 12, 13 [13, 14]) and calls upon God to turn again and rescue the vine which he planted (vv. 14, 15 [14, 15]). In addition the Psalm talks of the fact that the vine has been burned with fire (ἐμπεπυρισμένη, v. 16 [17]). Dodd points out that, in its parallelism, the LXX version of Psalm 80 seems to equate the image of the vine with the concept of the Son of man (v. 15 [16]).[2]

Ps. 80.15 (LXX 79.15): καὶ κατάρτισαι αὐτήν, ἥν ἐφύτευσεν ἡ δεξιά σου, καὶ ἐπὶ υἱὸν ἀνθρώπου, ὃν ἐκραταίωσας σεαυτῷ.

Yet the connection of the Son of man with John 15 is highly speculative.[3] It would seem strange that John, who is keen to affirm that Jesus is the Son of man (cf. 3.13; 8.28; 9.35), should not make more of the link between the vine and that title if the primary reference in John 15 were to Psalm 80. As Borig comments:

> To look for a bridge via the designation 'Son of Man'... appears questionable, since this title does not surface in the vicinity of John 15.[4]

1. Both Dodd (*Interpretation*, p. 411) and Carson (*John*, p. 513) see this as the primary background for the vine imagery in Jn 15.
2. Cf. Dodd, *Interpretation*, p. 430.
3. Cf. Brown, *John*, II, p. 671.
4. Borig, *Weinstock*, p. 98. Borig himself suggests that there may be significance in the fact that the 'Son of man' title in Psalm 80 clearly refers to the king. He

For, tempting as the apparent link between the Son of man and the vine in that Psalm may be, there is no hint in the exposition of Jesus' claim to be the vine to suggest that the title Son of man is in view here.

However, what Dodd fails to point out is that the Hebrew of this verse speaks not of the Son of man, but of the Son. Thus the Hebrew parallels 'Vine' with 'Son' so that Ps. 80.15 and 16 of the Hebrew read:

אלהים צבאות שוב־נא	Turn again, O God of hosts!
הבט משמים וראה	Look down from heaven and see;
ופקד גפן זאת	have regard for this vine,
וכנה אשר־נטעה ימינך	the stock which thy right hand planted
וע־בן אמצתה לך	and upon the son whom thou hast reared for thyself.[1]

In this case the vine appears to be equated not with the Son of man but with the Son, which would fit both the context of John 15, in which Jesus' submission to the Father as the Son is implied (vv. 1, 8, 9, 10, 15), and Johannine Christology as a whole, even better than the concept of the Son of man.[2]

Despite the similarities cited above, it would not be correct to think that the vine imagery in Psalm 80 provides a direct parallel to the imagery of John 15. Borig is correct to comment:

suggests later that the vine-imagery 'corresponds to the kingly claim of Jesus, as it comes to its clearest expression in John 18.36f. It corresponds to our context when the kingly title of Jesus which is not rejected in 1.49 and 12.13 reads: "King of Israel"' (p. 107) (For a full discussion, see Borig, *Weinstock*, pp. 97-107). However, the kingly connection between Jn 15 and Ps. 80 is just as questionable as the connection with the title 'Son of man' and should be rejected on the same basis: Though John is willing to ascribe the title of 'King of Israel' (1.49; 12.13; cf. 18.36; 19.19) to Jesus, this title is not found in the context of John 15. Borig is, however, correct to point out that 'the object of the prayer shifts in the course of the Psalm from the entire people portrayed as a vine (or vineyard) to an individual person' (*Weinstock*, p. 80; cf. Schnackenburg, *John*, III, p. 106). This rules out the objection of Bernard (*John*, p. 478), who argued that the Old Testament should not be seen as the background to the vine imagery in John's Gospel since in the Old Testament the vine imagery concerns a nation.

1.   Verses 14 and 15 in the English. The RSV and NEB (also NRSV and REB) leave out the second phrase of v. 15, apparently regarding it as an incorrect duplication of v. 18b (see Brown, *John*, II, p. 671). The RV translates 'son' as branch, which seems to take 'son' more generally as offspring (the offshoot of the 'stock' in the first part of the verse presumably being a branch).

2.   Though the title 'Son' so common to the rest of the Gospel is not used, Jesus' Sonship is implied in Jn 15; see above.

> It must be stressed that, in the vine-imagery of Psalm 80, the idea of
> 'fruitbearing' so significant for John 15 and the manner of God's inter-
> vention determined by that, is completely ignored.[1]

In fact, this is one of the only places in the Old Testament vine-imagery
where the vine is actually yielding fruit. The Psalmist's complaint is
that though the people of Israel are bearing fruit, others are enjoying the
crop because the walls have been broken down (vv. 12, 13). The
emphasis of this Psalm is not on whether the vine is bearing fruit and so
is quite different from the emphasis in John 15. Although there is a
superficial parallel in the mention of fire in both passages, in John only
the unproductive branches are burned (v. 6). This is in contrast to the
idea in Psalm 80 that the whole vine has been burned with fire (v. 16).
On the basis of this, Psalm 80 can in no way be seen as the sole source
for the Johannine vine imagery, even though some of the similarities
are striking.[2]

Certain parallels with John 15 can be seen in the song of the vineyard
in Isa. 5.1-7. There the prophet tells a parable in which his beloved
plants a vineyard on a fertile hill. He cares for the vineyard but instead
of bearing good fruit it yields only bad fruit. In allegorical fashion the
prophet declares what has already been implied, namely that 'the
vineyard of the LORD of hosts is the house of Israel' (v. 7).[3] By
implication God is again the gardener. While the Psalmist questions
why the wall has been broken down (Ps. 80.12), the prophet makes it
clear that the purpose of the vineyard was to bear fruit (ἔμεινα τοῦ
ποιῆσαι σταφυλὴν, v. 2). It is because it produces bad fruit that the
wall is broken down around it (v. 5). This emphasis on fruitfulness is
the main subject of the vine imagery in John 15 (vv. 2, 4, 5, 8, 16).
However, there is a contrast between the imagery in John 15 and that of
Isaiah. For, in Isaiah, fruitfulness is contrasted with the production of
bad fruit (vv. 2, 4), while in John fruitfulness is contrasted with
fruitlessness (vv. 2, 4).

While Isa. 5.1-7 speaks of God's rejection of his vineyard, in Isa.

---

1.   Borig, *Weinstock*, p. 99.
2.   With Borig, *Weinstock*, p. 99.
3.   In some ways Isa. 5 functions in a similar way to Jn 10 where the 'parable'
is related and then is applied to the person of Jesus by means of ἐγώ εἰμι. In the
LXX of Isa. 5, the vineyard related in the 'parable' of vv. 1-6 is explicitly ascribed
to the house of Israel by means of the verb 'to be': ὁ γὰρ ἀμπελὼν Κυρίου
σαβαὼθ οἶκος τοῦ Ἰσραήλ ἐστι καὶ… (v. 7).

27.2-6 the LORD speaks of a day in which he will again take care of his vineyard.[1] The result of his care will be that 'In the days to come, Jacob shall take root, Israel shall blossom and put forth shoots, and fill the whole world with fruit' (v. 6). The LXX speaks of a 'good' vineyard (ἀμπελών καλὸς) and thus provides a correspondence to John where Jesus claims to be the 'true' vine (ἡ ἄμπελος ἡ ἀληθινὴ, v. 1). If the images of the vineyard in Isaiah are in mind in Jesus' claim to be the true vine, it follows that Jesus is not only taking on the role which Israel should have fulfilled in the past, but is also claiming that the day when the LORD would restore Israel as a fruitful vineyard is fulfilled in him.

Jaubert suggests that the distinction between the 'vine' and the 'vineyard' should discourage superficial analogies with those Old Testament passages which speak of 'vineyard' rather than 'vine'.[2] In a similar way John makes a distinction between the vine and the branches which is not present in the Old Testament picture of the vine. There the vine is seen as a unified whole.[3] Although it is important to recognize that John 15 concerns the vine and not the vineyard, three points allow for the possibility that Jesus' claim to be the true vine may still allude to the Old Testament's designation of Israel as the 'vineyard of the LORD of hosts' (v. 7) as well as to passages which refer more directly to the 'vine'.[4]

First, in the midst of a passage concerning the vineyard of the LORD, the LXX of Isa. 5.2 reads ἐφύτευσα ἄμπελον σωρηχ. Thus the LXX

---

1. Cf. J.N. Oswalt, *The Book of Isaiah: Chapters 1–39* (NICOT; Grand Rapids: Eerdmans, 1986), pp. 491-95. Oswalt comments: 'Whether consciously or unconsciously, vv. 2-6 stand over against the picture of the vineyard in 5.1-7. There the vineyard had revealed a fundamentally perverse nature with the result that the farmer had abandoned it to the wild. Here as there the vineyard is Israel and the farmer is God' (p. 493).

2. Jaubert, *La Vigne*, p. 93.

3. Cf. Borig, *Weinstock*, p. 95.

4. In pointing to Isa. 5.1-7 as background material for Jn 15, many commentators assume that this is the case (cf. Barrett, *John*, p. 472; Carson, *John*, p. 513; Schnackenburg, *John*, III, p. 105). However, the strict emphasis in John on the vine and the branches, and the fact that fruitfulness results from remaining in the vine leads Lindars (*John*, p. 487) to call into question whether John is using any Old Testament categories at all in the image of the vine. He prefers to see the categories in Jn 15 as moral, entirely concerning personal relationships and not contrasting the old with the new.

speaks in terms of a single vine, while the context calls for this vine to refer to the whole vineyard.[1] This suggests that the distinction between ἄμπελος and ἀμπελών may not be as great as first perceived.[2]

Secondly, Borig points out that the distinction between the vine and the branches in John 15 comes about because of John's particular emphasis on the role of the Son:

> At the moment when the person of Jesus is included in a [fruit-] bearing capacity in the vine-imagery, this [person] must be disassociated from the disciples within the vine-imagery in a quite new way, on the basis of the theological greatness in which the Fourth Gospel sketches the character of the Son.[3]

Borig also argues that, while the differentiation between the role of the vine and its shoots is not explicit in the Old Testament, it is implicit if the Old Testament imagery is taken to its logical conclusion. Thus the shoots which spread from the Euphrates to the Mediterranean (Ps. 80.11, 12) must be the individual members of Israel itself.[4]

---

1. The Hebrew שׁרק ויטעהו is also singular and thus literally means 'He planted it [i.e. the vineyard] a soreq'. From this it is hard to determine whether the singular 'soreq' should be regarded as a vine in its own right (so RV) or as an adjectival noun describing the vineyard. Either way it should be seen as a collective noun referring to the whole vineyard, thus the RSV translates it in the plural. 'Soreq' refers to a particularly choice type of vine (cf. Jer. 2.21; also Gen. 49.11; BDB, p. 977).

2. That 'vine' and 'vineyard' may be used interchangeably is possibly confirmed by the fact that the Old Latin, Old Syriac (Curetonian mss.), Ethiopic and Tatian read 'vineyard' in Jn 15.1; cf. Brown, who comments, 'Sometimes in the popular Greek attested in the papyri *ampelos*, "vine", takes on the meaning of *ampelon*, "vineyard"' (*John*, II, p. 660). Examples of this are given by Moulton and Milligan: 'In P Petr I.29[4] (iii/BC) πεφύτευται δὲ καὶ ἡ ἄμπελος πᾶσα, ἅ, 'a. is used in a collective sense: cf. P Flor I.50[2] (AD 268) ἐξ ἴσου τ[ῆς ἀμπέ]λου μεριζομένος. This use of ἄμπελος (so MGr ἀμπέλι), which makes it equivalent to ἀμπελὼν, occurs also in the Median parchments. P Said Khan (BC 88 and 22) [contains] deeds concerning the transfer of a "vineyard", which is never called ἀμπελών in the documents' (J.H. Moulton and G. Milligan, *A Vocabulary of the Greek Testament* [London: Hodder and Stoughton, 1930], p. 27).

3. Borig, *Weinstock*, p. 95.

4. Borig, *Weinstock*, p. 95. He also suggests that the same is true when the 'remnant' of Israel are seen as a stump (Isa. 6.13; 37.31) (p. 96). This stump represents the whole, true Israel which will yet emerge as a whole plant. Borig also asserts that the κλήματα (branches) mentioned in Ps. 80.12 are to be seen as individual members of God's people, so that a direct link is established between the application of the imagery in the Psalm and Jn 15 (*Weinstock*, pp. 98, 99).

Thirdly, the connection between the vine–vineyard imagery in the Old Testament and the vine imagery of John 15 is not exclusively concerned with the vine itself but with the bearing of fruit. Israel was neither a true vine nor a true vineyard because it did not bear the fruit despite the care of the gardener. In contrast, Jesus is the true vine and, as long as the branches remain in him, they will not simply bear fruit but much fruit (καρπὸν πολὺν, vv. 5, 8). The allusion to the Old Testament is thus not only concerned with the vine but with the context in which that vine imagery occurs.[1]

Jer. 2.21 speaks of a vine rather than a vineyard and so provides a closer verbal link with John 15.[2] As in the other Old Testament passages the LORD is seen as the gardener. The vine that he planted had been of 'true' stock but it had become wild:

Jer. 2.21:   ἐγὼ δὲ ἐφύτευσά σε ἄμπελον καρποφόρον πᾶσαν ἀληθινὴν· πῶς
            ἐστράφης εἰς πικρίαν, ἡ ἄμπελος ἡ ἀλλοτρία.

In its translation the LXX seems to have amalgamated the two Hebrew phrases: שׂוֹרֵק כֻּלֹּה ('choice vine') and זֶרַע אֱמֶת ('pure seed'), and thus to have provided a close verbal link with John 15. The idea of fruitbearing, which is also closer to the Johannine image of the vine, is not present in the Hebrew where it is the seed which is true. The LXX also speaks of the vine becoming bitter (πικρίαν), again emphasizing that the vine's role is to produce fruit.

---

1.   It is this context as much as any other consideration that rules out the Mandaean vine imagery as background for Jn 15. The Mandaean vine is not concerned with the bearing of fruit but the giving of life (See *Ginza* 65.39-40 quoted in section on Gnosticism and Mandaism above, p. 30).

2.   Guilding (*Jewish Worship*, p. 97) points out that this passage from Jeremiah is the *haphtarah* to Deut. 9, which may have been read at Tabernacles (p. 95). She regards Jn 15.1–16.24 as 'the Tabernacles section of the Supper Discourses'. She thus suggests that 'In chapters 7-9 the ritual of Tabernacles and the lections read at that festival are seen as fulfilled in Jesus: in the present section, they are shown as fulfilled in the church. If Tabernacles, the feast of vintage, points to him who is the true vine, it typifies also those who are the branches' (p. 112). Although the Feast of Tabernacles is made explicit in 7.2 and Jesus seems to claim to fulfil its rituals in himself (7.37-39), the link with that Feast is far from clear in John 15. In John's chronology the discourse of John 15 in fact takes place in the season of Passover. Thus it is hardly likely that Jesus' claim to be the true vine should be seen as part of his claim to fulfil the feast of Tabernacles. It is far better to see in Jesus' words a claim to perform the role which Israel should have performed and thus to be the 'type' to which Israel's designation as the vine pointed.

If this passage is to be regarded as background material for John 15, the idea of the 'true' vine has been reinterpreted by John. In Jeremiah, as in Isaiah 5, the entirely true, fruitbearing vine does not fulfil its role and is in fact seen to be a 'false' vine because it produces bad fruit. In John, however, there is no question of the true vine bearing bad fruit. The emphasis is not on good fruit and bad fruit but on fruitfulness and fruitlessness. At the same time the emphasis is not on the vine's ability to bear fruit, but on that of each branch. Thus, while Jesus' claim to be the true vine may allude to the fact that he will fulfil the role which the vine in Jeremiah (and Isaiah 5) should have fulfilled, his interpretation of what this means concerns the fruitfulness of the individual disciples and not of the vine as a whole.[1]

By taking a common Old Testament image and applying it to the person of Jesus, the 'I am' saying of John 15 functions in a similar way to the previous 'I am' sayings. Yet the use of the Old Testament is even more allusive and complex here than in Jesus' claim to be the Good Shepherd. Again Jesus' claim alludes to more than one passage. However, it seems here that rather than emphasizing any passage in particular, it is the typological nature of the vine which is emphasized. While many of the individual concepts of the vine discourse are present in the Old Testament, it is not these small allusions that are important in Jesus' claim (though they may add support for the fact that John's language is steeped in Old Testament imagery).[2] John does not simply

---

1. To the passages outlined above may be added those of Jer. 12.10; Ezek. 15.1-8; 17.3-10;19.10-14 and Hos. 10.1, 2, which all contain vine/vineyard imagery. In Jer. 12.10, the LORD is again the owner of the vineyard and it is implied that the vineyard is to be regarded as Israel. This verse does not add anything to the previous vine/vineyard imagery, except by stating that it is the 'shepherds' who are accused of destroying the LORD's vineyard. However, there is no explicit link in Jn 15 with the shepherd imagery of Jn 10 to suggest that the vine imagery of Jn 15 alludes to this verse in Jeremiah. Ezek. 15 brings out the useless nature of the vine's wood which, even when whole, can be used for nothing (v. 5). This may have a parallel in Jesus' assertion that apart from him the disciples can do nothing (v. 5). As in Ezek. 15, so in John the useless branches are burned (v. 6). However, the useless nature of the branches in John 15 is probably not indebted to the imagery of Ezekiel but is simply an extension of John's own vine imagery. Neither of the other passages in Ezekiel (17.3-10; 19.10-14) or Hos. 10.1, 2 add anything of importance to the Old Testament vine imagery.

2. Borig, *Weinstock*, pp. 79-93, makes an almost exhaustive study of the Old Testament parallels to the individual concepts in the vine discourse.

use the Old Testament as a sort of 'reservoir for individual concepts in the imagery'.[1] Instead, he takes the essence of what is implied by that imagery, 'the picture of Israel as the vine of Yahweh', and applies the 'entire impression' to the person of Jesus.[2]

> Here, a single theme, used in the O.T. several times and in different ways, is brought out once in the special form demanded by its special context in the ministry of Jesus; light as it were, from numerous O.T. sources is brought to focus on that unique point.[3]

The focusing of this Old Testament theme on the person of Jesus is achieved here, as in John 10, through the words ἐγώ εἰμι. The fact that Jesus is designated as the 'true' vine, highlights the contrast with Israel, who had been of 'true' stock (Jer. 2.21) and yet had become a wild vine. The type that Israel should have been is taken up by Jesus who promises that his followers will share in the fruitfulness of the true vine if they remain in him as branches in a vine.

2. *Beyond the Old Testament: Fulfilment of Current Jewish Expectations*

John 11.25

When Jesus assures Martha that her brother will rise again, she replies, 'I know that he will rise again in the resurrection at the last day' (v. 24). It is in response to this declaration of belief in a final resurrection that Jesus himself claims to be both the Resurrection and the Life. Thus Jesus' 'I am' saying here takes Martha's words and reinterprets them to apply to himself in much the same way that the saying of 6.35 reinterpreted the crowd's quotation from Scripture. Just as Jesus took words spoken in the past tense (6.31), transferred them into the present (6.32, 33), and applied them to himself by means of ἐγώ εἰμι (6.35), so these words in 11.25 transform Martha's future expectation into a present reality that is fulfilled in the person of Jesus. However, unlike

---

1. Borig, *Weinstock*, p. 94.
2. Borig, *Weinstock*, p. 94. He also suggests that the vine-imagery of John 15 is not borrowed from one particular text (such as Psalm 80) but arises from 'an entire impression, which results from a large number of statements and connected ideas...' (*Weinstock*, p. 99).
3. Barrett, 'Old Testament', p. 165.

6.35, there is no direct quotation from the Old Testament which is applied to Jesus. It appears instead that this 'I am' saying reinterprets and applies to Jesus a current expectation as expressed by Martha. At the same time Jesus' reinterpretation of this current expectation may be seen to be based in the Old Testament.

There is no great distinction in John 11 between the noun 'resurrection' (vv. 24, 25) and the verb 'to rise' (vv. 23, 24). The shift to the noun form takes place in the application of the idea to a particular time (ἐν τῇ ἐσχάτῃ ἡμέρᾳ, v. 24) and does not originate with Jesus but with Martha. Before this, Jesus asks Martha whether she believes that her brother will 'rise again' (ἀναστήσεται, v. 23). Neither ἀνίστημι nor ἀνάστασις are common words in the Fourth Gospel.[1] However, there are two passages in which the concept of the resurrection is addressed. In the context of his claim to be the bread of life, Jesus has already promised that it is he who will raise people up on the last day (ἀναστήσω...ἐν τῇ ἐσχάτῃ ἡμέρᾳ, 6.39, 40, 44, 54). Even before that, in 5.25-29, he has claimed:

ἀμὴν ἀμὴν λέγω ὑμῖν ὅτι ἔρχεται ὥρα καὶ νῦν ἐστιν ὅτε οἱ νεκροὶ ἀκούσουσιν τῆς φωνῆς τοῦ υἱοῦ τοῦ θεοῦ καὶ οἱ ἀκούσαντες ζήσουσιν. ὥσπερ γὰρ ὁ πατὴρ ἔχει ζωὴν ἐν ἑαυτῷ, οὕτως καὶ τῷ υἱῷ ἔδωκεν ζωὴν ἔχειν ἐν ἑαυτῷ· καὶ ἐξουσίαν ἔδωκεν αὐτῷ κρίσιν ποιεῖν, ὅτι υἱὸς ἀνθρώπου ἐστίν. μὴ θαυμάζετε τοῦτο, ὅτι ἔρχεται ὥρα ἐν ᾗ πάντες οἱ ἐν τοῖς μνημείοις ἀκούσουσιν τῆς φωνῆς αὐτοῦ καὶ ἐκπορεύσονται, οἱ τὰ ἀγαθὰ ποιήσαντες εἰς ἀνάστασιν ζωῆς, οἱ δὲ τὰ φαῦλα πράξαντες εἰς ἀνάστασιν κρίσεως.	Truly, truly, I say to you, the hour is coming, and now is, when the dead will hear the voice of the Son of God, and those who hear will live. For, as the Father has life in himself, so he has granted the Son also to have life in himself, and has given him authority to execute judgment, because he is the Son of man. Do not marvel at this; for the hour is coming when all who are in the tombs will hear his voice and come forth, those who have done good to the resurrection of life, and those who have done evil, to the resurrection of judgment.

These earlier comments about the resurrection of the dead may themselves provide clues for the background of Jesus' claim in 11.25. In them Jesus has already declared that the hour of the final resurrection is now present and that it is he who has the authority to give judgment

---

1. Cf. Barrett, *John*, p. 395.

which will result either in the resurrection to life or the resurrection to judgment.[1]

While the verb 'to rise/raise up' (ἀνίστημι) is very common in the LXX (usually as a translation of the Hebrew verb קום) the noun (ἡ ἀνάστασις) is very rare and the concept of resurrection only seems to be hinted at in later books.[2] It is the scarcity of this noun which is one of the greatest arguments for looking outside the Old Testament for parallels to Jesus' claim in John 11.[3] The idea of resurrection clearly expressed in John 5, which is taken up in Jesus' claim to be the Resurrection in John 11, is hinted at in Daniel 12 and two passages in 2 Maccabees. The opening verses of Daniel 12 speak both of a resurrection to life and a resurrection to judgment, though the LXX uses ἀνίστημι in this context not of this 'resurrection' of the dead (v. 2) but of the 'raising' up of Michael (v. 1). The verb used by the LXX for the raising of the dead is a compound of John's more usual term ἐγείρω (cf. Jn 2.20-22; 5.21):[4]

Dan. 12.1, 2: καὶ ἐν τῷ καιρῷ ἐκείνῳ ἀναστήσεται Μιχαὴλ ὁ ἄρχων ὁ μέγας ὁ ἑστηκὼς ἐπὶ τοὺς υἱοὺς τοῦ λαοῦ σου· καὶ ἐν τῷ καιρῷ ἐκείνῳ σωθήσεται ὁ λαός σου, πᾶς ὁ γεγραμμένος ἐν τῇ βίβλῳ. καὶ

1. Reim thinks that the expectation of a resurrection in both Jn 5 and Jn 11 is dependent on the Synoptic tradition and compares Jn 5.29 with Mt. 25.46: 'And they will go away into eternal punishment, but the righteous to eternal life'. He suggests that this view is found in both Jewish and Christian tradition and that when Jn 11.25 is brought into consideration, it is seen that John used such traditional material (*Hintergrund*, p. 147).

2. P. Perkins (*Resurrection: New Testament Witness and Contemporary Reflection* [London: Geoffrey Chapman, 1984], p. 37) suggests that 'Resurrection symbolism first appears in Dan. 12'.

3. Bultmann (*John*, p. 402 n. 5, following Odeburg), sees ἀνάστασις as a technical word which does not express the action of 'raising' and is thus not so closely linked with the verb. For this reason he sees it as a parallel to the Mandaean term for Resurrection and not the raising of the dead as in Rabbinic sources. The close link between the term 'resurrection' and the verb 'to raise' in Jn 11 suggests that Bultmann's distinction between the verb and the noun is unwarranted.

4. In Dan. 12.2 ἐξεγερθήσονται translates the Hebrew יקיצו, which primarily carries the meaning of 'to wake up'. In this context it concerns resurrection. Instead of ἐξεγερθήσονται, Theodotian's translation of Dan. 12.2 uses ἀναστήσονται, thus providing a closer verbal parallel for both Jn 5 and Jn 11. Yet the fact that the LXX's ἐξεγείρω can mean 'to rouse from sleep' as well as 'to rouse from death' would fit well in the context of Jn 11, where Jesus declares that Lazarus has fallen asleep and that he is going to wake him (ἐξυπνίσω αὐτόν, v. 11).

πολλοὶ τῶν καθευδόντων ἐν τῆς γῆς χώματι ἐξεγερθήσονται, οὗτοι εἰς ζωὴν αἰώνιον καὶ οὗτοι εἰς ὀνειδισμὸν καὶ εἰς αἰσχύνην αἰώωιον.

The rousing of the dead foretold in Daniel will take place at a time of deliverance for the people (v. 1). In addition, Cavallin argues that this resurrection not only occurs at a time of deliverance but at the end time. He therefore suggests that:

> The resurrection is one of those events which accompany that decisive change of the ages, which is one of the most important characteristics of Jewish apocalyptic.[1]

If this is a correct interpretation of the significance of the resurrection in Daniel, certain parallels can be drawn with John 11. Since the raising of Lazarus is a key event for John in the build up to Jesus' crucifixion (cf. 11.46-53), Jesus' claim to be the resurrection and the life could be said to be in the context of deliverance and salvation. The logical connection of resurrection with the concept of eternal life also corresponds to the idea of a resurrection at the last day in the thinking of Martha in John 11 as well as Jesus' words in John 5 (see especially 5.29, εἰς ἀνάστασιν ζωῆς). Jesus' 'I am' saying at Jn 11.25 turns this future expectation into a present reality. In Jesus the decisive resurrection of the last day is brought into the present.

The concept of resurrection in 2 Maccabees 7 is similar to that expressed in Daniel 12, where both resurrection and judgment are conceived. As such it provides a more immediate link with John 5 than with John 11. However, the words of 2 Macc. 7.9 are pertinent to Martha's belief in a resurrection at the end time. In the context of an attempt to force seven brothers and their mother to eat pork, the king, having killed the first brother, tortures the second:

---

1. H.C.C. Cavallin, *Life after Death: Paul's Argument for the Resurrection of the Dead in 1 Cor 15: Part 1: An Enquiry into the Jewish Background*. (ConBNT, 7.1; Lund: Gleerup, 1974), p. 27. Cavallin remarks that 'The appearance of Michael corresponds to the parousia of Jesus, being the signal of the resurrection'. Cf. also G.W.E. Nickelsburg, *Resurrection, Immortality, and Eternal Life in Intertestamental Judaism* (Harvard Theological Studies, 26; London: Oxford University Press, 1972), p. 14.

2 Maccabees 7.9

Ἐν ἐσχάτῃ δὲ πνοῇ γενόμενος	And when he was at his last breath,
εἶπε, Σὺ μὲν ἀλάστωρ ἐκ τοῦ	he said, 'You accursed wretch, you
παρόντος ἡμᾶς ζῆν ἀπολύεις, ὁ δὲ	dismiss us from this present life, but
τοῦ κοσμου βασιλεὺς	the King of the universe will raise
ἀποθανόντας ἡμᾶς ὑπὲρ τῶν	us up to an everlasting renewal of
αὐτοῦ νόμων εἰς αἰώνιον	life, because we have died for his
ἀναβίωσιν ζωῆς ἡμᾶς ἀναστήσει	laws.' (NRSV)

A similar belief is expressed by the fourth brother (v. 14):

> One cannot but choose to die at the hands of mortals and to cherish the
> hope God gives of being raised again by him (ἀναστήσεσθαι). But for
> you there will be no resurrection to life (ἀνάστασις εἰς ζωὴν).

Cavallin points out that vv. 9b-11 clearly express a belief in a bodily
resurrection, where the third brother is to receive back the limbs which
he loses in the persecution. He is right, however, to acknowledge that
the idea of a bodily resurrection 'should not be overemphasized, since
in the context the function of resurrection belief is stressed, i.e., the
vindication of justice for the oppressed and tortured righteous'.[1]
Martha's statement of belief may be a similar expression of faith in the
final justice of God. She does not know that this restoration of life
(which she hopes for at the end times) is literally present in Jesus and
that she is about to see the bodily restoration of her brother in a way
that was envisaged in the book of Maccabees.[2]

---

1. Cavallin, *Life After Death*, pp. 112-13.
2. Hanson (*The Old Testament and Lazarus*, pp. 252-55) observes that the
difficult words of Jesus in 11.41 have an almost exact parallel in Ps. 118 (LXX 117).
He thus suggests that they are a quotation from that Psalm.

> John 11.41: πάτερ, εὐχαριστῶ σοι ὅτι ἤκουσάς μου
> Psalm 118.21a (117.21): ἐξομολογήσομαί σοι ὅτι ἐπήκουσάς μου

The differences between the choice of the verb and the choice of tense in Jn 11 and
the LXX version of this Psalm can be explained (Hanson, *The Old Testament and
Lazarus*, p. 254) if John knew the Hebrew of this verse. Because of similarities
between Jn 10.24-25; 11.41 and 12.13, Hanson suggests (p. 255) 'that John saw the
whole Psalm as giving the framework for what he recounts of Jesus in these
chapters'. If there is a link between this Psalm and Jn 11 it is possible that v. 17
may illumine Jesus' 'I am' saying. There the Psalmist declares: 'I shall not die, but
I shall live' (οὐκ ἀποθανοῦμαι, ἀλλὰ ζήσομαι) which bears a striking similarity
to the subclause of Jesus' 'I am' saying: ὁ πιστεύων εἰς ἐμὲ κἂν ἀποθάνῃ ζήσεται,
καὶ πᾶς ὁ ζῶν καὶ πιστεύων εἰς ἐμὶ οὐ μὴ ἀποθάνῃ εἰς τὸν αἰῶνα (11.25-26).

Davies suggests that John's understanding may have been influenced by the Wisdom literature of the Old Testament as well as by the reference in Daniel 12.[1] Although she acknowledges that Daniel 12 is the closest linguistic parallel to John and also the most immediate source for the idea of a 'post-mortem resurrection', she adds:

> Wisdom stories about the persecution and vindication of the righteous in this life (e.g. Joseph in Gen.37-50; Esther; Dan. 3 and 6; Susanna) and the poem depicting the fate of the servant in Isaiah 52-53 furnish the structure and the language for expressing belief in post-mortem vindication in the Wisdom of Solomon 1-6 and in Daniel 12, and hence provide the Fourth Gospel with a developed tradition for explaining the significance of the suffering of Jesus and his disciples.[2]

Although the passages from Daniel and Maccabees may provide the basis for the concept of a resurrection at the last day, it is by no means clear that Jesus' words in Jn 11.25 allude directly to either passage (or to any other Old Testament passage).[3] It seems better therefore to suggest that the belief expressed by Martha in Jn 11.24 constitutes a further development of those ideas within Judaism.

The belief in a resurrection at the last day similar to that of Martha is attested elsewhere in the New Testament (Lk. 14.14; Acts 24.15, 21; 1 Cor. 15.42; Phil. 3.11). In addition, the debate between the Pharisees and the Sadducees (cf. Mk 12.18-27 and parallels; Acts 23.6-8 and Josephus)[4] suggests that the 'I am' saying of 11.25 takes this current expectation and applies it to Jesus. However, the scope of this study

While it is possible that there is an allusion to this Psalm in the second half of Jesus' 'I am' saying, it seems more likely that the words are Johannine, following the pattern of the other 'I am' sayings and drawing out the logical implications of Jesus' claim for the reader. Hanson makes an even more speculative link between Jn 11 and Job 14.6 which he thinks explains the reason for Jesus' delay in going to Lazarus.

1.   Davies, *Rhetoric*, p. 80.

2.   Davies, *Rhetoric*, p. 80.

3.   However, Davies is surely right to think of the Old Testament as the basis on which John's understanding of the resurrection is founded. She comments that Jesus' reply to Martha in 11.23 'presupposes the scriptural hope of resurrection (Dan. 12.2; see Jn 6.39, 40, 44). Martha responds by confirming her belief in the future resurrection, "I know he will rise again in the resurrection at the last day" (11.24)' (*Rhetoric*, p. 371).

4.   Josephus, *Ant.* 13.171,173; *War* 2.163-64; Cf. F.F. Bruce *New Testament History* (London: Oliphants, 2nd rev. edn, 1977) pp. 67, 69.

prevents a full investigation of all that may have been implied by Martha's words.[1] The example of Jn 6.35 has shown that the 'I am' sayings of Jesus may express a current Jewish expectation (i.e., that manna from heaven would again be given in the messianic age)[2] at the same time as referring back to the Old Testament. This is also true of the saying of 4.26 in which Jesus claims to be the messiah for whom the Samaritan woman was waiting. The 'I am' saying of 11.25 fulfils a similar function by showing that the expectations current at the time of writing were fulfilled in Jesus. John thus points to a Jesus who has brought the Jewish expectations about the end time resurrection into the present in his own person.

1. For fuller discussions of what may have been the beliefs about resurrection by New Testament times see the works of Perkins, Cavallin and Nickelsburg cited above.

2. Cf. Brown, *John*, I, p. 265.

Chapter 8

RESULTS OF THIS INVESTIGATION

This study set out to investigate the function of the words ἐγώ εἰμι in
the Gospel of John. The first part (Chapters 2–4) concentrated on the
literary function of 'I am' in the Gospel itself. This meant that the text
itself could be used to determine both how ἐγώ εἰμι is used in John and
the background material for these sayings. The second part of the study
(Chapters 5–8) is devoted to the use the 'I am' sayings make of the Old
Testament as well as current Jewish expectations. The sayings accompanied by an image functioned in a slightly different way from those
without but there was seen to be an overlap in the function of the
different forms of sayings.

1. *Literary Studies*

The literary approach which formed the first part of this investigation
allowed the 'I am' sayings to be studied in the context of the larger
pericopes in which they occur. Such an approach also made it possible
to stand back and see how ἐγώ εἰμι functions in the Gospel as a whole.
This means that, rather than studying the sayings as abstract formulae,
their relationship with the other themes and characteristics of the Gospel
could be seen. As a result of this literary approach the following
important discoveries were made.

First, the 'I am' sayings were seen to reflect a consistent portrait of
Jesus. Through the use of ἐγώ εἰμι, his characterization as the dominant
person of the Gospel is reinforced and enhanced. In this, the role of the
other characters is often as a foil to Jesus, drawing out who the narrator
believes him to be. The words 'I am' focus the attention of the reader
on Jesus and his claims. Sometimes the use of ἐγώ εἰμι even has an
important role to play in the structure of a pericope. This is particularly
seen in the debate with the Jews in ch. 8, which begins and ends with a

claim made with the words ἐγώ εἰμι. Claims made by means of ἐγώ εἰμι are interspersed within the debate so that attention is clearly focused on Jesus and the validity of his claims. The function of ἐγώ εἰμι in the structure of the arrest scene is just as important, drawing attention to Jesus who is again dominant.[1]

Along with its role in the characterization of Jesus, it was discovered that ἐγώ εἰμι often plays a role in Johannine irony. While previous studies of the 'I am' sayings in John have allowed for the possibility that the words are used with a double meaning,[2] this study is the first to point out the importance of their role in Johannine irony. As O'Day has indicated, irony can form the locus of revelation for the reader of the Gospel, for the *how* of revelation is as significant as the *what*.[3] Such a use of irony is a particularly persuasive tool:

> For precisely in its restraint from dictation of a literal meaning to its readers, irony is able to move those readers to an intensely active state and to engage them in an open search for solid ground that will make them grateful when they find it.[4]

The precise role of the 'I am' sayings in this irony is often to resolve the ambiguity that has previously been raised (cf. 4.25, 26). This means that a claim made by means of ἐγώ εἰμι is often what provides the solid ground for which the reader searches.

Duke connects irony with the 'I am' sayings with an image in that they both form part of the Johannine duality:

> In summary, irony is one of several members of the Johannine literary family, all of which point in the same direction. The direction is beyond. It is mystery, height, depth - hidden significance in need of crucial illumination. All these 'devices' are, in other words, elements of an invitation to abide 'above', in the presence of him who is the revealing and penetrating light of the world.[5]

The use of the 'I am' sayings in the context of such irony thus constitutes an appeal for the reader to join the narrator's conceptual point of view.

---

1. Cf. Hinrichs' belief (*Ich Bin.*, pp. 23-28) that the 'I am' sayings point to the dominance of Jesus' word in John's Gospel.
2. Cf. Harner, *'I am'*, pp. 43, 45, 47-48; and Brown, *John*, I, p. 534.
3. Cf. O'Day, *Revelation*, pp. 50-51.
4. Duke, *Irony*, p. 37.
5. Duke, *Irony*, p. 147.

The introduction to this investigation asked whether the traditional distinction between the 'I am' sayings with an image and those without was in fact as strong as has sometimes been imagined. The literary study of ἐγώ εἰμι discovered that while there is an important difference in form, there are similarities in function which suggest that there is a deliberate interaction between the different forms of 'I am' saying. This was particularly seen in John 6, where the use of 'I am' on the lake continues to sound in the claims of the discourse, and in John 8, where different forms of 'I am' saying run through the chapter. It was therefore suggested that the 'I am' sayings without an image refer more to Jesus' identity itself, while the 'I am' sayings with an image refer more to his identity as it relates to his role among humanity. The ἐγώ εἰμι of 8.18 was found to form a bridge between the different uses of the words in that, while it was not formally the same as those sayings with an image, it concerned Jesus' role as a witness and not primarily his identity.

The literary study also suggested a close interaction between the 'I am' sayings and the major themes of the Gospel. Some possible implications of the connection with John's view of sonship, with the Logos of the Prologue, and with the offer of life are suggested below (Chapter 9). All that needs to be stated here is that Schweizer's basic belief in the unity of the Gospel is confirmed by such an observation.[1] The danger of seeking formal parallels to the 'I am' sayings without first seeing how they function in connection with the main themes of the Gospel itself has also been highlighted. Although formal parallels may help the understanding of 'I am' in John, due weight also needs to be given to the context in which the 'I am' sayings occur in order to determine whether such parallels are relevant.

Finally the literary study of the 'I am' sayings suggested that the immediate background for such sayings is in the Old Testament and Judaism. The sayings occur in the context of discussions on Jewish subjects (Jn 4, 6 and 8) involving the Jewish ancestors (Jacob, Jn 4; Moses, Jn 6; Abraham, Jn 8) and reflect Jewish expectations (Jn 6 and 11). Furthermore, Jesus explicitly tells the disciples that Jewish Scripture will be fulfilled in his betrayal and as a result they will believe that ἐγώ εἰμι (13.19).

---

1. Cf. Schweizer, *Ego Eimi*, p 108.

2. *Background to 'I Am'*

The second part of the investigation thus embarked on a study of the background material from the Old Testament which may be implied by Jesus' words. It was suggested that a distinction between the formulaic sayings with a predicate nominative and the various other forms of 'I am' sayings should be maintained for the purposes of classification. It was suggested that any background material proposed for these sayings should fit in with the distinction between the function of these different 'I am' sayings. An investigation into the background material implied by ἐγώ εἰμι was therefore undertaken with the idea that the 'I am' sayings may form a fulfilment motif. Following the conclusion of the literary studies, it was seen that the background to sayings without an image concern Jesus' *identity*, while those with an image concern his identity as it is worked out in his *role* among humanity.

In contrast to previous studies of ἐγώ εἰμι, it was suggested that it was not only the words 'I am' which pointed to the Old Testament, but also their formulation and context. This means that the Johannine Jesus does not appeal to all the uses of ἐγώ εἰμι in the Old Testament but to particular uses which function in a similar manner and context to his own. Although this study is by no means the first to suggest that the 'I am' sayings without an image appeal to the *ani hu* of Second Isaiah, the idea that it is *the whole phrase* and not only the words ἐγώ εἰμι that refer to the words of Isaiah is a significant advance in the study of the way John uses Isaiah. The formulation and context of the words in John points back to the whole context of the words in Isaiah. This means that the context of the Isaianic passages has direct implications for the understanding of Jesus' 'I am' sayings in John. The words in Isaiah were spoken in an eschatological and soteriological context and continue to have this force when applied to the person of Jesus. Furthermore the words in Isaiah were spoken exclusively by the LORD. By the application of such words to the Johannine Jesus, an identification with the words and salvation of the God of Isaiah is implied. It will be necessary as part of the conclusion of this investigation (Chapter 9) to consider how the specific use of Isaiah as the primary background to the 'I am' sayings without an image fits in with John's use of the Old Testament in general and Isaiah in particular.

This investigation has argued, following the work of Borgen on John 6,[1] that the 'I am' sayings with an image also appeal to the Old Testament. Jesus claims to be the Bread of which the Old Testament spoke, the Light of which Isaiah spoke, the Shepherd of whom Jeremiah and Ezekiel spoke, and the Vine of which many Old Testament passages spoke. In addition there may be allusions to the Isaianic concept of the 'way of the LORD' in Jesus' claim to be the Way, the Truth and Life. Jesus also takes the Jewish concept of resurrection of which Martha speaks and transforms it to refer to the present in his own person (11.25). In these sayings it is not the words 'I am' which are found in the Old Testament, but the images which accompany them. The words ἐγώ εἰμι thus act as a formula which applies Old Testament and Jewish concepts to the person of Jesus who embodies and fulfils them. Schweizer is right to think that in the Johannine theology, these images become the true reality when applied to Jesus.[2] The Old Testament images serve as types pointing to the reality which is found in Jesus.

It has thus been confirmed that there is no need to look to all the possible parallels of 'I am' sayings in order to understand how John uses the words. The Gospel itself provides clues which point to the Old Testament and Judaism as the correct conceptual background for the use of ἐγώ εἰμι. This confirms that the search for formal parallels to Johannine concepts and terms may be deceptive for, although the 'I am' sayings of Mandaism offer the closest formal similarities to John, they function in a quite different manner. The 'I am' sayings of Mandaism talk about bread, light and shepherds in purely cosmic terms and as offering sustenance, enlightenment and care. The 'I am' sayings of John do not rule out this cosmic aspect, but are pregnant with meaning in their allusion to the Old Testament. Bread was given by God daily to sustain the people of Israel on their escape from Egypt, bread became a symbol of God's sustenance to his people, bread also became associated with God's word and Law. The giving of bread from heaven may also have been a sign of the messiah's coming. The Old Testament and Jewish implications of Jesus' claim to be the bread are thus specific and not purely cosmic. The specific nature of Jesus' claims are also seen in the allusions other images make to the Old Testament. While the Mandaean sayings have a similar form, they do not contain such eschatological implications. For John the day when the Old Testament promises

1.   Borgen, *Bread*, esp. pp. 72-73.
2.   Schweizer, *Ego Eimi*, p. 124.

were to be fulfilled is present in the very person of Jesus to the extent that he can claim to be the reality of which the Old Testament images spoke.

The study of background material has thus shown that there is a distinction between the 'I am' sayings with an image and those without. However, both forms of saying require the Old Testament in order to be understood fully. Both imply that the fulfilment of Old Testament ideas, particularly concerning salvation, occur in Jesus. The distinction lies in the fact that, while the 'I am' sayings without an image point to formal parallels in the Old Testament to explain Jesus' identity, the 'I am' sayings with an image point to conceptual parallels to explain Jesus' role among humanity.

Although a distinction between Jesus' role and his identity is useful to categorize the functional difference between those 'I am' sayings with an image and those without, there are several occasions where these functions clearly overlap. In the link between the 'I am' sayings without an image and the prophecies of Second Isaiah, Jesus' words not only speak of a close identification with the God of the Old Testament but also concern the eschatological salvation promised to Israel. In other words, those sayings which speak primarily of Jesus' identity are, by implication, worked out in Jesus' role in bringing the salvation of God promised by Isaiah. Conversely, those sayings with images which primarily speak of Jesus' role, often implicitly speak of his identity. Thus the shepherd who cares for his sheep fulfils the role that Yahweh and his servant would perform in the prophecies of Ezekiel. By fulfilling such a role, Jesus identifies himself with the LORD and with his servant David. Likewise, it was the role of the Servant of the LORD in Isaiah to be a light to the nations. Thus, when Jesus claims to be that light, he implicitly assumes the identity of the Servant. In his role as the True Vine, Jesus also implies an identification with Israel. However, while Israel had not lived up to the calling to be God's vine, Jesus is the True Vine and those who remain in him will produce fruit.

Finally, it has been shown that the 'I am' sayings often create irony by their evocation of the Old Testament. The reader who knows the Old Testament sees two levels to Jesus' words and reinterprets the surface level of meaning in the light of the deeper meaning which the Old Testament gives to Jesus' words. Thus the Samaritan woman speaks of the Messiah but, by its formulation, Jesus' reply speaks of an identity with the words and person of Yahweh. By reference to the Old Testament, the significance of Jesus' words is radically reinterpreted, so that the reader who only sees the surface level of Jesus' 'I am' saying may recognize that Jesus is messiah without recognizing what sort of messiah the Johannine Jesus claims to be. A more revealing irony was seen at work in the 'I am' sayings of the shepherd discourse in which Jesus' words speak implicitly of the leaders of Israel who have failed to care for God's flock. The claim to be the Light of the World also pointed the finger at Jesus' opponents who claim to know that no prophet is to arise from Galilee but fail to see that Isaiah prophesied that a light would dawn in Galilee. Such a use of irony is entirely in keeping with the function that the 'I am' sayings were seen to have in the literary studies above.

Part IV

THE WORLD BEYOND THE TEXT:
CONCLUSIONS AND IMPLICATIONS

Chapter 9

POSSIBLE IMPLICATIONS FOR OTHER AREAS
OF JOHANNINE STUDY

1. *Possible Implications for John's Use of Isaiah
and the Old Testament*

In her discussion of the Implied Reader in the Fourth Gospel, Davies
states:

> Throughout the Gospel references to Scripture punctuate the narrative (e.g.
> 2.17; 5.39, 46-47; 6.31; 7.22, 38, 42; 12. 38-41) and these encourage
> readers to notice allusions to Scripture in other parts of the Gospel, like
> those to Ezekiel 34 in the discourse on the good shepherd (10.1-18), or
> those to Exodus 16 and Numbers 11 in Jesus' discourse on the bread of
> life and reactions to it. More than this, however, the very language of the
> Gospel, its vocabulary and some of its idioms, its focus through the
> omniscient narrator, its theological presuppositions, its themes and motifs,
> are all reminiscent of Scripture. It is Scripture which provides the familiar
> literary stock from which the Gospel grows. Readers who come to the
> Fourth Gospel without a knowledge of this Scripture will be very much
> more perplexed than those whose reading of Scripture has determined
> their outlook and expectations.[1]

In other words, the explicit references to the Jewish Scriptures,[2] may
alert the reader to more subtle allusions elsewhere. The evocative way
Old Testament themes are picked up by the 'I am' sayings confirms
this.[3]

---

1. Davies, *Rhetoric*, p. 355. Culpepper, too (*Anatomy*, p. 218), recognizes the
'the implied reader has extensive knowledge of the Old Testament.'
2. For example, the regular fulfilment formulae which punctuate Jesus' last
hours: 13.18; 17.12; 19.24, 36.
3. Ironically, Davies (*Rhetoric*, pp. 84-86) rejects the idea that the words ἐγώ εἰμι
alludes the the 'I am' sayings of Second Isaiah. However, her basic argument for the
necessity of the Old Testament for the implied reader would be strengthened rather

a. *Jesus' Role and John's Use of The Old Testament in General*
With the partial exception of the claim to be the Resurrection and the
Life, the 'I am' sayings with an image all transfer Old Testament concepts to the person of Jesus. Jesus transforms these categories to explain
his role among humanity. Such a role involves fulfilment, especially
typological fulfilment. For John, Jesus *is* all that the Old Testament
concept pointed to. As the fulfilment of these ideas, Jesus often also
replaces the original concept in himself, a feature characteristic to John's
general use of the Old Testament:

> One of the features of these allusions [to the Old Testament] is the manner
> in which Jesus is assumed to *replace* Old Testament figures and institutions.
> He is the new temple, the one of whom Moses wrote, the true bread from
> heaven, the true Son, the genuine vine, the tabernacle, the serpent in the
> wilderness, the passover.[1]

It is therefore right to conclude that the use that the 'I am' sayings with
an image concur with the way John makes use of the Old Testament
elsewhere. In these sayings as elsewhere, the Old Testament is 'so well
known and understood that John could use it not piecemeal but as a
whole'.[2]

b. *Jesus' Identity and the Use of Isaiah*
Although the ἐγώ εἰμι sayings without an image also make use of the
Old Testament, they seem to refer to a particular context: that of Isaiah
40–55. This same context also forms the foundational background to the
sayings with an image in 8.12 and 14.6.

Apart from allusions to Isaiah in the 'I am' sayings, John names the
prophet on four occasions in the context of a quotation from the book
of Isaiah. The first of these in 1.23, concerns the role of John the Baptist
as a witness to Jesus.[3] The other three occurrences of Isaiah's name all
occur within a few verses of each other, in Jn 12.38, 39 and 41. John
quotes from Isa. 53.1 and from Isa. 6.10.[4] In so doing, John puts the lack

than weakened by acknowledging such allusions in the 'I am' sayings without a
predicate.

1. Carson, *John*, p. 98.
2. Barrett, *John*, p. 30.
3. See A.T. Lincoln, 'Trials, Plots and the Narrative of the Fourth Gospel' *JSNT*
56 (1994), p. 25 and also the discussion of Jn 14.6 in Chapter 7 above.
4. In these verses, John, of course, makes no distinction between First and
Second Isaiah, seeing both parts of the prophetic book as pointing to the time of
Jesus. Of the 22 verses in the margin of the Nestlé-Aland *Novum Testamentum*

of belief on the part of Jesus' narrative audience down to the fulfilment of the words of Isaiah. These verses show that John not only founds his understanding of Jesus' identity on the words of Isaiah, but also explains the unbelief of Jesus' audience on the basis of the same prophet. Certainly no other Old Testament prophet is given such personal attention by John. He is the only prophet mentioned by name.

As a result of these references to Isaiah as well as the study of the 'I am' sayings, the question arises as to whether Isaiah is an especially important Old Testament book for John's understanding of Jesus' person and mission. In an important study of the relationship between the Fourth Gospel and Isaiah, F.W. Young put the same question:

> If it can be shown that uniquely Isaianic expressions are likewise uniquely Johannine then there is real reason to believe that John was influenced by Isaiah in a manner that is easily overlooked: that is, that he consciously utilized Isaiah as a source of language and ideology in his own effort to interpret the meaning of Jesus Christ in the Gospel which he produced.[1]

Young argues that Isaiah's vocabulary and ideology is echoed in the concept of the 'name' (cf. 5.43; 17.3, 11) which would be given at a future time to those who serve God (cf. Isa. 52.5; 55.13; 62.2; 65.15).[2] He further suggests that the idea of proclamation in Isaiah, expressed by the verb ἀναγγέλειν, is used in John of Jesus as the 'revealer'. He particularly refers to the context of the Samaritan woman, where he sees a connection with Isa. 52.5.[3] He also suggests a link between John 6 and Second Isaiah.[4] As a preliminary to his discussion of Isaiah's influence on John, Young argues that there was considerable speculation concerning the prophet Isaiah at the time the Fourth Gospel was written, such that it is likely John also knew of these traditions about Isaiah.[5]

Graece, which may allude to at least 29 verses from Isaiah, 12 are from Isa. 40–55. These verses are: 1.1 (referring to Isa. 9.1); 1.23 (40.3); 1.29 (53.7); 1.32 (11.2); 2.11 (8.23 [9.1]); 4.14 (58.11); 4.23 (2.3); 5.28 (26.19); 5.44 (37.20); 6.45 (54.13); 7.24 (11.3); 8.12 (9.1; 42.8; 49.6; 60.13); 8.24 (43.10) 8.41 (63.16); 8.58 (43.10,13); 9.7 (8.6); 9.31 (1.15); 12.38 (53.1); 12.40 (6.10); 13.19 (46.10; 43.10); 16.22 (66.14 LXX); 17.12 (57.4 LXX); 18.20 (45.19).

1. F.W. Young, "Relationship', p. 222.
2. F.W. Young, "Relationship', pp. 222-24.
3. F.W. Young, "Relationship', pp. 224-26. Young makes no mention of the significance of ἐγώ εἰμι for John.
4. See Discussion of John 6 in Chapter 7 above.
5. Cf. F.W. Young, "Relationship', pp. 215-21.

In a recent article on the 'cosmic lawsuit' motif within the Gospel of John, Lincoln confirms that Deutero-Isaiah is especially important for John.[1] He argues that the extended metaphor of a cosmic lawsuit pervades the whole Gospel and also occurs at significant points within the narrative, forming an essential theme of the main plot as well as of subtle counterplots.[2] While Jesus' opponents 'interpret Jesus and his followers in the light of Moses or Torah and judge him to be a false prophet who has led his followers astray', Lincoln thinks that

> The implied author wishes to move away from this limited perspective and set it in a broader context. In order to do this, he brings to bear another legal model from Scripture, the covenant lawsuit, and it is Isaiah 40-55 that provides the resources.[3]

If such is the case, the background which proved to be so significant for the 'I am' sayings without an image, also forms the essential basis of themes such as 'truth', 'witness' and 'judgment'. After a study of the 'lawsuit motif' within Isaiah 40–55, Lincoln states:

> The implied reader who is also an informed reader, and who has not only received Jesus' witness that the Scriptures testify on his behalf (5.39; cf. also, e.g., 2.17, 22; 7.39; 12.16), but has also picked up on the narrator's three direct citations from Isaiah 40-55 (40.3 in Jn 1.23; 53.1 in Jn 12.38; and 54.13 in Jn 6.45), will not fail to have heard resounding echoes from these chapters.

Whether or not Lincoln's contention that the 'cosmic lawsuit' forms an essential part of the plot of the Fourth Gospel is accepted,[4] he is surely correct to see Isaiah 40–55 as the conceptual background to the themes connected with such a trial.[5] This suggests that Isaiah 40–55, forms an

---

1.   Lincoln ('Trials', p. 4 n. 3) acknowledges the work of A.E. Harvey, *Jesus on Trial* , which makes the case for regarding 'the presentation of Jesus' public ministry in terms of a trial'.

2.   Lincoln, 'Trials', pp. 3-20.

3.   Lincoln, 'Trials', p. 20.

4.   Lincoln's study of the plot of the Gospel both in terms of commission, complication and resolution ('Trials', pp. 12-14), as well as in terms of Greimas's actantial model (pp. 14-18), is enlightening and confirms the importance of the 'trial motif' in the whole Gospel. However, there may well be other equally deserving candidates for the 'object' of Jesus' mission, such as knowledge of God (cf. 1.18; 14.7), salvation (3.16) and the offer of life (20.31; 10.10).

5.   See the discussion of Jesus' identity above (Chapter 6) which shows how often the themes of witness and judgment appear in the context of 'I am' sayings both in Isaiah and in John.

essential foundation to understanding John's whole picture of Jesus.

Thus the 'I am' sayings without a predicate are not alone in the use of Isaiah 40–55 as background material. Themes such as witness, judgment, light, darkness and the extended metaphor of a cosmic trial all derive from this specific Old Testament context. It is also probable that John's use of the 'name' is indebted to Isaiah and that other subtleties of vocabulary derive from the same prophet. Moreover, as Lincoln has pointed out, Deutero-Isaiah seems to form a foundational storey, on which the narrative of the Fourth Gospel is founded. This is in accord with the argument set out above, namely that when John alludes to Old Testament passages by means of an 'I am' saying it is not only to the words ἐγώ εἰμι themselves but also to the context in which they occur. John not only used Isaiah in his portrait of Jesus, but expected his audience to be familiar with Isaiah's thought world. In other words, 'he consciously utilized Isaiah as a source of language and ideology' in his interpretation of Jesus as the Christ.[1]

The specific relationship between Isaiah and John needs to be addressed briefly in conclusion. It is certain that John's interpretation of Isaiah is to be interpreted in and through the person of Jesus. Young is therefore correct to suggest that it is his Christology which in part shapes John's interpretation of Isaiah.[2] However, if it is true that his Christology determines his interpretation of Isaiah, it is equally true that John's understanding of Isaiah shapes his Christology. Jesus is to be understood in the light of the words of the exclusive God of Isaiah. This is abundantly clear in the way the 'I am' sayings of Deutero-Isaiah seem to form a foundational storey, by which the 'I am' sayings of the Gospel are to be understood. Lincoln suggests that this is also true of the rest of the Gospel narrative. In other words, John's conceptual point of view is shaped by Isaiah to such an extent that it may not be an exaggeration to say that

1. F.W. Young, "Relationship', p. 222.

2. F.W. Young, "Relationship', p. 231, asks: 'is John's principle of interpretation dependent on Isaiah or is there some principle extraneous if not alien to Isaiah with which he comes to his interpretation. The immediate answer would seem to be that John was dependent on his Christology for his interpretation of Isaiah.' Young goes on to suggest that another, perhaps equally important, reason for John's interpretation may have been 'that the type of interpretation represented by John was already part of an "Isaiah tradition" in existence before John wrote. While he came to Isaiah with his Christology he came to it via a type of interpretation which had become a modus for reading the prophet.'

'the very language of the Gospel, its vocabulary and some of its idioms, its focus through the omniscient narrator, its theological presuppositions, its themes and motifs, are all reminiscent' not only of Scripture[1] but, more specifically, of Isaiah.[2] Some possible implications for John's audience and Christology are tentatively suggested below.

2. *Possible Implications for John's Purpose and Audience*

It is not within the scope of this investigation to discuss the question of the purpose or audience of John. Nor do the limits of this investigation allow for a discussion of whether Jesus' words stem from the time of the community or whether they go back to Jesus himself. Such questions would provide enough material for a separate study. However, the following tentative observations arising from the study of the function of ἐγώ εἰμι may have implications for these areas of Johannine research.

'I Am' as Proclamation: The Fulfilment of Jewish Scriptures and Expectations

It has consistently been emphasized that the 'I am' sayings contribute to the portrayal of the dominance of Jesus. Through them attention is focused on the character of Jesus. By them the very nature of Jesus is proclaimed to the reader. It has also been suggested, through the study of background material, that the 'I am' sayings function to identify Jesus with certain images and concepts from the Old Testament as well as current Jewish expectation. The Old Testament images and concepts function as types. Jesus is portrayed as the fulfilment and even the embodiment of these Old Testament and Jewish concepts. By means of the 'I am' sayings without an image, Jesus is even identified with the God of the Old Testament.[3] Furthermore the reason that the Gospel is

---

1. Davies, *Rhetoric*, p. 355.

2. It remains for further studies to ascertain how far aspects other than the 'I am' sayings of Isaiah have shaped John's Christology. Both F.W. Young ('Relationship', p. 227) and Lincoln ('Trials', pp. 24-26) have hinted that there may be a link between Isaiah and the concept of the Logos.

3. This dependence on the Old Testament concurs with the Fourth Gospel's basic conceptual point of view: Moses wrote of Jesus (5.46); Abraham rejoiced to see his day (8.56); Isaiah saw his glory (12.41). Cf. Culpepper, *Anatomy*, p. 215: 'The Jewish groups are all recognised by the reader. No explanation is needed regarding the Jews, priests, or Levites. Similarly, the reader knows who the Pharisees, rulers of the Jews (3.1; 7.26), chief priests (7.32), and high priest (11.49) are.'

written is so that the readers may believe that Jesus is the Christ (20.31), the messiah whom the Samaritan woman was waiting for (4.25, 26). Thus, the 'I am' sayings not only proclaim Jesus to the reader, they proclaim a Jesus who must be understood in the light of the Old Testament and Judaism.

While it is possible that the Gospel was written to persuade non-Jewish people that Jesus is to be understood in the light of the Old Testament, the way that the 'I am' sayings use the Old Testament implies that the readers have a detailed knowledge of the Jewish Scriptures and of Jewish customs. Such a detailed knowledge of the Old Testament is implied by the ironic way that a knowledge of Old Testament ideas is played off against a 'surface' level of meaning, as in the ironic challenge of the Pharisees that Nicodemus should 'Search and see that no prophet is to arise from Galilee' (7.52). The reader who really knows the Scripture will know that a Light is to arise from Galilee of the Gentiles (Isa. 9.1, 2), a light which turns out to be more than a prophet, a light that is to be a child who will be called 'Wonderful Counsellor, Mighty God, Everlasting Father, Prince of peace' (v. 6). Though the Old Testament is nowhere mentioned in the Shepherd discourse, a knowledge of the prophecies of Ezekiel concerning the leaders who mistreat God's flock allows the reader to see a specific reference to Jesus' narrative audience when Jesus claims to be the Good Shepherd in contrast to the hirelings who leave the sheep when they themselves are threatened (10.11, 12). Verbal allusions in the phrasing of the 'I am' sayings without a predicate nominative further suggest that the implied reader is well versed in the Old Testament: 'These references and the repeated quotations and allusions to the Old Testament scriptures imply that the fulfilment of scripture will confirm for the reader the truth of the evangelist's interpretation of the events'.[1] This indicates that the audience most likely to understand the implications of the 'I am' sayings knows the Old Testament and is therefore probably either Jewish or Christian.[2]

Not only has the study of the 'I am' sayings shown their essential Jewishness, it has at times suggested that the version of the Old Testament

---

1.   Culpepper, *Anatomy*, p. 220.

2.   Cf. S. Pancaro, 'The Relationship of the Church to Israel in the Gospel of St John' *NTS* 21 (1974–75), pp. 396-405. Pancaro maintains that John is 'a Jew writing for a Jewish audience' (p. 396). Against this cf. Culpepper, *Anatomy*, pp. 219-22, who thinks that the overall evidence of John's use of the Old Testament implies a Christian rather than a Jewish audience.

to which Jesus' words allude is not primarily the Hebrew text but the Septuagint (LXX). The close correspondence between the wording of the LXX of Isa. 52.6 and the wording of Jn 4.26 implies that John's audience probably knew the LXX. Likewise, the version of Isa. 43.10 assumed in the sayings of Jn 8.24, 28 appears closer to the LXX than to the Hebrew. It is difficult to determine how much significance should be placed on the fact that the 'I am' sayings seem to assume a knowledge of the LXX rather than (or as well as) the Hebrew text. It could be that this points to a non-Palestinian Jewish audience. This would be affirmed by the fact that the narrator feels it necessary to translate various Hebrew or Aramaic terms (cf. 1.38; 4.25; 11.16?).[1] However, since the Fourth Gospel is itself written in Greek (at least in its present form), a knowledge of the Greek Old Testament may prove nothing more about the audience of the Gospel than does the fact that it is written in Greek and not Hebrew or Aramaic. If the audience understood Greek, it seems reasonable to assume that the Old Testament version they would use would be the Greek rather than (or in addition to) the Hebrew.[2]

The use of 'I am' in connection with irony may provide a more fruitful avenue to discovering John's likely audience than the fact that it is conversant with the LXX. Duke points out that many of the ironies of the Fourth Gospel are conceptually Jewish, while they are formally Hellenistic.[3] This suggests to him that while the audience were thoroughly

1.   Cf. Culpepper, *Anatomy*, pp. 218-19. Culpepper also points out that while 'the narrator assumes that the reader has a general geography of the gospel story... For the name 'Jerusalem' the narrator uses the Hellenized form Ἰερασόλυμα exclusively (twelve times) rather than the more Semitic Ἰερυσαλήμ, which is preferred by the author of Luke–Acts. The choice of the Hellenized form may arise from the idiom of the evangelist or that of his intended readers' (p. 216). On this point, it may be significant that John explains that the Sea of Galilee is the Sea of Tiberias. Cf. Culpepper, *Anatomy*, p. 217; cf. also Davies, *Rhetoric*, pp. 265-75, for Hellenistic and other influences on John.

2.   Cf. Hengel's suggestion (*Hellenisation*, esp. pp. 52-56) that Judea of the first century was considerably Hellenized and therefore it is wrong to make a strong distinction between a 'Hellenistic' and a 'Palestinian' Judaism. Cf. also J.A.T. Robinson, *Priority*, pp. 36-41.

3.   Duke accepts that 'ironies of reversal...are thoroughly consistent with Hebrew thought. Likewise there is nothing distinctively Greek about "ironies of simple incongruity" (e.g. 10.32) or "irony of events" (e.g. Jesus' death effecting the opposite of his enemies' desire), or even "general dramatic irony" (when readers know what characters do not). There is however, an element foreign to typical biblical irony—in John's persistent focusing and underlining of irony by the unwitting

conversant in Judaism, they were also aware of Greek literary devices. He concludes that 'while the techniques employed in John's irony are those of the Hellenistic world, the themes, the targets, and the frequent presuppositions of John's irony all point to a setting very much shaped by Judaism'.[1] The use of 'I am' in conjunction with irony may therefore also imply a knowledge of Greek literary technique on the part of John's audience. It is possible that a similar phenomenon occurs with the 'I am' sayings themselves. While the Old Testament and Jewish background to the 'I am' sayings has accounted for the form of ἐγώ εἰμι without a predicate nominative and also for the content of the sayings with or without an image, it has not really accounted for the *form* of the sayings with an image. The closest formal parallels to the 'I am' sayings with a predicate nominative have not been found in Judaism but in Mandaism.[2] Could it be that the content of the 'I am' sayings with a predicate is Jewish while their form is in fact Hellenistic? This is certainly the view of Schnackenburg.[3] Further investigation into the use of ἐγώ εἰμι in the world of Hellenism is needed to confirm whether there are indeed close formal parallels to the 'I am' sayings of John in the rest of Greek literature. Following Borgen's contention that the words 'I am' may themselves be part of a midrashic formula, there is also a need for further investigation to see if there are formal similarities within Judaism.[4]

In conclusion it can be said that the role of the 'I am' sayings is to proclaim Jesus to the reader. The Jesus so proclaimed is one who fulfils and embodies various concepts within the Old Testament and Judaism and so is to be understood from a Jewish rather than a Gnostic or Hellenistic point of view. There are, however, hints within the 'I am' sayings (their allusions to the LXX rather than the Hebrew, their use of irony and possibly the form of the sayings with a predicate nominative) that the audience may not be Palestinian or that it is at least conversant

---

speeches of his characters. In this "specific dramatic irony," unsuspected *double entendre* abounds, so that the reader may savour the utmost truth which the characters cannot or will not see' (*Irony*, p. 140). It has been seen above that such irony does occur in conjunction with Jesus' use of ἐγώ εἰμι.

1.   Duke, *Irony*, p. 142.
2.   See e.g. Schweizer, *Ego Eimi*, pp. 36, 37, and Schulz, *Komposition*, pp. 91, 92.
3.   Schnackenburg, *John*, II, p. 86.
4.   Cf.Borgen, *Bread*, pp. 72. See discussion above. Meanwhile, the Mandaean sayings remain the closest in form to those of John.

with the techniques of Greek literature. Members of the Jewish dispersion[1] or of the wider Christian church would probably provide the audience most likely to understand all the implications of the 'I am' sayings.

'I Am' as Polemic: The Exclusiveness of Jesus and the Obsolescence of Judaism

If the purpose of the 'I am' sayings is to proclaim that in Jesus the concepts of the Old Testament and Judaism are fulfilled, that necessarily implies that Judaism (as traditionally understood) is obsolete. This means that the 'I am' sayings should in some way be regarded as polemic. Such a polemical point of view may be seen in the Shepherd discourse, where ironic allusions to the Old Testament imply that the 'thieves', 'robbers' and 'hirelings' of whom Jesus speaks are the leaders of Israel, 'the Pharisees' to whom Jesus speaks. Those who came before Jesus claiming to care for the sheep were no more than thieves and hirelings. In addition, many of the claims of John 8 appear deliberately provocative. The first verse of the debate with the Jews (8.12) provokes a response among the Jews, who think Jesus has no right to make such a claim. Jesus then claims that the Jews will die in their sins unless they believe that ἐγώ εἰμι (8.24). This provokes a question about Jesus' identity (v. 25) and is followed by the assertion that they will discover who he is when they 'lift him up' (8.28). Following this, the debate switches to the question of the true descendants of Abraham. Finally Jesus declares: 'Before Abraham was, I am' (v. 58). Such a claim provokes Jesus' narrative audience to stone him for blasphemy. In other words, the claims made by means of ἐγώ εἰμι are unacceptable to his Jewish audience.

Furthermore, Jesus' re-interpretation of the concept of the bread in John 6 implies that the traditional Jewish interpretation of 'bread from heaven' is no longer applicable: 'Truly, truly I say to you, it was not Moses who gave you the bread from heaven; my Father gives the true bread from heaven' (6.32). As the only way to the Father (14.6), traditional Jewish approaches to God become obsolete. As the gate (10.7, 9) traditional ways of salvation are no longer applicable. Those who do not enter the sheepfold by the door but climb in by another way are thieves and robbers (10.1). Only a belief in Jesus will prevent the Jews from dying in their sins (8.28).

---

1. Cf. Van Unnik, *Purpose*, pp. 382-411; J.A.T. Robinson, 'The Destination and Purpose of St John's Gospel', *NTS* 6 (1960), pp. 117-31.

Duke is correct to point out that irony has a role to play in polemic.[1] It points the finger at those who claim to see but are in fact blind (9.41). It allows the readers to see that those who are supposed to be the teachers of Israel do not understand the true meaning of Jesus' words (3.10). Those who claim to be leaders are ironically seen to be thieves and robbers (10.1, 2, 7, 8). It even shows that they are the ones who have not truly understood the Scriptures (5.46; cf. 7.52; 8.12).

While any investigation into the Johannine audience should take into account this polemical aspect of the 'I am' sayings, it should be stressed that the exclusive, polemical aspect of the 'I am' sayings is often the necessary by-product of John's proclamation of Jesus as the fulfilment of the Jewish Scriptures and is not the main emphasis of the Evangelist.[2] The Old Testament idea of bread from heaven is obsolete in as much as it was a type of the real, true bread which is Jesus. Just as the signs which Jesus performs point to a reality beyond themselves, so the images of the Old Testament and Judaism point beyond themselves to the reality which is Jesus. Although Jesus takes on the role of Israel in his claim to be the 'true' vine, the emphasis of the episode is on what Jesus offers to the disciples and not on the ineffectiveness of what has gone before.

'I Am' as Promise: The Encouragement of Believers
An investigation of the Johannine audience should also take into account the soteriological sub-clauses attached to the sayings with an image. These sub-clauses act both as invitation and as promise.

As the True Vine, Jesus emphasizes that the believers should remain in him (15.4). Those who obey this command are given the promise that they will bear much fruit (v. 5). In addition they are promised that their prayers in Jesus' name will be answered (v. 7). The narrative audience for these promises is the disciples. However, the general nature of the sub-clause (ὁ μένων ἐν ἐμοί, v. 5) and the addition of the word 'anyone' (ἐὰν μὴ τις μένῃ ἐν ἐμοί, v. 6) in the following phrase may suggest that the implied reader should apply these words to himself/ herself. If so, the words of Jesus must be interpreted as a promise to believers who read the Gospel. As the Good Shepherd, Jesus also

---

1. Duke, *Irony*, pp. 149-50.
2. Cf. Kundzins, *Die Ego-Eimi-Spruche*, pp. 99, 100, who emphasizes that the 'I am' sayings can imply the fulfilment of expectation and do not necessarily imply contrast.

promises to care for the sheep. He lays down his life for the sheep
(10.11) and is portrayed in an intimate relationship with them (v. 14).
This care for his sheep goes beyond those who are present as part of the
narrative audience (v. 16). These words suggest that the believing reader
is meant to take comfort from Jesus' promises of care and intimate
relationship. As the Resurrection and the Life, Jesus offers Martha life
that surpasses death (11.25). Again the sub-clause of Jesus' words goes
beyond the narrative audience and appeals to the reader of the Gospel.
Those who believe with Martha (v. 27) that Jesus is the Christ, the Son
of God, who is coming into the world are promised that, though they
die, yet shall they live and whoever lives and believes in Jesus will never
die (v. 26).

That some of the promises in the sub-clauses of the 'I am' are made
to believers may suggest that the words of the Johannine Jesus are
addressed to members of the believing community who need to be
encouraged in their faith. Through the 'I am' sayings benefits are
offered to those readers who have already joined the narrative audience
of the farewell discourses and consider themselves to be disciples. The
words spoken by the Johannine Jesus to the original disciples are related
directly by the narrator. With the narrative audience, the readers are
offered the opportunity of hearing the claims of Jesus and continuing in
their belief.

'I Am' as Invitation: A Missionary Perspective
Hand in hand with those sub-clauses, which promise encouragement to
believers, go those which act as an invitation to the reader. The
soteriological nature of the 'I am' sayings will be discussed below (see
'The "I am" sayings and Christology' below). All that needs to be said
here is that the offer of life made through the 'I am' sayings is not only
addressed to believers but also to unbelievers. Thus as the Bread of Life,
Jesus offers nourishment to those who come to him (6.35). He promises
that he will not cast out those who come to him in response to this
invitation (v. 37). As the Light of the World, Jesus offers the light of life
to those who follow him (8.12). As the Door, he offers salvation and safe
pasture to those who enter by him (10.9). Again, Duke is correct to
point out that irony has a role in such an appeal to the reader.[1] The
reader is given information that the narrative audience could not possibly

---

1. Duke, *Irony*, pp. 36-41. Cf. also O'Day, *Revelation*, pp. 113-14.

possess and through such privileged knowledge is urged to adopt the point of view of the narrator. The ironic interplay, of which the 'I am' sayings so often form a part, urges the reader to believe that Jesus is the Christ, the Son of God and that by believing, he/she may have life in his name (20.31). It is perhaps John's insistence on correct belief that allows the 'I am' sayings to appeal to both the reader who already believes as well as the one who has no belief or an insufficient belief in who Jesus is.

Any investigation into John's audience should give due weight to this apparently missionary appeal to the reader of the Gospel. Such a missionary appeal is accompanied by the warning that those who do not believe what Jesus claims for himself through ἐγώ εἰμι will die in their sins (8.24). The proclamation of Jesus as the fulfilment of the Old Testament and Judaism and the missionary aspect to the soteriological sub-clauses may suggest that the 'I am' sayings come from a level of tradition in which the audience of John's Gospel included non-believers as well as believers. Whether this implies that the Gospel itself had a dual purpose as an appeal to those as yet outside the believing community as well as those within must be the subject of further investigation of the purpose of the Gospel as a whole. Here it need only be noted that the purpose of the 'I am' sayings appears to be primarily that of persuading the reader that the significance of Jesus is to be seen in his fulfilment of Old Testament and Jewish ideas. Although this is exclusive, and so in some way polemic, it still appears to be an appeal to those outside the community of faith as well as to those within it.

3. *The 'I Am' Sayings and Christology: How the 'I Am' Sayings Fit in with John's View of Jesus*

The Johannine View of Sonship
It has been noted in the above study that John's use of ἐγώ εἰμι is often closely tied with the concept of sonship. This link between ἐγώ εἰμι and Jesus' sonship is seen most clearly in the 'I am' saying of 8.28:

> When you have lifted up the Son of Man, then you will know that I am, and that I do nothing on my own authority but speak thus as the Father taught me (cf. v. 18).

Here the presentation of Jesus by means of ἐγώ εἰμι coincides with the revelation of his unique co-operation with the Father. A similar co-operation between Jesus and the Father is also seen in the earlier 'I am' saying of v. 18 in which Jesus claims that it is not he alone who witnesses (cf. v. 16) but that the Father who sent him also bears witness to him (καὶ μαρτυρεῖ περὶ ἐμοῦ ὁ πέμψας με παπήρ). These 'I am' sayings thus show that Jesus functions in complete dependence on the Father and so demonstrate a functional unity between Jesus and God. Jesus says what the Father says (cf. 3.34). Jesus does what the Father does (cf. 5.30).

Jesus' close relationship with his Father is also seen in the 'I am' sayings with an image. As the Good Shepherd (10.14), he willingly lays down his life only to take it up again. This is in direct obedience to the charge he received from his Father (v. 18) who knows him and whom he knows as intimately as he knows his sheep (v. 15). His relationship with the Father is so close that he is the only Way by which people may approach God (14.6). If his hearers had known him, they would have known the Father (v. 7). Furthermore they do not need to see the Father because they have seen Jesus (vv. 8-10).

However, it must be asked whether John's view of sonship is restricted to a functional unity between Jesus and the Father or whether it involves an ontological identification of Jesus with God. One of the characteristics of John's Gospel is that Jesus is portrayed not only as the 'Son of God' but simply as the 'Son'.[1] Jesus' relationship with his Father is 'unique' (μονογενής, 1.14, 18; 3.16, 18). This unique sonship is closely liked with the idea of pre-existence.[2] The prologue announces that the Son is the only one who can reveal the Father because he is the only one who has seen God (1.18). He came from God and he is returning to God (16.28). When the 'hour has come' Jesus prays that the Father would glorify him on earth with the glory which he had with God before the world was made (17.5).

The claim to unique sonship reaches its climax at the end of the Shepherd discourse, where, in response to the Jews' wish for Jesus to tell them whether he was the Christ, he replies:

> I told you and you do not believe. The works I do in my Father's name,
> they bear witness to me...I and the Father are one (10.25, 30).

---

1.   J.D.G. Dunn states 'No other documents in the N.T. regard the Son of God confession so highly as the Johannine writings' (*Christology in the Making: An Inquiry into the Origins of the Doctrine of the Incarnation.* [London: SCM Press, 2nd edn, 1989], p. 56). Cf. M. de Jonge, *Jesus: Stranger from Heaven and Son of God* (trans. and ed. J.E.Steeley; Missoula, MT: Scholars Press, 1977), p. 141.

2.   Cf. Dunn, *Christology* , p. 56. Dunn cites 6.38; 8.23, 38, 42, 58; 10.36; 16.28 as examples of the Son's pre-existence.

The Jews understand such a claim of unity with the Father as blasphemy (v. 33), which is the reason they take up stones to stone Jesus (v. 31). The similar reaction of the Jews to Jesus' claim in 8.58 suggest that they see a similar blasphemy in his words there. Significantly this 'I am' saying is linked both with his relationship to his Father (8.54) and with pre-existence. The fact that the Jews see the claims of 8.58 and 10.30 as blasphemy raises the possibility that Jesus' Sonship should be seen not only in terms of functional identification with God but also of ontological identification.

The study of the background to the 'I am' sayings without an image makes even greater the possibility that Jesus' unity with the Father involves an ontological and not merely a functional unity. The fact that the words ἐγώ εἰμι on the lips of Jesus allude to the *ani hu* of Isaiah which spoke of Yahweh's exclusive right to save suggests that the Johannine church acknowledged an ontological and not just a functional union between Jesus and the Father. From the viewpoint of John's Christology, Jesus is unique not simply because of what God has done through him but because he himself is divine.[1] Jn 8.58 speaks of Jesus' divine nature which existed before Abraham. The words πρὶν ᾽Αβραὰμ γενέσθαι ἐγώ εἰμί were abhorrent to Jesus' narrative audience for they spoke of an ontological identification of Jesus with God.[2] That God should become flesh is a detestable suggestion; that anyone should claim to be identified with God is blasphemous.[3] The use of ἐγώ εἰμι as an allusion to the *ani hu* of Isaiah, together with John's view of sonship, speaks of Jesus' identification with the words, work and very nature of God. However, John's view of Jesus' unique sonship justifies his use of ἐγώ εἰμι. Because he whom God has sent (i.e. the Son) utters the words of God (3.34), the Johannine Jesus is able to take words reserved exclusively for YHWH and use them of himself and his own ministry.

Both John's view of sonship and his use of ἐγώ εἰμι present a

---

1. Cf. C.J.H. Wright, *What's so Unique about Jesus?* (Eastbourne: MARC, 1990), p. 22.

2. Against this, see Davies, *Rhetoric*, pp. 84-86, who argues that πρὶν ᾽Αβραὰμ γενέσθαι ἐγώ εἰμι is no more than a claim to superiority over Abraham.

3. I am indebted to I.H. Marshall for pointing out that the phrase 'to identify oneself with God' is ambiguous and not in itself blasphemous if it only implies empathy or moral identification with God. The narrative audience must in both 8.58 and 10.33 see more than the implication that Jesus is a godly man for that would present no reason to stone him.

portrait of Jesus which is unacceptable to the narrative audience and is interpreted as blasphemy. This suggests that Dunn may be too cautious in thinking that in the Fourth Gospel 'we have not yet reached the concept of an ontological union between Father and Son, of a oneness of essence and substance'.[1] While Jesus' claim that he is one with the Father (10.30) certainly concerns functional identity with God, it surely involves more than that. The Jews themselves seem to take Jesus' claim as a claim to ontological identification with God (10.33) and it is almost certain that their reaction to the 'I am' saying in 8.58 should be interpreted in the same way. For John, the Jews were mistaken, not in their recognition of Jesus' claim to ontological union with the Father, but in the fact that they recognized the implications of Jesus' claim without acknowledging that he had a right to make such a claim.

'I Am' and the Logos

The suggestion that the 'I am' sayings imply an ontological identification of Jesus with God in the Fourth Gospel calls to mind the words of the prologue. Even though the term λόγος is only used of the pre-existent Christ in the Prologue, it is an important concept in the rest of the Gospel.[2] The literary study of the function of ἐγώ εἰμι in John suggested that the saying of 8.58 deliberately recalls the contrast of the prologue between the Word who was (ἦν, vv. 1, 2) and creation which came into being through him (ἐγένετο, v. 4). In addition the literary studies suggested that Jesus fulfils the words of the prologue in his claim to be the Light (8.12), the Life (11.25; 14.6; cf. 6.35) and the Truth (14.6; cf. 6.32ff). All these concepts which Jesus applies to himself by means of ἐγώ εἰμι are attributed to the Word of the prologue. The relationship set out in the Prologue between the Word and God, in which the Word can even be described as God, is echoed in the rest of the Gospel by the words ἐγώ εἰμι which were used exclusively of God in Isaiah.

---

1. Dunn, *Christology*, p. 58. Dunn is mistaken if he means by this statement that there is no concept of ontological union between the Father and the Son. However, he is correct if he is suggesting that the ontological union between Father and Son is not as developed as in the later creeds of the church. Although the ontological union between Father and Son expressed in John is certainly not in the formalized form that was later adopted by the council of Nicea (e.g. 'Of one being with the Father'), it is not entirely absent.

2. Though possibly overstated, the work of Hinrichs, *Ich Bin*, has shown the fundamental importance of the 'word' of Jesus in the Gospel of John.

Alongside the Johannine concept of the λόγος, Jesus' use of 'I am' makes sense. Jesus can only claim a phrase that was reserved for YHWH and apply it to himself because he is not only YHWH's Son but is in fact YHWH speaking.[1] In the words of Brown: 'The word that existed in God's presence before creation has become flesh in Jesus (1.1,14)... indeed, he can speak as the divine "I AM."'[2] The connection between Jesus' use of 'I am' and the Logos of the prologue again suggests that the Johannine church believed in an ontological identification of the historical person Jesus and the Jewish God. Without the Son coming to dwell among humanity, the Father would not have been made known (1.14, 18). For John, the reason the Son can make the Father known is not only because he was in the bosom of the Father, but because he is also the Word who was in the beginning with God. He is even described as God (1.1).[3] It is this ontological identification with God that is the basis for the use of the 'I am' sayings outlined above. For John this is also the basis of his Christology. This underlying conviction that Jesus is God become flesh is why John allows Jesus to confirm Thomas's confession 'My Lord and My God!' (20.28, 29).

In the Logos of the prologue both the divinity (1.1-4)[4] and the humanity (1.14) of Jesus is stressed. In the Fourth Gospel's exposition of Jesus' ministry, the narrator wishes to show that Jesus is neither just a teacher nor just a prophet nor even what was expected of the Christ

1.   For a similar Christology see Heb. 1.1, 2. The relationship between the Christologies of the epistle to the Hebrews and John seems to be an area of study which is ripe for further investigation. For the possible relationship between the Logos of the prologue and the words of Isa. 40–55, see Lincoln, 'Trials', p. 25.

2.   R.E. Brown, *The Community of the Beloved Disciple* (London: Geoffrey Chapman, 1979), p. 45.

3.   For a discussion of how θεὸς without the article should be rendered, cf. B.A. Mastin, 'A Neglected Feature of the Christology of the Fourth Gospel', *NTS* 22 (1976) pp. 32-51; also Morris, *John*, p. 77 n. 15.

4.   Davies points out that the phrase θεὸς ἦν ὁ λόγος 'cannot be interpreted as a declaration of complete identity, equivalent to ὁ λόγος ἦν ὁ θεός because this would involve a direct contradiction of the previous clause [i.e. ὁ λόγος ἦν πρὸς τὸν θεόν]...On the other hand, the statement does not mean that ὁ λόγος was "a god" or "divine". As Harner (1973) has shown, θεὸς ἦν ὁ λόγος, with an anarthrous predicate *before* the verb, means something between theses two extremes: ὁ λόγος has the nature of θεός but the terms are not synonymous, not exactly equivalent or interchangeable' (*Rhetoric*, p. 81). The use of ἐγώ εἰμι by Jesus' should be seen in a similar way. There is always a distinction between Jesus and the Father and yet there is also a unity of nature.

(10.24) but is essentially different in character (8.38). This difference in nature stems from a difference in origin. Because Jesus is from above, he has the nature of one from above (8.23). Jesus' claim that he is before Abraham was born (8.58) betrays that his very nature is different to the nature of the Jews. However, the Logos in the prologue does not only express an essential difference between Jesus and the world, but also a bridging of that difference. The Word is not God in his distant glory but is God identifying himself with the world and thus communicating with it (cf. 3.16).[1] The Word became flesh (1.14). The Word made the unknowable known (1.18). Just as a person's innermost thoughts can only be made known by their words, so the reader can only know the innermost thoughts of the Father by listening to and understanding his Word. Jesus is the expression of the Father and thus is the Father's word. As well as expressing that Jesus is divine, the term λόγος expresses that Jesus is the tangible revelation of God. While the Father may not be tangible, Jesus makes him tangible.

The study of the possible Old Testament background to Jesus' strange phrase in 4.26 takes on even more significance in the light of the connection between the Logos of the prologue and Jesus' use of 'I am'. For when Jesus states that it is he who speaks, he confirms that he is the very expression of YHWH, who was the one would speak in the day of salvation. As the very expression, the Word, of God, Jesus can take what was originally applied to God and use it to refer to himself (cf. 3.34).

It is most striking that by the use of ἐγώ εἰμι in John, Jesus takes on himself a phrase from Isaiah reserved for Yahweh alone. Although the use of ἐγώ εἰμι is not limited exclusively to Jesus in John's Gospel (cf. 9.9), *the way it is used on Jesus' lips* identifies him so closely with Yahweh's saving action and even with Yahweh himself that it is equivalent to the claim 'I and the Father are one' (10.30). The Jews perceive that by those words Jesus, a man, makes himself God (ὅτι σὺ ἄνθρωπος ὢν ποιεῖς σεαυτὸν θεόν, 10.33) and so they attempt to stone him. Such a reaction confirms to the reader that the Jews see a similar blasphemy in the words of 8.58. If in Isaiah *ani hu* is a phrase that the LORD speaks in defence of his exclusive right over his people, it surely holds true that it would be a matter of 'presumptuous pride' for someone to take these words from such a context and apply them to himself. When Jesus uses the phrase, the Jews see it from such a

1.   Cf. Barrett, *John*, p. 73.

perspective. However, from the Gospel's point of view, it is not Jesus who makes himself God but the reverse. It is the Word, who was in the beginning with God and was to be identified as God, who has made himself flesh (σὰρξ ἐγένετο, 1.14).[1]

The 'I Am' Sayings and Salvation

Whatever else is said about the purpose of John's Gospel, it is certain that it is soteriological in nature.[2] The narrator explains that the Gospel is written that 'you may believe that Jesus is the Christ, the Son of God, and that believing you may have life in his name' (20.31). Moreover, the Gospel contends that God did not send his Son into the world to judge it but to save it (3.17; 12.47). Such salvation is 'from the Jews' (4.22). The framework for understanding salvation in John is thus self-confessedly Jewish.[3] It is within this Jewish framework of salvation that the 'I am' sayings fall.

The study of the background to the 'I am' sayings noted that the *ani hu* of Isaiah presents 'Yahweh as lord of history and therefore as redeemer of Israel' (cf. Isa. 41.4; 43.10, 13; 51.12; 52.6).[4] The 'I am' sayings without an image, which primarily concern Jesus' identity rather than his role, thus portray an identity which is soteriological. It was indicated above that the 'I am' saying of 4.26 may allude to the day when the LORD was to redeem Jerusalem and by implication identify Jesus with that redemption. The 'I am' sayings of John, like those in Isaiah, are fulfilled in an act of history. The Jews will 'know that I am' (8.28) when Jesus is 'lifted up' by them. The disciples 'will believe that I am' (13.19) in the events following Jesus' betrayal. In his betrayal, passion and crucifixion as well as his exaltation both his opponents and his followers will realize that Jesus is identified with the salvation of Yahweh. They will realize that by taking the words of the LORD upon himself it is he (and he alone) who blots out sins (cf. 8.24) because it is he alone who is one with the Father. Thus the Johannine ἐγώ εἰμι contains the same soteriological overtones of the Isaianic *ani hu*.

The 'I am' sayings with an image confirm and reinforce the soteriolo-

---

1.   For a discussion of whether John's view of Jesus goes beyond the bounds of Jewish monotheism see Dunn, *Christology*, pp. 129-31, 163-67, 241; Dodd, *Interpretation*, pp. 324-28; Schnackenburg, *John*, II, p. 102.

2.   Cf. Barrett, *John*, pp. 78-79.

3.   Cf. Carson, *John*, p. 97.

4.   Harner, *'I am'*, p. 7.

gical use of ἐγώ εἰμι. Jesus in John's Gospel is also portrayed as the life-giver. Thus Morris comments on the Logos (1.4): 'It is only because there is life in the Logos that there is life in anything on earth at all. Life does not exist in its own right. It is not even spoken of as made "by" or "through" the Word, but as existing in him'.[1] Jesus offers the woman at the well living water (4.10, 14). He gives the people the bread of life (6.35) which is himself. He offers his life so that his sheep might have life in all its fulness (ἐγώ ἦλθον ἵνα ζωὴν ἔχωσιν καὶ περισσὸν ἔχωσιν, 10.10). What is more, by means of the words ἐγώ εἰμι, Jesus claims to be the Life (11.25; 14.6). However, the ability to give life is presented as a divine prerogative. Only because of Jesus' unique relationship with the Father can he give life (5.26). The 'I am' sayings with an image have a positive soteriological function in offering those things associated with Life. Through them Jesus provides light (8.12; 9.5), nourishment (6.35; cf. 15.1), protection (10.9, 11) and a relationship (10.14; cf. 14.7), resurrection (11.25), truth (14.6) and guidance (10.11; 14.6), but above all life (11.25; 14.6; cf. 6.35ff.). The offer of life comes not only through the 'I am' sayings themselves but also through the soteriological sub-clauses which accompany them. As the Light of the World, Jesus offers the light of life (8.12b); as the door Jesus specifically offers salvation (10.9); as the Resurrection and the Life, Jesus offers a life that transcends death (11.25b, 26); and as the Vine he offers fruitfulness (15.5b). Hand in hand with life-giving as a soteriological function is set Jesus' ability to judge: 'the Father...has given him the authority to execute judgment, because he is the Son of man' (5.27). His right to execute judgment is seen in his claim to be the Light of the world (8.12), which provokes fierce debate about the role of Jesus' testimony.

The use of ἐγώ εἰμι on the lips of Jesus therefore concurs with the soteriological purpose of the Gospel. Through the 'I am' sayings of Jesus the author wants the reader to find life by believing that such life is in Jesus (1.4), is from Jesus (10.10) and is Jesus (11.25; 14.6). The author also stresses that this life is only in Jesus and thus it is only through Jesus that the readers can come to the Father (14.6) and to salvation (10.9).

1.   Morris, *John*, pp. 82-83.

BIBLIOGRAPHY

Aalen, S., '"Truth", a Key Word in St John's Gospel', in F.L. Cross, (ed.), *Studia Evangelica II* (Berlin: 1964), pp. 3-25.

Abbott, E.A., *Johannine Grammar* (London: A. & C. Black, 1906).

Abrams, M.H., *A Glossary of Literary Terms* (New York: Holt, Reinhart & Winston, 3rd edn, 1971).

Alexander, P. (ed.), *Textual Sources for the Study of Judaism* (Manchester: Manchester University Press, 1984).

Allen, L.C., *The Books of Joel, Obadiah, Jonah and Micah* (Grand Rapids: Eerdmans, 1976).

Allen, E., 'The Jewish Christian Church in the Fourth Gospel', *JBL* 74 (1955), pp. 88-92.

Appold, M.L., *The Oneness Motif in the Fourth Gospel* (WUNT, 2; Tübingen: Mohr, 1976).

Aristotle, *Nicomachean Ethics* (trans. H. Rackham; LCL Aristotle 19; London: Heinemann, 1926).

—*The Poetics: 'Longinus' on the Sublime: Demetrius on Style* (trans. W. Hamilton Fyfe; LCL Aristotle 23; London: Heinemann, 1927).

Ashton, J., *Understanding the Fourth Gospel* (Oxford: Oxford University Press, 1991).

Ball, R.M., 'St. John and the Institution of the Eucharist', *JSNT* 23 (1985), pp. 59-68.

Barrett, C.K., 'The Old Testament in the Fourth Gospel', *JTS* 48 (1947), pp. 155-69.

—*The New Testament Background: Selected Documents* (London: SPCK, 1957).

—*The Gospel of John and Judaism* (London: SPCK, 1975).

—*The Gospel according to St John* (London: SPCK, 2nd edn, 1978).

Beasley-Murray, G.R., *John* (WBC, 36; Waco, TXs: Word Books, 1987).

—*The Gospel of Life: Theology in the Fourth Gospel* (Peabody, MA: Hendrickson, 1991).

Becker, J., 'Die Abschiedsreden Jesu im Johannesevangelium', *ZNW* 61 (1970), pp. 215-46.

—*Das Evangelium des Johannes. I. Kapitel 1-10* (Ökumenischer Taschenbuch zum Neuen Testament; Gütersloh: Gütersloher Verlagshaus, 1979).

—'Ich bin die Auferstehung und das Leben', *ThZ* 39 (1983), pp. 136-51.

Benoit, P., 'La Divinité de Jésus dans les Évangiles Synoptiques', *Lumière et Vie* 9 (1953), pp. 43-74.

Berlin, A., *Poetics and Interpretation of Biblical Narrative* (Bible and Literature; Sheffield: Almond Press, 1983).

Bernard, J.H., *The Gospel according to St John* (ed. A.H. McNeile; ICC, 30; Edinburgh: T. & T. Clark, 1928).

Beutler, J., and R.T. Fortna (eds.), *The Shepherd Discourse of John 10 and its Context:*

Studies by Members of the Johannine Writings Seminar (SNTSMS, 67; Cambridge: Cambridge University Press, 1991).

Bishop, E.F.F., ''He that Eateth Bread with me Hath Lifted Up his Heel against me'': John 13.8', *ExpTim* 70 (1958–59), pp. 331-33.

Black, M., 'The Theological Appropriation of the Old Testament by the New Testament', *SJT* 39 (1986), pp. 1-17.

Boismard, M.E., 'Le Lavement Des Pieds (Jn, XIII, 1-17)', *RB* 71 (1964), pp. 5-24.

Booth, K.N., 'The Self-Proclamation of Jesus in St. John's Gospel', *Colloqium* 7.2 (1975), pp. 36-47.

Booth, W.C., *The Rhetoric of Fiction* (Chicago: Chicago University Press, 1961).

Borgen, P., *Bread from Heaven: An Exegetical Study of the Concept of Manna in the Gospel of John and the Writings of Philo* (NovTSup, 10; Leiden: Brill, 1965).

—*Logos was the True Light: And Other Essays on the Gospel of John* (Trondheim: Tapir, 1983).

—*Philo, John and Paul: New Perspectives on Judaism and Early Christianity* (Brown Judaic Studies, 131; Atlanta, GA: Scholars Press, 1987).

Borig, R., *Der Wahre Weinstock: Studien zum Alten und Neuen Testament* (Münich: Kösel, 1967).

Bowker, J., *The Targums and Rabbinic Literature* (Cambridge: Cambridge University Press, 1969).

Braine, D.D.C., 'The Inner Jewishness of St. John's Gospel', *SNTU* 13 (1988), pp. 101-55.

Braun, F.-M., *Jean le Théologien. II. Les grandes traditions d'Isräel et l'accord des Écritures selon le Quatrième Évangile* (Etudes Bibliques; Paris: J. Gabbala et Cie, 1964).

Brinktrine, J., 'Die Selbstaussage Jesu Ego Eimi', *Theologie und Glaube* 47 (1957), pp. 34-36.

Brooke, A.E., 'The Fragments of Heracleon', *Texts and Studies* 1.4 (1891), p. 83.

Brown, R.E., *The Gospel according to John* (2 vols.; AB, 29; New York: Doubleday, 1970–1971).

—*The Community of the Beloved Disciple* (London: Geoffrey Chapman, 1979).

Bruce, F.F., *New Testament History* (London: Oliphants, 2nd rev. edn, 1977).

—*The Gospel of John* (Basingstoke: Pickering and Inglis, 1983).

Büchsel, F., 'εἰμι', *TDNT*, II, pp. 398-400.

Bühner, J.A., *Der Gesandte und Sein Weg* (WUNT, 2 Reihe; Tübingen: Mohr, 1977).

Bultmann, R., 'Die Bedeutung der neuerschlossenen Mandäischen und Manichäischen Quellen für das Verständnis des Johannesevangeliums', *ZNW* 24 (1925), pp. 100-46.

—*Theology of the New Testament* (2 vols.; London: SCM Press, 1955).

—*The Gospel of John* (trans. G.R. Beasley-Murray; Oxford: Basil Blackwell, 1971 [1941]).

Cahill, P.J., 'Narrative Art in John IV', *Religious Studies Bulletin* 2 (1982), pp. 41-48.

Carson, D.A., 'John and the Johannine Epistles', in D.A. Carson and H.G.M. Williamson (eds.), *It is Written: Scripture Citing Scripture. Essays in Honour of Barnabas Lindars SSF* (Cambridge: Cambridge University Press, 1988), pp. 245-64.

—*The Gospel according to John* (Leicester: Inter-Varsity Press, 1991).

Cathcart, K.J., and R.J. Gordon (trans.), *The Targum of the Minor Prophets* (The Aramaic Bible, 14; Edinburgh: T. & T. Clark, 1989).

Cavallin, H.C.C., *Life after Death: Paul's Argument for the Resurrection of the Dead in 1 Cor 15: Part 1: An Enquiry into the Jewish Background* (ConBNT, 7.1; Lund: Gleerup, 1974).

Cerfaux, L., 'Le thème littéraire parabolique dans l'Évangile de Saint Jean', *ConNT* 11 (1947), pp. 15-25.

Charlier, J.P., 'L'Exégèse Johannique d'un précepte légal: Jean viii 17', *RB* 67 (1960), pp. 503-15.

Chatman, S., *Story and Discourse: Narrative Structure in Fiction and Film* (London: Ithaca, 1978).

Chilton, B.D., *A Galilean Rabbi and his Bible* (London: SPCK, 1984).

Chilton, B.D. (trans.), *The Isaiah Targum* (The Aramaic Bible, 11; Edinburgh: T. & T. Clark, 1987).

Coetzee, J.C., 'Jesus' Revelation in the Ego Eimi Sayings in John 8 and 9', in J.H. Petzer and P.J. Hartin (eds.), *A South African Perspective on the New Testament* (Leiden: Brill, 1986), pp. 170-77.

Cracknell, K., *Towards a New Relationship* (London: Epworth, 1986).

Crossan, J.D., 'It is Written: A Structuralist Analysis of John 6', *Semeia* 26 (1983), pp. 3-21.

Culpepper, R.A., *Anatomy of the Fourth Gospel* (Philadelphia: Fortress Press, 1983).

Dahl, N.A., 'The Johannine Church and History', in J. Ashton (ed.), *The Interpretation of John* (Issues in Religion and Theology, 9; London: SPCK, 1986), pp. 122-40.

Dahms, J.V., 'Isaiah 55.11 and the Gospel of John', *EvQ* 53 (1981), pp. 78-88.

Davies, M., *Rhetoric and Reference in the Fourth Gospel* (Sheffield: JSOT Press, 1992).

Daube, D., 'Ego eimi', *JTS* 50 (1949), pp. 56-57.

—'The "I am" of the Messianic Presence', in *idem*, *The New Testament and Rabbinic Judaism* (London: Athlone, 1956), pp. 325-29.

De Jonge, M., 'Jewish Expectations about the "Messiah" according to the Fourth Gospel', *NTS* 19 (1972–73), pp. 246-70.

—*Jesus as Prophet and King in the Fourth Gospel* (Leiden: Brill, 1973).

—*Jesus: Stranger from Heaven and Son of God* (trans. and ed. J.E. Steeley; Missoula, MT: Scholars Press, 1977).

Deissmann, A., *Light from the Ancient East* (New York: George H. Doran, 1927).

Delebeque, E., ' "Lazare est mort" (Note sur Jean 11.14-15)', *Bib* 67 (1986), pp. 89-97.

Derrett, J.D.M., 'The Good Shepherd: St. John's use of Jewish Halakah and Haggadah', *ST* 27 (1973), pp. 25-50.

Diodorus, *Diodorus Siculus I* (trans. C.H. Oldfather; LCL; London: Heinemann, 1933).

Dodd, C.H., *According to the Scriptures: The Sub-Structure of New Testament Theology* (London: Nisbet, 1952).

—*The Interpretation of the Fourth Gospel* (Cambridge: Cambridge University Press, 1953).

—*Historical Tradition in the Fourth Gospel* (Cambridge: Cambridge University Press, 1963).

Doeve, J.W., *Jewish Hermeneutics in the Synoptic Gospels and Acts* (Assen: Koninlijke, 1954).

Drower, E.S., *The Canonical Prayerbook of the Mandaeans* (Leiden: Brill, 1959).

Du Rand, J.A., 'The Characterization of Jesus as Depicted in the Narrative of the Fourth Gospel', *Neot* 19 (1985), pp. 18-36.

Duke, P.D., *Irony in the Fourth Gospel* (Atlanta: John Knox Press, 1985).

Dunkerly, R., 'Lazarus, John 11', *NTS* 5 (1959), pp. 321-27.

Dunn, J.D.G., 'The Washing of the Disciples' Feet in John 13.1-20', *ZNW* 61 (1970), pp. 247-52.

—*Christology in the Making: An Inquiry into the Origins of the Doctrine of the Incarnation* (London: SCM Press, 2nd edn, 1989).

Dupont-Sommer, A., *The Essene Writings from Qumran* (trans. G. Vermes; Oxford: Basil Blackwell, 1961).

Epstein, I. (ed.), *The Babylonian Talmud: Tractates Sukkah and Mo'ed Katan* (London: Soncino, 1984).

Erman, A., *Aegypten und Aegyptisches Leben im Altertum* (2 vols.; Tübingen: H. Laupp'schen, 1885).

—*The Literature of the Ancient Egyptians: Poems, Narratives, and Manuals of Instruction from the Third and Second Milennia B.C.* (trans. A.M. Black; London: Methuen, 1927).

Eslinger, L., 'The Wooing of the Woman at the Well: Jesus, the Reader and Reader-Response Criticism', *Literature and Theology* 1.2 (1987), pp. 167-83.

Evans, C.A., 'On the Quotation Formulas in the Fourth Gospel', *BZ* 26 (1982), pp. 79-83.

Fensham, F.S., '"I am the Way, the Truth and the Life": John 14.6', *Neot* 2 (1968), pp. 81-88.

Feuillet, A., *Johannine Studies* (Staten Island, NY: Alba House, 1965).

—'Les ego eimi christologiques du Quatrième Évangile: La révélation énigmatique de l'être divine de Jésus dans Jean et les synoptiques', *RSR* 54 (1966), pp. 5-22.

Field, F., *Notes on the Translation of the New Testament* (Cambridge: Cambridge University Press, 1889).

Forster, E.M., *Aspects of the Novel* (Harmondsworth: Penguin Books, 1962).

Freed, E.D., *Old Testament Quotations in the Gospel of John* (NovTSup, 11; Leiden: Brill, 1965).

—'The Son of Man in the Fourth Gospel', *JBL* 86 (1967), pp. 401-409.

—'Ego Eimi in John 1.20 and 4.25', *CBQ* 41 (1979), pp. 288-91.

—'Ego Eimi in John viii.24 in the Light of its Context and Jewish Messianic Belief', *JTS* 33 (1982), pp. 163-67.

—'Who or What was before Abraham in John 8.58?', *JSNT* 17 (1983), pp. 52-59.

Freedman, H. (trans.), *Midrash Rabbah: Genesis*, II (ed. H. Freedman and M. Simon; London: Soncino, 1939).

Genuyt, F., 'La porte et le pasteur (Jn 10,1-21): Étude sémiotique', in J. Delorme (ed.), *Les paraboles évangéliques: Perspectives nouvelles: XIIe Congrès de L'ACFEB, Lyons 1987* (Paris: Cerf, 1989), pp. 375-87.

Giblin, C.H., 'Confrontations in John 18.1-27', *Bib* 65 (1984), pp. 210-31.

Gärtner, B., *John 6 and the Jewish Passover* (ConBNT, 17; Lund: Gleerup, 1959).

Grant, R.M., *Gnosticism: A Source Book of the Heretical Writings from the Early Christian Period* (New York: Harper, 1961).

Grubb, E., 'The Raising of Lazarus (Jn 11)', *ExpTim* 33 (1921–22), pp. 401-407.

Guilding, A., *The Fourth Gospel and Jewish Worship: A Study of the Relation of St. John's Gospel to the Ancient Jewish Lectionary System* (Oxford: Clarendon Press, 1960).

Haenchen, E., *John* (2 vols.; Hermeneia; trans. R.W. Funk; Philadelphia: Fortress, 1984).

Hanson, A.T., 'The Old Testament Background to the Raising of Lazarus', in E.A. Livingstone (ed.), *Studia Evangelica VI* (Berlin: Akademie-Verlag, 1973), pp. 252-55.

—*The Prophetic Gospel* (Edinburgh: T.& T. Clark, 1991).

Harner, P.B., *The 'I am' of the Fourth Gospel* (Facet Books; Philadelphia: Fortress Press, 1970).

Hatch, E., and H. Redpath, *Concordance to the Septuagint* (3 vols.; Oxford: Clarendon Press, 1897).

Hawkins, D.J., 'Orthodoxy and Heresy in John 10.1-21 and 15.1-17', *EvQ* 47 (1975), pp. 208-13.

Heil, J.P., *Jesus Walking on the Sea: Meaning and Gospel Functions of Matt. 14.22-33, Mark 6.45-52 and John 6.15b-21* (AnBib, 87; Rome: Biblical Institute Press, 1981).

Henderson, A., 'Notes on John 11', *ExpTim* 32 (1920–21), pp. 123-26.

Hengel, M., *The 'Hellenisation' of Judaea in the First Century after Christ* (London: SCM Press, 1989).

—'Die Schriftauslegung des 4: Evangeliums auf dem Hintergrund der urchristlichen Exegese', *JBTh* 4 (1989), pp. 249-88.

Hennecke, E., and W. Schneemelcher, *The New Testament Apocrypha*.I.*Gospels and Related Writings* (trans. R.McL. Wilson; London: Lutterworth, 1963).

Higgins, A.J.B., 'The Words of Jesus according to John', *BJRL* 49 (1967), pp. 363-86.

Hinrichs, B., *'Ich Bin': Die Konsistenz des Johannes-Evangeliums in der Konzentration auf das Wort Jesus* (Stuttgarter Bibelstudien, 133; Stuttgart: Katholisches Bibelwerk, 1988).

Hoskyns, E.C., *The Fourth Gospel* (2 vols.; ed. F.N. Davey; London: Faber and Faber, 1939).

Innes, J. (trans.), *The Works of Aurelius Augustine: Bishop of Hippo*.II.*Lectures or Tractates on the Gospel according to St John.* (ed. M. Dods; Edinburgh: T. & T. Clark, 1874).

Janssens de Varabeke, A., 'La structure des scènes du récit de la Passion en Jn xviii-xix', *ETL* 38 (1962), pp. 504-22.

Jaubert, A., 'L'image de la vigne (Jean 15)', in F. Christ (ed.), *Oikonomia* (Festschrift O. Cullmann; Hamburg: Reich, 1957), pp. 93-99.

Josephus, *Jewish Antiquities XII–XIV* (trans. R. Marcus; LCL Josephus 7; Cambridge, MA: Harvard University Press, 1976).

—*The Jewish War I–II* (trans. H. St. J. Thackeray; LCL Josephus 2; Cambridge, MA: Harvard University Press, 1989).

Kaiser, O., *Isaiah 13–39* (trans. R.A. Wilson; London: SCM, 1974).

Kermode, F., 'John', in R. Alter and F. Kermode (eds.), *The Literary Guide to the Bible* (London: Collins, 1987), pp. 440-65.

Kern, W., 'Die symmmetrische Gesamtaufbau von Joh. 8,12-58', *ZKT* 78 (1956), pp. 451-54.

Knight, G.A.F., 'Ego Eimi', *NZTR* 1 (4,1966), pp. 219-24.

Knox, W.L., 'John 13.1-30', *HTR* 43 (1950), pp. 161-63.

Kremer, J., *Lazarus: Die Geschichte einer Auferstehung* (Stuttgart: Katholisches Bibelwerk, 1985).

Kundzins, K., 'Zur Diskussion über die Ego-Eimi-Spruche des Johannes-Evangeliums', in J. Köpp (ed.), *Charisteria* (Stockholm: 1954), pp. 95-107.

Kysar, R., *The Fourth Evangelist and his Gospel* (Minneapolis: Augsburg, 1975).

—*John* (Minneapolis: Augsburg, 1986).

Léon-Dufour, X., 'Jésus, le bon pasteur', in J. Delorme (ed.), *Les paraboles évangéliques: Perspectives nouvelles: XIIe Congrès de L'ACFEB, Lyons 1987* (Paris: Cerf, 1989), pp. 361-73.

Lidzbarski, M., *Das Johannesbuch der Mandäer* (Giessen: Alfred Töppelmann, 1915).

—*Mandäische Liturgien* (Abhandlungen der Königlichen Gesellschaft der Wissenschaften zu Göttingen Phil.-Hist Klasse BDXVII; Berlin: Weidmannschen, 1920).

—*Ginza, der Schatz oder das Grosse Buch der Mandäer* (Göttingen: Vandenhoeck & Ruprecht, 1925).

Lightfoot, R.H., *St John's Gospel* (ed. C.F. Evans; Oxford: Clarendon Press, 1986 [1953]).

Lincoln, A.T., 'Trials, Plots and the Narrative of the Fourth Gospel', *JSNT* 56 (1994), pp. 3-30.

Lindars, B., *Behind the Fourth Gospel: Studies in Creative Criticism* (London: SPCK, 1971).

—'Discourse and Tradition: The Use of the Sayings of Jesus in the Discourses of the Fourth Gospel', *JSNT* 13 (1981), pp. 83-101.

—*The Gospel of John* (NCB; London: Marshall, Morgan & Scott, 1986 [1972]).

Longenecker, R., *Biblical Exegesis in the Apostolic Period* (Grand Rapids: Eerdmans, 1975).

MacRae, G.W., 'The Ego-Proclamation in Gnostic Sources', in E. Bammel (ed.), *The Trial of Jesus* (London: SCM Press, 1970), pp. 123-39.

Malatesta, E., *St John's Gospel: 1920–1965* (AnBib, 32; Rome: Pontifical Biblical Institute, 1967).

Manson, W., 'The EGW EIMI of the Messianic Presence in the New Testament', *JTS* 48 (1947), pp. 137-45.

Marshall, I.H., 'The Problem of New Testament Exegesis (John 4.1-45)', *JETS* 17 (1974), pp. 67-73.

—'An Assessment of Recent Developments', in D. Carson and H.G.W. Williamson (eds.), *It is Written: Scripture Citing Scripture: Essays in Honour of Barnabas Lindars SSF* (Cambridge: Cambridge University Press, 1988), pp. 1-21.

Martin, J.P., 'History and Theology in the Lazarus Narrative: John 11.1-44', *SJT* 17 (1964), pp. 332ff.

Martyn, J.L., *History and Theology in the Fourth Gospel* (Nashville: Abingdon, 2nd edn, 1979).

Mastin, B.A., 'A Neglected Feature of the Christology of the Fourth Gospel', *NTS* 22 (1976), pp. 32-51.

Mays, J.L., *Micah* (London: SCM Press, 1976).

McArthur, H.K., 'Christological Perspectives in the Predicates of the Johannine Ego Eimi Sayings', in R.F. Berkey and S.A. Edwards (eds.), *Christological Perspectives: Festschrift H.K. McArthur* (New York: Pilgrim Press, 1982), pp. 95-111.

McCaffrey, J., *The House with Many Rooms: The Temple Theme of Jn 14.2-3* (AnBib, 114; Rome: Biblical Institute Press, 1988).

McCasland, S.V., 'The Way', *JBL* 77 (1958), pp. 222-30.

McKenzie, J.L., *Second Isaiah* (AB, 20; New York: Doubleday, 1968).

Meeks, W.A., 'The Man from Heaven in Johannine Sectarianism', *JBL* 91 (1972), pp. 44-72.

Mein, P., 'A Note on John xviii.6', *ExpTim* 65 (1953–54), pp. 286-87.

Menken, M.J.J., 'The Translation of Psalm 41.10 in John 12.18', *JSNT* 40 (1990) pp. 61-79

Michaelis, W., 'ὁδὸς', *TDNT*, V, pp. 48-96.

Mlakuzhyil, G., *The Christocentric Literary Structure of the Fourth Gospel* (Rome: Pontifical Biblical Institute, 1987).

Moloney, F.J., 'The Cross: The Revelation of the Son of Man as "Ego Eimi": John 8.28', in *idem*, *The Johannine Son of Man* (Biblioteca Di Scienze Religiose, 14; Rome: L.A.S., 1976), pp. 124-41.

Moore, S.D., *Literary Criticism and the Gospels* (New Haven: Yale University Press, 1989).

Morgan-Wynne, J.E., 'The Cross and the Revelation of Jesus as εγώ εἰμι in the Fourth Gospel (John 8.28)', in E.A. Livingstone (ed.), *Studia Biblica 1978. II. Papers on the Gospels. Sixth International Congress on Biblical Studies: Oxford 3-7 April 1978* (Sheffield: JSOT Press, 1980), pp. 219-26.

Morris, L., *The Gospel according to John* (NICNT; Grand Rapids: Eerdmans, 1971).

—'The "I am" Sayings', in *idem*, *Jesus is the Christ* (Leicester: Inter-Varsity Press, 1989), pp. 107-25.

Moule, C.F.D., 'The Meaning of "Life" in St. John (Jn 11.1-44)', *Theology* 78 (1975), pp. 114-25.

Moulton, J.H., and G. Milligan, *A Vocabulary of the Greek Testament* (London: Hodder & Stoughton, 1930).

Moulton, J.H., *A Grammar of New Testament Greek: Accidence and Word Formation with an Appendix on Semitisms in the New Testament*, II (with W.F. Howard; Edinburgh: T. & T. Clark, 1929).

—*A Grammar of New Testament Greek: Prolegomena*, I (Edinburgh: T. & T. Clark, 3rd edn, 1930).

—*A Grammar of New Testament Greek: Syntax*, III (by N. Turner; Edinburgh: T. & T. Clark, 1964).

Neyrey, J.H., 'Jacob Traditions and the Interpretation of John 4.10-26', *CBQ* 41 (1979), pp. 419-37.

—*An Ideology of Revolt* (Philadelphia: Fortress Press, 1988).

Nickelsburg, G.W.E., *Resurrection, Immortality, and Eternal Life in Intertestamental Judaism* (Harvard Theological Studies, 26; London: Oxford University Press, 1972).

Nock, A.D., and A. Festugière, *Corpus Hermeticum. I. Traités I-XII* (Collection des Universités de France; Paris: 1945).

Norden, E., *Agnostos Theos* (Leipzig/Stuttgart: 1913/1956).

O'Day, G.R., *Revelation in the Fourth Gospel* (Philadelphia: Fortress Press, 1986).

O'Grady, J.F., 'The Good Shepherd and the Vine and the Branches', *BTB* 8 (1978), pp. 86-88.

Olsson, B., *Structure and Meaning in the Fourth Gospel: A Text-linguistic Analysis of John 2.1-11 and 4.1-42* (ConBNT, 6; Lund: Gleerup, 1974).

Oswalt, J.N., *The Book of Isaiah: Chapters 1–39* (NICOT; Grand Rapids: Eerdmans, 1986).

Painter, J., *John: Witness and Theologian* (London: SPCK, 1979).

Pancaro, S., *The Law in the Fourth Gospel: The Torah and the Gospel, Moses and Jesus, Judaism and Christianity according to John* (SNT, 42; Leiden: Brill, 1975).

Perkins, P., *Resurrection: New Testament Witness and Contemporary Reflection* (London: Geoffrey Chapman, 1984).

Phillips, G.A., '"This is a Hard Saying. Who can be a Listener to it?": Creating a Reader in John 6', *Semeia* 26 (1983), pp. 23-56.

Philo, *Quod Deterius Potiori Insidiari Solet 47–48* (trans. F.H. Colson and G.H. Whitaker; LCL Philo 2; London: Heinnemann, 1979).

—*Legum Allegoria III. 162a* (trans. F.H. Colson and G.H. Whitaker; LCL Philo 1; London: Heinnemann, 1981).

—*De Somniis* (trans. F.H. Colson and G.H. Whitaker; LCL Philo 5; London: Heinemann, 1988).

Pieper, A., *Isaiah II* (trans. E.E. Kowalke; Milwaukee, WI: Northwestern Publishing House, 1979).

Plumb, C.L.B., 'The EGW EIMI Sayings in John's Gospel' (MPhil dissertation, University of Nottingham, 1990).

Pollard, T.E., 'The Raising of Lazarus', in E.A. Livingstone (ed.), *Studia Evangelica VI* (Berlin: Akademie Verlag, 1973), pp. 461-64.

Potterie, I., de la, 'Je suis la Voie, la Vérité et la Vie (Jn 14.6)', *NRT* 88 (1966), pp. 917-42.

—*La vérité dans Saint Jean* (AnBib, 73/74; Rome: Biblical Institute Press, 1977).

Proctor, J., 'The Way, the Truth and the Life: Interfaith Dialogue and the Fourth Gospel' (unpublished paper, 1991), pp. 18-19.

Rabinowitz, P.J., 'Truth in Fiction: A Re-examination of Audiences', *Critical Inquiry* 4 (1977), pp. 121-41.

Reese, J.M., 'Literary Structure of Jn 13.31-14.31; 16.5-6, 16-33', *CBQ* 34 (1972), pp. 321-31.

Rehm, B. (ed.), *Die Pseudoklementinen. I. Die Griechische christlichen Schriftsteller der ersten Jahrhunderte* (Berlin: Akademie Verlag, 1969).

Reim, G., *Studien zum alttestamentlichen Hintergrund des Johannesevangeliums* (SNTSMS, 22; Cambridge: Cambridge University Press, 1974).

—'Jesus as God in the Fourth Gospel: The Old Testament Background', *NTS* 30 (1984), pp. 158-60.

Rensberger, D., 'The Politics of John: The Trial of Jesus in the Fourth Gospel', *JBL* 103 (1984), pp. 395-411.

Richter, G., 'Die Gefangennahme Jesus nach dem Johannesevangelium (18.1-12)', *Bibel und Leben* 10 (1969), pp. 26-39.

Richter, J., 'Ani Hu und Ego Eimi' (unpublished dissertation, University of Erlangen, 1956).

Robert, R., 'Le malentendu sur le Nom Divin au Chapitre VIII du Quatrième Évangile', *Revue Thomiste* 88 (1988), pp. 278-87.

Robinson, J.M. (ed.), *The Nag Hammadi Library in English* (trans. Members of the Coptic Gnostic Library Project; Leiden: Brill, 1977).

Robinson, J.A.T., 'The Destination and Purpose of St. John's Gospel', *NTS* 6 (1960), pp. 117-31.

—*Redating the New Testament* (London: SCM, 1976).

—*The Priority of John* (ed. J.F. Coakley; London: SCM Press, 1985).

Romaniuk, K., '"I am the Resurrection and the Life": John 11.25', *Concilium* 10 (1970), pp. 68-77.

Rossup, J.E., *Abiding in Christ: Studies in John 15* (Grand Rapids: Eerdmans, 1973).

Sanders, J.N., and B.A. Mastin, *A Commentary on the Gospel according to St John* (London: A. & C. Black, 1968).

Schnackenburg, R., *The Gospel according to St John* (3 vols.; London: Burns and Oates, 1968–1982).

Schulz, S., *Komposition und Herkunft der Johanneischen Reden* (Stuttgart: Kohlhammer, 1960).

Schweizer, E., *Ego Eimi: Die religionsgeschichtliche Herkunft und theologische Bedeutung der johanneischen Bildreden, zugleich ein Beitrag zur Quellenfrage des vierten Evangeliums* (FRLANT, 56; Göttingen: Vandenhoeck & Ruprecht, 1939).

Segovia, F.F., 'John 13.1-20: The Footwashing in the Johannine Tradition', *ZNW* 73 (1982), pp. 31-51.

—'The Structure, Tendenz and Sitz im Leben of John 13.31–14.31', *JBL* 104 (1985), pp. 471-93.

Sidebottom, E.M., *The Christ of the Fourth Gospel* (London: SPCK, 1961).

Simmons, B.E., 'A Christology of the "I am" sayings in the Gospel of John', *Theological Educator* 38 (1988), pp. 94-103.

Simonis, A.J., *Die Hirtenrede im Johannes Evangelium* (Rome: Pontifical Biblical Institute, 1967).

Smalley, S.S., 'The Johannine Son of Man Sayings', *NTS 15* (1968–69), pp. 278-301.

—*John: Evangelist and Interpreter* (Exeter: Paternoster Press, 1978).

Smith, D.M., Jr, 'Johannine Christianity: Some Reflections on its Character and Delineation', *NTS* 21 (1975), pp. 222-48.

Smith, R.L., *Micah–Malachi* (WBC; Waco, TX: Word Books, 1984).

Staley, J.L., *The Print's First Kiss: A Rhetorical Investigation of the Implied Reader in the Fourth Gospel* (SBLDS, 82; Atlanta: Scholars Press, 1988)

Stauffer, E., 'Probleme der Priestertradition', *TLZ* 81 (1956), pp. 136-50 (esp. pp. 147-48).

—'ἐγώ', *TDNT*, II, pp. 343-62.

—'The Background to the Revelation' and 'I am He', in *idem, Jesus and his Story* (trans. D.M. Barton; London: SCM Press, 1960), pp. 142-59.

—*Jesus and his Story* (trans. D.M. Barton; London: SCM Press, 1960).

Stenning, J.F., *The Targum of Isaiah* (Oxford: Clarendon Press, 1953).

Stevens, C.T., 'The "I am" Formula in the Gospel of John', *Studia Biblica et Theologica* 7 (2,1977), pp. 19-30.

Stibbe, M.W.G., *John as Storyteller: Narrative Criticism and the Fourth Gospel* (SNTSMS, 73; Cambridge: Cambridge University Press, 1992).

Stierle, K., 'The Reading of Fictional Texts', in S.R. Suleiman and I. Crosman (eds.), *The Reader in the Text: Essays on Audience and Interpretation* (Princeton: Princeton University Press, 1980), pp. 94-95.

Strack, H.L., and P. Billerbeck, *Kommentar zum Neuen Testament aus Talmud und Midrasch* (7 vols.; Munich: C.H. Beck'sche, 1922–1961).

Suggit, J.N., 'The Raising of Lazarus', *ExpTim* 95 (1984), pp. 106-108.

Temple, S., 'The Two Traditions of the Last Supper, Betrayal, and Arrest', *NTS* 7 (1960), pp. 77-85.

Thayer, J.H., *A Greek-English Lexicon of the New Testament: Being Grimm Wilke's Clavis Novi Testamenti Translated and Enlarged* (Grand Rapids: Zondervan, 1983 [1885]).

Thomas, J.C., 'A Note on the Text of John 13.10', *NovT* 29.1 (1987), pp. 46-52.

—*Footwashing in John 13 and the Johannine Community* (JSNTSup, 61; Sheffield: JSOT Press, 1991).

Tragan, P.-R., *La parabole du «Pasteur» et ses explications: Jean, 10,1-18: La genèse, les milieux littéraires* (Studia Anselmiana, 67; Rome: Editrice Anselmiana, 1980).

Tresmontant, C., *The Hebrew Christ: Language in the Age of the Gospels* (Chicago: Franciscan Herald Press, 1989).

Turner, M., 'Atonement and the Death of Jesus in John: Some Questions to Bultmann and Forestell', *EvQ* 62 (1990), pp. 99-122.

Urban, L., and P. Henry, '"Before Abraham was I am": Does Philo explain John 8.56-58?', *Studia Philonica* 6 (1979–1980), pp. 157-95.

Van Belle, G., *Johannine Bibliography 1966–1985: A Cumulative Bibliography on the Fourth Gospel* (BEThL, 82; Leuven: Leuven University Press, 1988).

Van Unnik, W.C., 'The Purpose of St John's Gospel', in K. Aland *et al.* (eds.), *Studia Evangelica I* (Berlin: Akademie Verlag, 1959), pp. 382-411.

Verhoef, P.A., *The Books of Haggai and Malachi* (NICOT; Grand Rapids: Eerdmans, 1987).

Von Wahlde, U.C., 'Literary Structure and Theological Argument in Three Discourses with the Jews in the Fourth Gospel', *JBL* 103 (1984), pp. 575-84.

Wagner, G., *An Exegetical Bibliography of the New Testament: John and 1, 2, 3 John* (Macon, GA: Mercer University Press, 1987).

Watts, R., 'Camelot, Eskimos and the Grand Piano: The History of Hermeneutics in Biblical Studies: The Role of Ideology in New Testament Social Backgrounds' (unpublished lecture, Cambridge, 1990).

Wead, W.D., 'The Johannine Double Meaning', *ResQ* 13 (1970), pp. 106-120.

Webster, E.C., 'Pattern in the Fourth Gospel', in D. Clines (ed.), *Art and Meaning: Rhetoric in Biblical Literature* (JSOTSup, 19; Sheffield: JSOT Press, 1982).

Westcott, B.F., *The Gospel according to St John* (London: John Murray, 1882).

Westermann, C., *Isaiah 40–66* (trans. D.M.G. Stalker; London: SCM Press, 1966).

Wetter, G.P., '"Ich bin es", Eine Johanneische Formel', *TSK* 88 (1915), pp. 224-38.

Whitacre, R.A., *Johannine Polemic: The Role of Tradition and Theology* (SBLDS, 67; Chico, CA: Scholars Press, 1982).

Whybray, R.N., *Isaiah 40–66* (NCB; London: Oliphants, 1975).

Yamauchi, E.W., *Gnostic Ethics and Mandaean Origins* (Cambridge, MA: Harvard University Press, 1970).

—'Jewish Gnosticism? The Prologue of John, Mandaean Parallels, and the Trimorphic Protennoia', in R. Van den Broeck, and M.J. Vermaseren (eds.), *Studies in Gnosticism and Hellenistic Religions: Festschrift Gilles Quispel* (Leiden: Brill, 1981), pp. 467-97.

—*Pre-Christian Gnosticism* (Grand Rapids: Baker, 2nd edn, 1983).

Young, E.J., *The Book of Isaiah*, III (NICOT; Grand Rapids: Eerdmanns, 1972).

Young, F.W., 'A Study on the Relationship of Isaiah to the Fourth Gospel', *ZNW* 46 (1955), pp. 215-33.

Zickendraht, K., 'EGW EIMI', *TSK* 94 (1922), pp. 162-68.

Zimmerli, W., *I am Yahweh* (ed. W. Brueggemann; trans. D.W. Scott; Atlanta: John Knox Press, 1982).

Zimmermann, H., 'Das Absolute "Ego Eimi" als die neutestamentliche Offenbarungsformel', *BZ* 4 (1960), pp. 54-69, 266-76.

INDEXES

INDEX OF REFERENCES

OLD TESTAMENT

JOURNAL FOR THE STUDY OF THE NEW TESTAMENT SUPPLEMENT SERIES